JFP **19** (Supplement): 1–301, August 2009. © 2009 Cambridge University Press
doi:10.1017/S0956796809990074 Printed in the United Kingdom

Revised⁶ Report on the Algorithmic Language Scheme

Abstract

Programming languages should be designed not by piling feature on top of feature, but by removing the weaknesses and restrictions that make additional features appear necessary. Scheme demonstrates that a very small number of rules for forming expressions, with no restrictions on how they are composed, suffice to form a practical and efficient programming language that is flexible enough to support most of the major programming paradigms in use today.

Scheme was one of the first programming languages to incorporate first-class procedures as in the lambda calculus, thereby proving the usefulness of static scope rules and block structure in a dynamically typed language. Scheme was the first major dialect of Lisp to distinguish procedures from lambda expressions and symbols, to use a single lexical environment for all variables, and to evaluate the operator position of a procedure call in the same way as an operand position. By relying entirely on procedure calls to express iteration, Scheme emphasized the fact that tail-recursive procedure calls are essentially gotos that pass arguments. Scheme was the first widely used programming language to embrace first-class escape procedures, from which all previously known sequential control structures can be synthesized. A subsequent version of Scheme introduced the concept of exact and inexact number objects, an extension of Common Lisp's generic arithmetic. More recently, Scheme became the first programming language to support hygienic macros, which permit the syntax of a block-structured language to be extended in a consistent and reliable manner.

Revised^6 Report on the Algorithmic Language Scheme

MICHAEL SPERBER

DeinProgramm
(*e-mail:* `sperber@deinprogramm.de`)

R. KENT DYBVIG

Indiana University
(*e-mail:* `dyb@cs.indiana.edu`)

MATTHEW FLATT

University of Utah
(*e-mail:* `mflatt@cs.utah.edu`)

ANTON VAN STRAATEN

AppSolutions
(*e-mail:* `anton@appsolutions.com`)

ROBBY FINDLER	JACOB MATTHEWS
Northwestern University	*University of Chicago*
(*e-mail:* `robby@eecs.northwestern.edu`)	(*e-mail:* `jacobm@cs.uchicago.edu`)

(Authors, formal semantics)

RICHARD KELSEY, WILLIAM CLINGER, JONATHAN REES

(*Editors, Revised^5 Report on the Algorithmic Language Scheme*)

CAMBRIDGE
UNIVERSITY PRESS

Shaftesbury Road, Cambridge CB2 8EA, United Kingdom

One Liberty Plaza, 20th Floor, New York, NY 10006, USA

477 Williamstown Road, Port Melbourne, VIC 3207, Australia

314–321, 3rd Floor, Plot 3, Splendor Forum, Jasola District Centre, New Delhi – 110025, India

103 Penang Road, #05–06/07, Visioncrest Commercial, Singapore 238467

Cambridge University Press is part of Cambridge University Press & Assessment,
a department of the University of Cambridge.

We share the University's mission to contribute to society through the pursuit of
education, learning and research at the highest international levels of excellence.

www.cambridge.org
Information on this title: www.cambridge.org/9780521193993

© Cambridge University Press & Assessment 2009

First published 2009

A catalogue record for this publication is available from the British Library

ISBN   978-0-521-19399-3   Hardback
ISSN   0956-7968

A Supplement to the *Journal of Functional Programming*

Contents

PREFACE

This document contains the three parts comprising "R[6]RS", the sixth revision of a series of reports describing the programming language Scheme. These parts are the *Revised[6] Report on the Algorithmic Language Scheme* describing the language itself, the *Revised[6] Report on the Algorithmic Language Scheme — Libraries — describing the standard libraries, and *Revised[6] Report on the Algorithmic Language Scheme — Non-Normative Appendices* — with additional recommendations. A fourth report, not included in this document, gives some historical background and rationales for many aspects of the language and its libraries (Sperber *et al.*, 2007b). The historical background is summarized below.

These reports were originally published in 2007 on the www.r6rs.org web site, and were subsequently ratified by the Scheme community. Since then, a number of errors and inconsistencies have been found: these have been corrected for this document. Details on these corrections can be found on www.r6rs.org.

The individuals listed on the title page are not the sole authors of the text of the reports. Over the years, the following individuals were involved in discussions contributing to the design of the Scheme language, and were listed as authors of prior reports: Hal Abelson, Norman Adams, David Bartley, Gary Brooks, Daniel Friedman, Robert Halstead, Chris Hanson, Christopher Haynes, Eugene Kohlbecker, Don Oxley, Kent Pitman, Guillermo Rozas, Guy L. Steele Jr., Gerald Jay Sussman, and Mitchell Wand.

In order to highlight recent contributions, they are not listed as authors of this revision of the report. However, their contribution and service is gratefully acknowledged.

We intend this report to belong to the entire Scheme community, and so we grant permission to copy it in whole or in part without fee. In particular, we encourage implementors of Scheme to use this report as a starting point for manuals and other documentation, modifying it as necessary.

Historical background

The first description of Scheme was written by Gerald Jay Sussman and Guy Lewis Steele Jr. in 1975 (Sussman & Jr., 1975). A revised report by Steele and Sussman (Steele Jr. & Sussman, 1978) appeared in 1978 and described the evolution of the language as its MIT implementation was upgraded to support an innovative compiler (Steele Jr., 1978). Three distinct projects began in 1981 and 1982 to use variants of Scheme for courses at MIT, Yale, and Indiana University (Rees & IV, 1982; MIT Department of Electrical Engineering and Computer Science, 1984; Fessenden *et al.*, 1983). An introductory computer science textbook using Scheme was published in 1984 (Abelson *et al.*, 1996). A number of textbooks describing and using Scheme have been published since (Dybvig, 2003).

As Scheme became more widespread, local dialects began to diverge until students and researchers occasionally found it difficult to understand code written at other sites. Fifteen representatives of the major implementations of Scheme therefore met in October 1984 to work toward a better and more widely accepted standard for Scheme. Participating in this workshop were Hal Abelson, Norman Adams, David Bartley, Gary Brooks, William Clinger, Daniel Friedman, Robert Halstead, Chris Hanson, Christopher Haynes, Eugene Kohlbecker, Don Oxley, Jonathan Rees, Guillermo Rozas, Gerald Jay Sussman, and Mitchell Wand. Their report (Clinger, 1985), edited by Will Clinger, was published at MIT and Indiana University in the summer of 1985. Further revision took place in the spring of 1986 (Clinger & Rees, 1986) (edited by Jonathan Rees and Will Clinger), and in the spring of 1988 (Clinger & Rees, 1991b) (also edited by Will Clinger and Jonathan Rees). Another revision published in 1998, edited by Richard Kelsey, Will Clinger and Jonathan Rees, reflected further revisions agreed upon in a meeting at Xerox PARC in June 1992 (Kelsey *et al.*, 1998).

Attendees of the Scheme Workshop in Pittsburgh in October 2002 formed a Strategy Committee to discuss a process for producing new revisions of the report. The strategy committee drafted a charter for Scheme standardization. This charter, together with a process for selecting editorial committees for producing new revisions of the report, was confirmed by the attendees of the Scheme Workshop in Boston in November 2003. Subsequently, a Steering Committee according to the charter was selected, consisting of Alan Bawden, Guy L. Steele Jr., and Mitch Wand. An editorial committee charged with producing a new revision of the report was also formed at the end of 2003, consisting of Will Clinger, R. Kent Dybvig, Marc Feeley, Matthew Flatt, Richard Kelsey, Manuel Serrano, and Mike Sperber, with Marc Feeley acting as Editor-in-Chief. Richard Kelsey resigned from the committee in April 2005, and was replaced by Anton van Straaten. Marc Feeley and Manuel Serrano resigned from the committee in January 2006. Subsequently, the charter was revised to reduce the size of the editorial committee to five and to replace the office of Editor-in-Chief by a Chair and a Project Editor (Scheme Charter, 2006). R. Kent Dybvig served as Chair, and Mike Sperber served as Project Editor. Will Clinger resigned from the committee in May 2007. Parts of the report were posted as Scheme Requests for Implementation (SRFIs, see http://srfi.schemers.org/) and discussed by the community before being revised and finalized for the report (Flatt & Feeley, 2005; Clinger *et al.*, 2005; Clinger & Sperber, 2005; Flatt & Dybvig, 2005; Dybvig, 2006). Jacob Matthews and Robby Findler wrote the operational semantics for the language core, based on an earlier semantics for the language of the "Revised[5] Report" (Matthews & Findler, 2007).

Acknowledgements

Many people contributed significant help to this revision of the report. Specifically, we thank Aziz Ghuloum and André van Tonder for contributing reference implementations of the library system. We thank Alan Bawden, John Cowan, Sebastian Egner, Aubrey Jaffer, Shiro Kawai, Bradley Lucier, and André van Tonder for contributing insights on language design. Marc Feeley, Martin Gasbichler, Aubrey Jaffer, Lars T Hansen, Richard Kelsey, Olin Shivers, and André van Tonder wrote

SRFIs that served as direct input to the report. Casey Klein found and fixed several bugs in the formal semantics. Marcus Crestani, David Frese, Aziz Ghuloum, Arthur A. Gleckler, Eric Knauel, Jonathan Rees, and André van Tonder thoroughly proofread early versions of the report.

We would also like to thank the following people for their help in creating this report: Lauri Alanko, Eli Barzilay, Alan Bawden, Brian C. Barnes, Per Bothner, Trent Buck, Thomas Bushnell, Taylor Campbell, Ludovic Courtès, Pascal Costanza, John Cowan, Ray Dillinger, Jed Davis, J.A. "Biep" Durieux, Carl Eastlund, Sebastian Egner, Tom Emerson, Marc Feeley, Matthias Felleisen, Andy Freeman, Ken Friedenbach, Martin Gasbichler, Arthur A. Gleckler, Aziz Ghuloum, Dave Gurnell, Lars T Hansen, Ben Harris, Sven Hartrumpf, Dave Herman, Nils M. Holm, Stanislav Ievlev, James Jackson, Aubrey Jaffer, Shiro Kawai, Alexander Kjeldaas, Eric Knauel, Michael Lenaghan, Felix Klock, Donovan Kolbly, Marcin Kowalczyk, Thomas Lord, Bradley Lucier, Paulo J. Matos, Dan Muresan, Ryan Newton, Jason Orendorff, Erich Rast, Jeff Read, Jonathan Rees, Jorgen Schäfer, Paul Schlie, Manuel Serrano, Olin Shivers, Jonathan Shapiro, Jens Axel Søgaard, Jay Sulzberger, Pinku Surana, Mikael Tillenius, Sam Tobin-Hochstadt, David Van Horn, André van Tonder, Reinder Verlinde, Alan Watson, Andrew Wilcox, Jon Wilson, Lynn Winebarger, Keith Wright, and Chongkai Zhu.

Thanks are due as well to the following people for their help in creating the previous revisions of this report: Alan Bawden, Michael Blair, George Carrette, Andy Cromarty, Pavel Curtis, Jeff Dalton, Olivier Danvy, Ken Dickey, Bruce Duba, Marc Feeley, Andy Freeman, Richard Gabriel, Yekta Gürsel, Ken Haase, Robert Hieb, Paul Hudak, Morry Katz, Chris Lindblad, Mark Meyer, Jim Miller, Jim Philbin, John Ramsdell, Mike Shaff, Jonathan Shapiro, Julie Sussman, Perry Wagle, Daniel Weise, Henry Wu, and Ozan Yigit.

We thank Carol Fessenden, Daniel Friedman, and Christopher Haynes for permission to use text from the Scheme 311 version 4 reference manual. We thank Texas Instruments, Inc. for permission to use text from the *TI Scheme Language Reference Manual* (Texas Instruments, 1985). We gladly acknowledge the influence of manuals for MIT Scheme (MIT Department of Electrical Engineering and Computer Science, 1984), T (Rees *et al.*, 1984), Scheme 84 (Friedman *et al.*, 1985), Common Lisp (Steele Jr., 1990), Chez Scheme (Dybvig, 2005), PLT Scheme (Flatt, 2006), and Algol 60 (Backus *et al.*, 1963).

We also thank Betty Dexter for the extreme effort she put into setting this report in TEX, and Donald Knuth for designing the program that caused her troubles.

The Artificial Intelligence Laboratory of the Massachusetts Institute of Technology, the Computer Science Department of Indiana University, the Computer and Information Sciences Department of the University of Oregon, and the NEC Research Institute supported the preparation of this report. Support for the MIT work was provided in part by the Advanced Research Projects Agency of the Department of Defense under Office of Naval Research contract N00014-80-C-0505. Support for the Indiana University work was provided by NSF grants NCS 83-04567 and NCS 83-03325.

PART ONE
Language

Abstract

This part gives a defining description of the programming language Scheme. Scheme is a statically scoped and properly tail-recursive dialect of the Lisp programming language invented by Guy Lewis Steele Jr. and Gerald Jay Sussman. It was designed to have an exceptionally clear and simple semantics and few different ways to form expressions. A wide variety of programming paradigms, including functional, imperative, and message passing styles, find convenient expression in Scheme.

References to other parts of the document are identified by designations such as "library section" or "library chapter".

Guiding principles

To help guide the standardization effort, the editors have adopted a set of principles, presented below. Like the Scheme language defined in *Revised⁵ Report on the Algorithmic Language Scheme* (Kelsey *et al.*, 1998), the language described in this report is intended to:

- allow programmers to read each other's code, and allow development of portable programs that can be executed in any conforming implementation of Scheme;
- derive its power from simplicity, a small number of generally useful core syntactic forms and procedures, and no unnecessary restrictions on how they are composed;
- allow programs to define new procedures and new hygienic syntactic forms;
- support the representation of program source code as data;
- make procedure calls powerful enough to express any form of sequential control, and allow programs to perform non-local control operations without the use of global program transformations;
- allow interesting, purely functional programs to run indefinitely without terminating or running out of memory on finite-memory machines;
- allow educators to use the language to teach programming effectively, at various levels and with a variety of pedagogical approaches; and
- allow researchers to use the language to explore the design, implementation, and semantics of programming languages.

In addition, this report is intended to:

- allow programmers to create and distribute substantial programs and libraries, e.g., implementations of Scheme Requests for Implementation, that run without modification in a variety of Scheme implementations;

- support procedural, syntactic, and data abstraction more fully by allowing programs to define hygiene-bending and hygiene-breaking syntactic abstractions and new unique datatypes along with procedures and hygienic macros in any scope;
- allow programmers to rely on a level of automatic run-time type and bounds checking sufficient to ensure type safety; and
- allow implementations to generate efficient code, without requiring programmers to use implementation-specific operators or declarations.

While it was possible to write portable programs in Scheme as described in *Revised[5] Report on the Algorithmic Language Scheme*, and indeed portable Scheme programs were written prior to this report, many Scheme programs were not, primarily because of the lack of substantial standardized libraries and the proliferation of implementation-specific language additions.

In general, Scheme should include building blocks that allow a wide variety of libraries to be written, include commonly used user-level features to enhance portability and readability of library and application code, and exclude features that are less commonly used and easily implemented in separate libraries.

The language described in this report is intended to also be backward compatible with programs written in Scheme as described in *Revised[5] Report on the Algorithmic Language Scheme* to the extent possible without compromising the above principles and future viability of the language. With respect to future viability, the editors have operated under the assumption that many more Scheme programs will be written in the future than exist in the present, so the future programs are those with which we should be most concerned.

DESCRIPTION OF THE LANGUAGE

1 Overview of Scheme

This chapter gives an overview of Scheme's semantics. The purpose of this overview is to explain enough about the basic concepts of the language to facilitate understanding of the subsequent chapters of the report, which are organized as a reference manual. Consequently, this overview is not a complete introduction to the language, nor is it precise in all respects or normative in any way.

Following Algol, Scheme is a statically scoped programming language. Each use of a variable is associated with a lexically apparent binding of that variable.

Scheme has latent as opposed to manifest types (Waite & Goos, 1984). Types are associated with objects (also called values) rather than with variables. (Some authors refer to languages with latent types as untyped, weakly typed or dynamically typed languages.) Other languages with latent types are Python, Ruby, Smalltalk, and other dialects of Lisp. Languages with manifest types (sometimes referred to as strongly typed or statically typed languages) include Algol 60, C, C#, Java, Haskell, and ML.

All objects created in the course of a Scheme computation, including procedures and continuations, have unlimited extent. No Scheme object is ever destroyed. The reason that implementations of Scheme do not (usually!) run out of storage is that they are permitted to reclaim the storage occupied by an object if they can prove that the object cannot possibly matter to any future computation. Other languages in which most objects have unlimited extent include C#, Java, Haskell, most Lisp dialects, ML, Python, Ruby, and Smalltalk.

Implementations of Scheme must be properly tail-recursive. This allows the execution of an iterative computation in constant space, even if the iterative computation is described by a syntactically recursive procedure. Thus with a properly tail-recursive implementation, iteration can be expressed using the ordinary procedure-call mechanics, so that special iteration constructs are useful only as syntactic sugar.

Scheme was one of the first languages to support procedures as objects in their own right. Procedures can be created dynamically, stored in data structures, returned as results of procedures, and so on. Other languages with these properties include Common Lisp, Haskell, ML, Ruby, and Smalltalk.

One distinguishing feature of Scheme is that continuations, which in most other languages only operate behind the scenes, also have "first-class" status. First-class continuations are useful for implementing a wide variety of advanced control constructs, including non-local exits, backtracking, and coroutines.

In Scheme, the argument expressions of a procedure call are evaluated before the procedure gains control, whether the procedure needs the result of the evaluation or not. C, C#, Common Lisp, Python, Ruby, and Smalltalk are other languages that always evaluate argument expressions before invoking a procedure. This is distinct from the lazy-evaluation semantics of Haskell, or the call-by-name semantics of

Algol 60, where an argument expression is not evaluated unless its value is needed by the procedure.

Scheme's model of arithmetic provides a rich set of numerical types and operations on them. Furthermore, it distinguishes *exact* and *inexact* number objects: Essentially, an exact number object corresponds to a number exactly, and an inexact number object is the result of a computation that involved rounding or other errors.

1.1 Basic types

Scheme programs manipulate *objects*, which are also referred to as *values*. Scheme objects are organized into sets of values called *types*. This section gives an overview of the fundamentally important types of the Scheme language. More types are described in later chapters.

Note: As Scheme is latently typed, the use of the term *type* in this report differs from the use of the term in the context of other languages, particularly those with manifest typing.

Booleans A boolean is a truth value, and can be either true or false. In Scheme, the object for "false" is written #f. The object for "true" is written #t. In most places where a truth value is expected, however, any object different from #f counts as true.

Numbers Scheme supports a rich variety of numerical data types, including objects representing integers of arbitrary precision, rational numbers, complex numbers, and inexact numbers of various kinds. Chapter 3 gives an overview of the structure of Scheme's numerical tower.

Characters Scheme characters mostly correspond to textual characters. More precisely, they are isomorphic to the *scalar values* of the Unicode standard.

Strings Strings are finite sequences of characters with fixed length and thus represent arbitrary Unicode texts.

Symbols A symbol is an object representing a string, the symbol's *name*. Unlike strings, two symbols whose names are spelled the same way are never distinguishable. Symbols are useful for many applications; for instance, they may be used the way enumerated values are used in other languages.

Pairs and lists A pair is a data structure with two components. The most common use of pairs is to represent (singly linked) lists, where the first component (the "car") represents the first element of the list, and the second component (the "cdr") the rest of the list. Scheme also has a distinguished empty list, which is the last cdr in a chain of pairs that form a list.

Vectors Vectors, like lists, are linear data structures representing finite sequences of arbitrary objects. Whereas the elements of a list are accessed sequentially through the chain of pairs representing it, the elements of a vector are addressed by integer indices. Thus, vectors are more appropriate than lists for random access to elements.

Procedures Procedures are values in Scheme.

1.2 Expressions

The most important elements of Scheme code are *expressions*. Expressions can be *evaluated*, producing a *value*. (Actually, any number of values—see section 5.8.) The most fundamental expressions are literal expressions:

```
#t                                    ⟹ #t
23                                    ⟹ 23
```

This notation means that the expression #t evaluates to #t, that is, the value for "true", and that the expression 23 evaluates to a number object representing the number 23.

Compound expressions are formed by placing parentheses around their subexpressions. The first subexpression identifies an operation; the remaining subexpressions are operands to the operation:

```
(+ 23 42)                             ⟹ 65
(+ 14 (* 23 42))                      ⟹ 980
```

In the first of these examples, + is the name of the built-in operation for addition, and 23 and 42 are the operands. The expression (+ 23 42) reads as "the sum of 23 and 42". Compound expressions can be nested—the second example reads as "the sum of 14 and the product of 23 and 42".

As these examples indicate, compound expressions in Scheme are always written using the same prefix notation. As a consequence, the parentheses are needed to indicate structure. Consequently, "superfluous" parentheses, which are often permissible in mathematical notation and also in many programming languages, are not allowed in Scheme.

As in many other languages, whitespace (including line endings) is not significant when it separates subexpressions of an expression, and can be used to indicate structure.

1.3 Variables and binding

Scheme allows identifiers to stand for locations containing values. These identifiers are called variables. In many cases, specifically when the location's value is never modified after its creation, it is useful to think of the variable as standing for the value directly.

```
(let ((x 23)
      (y 42))
  (+ x y))                            ⟹ 65
```

In this case, the expression starting with `let` is a binding construct. The parenthesized structure following the `let` lists variables alongside expressions: the variable
x alongside 23, and the variable y alongside 42. The `let` expression binds x to 23,
and y to 42. These bindings are available in the *body* of the `let` expression, (+ x
y), and only there.

1.4 Definitions

The variables bound by a `let` expression are *local*, because their bindings are visible
only in the `let`'s body. Scheme also allows creating top-level bindings for identifiers
as follows:

```
(define x 23)
(define y 42)
(+ x y)                              ⟹ 65
```

(These are actually "top-level" in the body of a top-level program or library; see
section 1.12 below.)

The first two parenthesized structures are *definitions*; they create top-level bindings,
binding x to 23 and y to 42. Definitions are not expressions, and cannot appear in
all places where an expression can occur. Moreover, a definition has no value.

Bindings follow the lexical structure of the program: When several bindings with
the same name exist, a variable refers to the binding that is closest to it, starting
with its occurrence in the program and going from inside to outside, and referring
to a top-level binding if no local binding can be found along the way:

```
(define x 23)
(define y 42)
(let ((y 43))
  (+ x y))                           ⟹ 66

(let ((y 43))
  (let ((y 44))
    (+ x y)))                        ⟹ 67
```

1.5 Forms

While definitions are not expressions, compound expressions and definitions exhibit
similar syntactic structure:

```
(define x 23)
(* x 2)
```

While the first line contains a definition, and the second an expression, this distinction
depends on the bindings for `define` and `*`. At the purely syntactical level, both are
forms, and *form* is the general name for a syntactic part of a Scheme program. In
particular, 23 is a *subform* of the form (`define x 23`).

1.6 Procedures

Definitions can also be used to define procedures:

```
(define (f x)
  (+ x 42))

(f 23)                          ⟹ 65
```

A procedure is, slightly simplified, an abstraction of an expression over objects. In the example, the first definition defines a procedure called f. (Note the parentheses around f x, which indicate that this is a procedure definition.) The expression (f 23) is a procedure call, meaning, roughly, "evaluate (+ x 42) (the body of the procedure) with x bound to 23".

As procedures are objects, they can be passed to other procedures:

```
(define (f x)
  (+ x 42))

(define (g p x)
  (p x))

(g f 23)                        ⟹ 65
```

In this example, the body of g is evaluated with p bound to f and x bound to 23, which is equivalent to (f 23), which evaluates to 65.

In fact, many predefined operations of Scheme are provided not by syntax, but by variables whose values are procedures. The + operation, for example, which receives special syntactic treatment in many other languages, is just a regular identifier in Scheme, bound to a procedure that adds number objects. The same holds for * and many others:

```
(define (h op x y)
  (op x y))

(h + 23 42)                     ⟹ 65
(h * 23 42)                     ⟹ 966
```

Procedure definitions are not the only way to create procedures. A lambda expression creates a new procedure as an object, with no need to specify a name:

```
((lambda (x) (+ x 42)) 23)      ⟹ 65
```

The entire expression in this example is a procedure call; (lambda (x) (+ x 42)), evaluates to a procedure that takes a single number object and adds 42 to it.

1.7 Procedure calls and syntactic keywords

Whereas (+ 23 42), (f 23), and ((lambda (x) (+ x 42)) 23) are all examples of procedure calls, lambda and let expressions are not. This is because let, even

though it is an identifier, is not a variable, but is instead a *syntactic keyword*. A form
that has a syntactic keyword as its first subexpression obeys special rules determined
by the keyword. The `define` identifier in a definition is also a syntactic keyword.
Hence, definitions are also not procedure calls.

The rules for the `lambda` keyword specify that the first subform is a list of
parameters, and the remaining subforms are the body of the procedure. In `let`
expressions, the first subform is a list of binding specifications, and the remaining
subforms constitute a body of expressions.

Procedure calls can generally be distinguished from these *special forms* by looking
for a syntactic keyword in the first position of an form: if the first position does not
contain a syntactic keyword, the expression is a procedure call. (So-called *identifier
macros* allow creating other kinds of special forms, but are comparatively rare.) The
set of syntactic keywords of Scheme is fairly small, which usually makes this task
fairly simple. It is possible, however, to create new bindings for syntactic keywords;
see section 1.9 below.

1.8 Assignment

Scheme variables bound by definitions or `let` or `lambda` expressions are not actually bound directly to the objects specified in the respective bindings, but to
locations containing these objects. The contents of these locations can subsequently
be modified destructively via *assignment* :

```
(let ((x 23))
  (set! x 42)
  x)                               ⟹ 42
```

In this case, the body of the `let` expression consists of two expressions which
are evaluated sequentially, with the value of the final expression becoming the value
of the entire `let` expression. The expression (`set! x 42`) is an assignment, saying
"replace the object in the location referenced by x with 42". Thus, the previous value
of x, 23, is replaced by 42.

1.9 Derived forms and macros

Many of the special forms specified in this report can be translated into more basic
special forms. For example, a `let` expression can be translated into a procedure call
and a `lambda` expression. The following two expressions are equivalent:

```
(let ((x 23)
      (y 42))
  (+ x y))                        ⟹ 65

((lambda (x y) (+ x y)) 23 42)    ⟹ 65
```

Special forms like `let` expressions are called *derived forms* because their semantics
can be derived from that of other kinds of forms by a syntactic transformation.

Some procedure definitions are also derived forms. The following two definitions are equivalent:

```
(define (f x)
  (+ x 42))
```

```
(define f
  (lambda (x)
    (+ x 42)))
```

In Scheme, it is possible for a program to create its own derived forms by binding syntactic keywords to macros:

```
(define-syntax def
  (syntax-rules ()
    ((def f (p ...) body)
     (define (f p ...)
       body))))
```

```
(def f (x)
  (+ x 42))
```

The define-syntax construct specifies that a parenthesized structure matching the pattern (def f (p ...) body), where f, p, and body are pattern variables, is translated to (define (f p ...) body). Thus, the def form appearing in the example gets translated to:

```
(define (f x)
  (+ x 42))
```

The ability to create new syntactic keywords makes Scheme extremely flexible and expressive, allowing many of the features built into other languages to be derived forms in Scheme.

1.10 Syntactic data and datum values

A subset of the Scheme objects is called *datum values*. These include booleans, number objects, characters, symbols, and strings as well as lists and vectors whose elements are data. Each datum value may be represented in textual form as a *syntactic datum*, which can be written out and read back in without loss of information. A datum value may be represented by several different syntactic data. Moreover, each datum value can be trivially translated to a literal expression in a program by prepending a ' to a corresponding syntactic datum:

```
'23          ⟹ 23
'#t          ⟹ #t
'foo         ⟹ foo
'(1 2 3)     ⟹ (1 2 3)
'#(1 2 3)    ⟹ #(1 2 3)
```

The ' shown in the previous examples is not needed for representations of number objects or booleans. The syntactic datum foo represents a symbol with name "foo", and 'foo is a literal expression with that symbol as its value. (1 2 3) is a syntactic datum that represents a list with elements 1, 2, and 3, and '(1 2 3) is a literal expression with this list as its value. Likewise, #(1 2 3) is a syntactic datum that represents a vector with elements 1, 2 and 3, and '#(1 2 3) is the corresponding literal.

The syntactic data are a superset of the Scheme forms. Thus, data can be used to represent Scheme forms as data objects. In particular, symbols can be used to represent identifiers.

```
'(+ 23 42)                        ⟹ (+ 23 42)
'(define (f x) (+ x 42))          ⟹ (define (f x) (+ x 42))
```

This facilitates writing programs that operate on Scheme source code, in particular interpreters and program transformers.

1.11 Continuations

Whenever a Scheme expression is evaluated there is a *continuation* wanting the result of the expression. The continuation represents an entire (default) future for the computation. For example, informally the continuation of 3 in the expression

```
(+ 1 3)
```

adds 1 to it. Normally these ubiquitous continuations are hidden behind the scenes and programmers do not think much about them. On rare occasions, however, a programmer may need to deal with continuations explicitly. The call-with-current-continuation procedure (see section 11.15) allows Scheme programmers to do that by creating a procedure that reinstates the current continuation. The call-with-current-continuation procedure accepts a procedure, calls it immediately with an argument that is an *escape procedure*. This escape procedure can then be called with an argument that becomes the result of the call to call-with-current-continuation. That is, the escape procedure abandons its own continuation, and reinstates the continuation of the call to call-with-current-continuation.

In the following example, an escape procedure representing the continuation that adds 1 to its argument is bound to escape, and then called with 3 as an argument. The continuation of the call to escape is abandoned, and instead the 3 is passed to the continuation that adds 1:

```
(+ 1 (call-with-current-continuation
        (lambda (escape)
          (+ 2 (escape 3)))))        ⟹ 4
```

An escape procedure has unlimited extent: It can be called after the continuation it captured has been invoked, and it can be called multiple times. This makes call-with-current-continuation significantly more powerful than typical non-local control constructs such as exceptions in other languages.

1.12 Libraries

Scheme code can be organized in components called *libraries*. Each library contains definitions and expressions. It can import definitions from other libraries and export definitions to other libraries.

The following library called (hello) exports a definition called `hello-world`, and imports the base library (see chapter 11) and the simple I/O library (see library section 8.3). The `hello-world` export is a procedure that displays `Hello World` on a separate line:

```
(library (hello)
  (export hello-world)
  (import (rnrs base)
          (rnrs io simple))
  (define (hello-world)
    (display "Hello World")
    (newline)))
```

1.13 Top-level programs

A Scheme program is invoked via a *top-level program*. Like a library, a top-level program contains imports, definitions and expressions, and specifies an entry point for execution. Thus a top-level program defines, via the transitive closure of the libraries it imports, a Scheme program.

The following top-level program obtains the first argument from the command line via the `command-line` procedure from the (rnrs programs (6)) library (see library chapter 10). It then opens the file using `open-file-input-port` (see library section 8.2), yielding a *port*, i.e. a connection to the file as a data source, and calls the `get-bytes-all` procedure to obtain the contents of the file as binary data. It then uses `put-bytes` to output the contents of the file to standard output:

```
#!r6rs
(import (rnrs base)
        (rnrs io ports)
        (rnrs programs))
(let ((p (standard-output-port)))
  (put-bytevector p
                  (call-with-port
                      (open-file-input-port
                          (cadr (command-line)))
                      get-bytevector-all))
  (close-port p))
```

2 Requirement levels

The key words "must", "must not", "should", "should not", "recommended", "may", and "optional" in this report are to be interpreted as described in RFC 2119 (Bradner, 1997). Specifically:

must This word means that a statement is an absolute requirement of the specification.

must not This phrase means that a statement is an absolute prohibition of the specification.

should This word, or the adjective "recommended", means that valid reasons may exist in particular circumstances to ignore a statement, but that the implications must be understood and weighed before choosing a different course.

should not This phrase, or the phrase "not recommended", means that valid reasons may exist in particular circumstances when the behavior of a statement is acceptable, but that the implications should be understood and weighed before choosing the course described by the statement.

may This word, or the adjective "optional", means that an item is truly optional.

In particular, this report occasionally uses "should" to designate circumstances that are outside the specification of this report, but cannot be practically detected by an implementation; see section 5.4. In such circumstances, a particular implementation may allow the programmer to ignore the recommendation of the report and even exhibit reasonable behavior. However, as the report does not specify the behavior, these programs may be unportable, that is, their execution might produce different results on different implementations.

Moreover, this report occasionally uses the phrase "not required" to note the absence of an absolute requirement.

3 Numbers

This chapter describes Scheme's model for numbers. It is important to distinguish between the mathematical numbers, the Scheme objects that attempt to model them, the machine representations used to implement the numbers, and notations used to write numbers. In this report, the term *number* refers to a mathematical number, and the term *number object* refers to a Scheme object representing a number. This report uses the types *complex*, *real*, *rational*, and *integer* to refer to both mathematical numbers and number objects. The *fixnum* and *flonum* types refer to special subsets of the number objects, as determined by common machine representations.

3.1 Numerical tower

Numbers may be arranged into a tower of subsets in which each level is a subset of the level above it:

    number
    complex

> real
> rational
> integer

For example, 5 is an integer. Therefore 5 is also a rational, a real, and a complex. The same is true of the number objects that model 5.

Number objects are organized as a corresponding tower of subtypes defined by the predicates `number?`, `complex?`, `real?`, `rational?`, and `integer?`; see section 11.7.7. Integer number objects are also called *integer objects*.

There is no simple relationship between the subset that contains a number and its representation inside a computer. For example, the integer 5 may have several representations. Scheme's numerical operations treat number objects as abstract data, as independent of their representation as possible. Although an implementation of Scheme may use many different representations for numbers, this should not be apparent to a casual programmer writing simple programs.

3.2 Exactness

It is useful to distinguish between number objects that are known to correspond to a number exactly, and those number objects whose computation involved rounding or other errors. For example, index operations into data structures may need to know the index exactly, as may some operations on polynomial coefficients in a symbolic algebra system. On the other hand, the results of measurements are inherently inexact, and irrational numbers may be approximated by rational and therefore inexact approximations. In order to catch uses of numbers known only inexactly where exact numbers are required, Scheme explicitly distinguishes *exact* from *inexact* number objects. This distinction is orthogonal to the dimension of type.

A number object is exact if it is the value of an exact numerical literal or was derived from exact number objects using only exact operations. Exact number objects correspond to mathematical numbers in the obvious way.

Conversely, a number object is inexact if it is the value of an inexact numerical literal, or was derived from inexact number objects, or was derived using inexact operations. Thus inexactness is contagious.

Exact arithmetic is reliable in the following sense: If exact number objects are passed to any of the arithmetic procedures described in section 11.7.1, and an exact number object is returned, then the result is mathematically correct. This is generally not true of computations involving inexact number objects because approximate methods such as floating-point arithmetic may be used, but it is the duty of each implementation to make the result as close as practical to the mathematically ideal result.

3.3 Fixnums and flonums

A *fixnum* is an exact integer object that lies within a certain implementation-dependent subrange of the exact integer objects. (Library section 11.2 describes a library for computing with fixnums.) Likewise, every implementation must designate a subset of its inexact real number objects as *flonums*, and to convert certain external representations into flonums. (Library section 11.3 describes a library for computing with flonums.) Note that this does not imply that an implementation must use floating-point representations.

3.4 *Implementation requirements*

Implementations of Scheme must support number objects for the entire tower of subtypes given in section 3.1. Moreover, implementations must support exact integer objects and exact rational number objects of practically unlimited size and precision, and to implement certain procedures (listed in 11.7.1) so they always return exact results when given exact arguments. ("Practically unlimited" means that the size and precision of these numbers should only be limited by the size of the available memory.)

Implementations may support only a limited range of inexact number objects of any type, subject to the requirements of this section. For example, an implementation may limit the range of the inexact real number objects (and therefore the range of inexact integer and rational number objects) to the dynamic range of the flonum format. Furthermore the gaps between the inexact integer objects and rationals are likely to be very large in such an implementation as the limits of this range are approached.

An implementation may use floating point and other approximate representation strategies for inexact numbers. This report recommends, but does not require, that the IEEE floating-point standards be followed by implementations that use floating-point representations, and that implementations using other representations should match or exceed the precision achievable using these floating-point standards (IEEE754, 1985).

In particular, implementations that use floating-point representations must follow these rules: A floating-point result must be represented with at least as much precision as is used to express any of the inexact arguments to that operation. Potentially inexact operations such as sqrt, when applied to exact arguments, should produce exact answers whenever possible (for example the square root of an exact 4 ought to be an exact 2). However, this is not required. If, on the other hand, an exact number object is operated upon so as to produce an inexact result (as by sqrt), and if the result is represented in floating point, then the most precise floating-point format available must be used; but if the result is represented in some other way then the representation must have at least as much precision as the most precise floating-point format available.

It is the programmer's responsibility to avoid using inexact number objects with magnitude or significand too large to be represented in the implementation.

3.5 Infinities and NaNs

Some Scheme implementations, specifically those that follow the IEEE floating-point standards, distinguish special number objects called *positive infinity*, *negative infinity*, and *NaN*.

Positive infinity is regarded as an inexact real (but not rational) number object that represents an indeterminate number greater than the numbers represented by all rational number objects. Negative infinity is regarded as an inexact real (but not rational) number object that represents an indeterminate number less than the numbers represented by all rational numbers.

A NaN is regarded as an inexact real (but not rational) number object so indeterminate that it might represent any real number, including positive or negative infinity, and might even be greater than positive infinity or less than negative infinity.

3.6 Distinguished -0.0

Some Scheme implementations, specifically those that follow the IEEE floating-point standards, distinguish between number objects for 0.0 and −0.0, i.e., positive and negative inexact zero. This report will sometimes specify the behavior of certain arithmetic operations on these number objects. These specifications are marked with "if −0.0 is distinguished" or "implementations that distinguish −0.0".

4 Lexical syntax and datum syntax

The syntax of Scheme code is organized in three levels:

1. the *lexical syntax* that describes how a program text is split into a sequence of lexemes,
2. the *datum syntax*, formulated in terms of the lexical syntax, that structures the lexeme sequence as a sequence of *syntactic data*, where a syntactic datum is a recursively structured entity,
3. the *program syntax* formulated in terms of the read syntax, imposing further structure and assigning meaning to syntactic data.

Syntactic data (also called *external representations*) double as a notation for objects, and Scheme's (rnrs io ports (6)) library (library section 8.2) provides the get-datum and put-datum procedures for reading and writing syntactic data, converting between their textual representation and the corresponding objects. Each syntactic datum represents a corresponding *datum value*. A syntactic datum can be used in a program to obtain the corresponding datum value using quote (see section 11.4.1).

Scheme source code consists of syntactic data and (non-significant) comments. Syntactic data in Scheme source code are called *forms*. (A form nested inside another form is called a *subform*.) Consequently, Scheme's syntax has the property that any sequence of characters that is a form is also a syntactic datum representing some object. This can lead to confusion, since it may not be obvious out of context whether a given sequence of characters is intended to be a representation of objects or the text of a program. It is also a source of power, since it facilitates writing programs such as interpreters or compilers that treat programs as objects (or vice versa).

A datum value may have several different external representations. For example, both "#e28.000" and "#x1c" are syntactic data representing the exact integer object 28, and the syntactic data "(8 13)", "(08 13)", "(8 . (13 . ()))" all represent a list containing the exact integer objects 8 and 13. Syntactic data that represent equal objects (in the sense of equal?; see section 11.5) are always equivalent as forms of a program.

Because of the close correspondence between syntactic data and datum values, this report sometimes uses the term *datum* for either a syntactic datum or a datum value when the exact meaning is apparent from the context.

An implementation must not extend the lexical or datum syntax in any way, with one exception: it need not treat the syntax #!⟨identifier⟩, for any ⟨identifier⟩ (see section 4.2.4) that is not r6rs, as a syntax violation, and it may use specific #!-prefixed identifiers as flags indicating that subsequent input contains extensions to the standard lexical or datum syntax. The syntax #!r6rs may be used to signify that the input afterward is written with the lexical syntax and datum syntax described by this report. #!r6rs is otherwise treated as a comment; see section 4.2.3.

4.1 Notation

The formal syntax for Scheme is written in an extended BNF. Non-terminals are written using angle brackets. Case is insignificant for non-terminal names.

All spaces in the grammar are for legibility. ⟨Empty⟩ stands for the empty string.

The following extensions to BNF are used to make the description more concise: ⟨thing⟩* means zero or more occurrences of ⟨thing⟩, and ⟨thing⟩+ means at least one ⟨thing⟩.

Some non-terminal names refer to the Unicode scalar values of the same name: ⟨character tabulation⟩ (U+0009), ⟨linefeed⟩ (U+000A), ⟨line tabulation⟩ (U+000B), ⟨form feed⟩ (U+000C), ⟨carriage return⟩ (U+000D), ⟨space⟩ (U+0020), ⟨next line⟩ (U+0085), ⟨line separator⟩ (U+2028), and ⟨paragraph separator⟩ (U+2029).

4.2 Lexical syntax

The lexical syntax determines how a character sequence is split into a sequence of lexemes, omitting non-significant portions such as comments and whitespace. The character sequence is assumed to be text according to the Unicode standard (Unicode Consortium, 2007). Some of the lexemes, such as identifiers, representations of number objects, strings etc., of the lexical syntax are syntactic data in the datum syntax, and thus represent objects. Besides the formal account of the syntax, this section also describes what datum values are represented by these syntactic data.

The lexical syntax, in the description of comments, contains a forward reference to

⟨datum⟩, which is described as part of the datum syntax. Being comments, however, these ⟨datum⟩s do not play a significant role in the syntax.

Case is significant except in representations of booleans, number objects, and in hexadecimal numbers specifying Unicode scalar values. For example, #x1A and #X1a are equivalent. The identifier Foo is, however, distinct from the identifier FOO.

4.2.1 Formal account

⟨Interlexeme space⟩ may occur on either side of any lexeme, but not within a lexeme. ⟨Identifier⟩s, ., ⟨number⟩s, ⟨character⟩s, and ⟨boolean⟩s, must be terminated by a ⟨delimiter⟩ or by the end of the input.

The following two characters are reserved for future extensions to the language: { }

⟨lexeme⟩ ⟶ ⟨identifier⟩ | ⟨boolean⟩ | ⟨number⟩
    | ⟨character⟩ | ⟨string⟩
    | (|) | [|] | #(| #vu8(| ' | ` | , | ,@ | .
    | #' | #` | #, | #,@
⟨delimiter⟩ ⟶ (|) | [|] | " | ; | #
    | ⟨whitespace⟩
⟨whitespace⟩ ⟶ ⟨character tabulation⟩
    | ⟨linefeed⟩ | ⟨line tabulation⟩ | ⟨form feed⟩
    | ⟨carriage return⟩ | ⟨next line⟩
    | ⟨any character whose category is Zs, Zl, or Zp⟩
⟨line ending⟩ ⟶ ⟨linefeed⟩ | ⟨carriage return⟩
    | ⟨carriage return⟩ ⟨linefeed⟩ | ⟨next line⟩
    | ⟨carriage return⟩ ⟨next line⟩ | ⟨line separator⟩
⟨comment⟩ ⟶ ; ⟨all subsequent characters up to a
                ⟨line ending⟩ or ⟨paragraph separator⟩⟩
    | ⟨nested comment⟩
    | #; ⟨interlexeme space⟩ ⟨datum⟩
    | #!r6rs
⟨nested comment⟩ ⟶ #| ⟨comment text⟩
                ⟨comment cont⟩* |#
⟨comment text⟩ ⟶ ⟨character sequence not containing
             #| or |#⟩
⟨comment cont⟩ ⟶ ⟨nested comment⟩ ⟨comment text⟩
⟨atmosphere⟩ ⟶ ⟨whitespace⟩ | ⟨comment⟩
⟨interlexeme space⟩ ⟶ ⟨atmosphere⟩*

⟨identifier⟩ ⟶ ⟨initial⟩ ⟨subsequent⟩*
    | ⟨peculiar identifier⟩
⟨initial⟩ ⟶ ⟨constituent⟩ | ⟨special initial⟩
    | ⟨inline hex escape⟩
⟨letter⟩ ⟶ a | b | c | ... | z

```
     | A | B | C | ... | Z
```
⟨constituent⟩ ⟶ ⟨letter⟩
    | ⟨any character whose Unicode scalar value is greater than
        127, and whose category is Lu, Ll, Lt, Lm, Lo, Mn,
        Nl, No, Pd, Pc, Po, Sc, Sm, Sk, So, or Co⟩
⟨special initial⟩ ⟶ ! | $ | % | & | * | / | : | < | =
    | > | ? | ^ | _ | ~
⟨subsequent⟩ ⟶ ⟨initial⟩ | ⟨digit⟩
    | ⟨any character whose category is Nd, Mc, or Me⟩
    | ⟨special subsequent⟩
⟨digit⟩ ⟶ 0 | 1 | 2 | 3 | 4 | 5 | 6 | 7 | 8 | 9
⟨hex digit⟩ ⟶ ⟨digit⟩
    | a | A | b | B | c | C | d | D | e | E | f | F
⟨special subsequent⟩ ⟶ + | - | . | @
⟨inline hex escape⟩ ⟶ \x⟨hex scalar value⟩;
⟨hex scalar value⟩ ⟶ ⟨hex digit⟩$^{+}$
⟨peculiar identifier⟩ ⟶ + | - | ... | -> ⟨subsequent⟩*
⟨boolean⟩ ⟶ #t | #T | #f | #F
⟨character⟩ ⟶ #\⟨any character⟩
    | #\⟨character name⟩
    | #\x⟨hex scalar value⟩
⟨character name⟩ ⟶ nul | alarm | backspace | tab
    | linefeed | newline | vtab | page | return
    | esc | space | delete
⟨string⟩ ⟶ " ⟨string element⟩* "
⟨string element⟩ ⟶ ⟨any character other than " or \⟩
    | \a | \b | \t | \n | \v | \f | \r
    | \" | \\
    | \⟨intraline whitespace⟩*⟨line ending⟩
        ⟨intraline whitespace⟩*
    | ⟨inline hex escape⟩
⟨intraline whitespace⟩ ⟶ ⟨character tabulation⟩
    | ⟨any character whose category is Zs⟩
```

A ⟨hex scalar value⟩ represents a Unicode scalar value between 0 and #x10FFFF, excluding the range [#xD800, #xDFFF].

The rules for ⟨num $R$⟩, ⟨complex $R$⟩, ⟨real $R$⟩, ⟨ureal $R$⟩, ⟨uinteger $R$⟩, and ⟨prefix $R$⟩ below should be replicated for $R = 2, 8, 10$, and 16. There are no rules for ⟨decimal 2⟩, ⟨decimal 8⟩, and ⟨decimal 16⟩, which means that number representations containing decimal points or exponents must be in decimal radix.

In the following rules, case is insignificant.

```
⟨number⟩ ⟶ ⟨num 2⟩ | ⟨num 8⟩
    | ⟨num 10⟩ | ⟨num 16⟩
⟨num R⟩ ⟶ ⟨prefix R⟩ ⟨complex R⟩
⟨complex R⟩ ⟶ ⟨real R⟩ | ⟨real R⟩ @ ⟨real R⟩
```
```

    | ⟨real R⟩ + ⟨ureal R⟩ i | ⟨real R⟩ - ⟨ureal R⟩ i
    | ⟨real R⟩ + ⟨naninf⟩ i | ⟨real R⟩ - ⟨naninf⟩ i
    | ⟨real R⟩ + i | ⟨real R⟩ - i
    | + ⟨ureal R⟩ i | - ⟨ureal R⟩ i
    | + ⟨naninf⟩ i | - ⟨naninf⟩ i
    | + i | - i

⟨real R⟩ ⟶ ⟨sign⟩ ⟨ureal R⟩
    | + ⟨naninf⟩ | - ⟨naninf⟩

⟨naninf⟩ ⟶ nan.0 | inf.0

⟨ureal R⟩ ⟶ ⟨uinteger R⟩
    | ⟨uinteger R⟩ / ⟨uinteger R⟩
    | ⟨decimal R⟩ ⟨mantissa width⟩

⟨decimal 10⟩ ⟶ ⟨uinteger 10⟩ ⟨suffix⟩
    | . ⟨digit 10⟩⁺ ⟨suffix⟩
    | ⟨digit 10⟩⁺ . ⟨digit 10⟩* ⟨suffix⟩

⟨uinteger R⟩ ⟶ ⟨digit R⟩⁺

⟨prefix R⟩ ⟶ ⟨radix R⟩ ⟨exactness⟩
    | ⟨exactness⟩ ⟨radix R⟩

⟨suffix⟩ ⟶ ⟨empty⟩
    | ⟨exponent marker⟩ ⟨sign⟩ ⟨digit 10⟩⁺

⟨exponent marker⟩ ⟶ e | s | f
    | d | l

⟨mantissa width⟩ ⟶ ⟨empty⟩
    | | ⟨digit 10⟩⁺

⟨sign⟩ ⟶ ⟨empty⟩ | + | -

⟨exactness⟩ ⟶ ⟨empty⟩
    | #i | #e

⟨radix 2⟩ ⟶ #b

⟨radix 8⟩ ⟶ #o

⟨radix 10⟩ ⟶ ⟨empty⟩ | #d

⟨radix 16⟩ ⟶ #x

⟨digit 2⟩ ⟶ 0 | 1

⟨digit 8⟩ ⟶ 0 | 1 | 2 | 3 | 4 | 5 | 6 | 7

⟨digit 10⟩ ⟶ ⟨digit⟩

⟨digit 16⟩ ⟶ ⟨hex digit⟩

4.2.2 Line endings

Line endings are significant in Scheme in single-line comments (see section 4.2.3) and within string literals. In Scheme source code, any of the line endings in ⟨line ending⟩ marks the end of a line. Moreover, the two-character line endings ⟨carriage return⟩ ⟨linefeed⟩ and ⟨carriage return⟩ ⟨next line⟩ each count as a single line ending.

In a string literal, a ⟨line ending⟩ not preceded by a \ stands for a linefeed character, which is the standard line-ending character of Scheme.

4.2.3 Whitespace and comments

Whitespace characters are spaces, linefeeds, carriage returns, character tabulations, form feeds, line tabulations, and any other character whose category is Zs, Zl, or Zp. Whitespace is used for improved readability and as necessary to separate lexemes from each other. Whitespace may occur between any two lexemes, but not within a lexeme. Whitespace may also occur inside a string, where it is significant.

The lexical syntax includes several comment forms. In all cases, comments are invisible to Scheme, except that they act as delimiters, so, for example, a comment cannot appear in the middle of an identifier or representation of a number object.

A semicolon (;) indicates the start of a line comment. The comment continues to the end of the line on which the semicolon appears.

Another way to indicate a comment is to prefix a ⟨datum⟩ (cf. section 4.3.1) with #;, possibly with ⟨interlexeme space⟩ before the ⟨datum⟩. The comment consists of the comment prefix #; and the ⟨datum⟩ together. This notation is useful for "commenting out" sections of code.

Block comments may be indicated with properly nested #| and |# pairs.

```
#|
    The FACT procedure computes the factorial
    of a non-negative integer.
|#
(define fact
  (lambda (n)
    ;; base case
    (if (= n 0)
        #;(= n 1)
        1          ; identity of *
        (* n (fact (- n 1)))))))
```

The lexeme #!r6rs, which signifies that the program text that follows is written with the lexical and datum syntax described in this report, is also otherwise treated as a comment.

4.2.4 Identifiers

Most identifiers allowed by other programming languages are also acceptable to Scheme. In general, a sequence of letters, digits, and "extended alphabetic characters" is an identifier when it begins with a character that cannot begin a representation of a number object. In addition, +, -, and ... are identifiers, as is a sequence of letters, digits, and extended alphabetic characters that begins with the two-character sequence ->. Here are some examples of identifiers:

```
lambda          q                soup
list->vector    +                V17a
<=              a34kTMNs         ->-
the-word-recursion-has-many-meanings
```

Extended alphabetic characters may be used within identifiers as if they were letters. The following are extended alphabetic characters:

```
! $ % & * + - . / : < = > ? @ ^ _ ~
```

Moreover, all characters whose Unicode scalar values are greater than 127 and whose Unicode category is Lu, Ll, Lt, Lm, Lo, Mn, Mc, Me, Nd, Nl, No, Pd, Pc, Po, Sc, Sm, Sk, So, or Co can be used within identifiers. In addition, any character can be used within an identifier when specified via an ⟨inline hex escape⟩. For example, the identifier H\x65;llo is the same as the identifier Hello, and the identifier \x3BB; is the same as the identifier λ.

Any identifier may be used as a variable or as a syntactic keyword (see sections 5.2 and 9.2) in a Scheme program. Any identifier may also be used as a syntactic datum, in which case it represents a *symbol* (see section 11.10).

4.2.5 Booleans

The standard boolean objects for true and false have external representations #t and #f.

4.2.6 Characters

Characters are represented using the notation #\⟨character⟩ or #\⟨character name⟩ or #\x⟨hex scalar value⟩.

For example:

```
#\a          lower case letter a
#\A          upper case letter A
#\(          left parenthesis
#\           space character
#\nul        U+0000
#\alarm      U+0007
#\backspace  U+0008
#\tab        U+0009
#\linefeed   U+000A
#\newline    U+000A
#\vtab       U+000B
#\page       U+000C
#\return     U+000D
#\esc        U+001B
#\space      U+0020
             preferred way to write a space
```

`#\delete`	U+007F
`#\xFF`	U+00FF
`#\x03BB`	U+03BB
`#\x00006587`	U+6587
`#\λ`	U+03BB
`#\x0001z`	&lexical *exception*
`#\λx`	&lexical *exception*
`#\alarmx`	&lexical *exception*
`#\alarm x`	U+0007
	followed by x
`#\Alarm`	&lexical *exception*
`#\alert`	&lexical *exception*
`#\xA`	U+000A
`#\xFF`	U+00FF
`#\xff`	U+00FF
`#\x ff`	U+0078
	followed by another datum, ff
`#\x(ff)`	U+0078
	followed by another datum,
	a parenthesized ff
`#\(x)`	&lexical *exception*
`#\(x`	&lexical *exception*
`#\((x)`	U+0028
	followed by another datum,
	parenthesized x
`#\x00110000`	&lexical *exception*
	out of range
`#\x000000001`	U+0001
`#\xD800`	&lexical *exception*
	in excluded range

(The notation &lexical *exception* means that the line in question is a lexical syntax violation.)

Case is significant in #\⟨character⟩, and in #\⟨character name⟩, but not in the ⟨hex scalar value⟩ part of #\x⟨hex scalar value⟩. A ⟨character⟩ must be followed by a ⟨delimiter⟩ or by the end of the input. This rule resolves various ambiguous cases involving named characters, requiring, for example, the sequence of characters "#\space" to be interpreted as the space character rather than as the character "#\s" followed by the identifier "pace".

Note: The #\newline notation is retained for backward compatibility. Its use is deprecated; #\linefeed should be used instead.

4.2.7 Strings

String are represented by sequences of characters enclosed within doublequotes (").
Within a string literal, various escape sequences represent characters other than
themselves. Escape sequences always start with a backslash (\):

- \a : alarm, U+0007
- \b : backspace, U+0008
- \t : character tabulation, U+0009
- \n : linefeed, U+000A
- \v : line tabulation, U+000B
- \f : formfeed, U+000C
- \r : return, U+000D
- \" : doublequote, U+0022
- \\ : backslash, U+005C
- \⟨intraline whitespace⟩⟨line ending⟩
  ⟨intraline whitespace⟩ : nothing
- \x⟨hex scalar value⟩; : specified character (note the terminating semi-colon).

These escape sequences are case-sensitive, except that the alphabetic digits of a
⟨hex scalar value⟩ can be uppercase or lowercase.

Any other character in a string after a backslash is a syntax violation. Except for
a line ending, any character outside of an escape sequence and not a doublequote
stands for itself in the string literal. For example the single-character string literal
"λ" (doublequote, a lower case lambda, doublequote) represents the same string as
"\x03bb;". A line ending that does not follow a backslash stands for a linefeed
character.

Examples:

"abc"	U+0061, U+0062, U+0063
"\x41;bc"	"Abc" ; U+0041, U+0062, U+0063
"\x41; bc"	"A bc"
	U+0041, U+0020, U+0062, U+0063
"\x41bc;"	U+41BC
"\x41"	&lexical *exception*
"\x;"	&lexical *exception*
"\x41bx;"	&lexical *exception*
"\x00000041;"	"A" ; U+0041
"\x0010FFFF;"	U+10FFFF
"\x00110000;"	&lexical *exception*
	out of range
"\x000000001;"	U+0001
"\xD800;"	&lexical *exception*
	in excluded range
"A	
bc"	U+0041, U+000A, U+0062, U+0063
	if no space occurs after the A

4.2.8 Numbers

The syntax of external representations for number objects is described formally by the ⟨number⟩ rule in the formal grammar. Case is not significant in external representations of number objects.

A representation of a number object may be written in binary, octal, decimal, or hexadecimal by the use of a radix prefix. The radix prefixes are #b (binary), #o (octal), #d (decimal), and #x (hexadecimal). With no radix prefix, a representation of a number object is assumed to be expressed in decimal.

A representation of a number object may be specified to be either exact or inexact by a prefix. The prefixes are #e for exact, and #i for inexact. An exactness prefix may appear before or after any radix prefix that is used. If the representation of a number object has no exactness prefix, the constant is inexact if it contains a decimal point, an exponent, or a nonempty mantissa width; otherwise it is exact.

In systems with inexact number objects of varying precisions, it may be useful to specify the precision of a constant. For this purpose, representations of number objects may be written with an exponent marker that indicates the desired precision of the inexact representation. The letters s, f, d, and l specify the use of *short*, *single*, *double*, and *long* precision, respectively. (When fewer than four internal inexact representations exist, the four size specifications are mapped onto those available. For example, an implementation with two internal representations may map short and single together and long and double together.) In addition, the exponent marker e specifies the default precision for the implementation. The default precision has at least as much precision as *double*, but implementations may wish to allow this default to be set by the user.

> 3.1415926535898F0
>> Round to single, perhaps 3.141593
> 0.6L0
>> Extend to long, perhaps .600000000000000

A representation of a number object with nonempty mantissa width, $x \mid p$, represents the best binary floating-point approximation of x using a p-bit significand. For example, 1.1|53 is a representation of the best approximation of 1.1 in IEEE double precision. If x is an external representation of an inexact real number object that contains no vertical bar, then its numerical value should be computed as though it had a mantissa width of 53 or more.

Implementations that use binary floating-point representations of real number objects should represent $x \mid p$ using a p-bit significand if practical, or by a greater precision if a p-bit significand is not practical, or by the largest available precision if p or more bits of significand are not practical within the implementation.

Note: The precision of a significand should not be confused with the number of bits used to represent the significand. In the IEEE floating-point standards, for example, the significand's most significant bit is implicit in single and double precision but is explicit in extended precision. Whether that bit is implicit or explicit does not affect the mathematical precision. In implementations that use binary floating point, the default precision can be calculated by calling the following procedure:

```
(define (precision)
  (do ((n 0 (+ n 1))
       (x 1.0 (/ x 2.0)))
      ((= 1.0 (+ 1.0 x)) n)))
```

Note: When the underlying floating-point representation is IEEE double precision, the |p suffix should not always be omitted: Denormalized floating-point numbers have diminished precision, and therefore their external representations should carry a |p suffix with the actual width of the significand.

The literals +inf.0 and -inf.0 represent positive and negative infinity, respectively. The +nan.0 literal represents the NaN that is the result of (/ 0.0 0.0), and may represent other NaNs as well. The -nan.0 literal also represents a NaN.

If *x* is an external representation of an inexact real number object and contains no vertical bar and no exponent marker other than e, the inexact real number object it represents is a flonum (see library section 11.3). Some or all of the other external representations of inexact real number objects may also represent flonums, but that is not required by this report.

4.3 Datum syntax

The datum syntax describes the syntax of syntactic data in terms of a sequence of ⟨lexeme⟩s, as defined in the lexical syntax.

Syntactic data include the lexeme data described in the previous section as well as the following constructs for forming compound data:

- pairs and lists, enclosed by ( ) or [ ] (see section 4.3.2)
- vectors (see section 4.3.3)
- bytevectors (see section 4.3.4)

4.3.1 Formal account

The following grammar describes the syntax of syntactic data in terms of various kinds of lexemes defined in the grammar in section 4.2:

⟨datum⟩ ⟶ ⟨lexeme datum⟩
   | ⟨compound datum⟩
⟨lexeme datum⟩ ⟶ ⟨boolean⟩ | ⟨number⟩
   | ⟨character⟩ | ⟨string⟩ | ⟨symbol⟩
⟨symbol⟩ ⟶ ⟨identifier⟩
⟨compound datum⟩ ⟶ ⟨list⟩ | ⟨vector⟩ | ⟨bytevector⟩
⟨list⟩ ⟶ (⟨datum⟩*) | [⟨datum⟩*]
   | (⟨datum⟩$^+$. ⟨datum⟩) | [⟨datum⟩$^+$. ⟨datum⟩]
   | ⟨abbreviation⟩
⟨abbreviation⟩ ⟶ ⟨abbrev prefix⟩ ⟨datum⟩
⟨abbrev prefix⟩ ⟶ ' | ` | , | ,@

```
      | #' | #` | #, | #,@
⟨vector⟩ ⟶ #(⟨datum⟩*)
⟨bytevector⟩ ⟶ #vu8(⟨u8⟩*)
⟨u8⟩ ⟶ ⟨any ⟨number⟩ representing an exact
              integer in {0,...,255})
```

4.3.2 Pairs and lists

List and pair data, representing pairs and lists of values (see section 11.9) are represented using parentheses or brackets. Matching pairs of brackets that occur in the rules of ⟨list⟩ are equivalent to matching pairs of parentheses.

The most general notation for Scheme pairs as syntactic data is the "dotted" notation (⟨datum$_1$⟩ . ⟨datum$_2$⟩) where ⟨datum$_1$⟩ is the representation of the value of the car field and ⟨datum$_2$⟩ is the representation of the value of the cdr field. For example (4 . 5) is a pair whose car is 4 and whose cdr is 5.

A more streamlined notation can be used for lists: the elements of the list are simply enclosed in parentheses and separated by spaces. The empty list is represented by () . For example,

    (a b c d e)

and

    (a . (b . (c . (d . (e . ())))))

are equivalent notations for a list of symbols.

The general rule is that, if a dot is followed by an open parenthesis, the dot, open parenthesis, and matching closing parenthesis can be omitted in the external representation.

The sequence of characters "(4 . 5)" is the external representation of a pair, not an expression that evaluates to a pair. Similarly, the sequence of characters "(+ 2 6)" is *not* an external representation of the integer 8, even though it *is* an expression (in the language of the (rnrs base (6)) library) evaluating to the integer 8; rather, it is a syntactic datum representing a three-element list, the elements of which are the symbol + and the integers 2 and 6.

4.3.3 Vectors

Vector data, representing vectors of objects (see section 11.13), are represented using the notation #(⟨datum⟩ ...). For example, a vector of length 3 containing the number object for zero in element 0, the list (2 2 2 2) in element 1, and the string "Anna" in element 2 can be represented as follows:

    #(0 (2 2 2 2) "Anna")

This is the external representation of a vector, not an expression that evaluates to a vector.

4.3.4 Bytevectors

Bytevector data, representing bytevectors (see library chapter 2), are represented using the notation #vu8(⟨u8⟩ ...), where the ⟨u8⟩s represent the octets of the bytevector. For example, a bytevector of length 3 containing the octets 2, 24, and 123 can be represented as follows:

```
#vu8(2 24 123)
```

This is the external representation of a bytevector, and also an expression that evaluates to a bytevector.

4.3.5 Abbreviations

```
'⟨datum⟩
`⟨datum⟩
,⟨datum⟩
,@⟨datum⟩
#'⟨datum⟩
#`⟨datum⟩
#,⟨datum⟩
#,@⟨datum⟩
```

Each of these is an abbreviation:
'⟨datum⟩ for (quote ⟨datum⟩),
`⟨datum⟩ for (quasiquote ⟨datum⟩),
,⟨datum⟩ for (unquote ⟨datum⟩),
,@⟨datum⟩ for (unquote-splicing ⟨datum⟩),
#'⟨datum⟩ for (syntax ⟨datum⟩),
#`⟨datum⟩ for (quasisyntax ⟨datum⟩),
#,⟨datum⟩ for (unsyntax ⟨datum⟩), and
#,@⟨datum⟩ for (unsyntax-splicing ⟨datum⟩).

5 Semantic concepts

5.1 Programs and libraries

A Scheme program consists of a *top-level program* together with a set of *libraries*, each of which defines a part of the program connected to the others through explicitly specified exports and imports. A library consists of a set of export and import specifications and a body, which consists of definitions, and expressions. A top-level program is similar to a library, but has no export specifications. Chapters 7 and 8 describe the syntax and semantics of libraries and top-level programs, respectively. Chapter 11 describes a base library that defines many of the constructs traditionally associated with Scheme. A separate report (Sperber *et al.*, 2007a) describes the various *standard libraries* provided by a Scheme system.

The division between the base library and the other standard libraries is based on use, not on construction. In particular, some facilities that are typically implemented as "primitives" by a compiler or the run-time system rather than in terms of other standard procedures or syntactic forms are not part of the base library, but are defined in separate libraries. Examples include the fixnums and flonums libraries, the exceptions and conditions libraries, and the libraries for records.

5.2 Variables, keywords, and regions

Within the body of a library or top-level program, an identifier may name a kind of syntax, or it may name a location where a value can be stored. An identifier that names a kind of syntax is called a *keyword*, or *syntactic keyword*, and is said to be *bound* to that kind of syntax (or, in the case of a syntactic abstraction, a *transformer* that translates the syntax into more primitive forms; see section 9.2). An identifier that names a location is called a *variable* and is said to be *bound* to that location. At each point within a top-level program or a library, a specific, fixed set of identifiers is bound. The set of these identifiers, the set of *visible bindings*, is known as the *environment* in effect at that point.

Certain forms are used to create syntactic abstractions and to bind keywords to transformers for those new syntactic abstractions, while other forms create new locations and bind variables to those locations. Collectively, these forms are called *binding constructs*. Some binding constructs take the form of *definitions*, while others are expressions. With the exception of exported library bindings, a binding created by a definition is visible only within the body in which the definition appears, e.g., the body of a library, top-level program, or lambda expression. Exported library bindings are also visible within the bodies of the libraries and top-level programs that import them (see chapter 7).

Expressions that bind variables include the lambda, let, let*, letrec, letrec*, let-values, and let*-values forms from the base library (see sections 11.4.2, 11.4.6). Of these, lambda is the most fundamental. Variable definitions appearing within the body of such an expression, or within the bodies of a library or top-level program, are treated as a set of letrec* bindings. In addition, for library bodies, the variables exported from the library can be referenced by importing libraries and top-level programs.

Expressions that bind keywords include the let-syntax and letrec-syntax forms (see section 11.18). A define form (see section 11.2.1) is a definition that creates a variable binding (see section 11.2), and a define-syntax form is a definition that creates a keyword binding (see section 11.2.2).

Scheme is a statically scoped language with block structure. To each place in a top-level program or library body where an identifier is bound there corresponds a *region* of code within which the binding is visible. The region is determined by the particular binding construct that establishes the binding; if the binding is established by a lambda expression, for example, then its region is the entire lambda expression. Every mention of an identifier refers to the binding of the identifier that establishes the innermost of the regions containing the use. If a use of an identifier appears in a place where none of the surrounding expressions contains a binding for the identifier, the use may refer to a binding established by a definition or import at the top of the enclosing library or top-level program (see chapter 7). If there is no binding for the identifier, it is said to be *unbound*.

5.3 Exceptional situations

A variety of exceptional situations are distinguished in this report, among them violations of syntax, violations of a procedure's specification, violations of implementation restrictions, and exceptional situations in the environment. When an exceptional situation is detected by the implementation, an *exception is raised*, which means that a special procedure called the *current exception handler* is called. A program can also raise an exception, and override the current exception handler; see library section 7.1.

When an exception is raised, an object is provided that describes the nature of the exceptional situation. The report uses the condition system described in library section 7.2 to describe exceptional situations, classifying them by condition types.

Some exceptional situations allow continuing the program if the exception handler takes appropriate action. The corresponding exceptions are called *continuable*. For most of the exceptional situations described in this report, portable programs cannot rely upon the exception being continuable at the place where the situation was detected. For those exceptions, the exception handler that is invoked by the exception should not return. In some cases, however, continuing is permissible, and the handler may return. See library section 7.1.

Implementations must raise an exception when they are unable to continue correct execution of a correct program due to some *implementation restriction*. For example, an implementation that does not support infinities must raise an exception with condition type &implementation-restriction when it evaluates an expression whose result would be an infinity.

Some possible implementation restrictions such as the lack of representations for NaNs and infinities (see section 11.7.2) are anticipated by this report, and implementations typically must raise an exception of the appropriate condition type if they encounter such a situation.

This report uses the phrase "an exception is raised" synonymously with "an exception must be raised". This report uses the phrase "an exception with condition type t" to indicate that the object provided with the exception is a condition object of the specified type. The phrase "a continuable exception is raised" indicates an exceptional situation that permits the exception handler to return.

5.4 Argument checking

Many procedures specified in this report or as part of a standard library restrict the arguments they accept. Typically, a procedure accepts only specific numbers and types of arguments. Many syntactic forms similarly restrict the values to which one or more of their subforms can evaluate. These restrictions imply responsibilities for both the programmer and the implementation. Specifically, the programmer is responsible for ensuring that the values indeed adhere to the restrictions described in the specification. The implementation must check that the restrictions in the specification are indeed met, to the extent that it is reasonable, possible, and necessary to allow the specified operation to complete successfully. The implementation's responsibilities are specified in more detail in chapter 6 and throughout the report.

Note that it is not always possible for an implementation to completely check the restrictions set forth in a specification. For example, if an operation is specified to accept a procedure with specific properties, checking of these properties is undecidable in general. Similarly, some operations accept both lists and procedures that are called by these operations. Since lists can be mutated by the procedures through the (rnrs mutable-pairs (6)) library (see library chapter 17), an argument that is a list when the operation starts may become a non-list during the execution of the operation. Also, the procedure might escape to a different continuation, preventing the operation from performing more checks. Requiring the operation to check that the argument is a list after each call to such a procedure would be impractical. Furthermore, some operations that accept lists only need to traverse these lists partially to perform their function; requiring the implementation to traverse the remainder of the list to verify that all specified restrictions have been met might violate reasonable performance assumptions. For these reasons, the programmer's obligations may exceed the checking obligations of the implementation.

When an implementation detects a violation of a restriction for an argument, it must raise an exception with condition type &assertion in a way consistent with the safety of execution as described in section 5.6.

5.5 Syntax violations

The subforms of a special form usually need to obey certain syntactic restrictions. As forms may be subject to macro expansion, which may not terminate, the question of whether they obey the specified restrictions is undecidable in general.

When macro expansion terminates, however, implementations must detect violations of the syntax. A *syntax violation* is an error with respect to the syntax of library bodies, top-level bodies, or the "syntax" entries in the specification of the base library or the standard libraries. Moreover, attempting to assign to an immutable variable (i.e., the variables exported by a library; see section 7.1) is also considered a syntax violation.

If a syntax violation occurs, the implementation must raise an exception with condition type &syntax, and execution of that top-level program or library must not be allowed to begin.

5.6 Safety

The standard libraries whose exports are described by this document are said to be *safe libraries*. Libraries and top-level programs that import only from safe libraries are also said to be safe.

As defined by this document, the Scheme programming language is safe in the following sense: The execution of a safe top-level program cannot go so badly wrong as to crash or to continue to execute while behaving in ways that are inconsistent with the semantics described in this document, unless an exception is raised.

Violations of an implementation restriction must raise an exception with condition type &implementation-restriction, as must all violations and errors that would otherwise threaten system integrity in ways that might result in execution that is inconsistent with the semantics described in this document.

The above safety properties are guaranteed only for top-level programs and libraries that are said to be safe. In particular, implementations may provide access to unsafe libraries in ways that cannot guarantee safety.

5.7 Boolean values

Although there is a separate boolean type, any Scheme value can be used as a boolean value for the purpose of a conditional test. In a conditional test, all values count as true in such a test except for #f. This report uses the word "true" to refer to any Scheme value except #f, and the word "false" to refer to #f.

5.8 Multiple return values

A Scheme expression can evaluate to an arbitrary finite number of values. These values are passed to the expression's continuation.

Not all continuations accept any number of values. For example, a continuation that accepts the argument to a procedure call is guaranteed to accept exactly one value. The effect of passing some other number of values to such a continuation is unspecified. The call-with-values procedure described in section 11.15 makes it possible to create continuations that accept specified numbers of return values. If the number of return values passed to a continuation created by a call to call-with-values is not accepted by its consumer that was passed in that call, then an exception is raised. A more complete description of the number of values accepted by different continuations and the consequences of passing an unexpected number of values is given in the description of the values procedure in section 11.15.

A number of forms in the base library have sequences of expressions as subforms that are evaluated sequentially, with the return values of all but the last expression being discarded. The continuations discarding these values accept any number of values.

5.9 Unspecified behavior

If an expression is said to "return unspecified values", then the expression must evaluate without raising an exception, but the values returned depend on the implementation; this report explicitly does not say how many or what values should be returned. Programmers should not rely on a specific number of return values or the specific values themselves.

5.10 Storage model

Variables and objects such as pairs, vectors, bytevectors, strings, hashtables, and records implicitly refer to locations or sequences of locations. A string, for example, contains as many locations as there are characters in the string. (These locations need not correspond to a full machine word.) A new value may be stored into one of these locations using the `string-set!` procedure, but the string contains the same locations as before.

An object fetched from a location, by a variable reference or by a procedure such as `car`, `vector-ref`, or `string-ref`, is equivalent in the sense of eqv? (section 11.5) to the object last stored in the location before the fetch.

Every location is marked to show whether it is in use. No variable or object ever refers to a location that is not in use. Whenever this report speaks of storage being allocated for a variable or object, what is meant is that an appropriate number of locations are chosen from the set of locations that are not in use, and the chosen locations are marked to indicate that they are now in use before the variable or object is made to refer to them.

It is desirable for constants (i.e. the values of literal expressions) to reside in read-only memory. To express this, it is convenient to imagine that every object that refers to locations is associated with a flag telling whether that object is mutable or immutable. Literal constants, the strings returned by `symbol->string`, records with no mutable fields, and other values explicitly designated as immutable are immutable objects, while all objects created by the other procedures listed in this report are mutable. An attempt to store a new value into a location referred to by an immutable object should raise an exception with condition type `&assertion`.

5.11 Proper tail recursion

Implementations of Scheme must be *properly tail-recursive*. Procedure calls that occur in certain syntactic contexts called *tail contexts* are *tail calls*. A Scheme implementation is properly tail-recursive if it supports an unbounded number of active tail calls. A call is *active* if the called procedure may still return. Note that this includes regular returns as well as returns through continuations captured earlier by `call-with-current-continuation` that are later invoked. In the absence of captured continuations, calls could return at most once and the active calls would be those that had not yet returned. A formal definition of proper tail recursion can be found in Clinger's paper (Clinger, 1998). The rules for identifying tail calls in constructs from the (`rnrs base (6)`) library are described in section 11.20.

5.12 Dynamic extent and the dynamic environment

For a procedure call, the time between when it is initiated and when it returns is called its *dynamic extent*. In Scheme, `call-with-current-continuation` (section 11.15) allows reentering a dynamic extent after its procedure call has returned. Thus, the dynamic extent of a call may not be a single, connected time period.

Some operations described in the report acquire information in addition to their explicit arguments from the *dynamic environment*. For example, `call-with-current-continuation` accesses an implicit context established by `dynamic-wind` (section 11.15), and the `raise` procedure (library section 7.1) accesses the current exception handler. The operations that modify the dynamic environment do so dynamically, for the dynamic extent of a call to a procedure like `dynamic-wind` or `with-exception-handler`. When such a call returns, the previous dynamic environment is restored. The dynamic environment can be thought of as part of the dynamic extent of a call. Consequently, it is captured by `call-with-current-continuation`, and restored by invoking the escape procedure it creates.

6 Entry format

The chapters that describe bindings in the base library and the standard libraries are organized into entries. Each entry describes one language feature or a group of related features, where a feature is either a syntactic construct or a built-in procedure. An entry begins with one or more header lines of the form

template   *category*

The *category* defines the kind of binding described by the entry, typically either "syntax" or "procedure". An entry may specify various restrictions on subforms or arguments. For background on this, see section 5.4.

6.1 Syntax entries

If *category* is "syntax", the entry describes a special syntactic construct, and the template gives the syntax of the forms of the construct. The template is written in a notation similar to a right-hand side of the BNF rules in chapter 4, and describes the set of forms equivalent to the forms matching the template as syntactic data. Some "syntax" entries carry a suffix (expand), specifying that the syntactic keyword of the construct is exported with level 1. Otherwise, the syntactic keyword is exported with level 0; see section 7.2.

Components of the form described by a template are designated by syntactic variables, which are written using angle brackets, for example, ⟨expression⟩, ⟨variable⟩. Case is insignificant in syntactic variables. Syntactic variables stand for other forms, or sequences of them. A syntactic variable may refer to a non-terminal in the grammar for syntactic data (see section 4.3.1), in which case only forms matching that non-terminal are permissible in that position. For example, ⟨identifier⟩ stands for a form which must be an identifier. Also, ⟨expression⟩ stands for any form which is a syntactically valid expression. Other non-terminals that are used in templates are defined as part of the specification.

The notation

   ⟨thing$_1$⟩ ...

indicates zero or more occurrences of a ⟨thing⟩, and

   ⟨thing$_1$⟩ ⟨thing$_2$⟩ ...

indicates one or more occurrences of a ⟨thing⟩.

It is the programmer's responsibility to ensure that each component of a form has the shape specified by a template. Descriptions of syntax may express other restrictions on the components of a form. Typically, such a restriction is formulated as a phrase of the form "⟨x⟩ must be a ... ". Again, these specify the programmer's responsibility. It is the implementation's responsibility to check that these restrictions are satisfied, as long as the macro transformers involved in expanding the form terminate. If the implementation detects that a component does not meet the restriction, an exception with condition type &syntax is raised.

6.2 Procedure entries

If *category* is "procedure", then the entry describes a procedure, and the header line gives a template for a call to the procedure. Parameter names in the template are *italicized*. Thus the header line

```
(vector-ref vector k)                                          procedure
```

indicates that the built-in procedure vector-ref takes two arguments, a vector *vector* and an exact non-negative integer object k (see below). The header lines

```
(make-vector k)                                                procedure
(make-vector k fill)                                           procedure
```

indicate that the make-vector procedure takes either one or two arguments. The parameter names are case-insensitive: *Vector* is the same as *vector*.

As with syntax templates, an ellipsis ... at the end of a header line, as in

```
(= z₁ z₂ z₃ ...)                                               procedure
```

indicates that the procedure takes arbitrarily many arguments of the same type as specified for the last parameter name. In this case, = accepts two or more arguments that must all be complex number objects.

A procedure that detects an argument that it is not specified to handle must raise an exception with condition type &assertion. Also, the argument specifications are exhaustive: if the number of arguments provided in a procedure call does not match any number of arguments accepted by the procedure, an exception with condition type &assertion must be raised.

For succinctness, the report follows the convention that if a parameter name is also the name of a type, then the corresponding argument must be of the named type. For example, the header line for vector-ref given above dictates that the first argument to vector-ref must be a vector. The following naming conventions imply type restrictions:

obj	any object
z	complex number object
x	real number object
y	real number object
q	rational number object
n	integer object
k	exact non-negative integer object
bool	boolean (#f or #t)
octet	exact integer object in $\{0, \ldots, 255\}$
byte	exact integer object in $\{-128, \ldots, 127\}$
char	character (see section 11.11)
pair	pair (see section 11.9)
vector	vector (see section 11.13)
string	string (see section 11.12)
condition	condition (see library section 7.2)
bytevector	bytevector (see library chapter 2)
proc	procedure (see section 1.6)

Other type restrictions are expressed through parameter-naming conventions that are described in specific chapters. For example, library chapter 11 uses a number of special parameter variables for the various subsets of the numbers.

With the listed type restrictions, it is the programmer's responsibility to ensure that the corresponding argument is of the specified type. It is the implementation's responsibility to check for that type.

A parameter called *list* means that it is the programmer's responsibility to pass an argument that is a list (see section 11.9). It is the implementation's responsibility to check that the argument is appropriately structured for the operation to perform its function, to the extent that this is possible and reasonable. The implementation must at least check that the argument is either an empty list or a pair.

Descriptions of procedures may express other restrictions on the arguments of a procedure. Typically, such a restriction is formulated as a phrase of the form "*x* must be a ... " (or otherwise using the word "must").

6.3 Implementation responsibilities

In addition to the restrictions implied by naming conventions, an entry may list additional explicit restrictions. These explicit restrictions usually describe both the programmer's responsibilities, who must ensure that the subforms of a form are appropriate, or that an appropriate argument is passed, and the implementation's responsibilities, which must check that subform adheres to the specified restrictions (if macro expansion terminates), or if the argument is appropriate. A description may explicitly list the implementation's responsibilities for some arguments or subforms in a paragraph labeled "*Implementation responsibilities*". In this case, the responsibilities specified for these subforms or arguments in the rest of the description are only for the programmer. A paragraph describing implementation responsibility does not affect the implementation's responsibilities for checking subforms or arguments not mentioned in the paragraph.

6.4 Other kinds of entries

If *category* is something other than "syntax" and "procedure", then the entry describes a non-procedural value, and the *category* describes the type of that value. The header line

&who   condition type

indicates that &who is a condition type. The header line

unquote   auxiliary syntax

indicates that unquote is a syntax binding that may occur only as part of specific surrounding expressions. Any use as an independent syntactic construct or identifier is a syntax violation. As with "syntax" entries, some "auxiliary syntax" entries carry a suffix (expand), specifying that the syntactic keyword of the construct is exported with level 1.

6.5 Equivalent entries

The description of an entry occasionally states that it is *the same* as another entry. This means that both entries are equivalent. Specifically, it means that if both entries have the same name and are thus exported from different libraries, the entries from both libraries can be imported under the same name without conflict.

6.6 Evaluation examples

The symbol "$\Longrightarrow$" used in program examples can be read "evaluates to". For example,

(* 5 8) $\Longrightarrow$ 40

means that the expression (* 5 8) evaluates to the object 40. Or, more precisely: the expression given by the sequence of characters "(* 5 8)" evaluates, in an environment that imports the relevant library, to an object that may be represented externally by the sequence of characters "40". See section 4.3 for a discussion of external representations of objects.

The "$\Longrightarrow$" symbol is also used when the evaluation of an expression causes a violation. For example,

(integer->char #xD800) $\Longrightarrow$ &assertion *exception*

means that the evaluation of the expression (integer->char #xD800) must raise an exception with condition type &assertion.

Moreover, the "$\Longrightarrow$" symbol is also used to explicitly say that the value of an expression in unspecified. For example:

```
(eqv? "" "")                          ⟹  unspecified
```

Mostly, examples merely illustrate the behavior specified in the entry. In some cases, however, they disambiguate otherwise ambiguous specifications and are thus normative. Note that, in some cases, specifically in the case of inexact number objects, the return value is only specified conditionally or approximately. For example:

```
(atan -inf.0)              ⟹  -1.5707963267948965 ; approximately
```

6.7 *Naming conventions*

By convention, the names of procedures that store values into previously allocated locations (see section 5.10) usually end in "!".

By convention, "->" appears within the names of procedures that take an object of one type and return an analogous object of another type. For example, list->vector takes a list and returns a vector whose elements are the same as those of the list.

By convention, the names of predicates—procedures that always return a boolean value—end in "?" when the name contains any letters; otherwise, the predicate's name does not end with a question mark.

By convention, the components of compound names are separated by "-" In particular, prefixes that are actual words or can be pronounced as though they were actual words are followed by a hyphen, except when the first character following the hyphen would be something other than a letter, in which case the hyphen is omitted. Short, unpronounceable prefixes ("fx" and "fl") are not followed by a hyphen.

By convention, the names of condition types start with "&".

7 Libraries

Libraries are parts of a program that can be distributed independently. The library system supports macro definitions within libraries, macro exports, and distinguishes the phases in which definitions and imports are needed. This chapter defines the notation for libraries and a semantics for library expansion and execution.

7.1 *Library form*

A library definition must have the following form:

```
(library ⟨library name⟩
  (export ⟨export spec⟩ ...)
  (import ⟨import spec⟩ ...)
  ⟨library body⟩)
```

A library declaration contains the following elements:

- The ⟨library name⟩ specifies the name of the library (possibly with version).
- The export subform specifies a list of exports, which name a subset of the bindings defined within or imported into the library.

- The `import` subform specifies the imported bindings as a list of import dependencies, where each dependency specifies:
  — the imported library's name, and, optionally, constraints on its version,
  — the relevant levels, e.g., expand or run time (see section 7.2, and
  — the subset of the library's exports to make available within the importing library, and the local names to use within the importing library for each of the library's exports.
- The ⟨library body⟩ is the library body, consisting of a sequence of definitions followed by a sequence of expressions. The definitions may be both for local (unexported) and exported bindings, and the expressions are initialization expressions to be evaluated for their effects.

An identifier can be imported with the same local name from two or more libraries or for two levels from the same library only if the binding exported by each library is the same (i.e., the binding is defined in one library, and it arrives through the imports only by exporting and re-exporting). Otherwise, no identifier can be imported multiple times, defined multiple times, or both defined and imported. No identifiers are visible within a library except for those explicitly imported into the library or defined within the library.

A ⟨library name⟩ uniquely identifies a library within an implementation, and is globally visible in the `import` clauses (see below) of all other libraries within an implementation. A ⟨library name⟩ has the following form:

   (⟨identifier₁⟩ ⟨identifier₂⟩ ... ⟨version⟩)

where ⟨version⟩ is empty or has the following form:

   (⟨sub-version⟩ ...)

Each ⟨sub-version⟩ must represent an exact nonnegative integer object. An empty ⟨version⟩ is equivalent to ().

An ⟨export spec⟩ names a set of imported and locally defined bindings to be exported, possibly with different external names. An ⟨export spec⟩ must have one of the following forms:

   ⟨identifier⟩
   (rename (⟨identifier₁⟩ ⟨identifier₂⟩) ...)

In an ⟨export spec⟩, an ⟨identifier⟩ names a single binding defined within or imported into the library, where the external name for the export is the same as the name of the binding within the library. A `rename` spec exports the binding named by ⟨identifier₁⟩ in each (⟨identifier₁⟩ ⟨identifier₂⟩) pairing, using ⟨identifier₂⟩ as the external name.

Each ⟨import spec⟩ specifies a set of bindings to be imported into the library, the levels at which they are to be available, and the local names by which they are to be known. An ⟨import spec⟩ must be one of the following:

   ⟨import set⟩
   (for ⟨import set⟩ ⟨import level⟩ ...)

An ⟨import level⟩ is one of the following:

```
run
expand
(meta ⟨level⟩)
```

where ⟨level⟩ represents an exact integer object.

As an ⟨import level⟩, run is an abbreviation for (meta 0), and expand is an abbreviation for (meta 1). Levels and phases are discussed in section 7.2.

An ⟨import set⟩ names a set of bindings from another library and possibly specifies local names for the imported bindings. It must be one of the following:

```
⟨library reference⟩
(library ⟨library reference⟩)
(only ⟨import set⟩ ⟨identifier⟩ ...)
(except ⟨import set⟩ ⟨identifier⟩ ...)
(prefix ⟨import set⟩ ⟨identifier⟩)
(rename ⟨import set⟩ (⟨identifier₁⟩ ⟨identifier₂⟩) ...)
```

A ⟨library reference⟩ identifies a library by its name and optionally by its version. It has one of the following forms:

```
(⟨identifier₁⟩ ⟨identifier₂⟩ ...)
(⟨identifier₁⟩ ⟨identifier₂⟩ ... ⟨version reference⟩)
```

A ⟨library reference⟩ whose first ⟨identifier⟩ is for, library, only, except, prefix, or rename is permitted only within a library ⟨import set⟩. The ⟨import set⟩ (library ⟨library reference⟩) is otherwise equivalent to ⟨library reference⟩.

A ⟨library reference⟩ with no ⟨version reference⟩ (first form above) is equivalent to a ⟨library reference⟩ with a ⟨version reference⟩ of (). A ⟨version reference⟩ specifies a set of ⟨version⟩s that it matches. The ⟨library reference⟩ identifies all libraries of the same name and whose version is matched by the ⟨version reference⟩. A ⟨version reference⟩ has the following form:

```
(⟨sub-version reference₁⟩ ... ⟨sub-version reference_n⟩)
(and ⟨version reference⟩ ...)
(or ⟨version reference⟩ ...)
(not ⟨version reference⟩)
```

A ⟨version reference⟩ of the first form matches a ⟨version⟩ with at least n elements, whose ⟨sub-version reference⟩s match the corresponding ⟨sub-version⟩s. An and ⟨version reference⟩ matches a version if all ⟨version references⟩ following the and match it. Correspondingly, an or ⟨version reference⟩ matches a version if one of ⟨version references⟩ following the or matches it, and a not ⟨version reference⟩ matches a version if the ⟨version reference⟩ following it does not match it.

A ⟨sub-version reference⟩ has one of the following forms:

```
⟨sub-version⟩
(>= ⟨sub-version⟩)
(<= ⟨sub-version⟩)
```

```
(and ⟨sub-version reference⟩ ...)
(or ⟨sub-version reference⟩ ...)
(not ⟨sub-version reference⟩)
```

A ⟨sub-version reference⟩ of the first form matches a ⟨sub-version⟩ if it is equal to it. A >= ⟨sub-version reference⟩ form matches a sub-version if it is greater or equal to the ⟨sub-version⟩ following it; analogously for <=. An and ⟨sub-version reference⟩ matches a sub-version if all of the subsequent ⟨sub-version reference⟩s match it. Correspondingly, an or ⟨sub-version reference⟩ matches a sub-version if one of the subsequent ⟨sub-version reference⟩s matches it, and a not ⟨sub-version reference⟩ matches a sub-version if the subsequent ⟨sub-version reference⟩ does not match it.

Examples:

version reference	version	match?
()	(1)	yes
(1)	(1)	yes
(1)	(2)	no
(2 3)	(2)	no
(2 3)	(2 3)	yes
(2 3)	(2 3 5)	yes
(or (1 (>= 1)) (2))	(2)	yes
(or (1 (>= 1)) (2))	(1 1)	yes
(or (1 (>= 1)) (2))	(1 0)	no
((or 1 2 3))	(1)	yes
((or 1 2 3))	(2)	yes
((or 1 2 3))	(3)	yes
((or 1 2 3))	(4)	no

When more than one library is identified by a library reference, the choice of libraries is determined in some implementation-dependent manner.

To avoid problems such as incompatible types and replicated state, implementations should prohibit the two libraries whose library names consist of the same sequence of identifiers but whose versions do not match to co-exist in the same program.

By default, all of an imported library's exported bindings are made visible within an importing library using the names given to the bindings by the imported library. The precise set of bindings to be imported and the names of those bindings can be adjusted with the only, except, prefix, and rename forms as described below.

- An only form produces a subset of the bindings from another ⟨import set⟩, including only the listed ⟨identifier⟩s. The included ⟨identifier⟩s must be in the original ⟨import set⟩.
- An except form produces a subset of the bindings from another ⟨import set⟩, including all but the listed ⟨identifier⟩s. All of the excluded ⟨identifier⟩s must be in the original ⟨import set⟩.
- A prefix form adds the ⟨identifier⟩ prefix to each name from another ⟨import set⟩.

- A rename form, (rename (⟨identifier₁⟩ ⟨identifier₂⟩) ...), removes the bindings for ⟨identifier₁⟩ ... to form an intermediate ⟨import set⟩, then adds the bindings back for the corresponding ⟨identifier₂⟩ ... to form the final ⟨import set⟩. Each ⟨identifier₁⟩ must be in the original ⟨import set⟩, each ⟨identifier₂⟩ must not be in the intermediate ⟨import set⟩, and the ⟨identifier₂⟩s must be distinct.

It is a syntax violation if a constraint given above is not met.

The ⟨library body⟩ of a library form consists of forms that are classified as *definitions* or *expressions*. Which forms belong to which class depends on the imported libraries and the result of expansion—see chapter 10. Generally, forms that are not definitions (see section 11.2 for definitions available through the base library) are expressions.

A ⟨library body⟩ is like a ⟨body⟩ (see section 11.3) except that a ⟨library body⟩s need not include any expressions. It must have the following form:

⟨definition⟩ ... ⟨expression⟩ ...

When begin, let-syntax, or letrec-syntax forms occur in a library body prior to the first expression, they are spliced into the body; see section 11.4.7. Some or all of the body, including portions wrapped in begin, let-syntax, or letrec-syntax forms, may be specified by a syntactic abstraction (see section 9.2).

The transformer expressions and bindings are evaluated and created from left to right, as described in chapter 10. The expressions of variable definitions are evaluated from left to right, as if in an implicit letrec*, and the body expressions are also evaluated from left to right after the expressions of the variable definitions. A fresh location is created for each exported variable and initialized to the value of its local counterpart. The effect of returning twice to the continuation of the last body expression is unspecified.

Note: The names library, export, import, for, run, expand, meta, import, export, only, except, prefix, rename, and, or, not, >=, and <= appearing in the library syntax are part of the syntax and are not reserved, i.e., the same names can be used for other purposes within the library or even exported from or imported into a library with different meanings, without affecting their use in the library form.

Bindings defined with a library are not visible in code outside of the library, unless the bindings are explicitly exported from the library. An exported macro may, however, *implicitly export* an otherwise unexported identifier defined within or imported into the library. That is, it may insert a reference to that identifier into the output code it produces.

All explicitly exported variables are immutable in both the exporting and importing libraries. It is thus a syntax violation if an explicitly exported variable appears on the left-hand side of a set! expression, either in the exporting or importing libraries.

All implicitly exported variables are also immutable in both the exporting and importing libraries. It is thus a syntax violation if a variable appears on the left-hand side of a set! expression in any code produced by an exported macro outside of the library in which the variable is defined. It is also a syntax violation if a reference to an assigned variable appears in any code produced by an exported macro outside of the library in which the variable is defined, where an assigned variable is one that appears on the left-hand side of a set! expression in the exporting library.

All other variables defined within a library are mutable.

7.2 *Import and export levels*

Expanding a library may require run-time information from another library. For example, if a macro transformer calls a procedure from library A, then the library A must be instantiated before expanding any use of the macro in library B. Library A may not be needed when library B is eventually run as part of a program, or it may be needed for run time of library B, too. The library mechanism distinguishes these times by phases, which are explained in this section.

Every library can be characterized by expand-time information (minimally, its imported libraries, a list of the exported keywords, a list of the exported variables, and code to evaluate the transformer expressions) and run-time information (minimally, code to evaluate the variable definition right-hand-side expressions, and code to evaluate the body expressions). The expand-time information must be available to expand references to any exported binding, and the run-time information must be available to evaluate references to any exported variable binding.

A *phase* is a time at which the expressions within a library are evaluated. Within a library body, top-level expressions and the right-hand sides of define forms are evaluated at run time, i.e., phase 0, and the right-hand sides of define-syntax forms are evaluated at expand time, i.e., phase 1. When define-syntax, let-syntax, or letrec-syntax forms appear within code evaluated at phase n, the right-hand sides are evaluated at phase $n + 1$.

These phases are relative to the phase in which the library itself is used. An *instance* of a library corresponds to an evaluation of its variable definitions and expressions in a particular phase relative to another library—a process called *instantiation*. For example, if a top-level expression in a library B refers to a variable export from another library A, then it refers to the export from an instance of A at phase 0 (relative to the phase of B). But if a phase 1 expression within B refers to the same binding from A, then it refers to the export from an instance of A at phase 1 (relative to the phase of B).

A *visit* of a library corresponds to the evaluation of its syntax definitions in a particular phase relative to another library—a process called *visiting*. For example, if a top-level expression in a library B refers to a macro export from another library A, then it refers to the export from a visit of A at phase 0 (relative to the phase of B), which corresponds to the evaluation of the macro's transformer expression at phase 1.

A *level* is a lexical property of an identifier that determines in which phases it can be referenced. The level for each identifier bound by a definition within a library is 0; that is, the identifier can be referenced only at phase 0 within the library. The level for each imported binding is determined by the enclosing `for` form of the `import` in the importing library, in addition to the levels of the identifier in the exporting library. Import and export levels are combined by pairwise addition of all level combinations. For example, references to an imported identifier exported for levels p_a and p_b and imported for levels q_a, q_b, and q_c are valid at levels $p_a + q_a$, $p_a + q_b$, $p_a + q_c$, $p_b + q_a$, $p_b + q_b$, and $p_b + q_c$. An ⟨import set⟩ without an enclosing `for` is equivalent to (`for` ⟨import set⟩ `run`), which is the same as (`for` ⟨import set⟩ (`meta 0`)).

The export level of an exported binding is 0 for all bindings that are defined within the exporting library. The export levels of a reexported binding, i.e., an export imported from another library, are the same as the effective import levels of that binding within the reexporting library.

For the libraries defined in the library report, the export level is 0 for nearly all bindings. The exceptions are `syntax-rules`, `identifier-syntax`, ..., and `_` from the (`rnrs base (6)`) library, which are exported with level 1, `set!` from the (`rnrs base (6)`) library, which is exported with levels 0 and 1, and all bindings from the composite (`rnrs (6)`) library (see library chapter 15), which are exported with levels 0 and 1.

Macro expansion within a library can introduce a reference to an identifier that is not explicitly imported into the library. In that case, the phase of the reference must match the identifier's level as shifted by the difference between the phase of the source library (i.e., the library that supplied the identifier's lexical context) and the library that encloses the reference. For example, suppose that expanding a library invokes a macro transformer, and the evaluation of the macro transformer refers to an identifier that is exported from another library (so the phase-1 instance of the library is used); suppose further that the value of the binding is a syntax object representing an identifier with only a level-n binding; then, the identifier must be used only at phase $n + 1$ in the library being expanded. This combination of levels and phases is why negative levels on identifiers can be useful, even though libraries exist only at non-negative phases.

If any of a library's definitions are referenced at phase 0 in the expanded form of a program, then an instance of the referenced library is created for phase 0 before the program's definitions and expressions are evaluated. This rule applies transitively: if the expanded form of one library references at phase 0 an identifier from another library, then before the referencing library is instantiated at phase n, the referenced library must be instantiated at phase n. When an identifier is referenced at any phase n greater than 0, in contrast, then the defining library is instantiated at phase n at some unspecified time before the reference is evaluated. Similarly, when a macro keyword is referenced at phase n during the expansion of a library, then the defining library is visited at phase n at some unspecified time before the reference is evaluated.

An implementation may distinguish instances/visits of a library for different phases or to use an instance/visit at any phase as an instance/visit at any other phase. An implementation may further expand each `library` form with distinct visits of libraries in any phase and/or instances of libraries in phases above 0. An

implementation may create instances/visits of more libraries at more phases than
required to satisfy references. When an identifier appears as an expression in a
phase that is inconsistent with the identifier's level, then an implementation may
raise an exception either at expand time or run time, or it may allow the reference.
Thus, a library whose meaning depends on whether the instances of a library are
distinguished or shared across phases or library expansions may be unportable.

7.3 Examples

Examples for various ⟨import spec⟩s and ⟨export spec⟩s:

```
(library (stack)
   (export make push! pop! empty!)
   (import (rnrs)
           (rnrs mutable-pairs))

   (define (make) (list '()))
   (define (push! s v) (set-car! s (cons v (car s))))
   (define (pop! s) (let ([v (caar s)])
                      (set-car! s (cdar s))
                      v))
   (define (empty! s) (set-car! s '())))

(library (balloons)
   (export make push pop)
   (import (rnrs))

   (define (make w h) (cons w h))
   (define (push b amt)
     (cons (- (car b) amt) (+ (cdr b) amt)))
   (define (pop b) (display "Boom! ")
                   (display (* (car b) (cdr b)))
                   (newline)))

(library (party)
   ;; Total exports:
   ;; make, push, push!, make-party, pop!
   (export (rename (balloon:make make)
                   (balloon:push push))
           push!
           make-party
           (rename (party-pop! pop!)))
   (import (rnrs)
           (only (stack) make push! pop!) ; not empty!
           (prefix (balloons) balloon:))
```

```
;; Creates a party as a stack of balloons,
;; starting with two balloons
(define (make-party)
  (let ([s (make)]) ; from stack
    (push! s (balloon:make 10 10))
    (push! s (balloon:make 12 9))
    s))
(define (party-pop! p)
  (balloon:pop (pop! p))))


(library (main)
  (export)
  (import (rnrs) (party))

  (define p (make-party))
  (pop! p)              ; displays "Boom! 108"
  (push! p (push (make 5 5) 1))
  (pop! p))             ; displays "Boom! 24"
```

Examples for macros and phases:

```
(library (my-helpers id-stuff)
  (export find-dup)
  (import (rnrs))

  (define (find-dup l)
    (and (pair? l)
         (let loop ((rest (cdr l)))
           (cond
             [(null? rest) (find-dup (cdr l))]
             [(bound-identifier=? (car l) (car rest))
              (car rest)]
             [else (loop (cdr rest))])))))

(library (my-helpers values-stuff)
  (export mvlet)
  (import (rnrs) (for (my-helpers id-stuff) expand))

  (define-syntax mvlet
    (lambda (stx)
      (syntax-case stx ()
        [(_ [(id ...) expr] body0 body ...)
         (not (find-dup (syntax (id ...))))
         (syntax
```

```
        (call-with-values
            (lambda () expr)
            (lambda (id ...) body0 body ...))))])))))

(library (let-div)
  (export let-div)
  (import (rnrs)
          (my-helpers values-stuff)
          (rnrs r5rs))

  (define (quotient+remainder n d)
    (let ([q (quotient n d)])
      (values q (- n (* q d)))))
  (define-syntax let-div
    (syntax-rules ()
      [(_ n d (q r) body0 body ...)
       (mvlet [(q r) (quotient+remainder n d)]
         body0 body ...)])))
```

8 Top-level programs

A *top-level program* specifies an entry point for defining and running a Scheme program. A top-level program specifies a set of libraries to import and code to run. Through the imported libraries, whether directly or through the transitive closure of importing, a top-level program defines a complete Scheme program.

8.1 Top-level program syntax

A top-level program is a delimited piece of text, typically a file, that has the following form:

⟨import form⟩ ⟨top-level body⟩

An ⟨import form⟩ has the following form:

(import ⟨import spec⟩ ...)

A ⟨top-level body⟩ has the following form:

⟨top-level body form⟩ ...

A ⟨top-level body form⟩ is either a ⟨definition⟩ or an ⟨expression⟩.

The ⟨import form⟩ is identical to the import clause in libraries (see section 7.1), and specifies a set of libraries to import. A ⟨top-level body⟩ is like a ⟨library body⟩ (see section 7.1), except that definitions and expressions may occur in any order. Thus, the syntax specified by ⟨top-level body form⟩ refers to the result of macro expansion.

When uses of begin, let-syntax, or letrec-syntax from the (rnrs base (6)) library occur in a top-level body prior to the first expression, they are spliced into the body; see section 11.4.7. Some or all of the body, including portions wrapped in begin, let-syntax, or letrec-syntax forms, may be specified by a syntactic abstraction (see section 9.2).

8.2 *Top-level program semantics*

A top-level program is executed by treating the program similarly to a library, and evaluating its definitions and expressions. The semantics of a top-level body may be roughly explained by a simple translation into a library body: Each ⟨expression⟩ that appears before a definition in the top-level body is converted into a dummy definition

    (define ⟨variable⟩ (begin ⟨expression⟩ ⟨unspecified⟩))

where ⟨variable⟩ is a fresh identifier and ⟨unspecified⟩ is a side-effect-free expression returning an unspecified value. (It is generally impossible to determine which forms are definitions and expressions without concurrently expanding the body, so the actual translation is somewhat more complicated; see chapter 10.)

On platforms that support it, a top-level program may access its command line by calling the command-line procedure (see library section 10).

9 Primitive syntax

After the import form within a library form or a top-level program, the forms that constitute the body of the library or the top-level program depend on the libraries that are imported. In particular, imported syntactic keywords determine the available syntactic abstractions and whether each form is a definition or expression. A few form types are always available independent of imported libraries, however, including constant literals, variable references, procedure calls, and macro uses.

9.1 *Primitive expression types*

The entries in this section all describe expressions, which may occur in the place of ⟨expression⟩ syntactic variables. See also section 11.4.

Constant literals

⟨number⟩	syntax
⟨boolean⟩	syntax
⟨character⟩	syntax
⟨string⟩	syntax
⟨bytevector⟩	syntax

An expression consisting of a representation of a number object, a boolean, a character, a string, or a bytevector, evaluates "to itself".

```
145932                              ⟹   145932
#t                                  ⟹   #t
"abc"                               ⟹   "abc"
#vu8(2 24 123)                      ⟹   #vu8(2 24 123)
```

As noted in section 5.10, the value of a literal expression is immutable.

Variable references

⟨variable⟩   syntax

An expression consisting of a variable (section 5.2) is a variable reference if it is not a macro use (see below). The value of the variable reference is the value stored in the location to which the variable is bound. It is a syntax violation to reference an unbound variable.

The following example examples assumes the base library has been imported:

```
(define x 28)
x                                   ⟹   28
```

Procedure calls

(⟨operator⟩ ⟨operand₁⟩ ...)   syntax

A procedure call consists of expressions for the procedure to be called and the arguments to be passed to it, with enclosing parentheses. A form in an expression context is a procedure call if ⟨operator⟩ is not an identifier bound as a syntactic keyword (see section 9.2 below).

When a procedure call is evaluated, the operator and operand expressions are evaluated (in an unspecified order) and the resulting procedure is passed the resulting arguments.

The following examples assume the (rnrs base (6)) library has been imported:

```
(+ 3 4)                             ⟹   7
((if #f + *) 3 4)                   ⟹   12
```

If the value of ⟨operator⟩ is not a procedure, an exception with condition type &assertion is raised. Also, if ⟨operator⟩ does not accept as many arguments as there are ⟨operand⟩s, an exception with condition type &assertion is raised.

Note: In contrast to other dialects of Lisp, the order of evaluation is unspecified, and the operator expression and the operand expressions are always evaluated with the same evaluation rules.

Although the order of evaluation is otherwise unspecified, the effect of any concurrent evaluation of the operator and operand expressions is constrained to be consistent with some sequential order of evaluation. The order of evaluation may be chosen differently for each procedure call.

Note: In many dialects of Lisp, the form () is a legitimate expression. In Scheme, expressions written as list/pair forms must have at least one subexpression, so () is not a syntactically valid expression.

9.2 *Macros*

Libraries and top-level programs can define and use new kinds of derived expressions and definitions called *syntactic abstractions* or *macros*. A syntactic abstraction is created by binding a keyword to a *macro transformer* or, simply, *transformer*. The transformer determines how a use of the macro (called a *macro use*) is transcribed into a more primitive form.

Most macro uses have the form:

(⟨keyword⟩ ⟨datum⟩ ...)

where ⟨keyword⟩ is an identifier that uniquely determines the kind of form. This identifier is called the *syntactic keyword*, or simply *keyword*, of the macro. The number of ⟨datum⟩s and the syntax of each depends on the syntactic abstraction.

Macro uses can also take the form of improper lists, singleton identifiers, or `set!` forms, where the second subform of the `set!` is the keyword (see section 11.19) library section 12.3):

(⟨keyword⟩ ⟨datum⟩ ... . ⟨datum⟩)
⟨keyword⟩
(set! ⟨keyword⟩ ⟨datum⟩)

The `define-syntax`, `let-syntax` and `letrec-syntax` forms, described in sections 11.2.2 and 11.18, create bindings for keywords, associate them with macro transformers, and control the scope within which they are visible.

The `syntax-rules` and `identifier-syntax` forms, described in section 11.19, create transformers via a pattern language. Moreover, the `syntax-case` form, described in library chapter 12, allows creating transformers via arbitrary Scheme code.

Keywords occupy the same name space as variables. That is, within the same scope, an identifier can be bound as a variable or keyword, or neither, but not both, and local bindings of either kind may shadow other bindings of either kind.

Macros defined using `syntax-rules` and `identifier-syntax` are "hygienic" and "referentially transparent" and thus preserve lexical scoping (Kohlbecker Jr., 1986; Kohlbecker *et al.*, 1986; Bawden & Rees, 1988; Clinger & Rees, 1991a; Dybvig *et al.*, 1992):

- If a macro transformer inserts a binding for an identifier (variable or keyword) not appearing in the macro use, the identifier is in effect renamed throughout its scope to avoid conflicts with other identifiers.
- If a macro transformer inserts a free reference to an identifier, the reference refers to the binding that was visible where the transformer was specified, regardless of any local bindings that may surround the use of the macro.

Macros defined using the `syntax-case` facility are also hygienic unless `datum->syntax` (see library section 12.6) is used.

10 Expansion process

Macro uses (see section 9.2) are expanded into *core forms* at the start of evaluation (before compilation or interpretation) by a syntax *expander*. The set of core forms is implementation-dependent, as is the representation of these forms in the expander's output. If the expander encounters a syntactic abstraction, it invokes the associated transformer to expand the syntactic abstraction, then repeats the expansion process for the form returned by the transformer. If the expander encounters a core form, it recursively processes its subforms that are in expression or definition context, if any, and reconstructs the form from the expanded subforms. Information about identifier bindings is maintained during expansion to enforce lexical scoping for variables and keywords.

To handle definitions, the expander processes the initial forms in a ⟨body⟩ (see section 11.3) or ⟨library body⟩ (see section 7.1) from left to right. How the expander processes each form encountered depends upon the kind of form.

macro use The expander invokes the associated transformer to transform the macro use, then recursively performs whichever of these actions are appropriate for the resulting form.

`define-syntax` **form** The expander expands and evaluates the right-hand-side expression and binds the keyword to the resulting transformer.

`define` **form** The expander records the fact that the defined identifier is a variable but defers expansion of the right-hand-side expression until after all of the definitions have been processed.

`begin` **form** The expander splices the subforms into the list of body forms it is processing. (See section 11.4.7.)

`let-syntax` **or** `letrec-syntax` **form** The expander splices the inner body forms into the list of (outer) body forms it is processing, arranging for the keywords bound by the `let-syntax` and `letrec-syntax` to be visible only in the inner body forms.

expression, i.e., nondefinition The expander completes the expansion of the deferred right-hand-side expressions and the current and remaining expressions in the body, and then creates the equivalent of a `letrec*` form from the defined variables, expanded right-hand-side expressions, and expanded body expressions.

For the right-hand side of the definition of a variable, expansion is deferred until after all of the definitions have been seen. Consequently, each keyword and variable reference within the right-hand side resolves to the local binding, if any.

A definition in the sequence of forms must not define any identifier whose binding is used to determine the meaning of the undeferred portions of the definition or any definition that precedes it in the sequence of forms. For example, the bodies of the following expressions violate this restriction.

```
(let ()
  (define define 17)
  (list define))
```

```
(let-syntax ([def0 (syntax-rules ()
                     [(_ x) (define x 0)])])
  (let ([z 3])
    (def0 z)
    (define def0 list)
    (list z)))

  (let ()
    (define-syntax foo
      (lambda (e)
        (+ 1 2)))
    (define + 2)
    (foo))
```

The following do not violate the restriction.

```
(let ([x 5])
  (define lambda list)
  (lambda x x))                          ⟹  (5 5)


(let-syntax ([def0 (syntax-rules ()
                     [(_ x) (define x 0)])])
  (let ([z 3])
    (define def0 list)
    (def0 z)
    (list z)))                           ⟹   (3)


(let ()
  (define-syntax foo
    (lambda (e)
      (let ([+ -]) (+ 1 2))))
  (define + 2)
  (foo))                                 ⟹  -1
```

The implementation should treat a violation of the restriction as a syntax violation.

Note that this algorithm does not directly reprocess any form. It requires a single left-to-right pass over the definitions followed by a single pass (in any order) over the body expressions and deferred right-hand sides.

Example:

```
(lambda (x)
  (define-syntax defun
    (syntax-rules ()
      [(_ x a e) (define x (lambda a e))]))
  (defun even? (n) (or (= n 0) (odd? (- n 1))))
  (define-syntax odd?
    (syntax-rules () [(_ n) (not (even? n))]))
```

```
(odd? (if (odd? x) (* x x) x)))
```

In the example, the definition of defun is encountered first, and the keyword defun is associated with the transformer resulting from the expansion and evaluation of the corresponding right-hand side. A use of defun is encountered next and expands into a define form. Expansion of the right-hand side of this define form is deferred. The definition of odd? is next and results in the association of the keyword odd? with the transformer resulting from expanding and evaluating the corresponding right-hand side. A use of odd? appears next and is expanded; the resulting call to not is recognized as an expression because not is bound as a variable. At this point, the expander completes the expansion of the current expression (the call to not) and the deferred right-hand side of the even? definition; the uses of odd? appearing in these expressions are expanded using the transformer associated with the keyword odd?. The final output is the equivalent of

```
(lambda (x)
  (letrec* ([even?
             (lambda (n)
               (or (= n 0)
                   (not (even? (- n 1)))))])
    (not (even? (if (not (even? x)) (* x x) x)))))
```

although the structure of the output is implementation-dependent.

Because definitions and expressions can be interleaved in a ⟨top-level body⟩ (see chapter 8), the expander's processing of a ⟨top-level body⟩ is somewhat more complicated. It behaves as described above for a ⟨body⟩ or ⟨library body⟩ with the following exceptions: When the expander finds a nondefinition, it defers its expansion and continues scanning for definitions. Once it reaches the end of the set of forms, it processes the deferred right-hand-side and body expressions, then generates the equivalent of a letrec* form from the defined variables, expanded right-hand-side expressions, and expanded body expressions. For each body expression ⟨expression⟩ that appears before a variable definition in the body, a dummy binding is created at the corresponding place within the set of letrec* bindings, with a fresh temporary variable on the left-hand side and the equivalent of (begin ⟨expression⟩ ⟨unspecified⟩), where ⟨unspecified⟩ is a side-effect-free expression returning an unspecified value, on the right-hand side, so that left-to-right evaluation order is preserved. The begin wrapper allows ⟨expression⟩ to evaluate to an arbitrary number of values.

11 Base library

This chapter describes Scheme's (rnrs base (6)) library, which exports many of the procedure and syntax bindings that are traditionally associated with Scheme.

Section 11.20 defines the rules that identify tail calls and tail contexts in constructs from the (rnrs base (6)) library.

11.1 Base types

No object satisfies more than one of the following predicates:

```
boolean?        pair?
symbol?         number?
char?           string?
vector?         procedure?
null?
```

These predicates define the base types *boolean*, *pair*, *symbol*, *number*, *char* (or *character*), *string*, *vector*, and *procedure*. Moreover, the empty list is a special object of its own type.

Note that, although there is a separate boolean type, any Scheme value can be used as a boolean value for the purpose of a conditional test; see section 5.7.

11.2 Definitions

Definitions may appear within a ⟨top-level body⟩ (section 8.1), at the top of a ⟨library body⟩ (section 7.1), or at the top of a ⟨body⟩ (section 11.3).

A ⟨definition⟩ may be a variable definition (section 11.2.1) or keyword definition (section 11.2.1). Macro uses that expand into definitions or groups of definitions (packaged in a begin, let-syntax, or letrec-syntax form; see section 11.4.7) may also appear wherever other definitions may appear.

11.2.1 Variable definitions

The define form described in this section is a ⟨definition⟩ used to create variable bindings and may appear anywhere other definitions may appear.

(define ⟨variable⟩ ⟨expression⟩)	syntax
(define ⟨variable⟩)	syntax
(define (⟨variable⟩ ⟨formals⟩) ⟨body⟩)	syntax
(define (⟨variable⟩ . ⟨formal⟩) ⟨body⟩)	syntax

The first from of define binds ⟨variable⟩ to a new location before assigning the value of ⟨expression⟩ to it.

```
(define add3
  (lambda (x) (+ x 3)))
(add3 3)                          ⟹  6
(define first car)
(first '(1 2))                    ⟹  1
```

The continuation of ⟨expression⟩ should not be invoked more than once.

Implementation responsibilities: Implementations should detect that the continuation of ⟨expression⟩ is invoked more than once. If the implementation detects this, it must raise an exception with condition type &assertion.

The second form of define is equivalent to

```
(define ⟨variable⟩ ⟨unspecified⟩)
```

where ⟨unspecified⟩ is a side-effect-free expression returning an unspecified value.

In the third form of `define`, ⟨formals⟩ must be either a sequence of zero or more variables, or a sequence of one or more variables followed by a dot . and another variable (as in a lambda expression, see section 11.4.2). This form is equivalent to

```
(define ⟨variable⟩
   (lambda (⟨formals⟩) ⟨body⟩)).
```

In the fourth form of `define`, ⟨formal⟩ must be a single variable. This form is equivalent to

```
(define ⟨variable⟩
   (lambda ⟨formal⟩ ⟨body⟩)).
```

11.2.2 Syntax definitions

The `define-syntax` form described in this section is a ⟨definition⟩ used to create keyword bindings and may appear anywhere other definitions may appear.

`(define-syntax ⟨keyword⟩ ⟨expression⟩)`   syntax

Binds ⟨keyword⟩ to the value of ⟨expression⟩, which must evaluate, at macro-expansion time, to a transformer. Macro transformers can be created using the `syntax-rules` and `identifier-syntax` forms described in section 11.19. See library section 12.3 for a more complete description of transformers.

Keyword bindings established by `define-syntax` are visible throughout the body in which they appear, except where shadowed by other bindings, and nowhere else, just like variable bindings established by `define`. All bindings established by a set of definitions, whether keyword or variable definitions, are visible within the definitions themselves.

Implementation responsibilities: The implementation should detect if the value of ⟨expression⟩ cannot possibly be a transformer.

Example:

```
(let ()
  (define even?
    (lambda (x)
      (or (= x 0) (odd? (- x 1)))))
  (define-syntax odd?
    (syntax-rules ()
      ((odd? x) (not (even? x)))))
  (even? 10))                              ⟹ #t
```

An implication of the left-to-right processing order (section 10) is that one definition can affect whether a subsequent form is also a definition.

Example:

```
(let ()
  (define-syntax bind-to-zero
    (syntax-rules ()
      ((bind-to-zero id) (define id 0))))
  (bind-to-zero x)
  x)                                    ⟹ 0
```

The behavior is unaffected by any binding for bind-to-zero that might appear outside of the let expression.

11.3 Bodies

The ⟨body⟩ of a lambda, let, let*, let-values, let*-values, letrec, or letrec* expression, or that of a definition with a body consists of zero or more definitions followed by one or more expressions.

⟨definition⟩ ... ⟨expression₁⟩ ⟨expression₂⟩ ...

Each identifier defined by a definition is local to the ⟨body⟩. That is, the identifier is bound, and the region of the binding is the entire ⟨body⟩ (see section 5.2).

Example:

```
(let ((x 5))
  (define foo (lambda (y) (bar x y)))
  (define bar (lambda (a b) (+ (* a b) a)))
  (foo (+ x 3)))                        ⟹   45
```

When begin, let-syntax, or letrec-syntax forms occur in a body prior to the first expression, they are spliced into the body; see section 11.4.7. Some or all of the body, including portions wrapped in begin, let-syntax, or letrec-syntax forms, may be specified by a macro use (see section 9.2).

An expanded ⟨body⟩ (see chapter 10) containing variable definitions can always be converted into an equivalent letrec* expression. For example, the let expression in the above example is equivalent to

```
(let ((x 5))
  (letrec* ((foo (lambda (y) (bar x y)))
            (bar (lambda (a b) (+ (* a b) a))))
    (foo (+ x 3))))
```

11.4 Expressions

The entries in this section describe the expressions of the (rnrs base (6)) library, which may occur in the position of the ⟨expression⟩ syntactic variable in addition to the primitive expression types as described in section 9.1.

11.4.1 Quotation

(quote ⟨datum⟩)   syntax

   Syntax: ⟨Datum⟩ should be a syntactic datum.

Semantics: (quote ⟨datum⟩) evaluates to the datum value represented by ⟨datum⟩ (see section 4.3). This notation is used to include constants.

(quote a)	⟹	a
(quote #(a b c))	⟹	#(a b c)
(quote (+ 1 2))	⟹	(+ 1 2)

As noted in section 4.3.5, (quote ⟨datum⟩) may be abbreviated as '⟨datum⟩:

'"abc"	⟹	"abc"
'145932	⟹	145932
'a	⟹	a
'#(a b c)	⟹	#(a b c)
'()	⟹	()
'(+ 1 2)	⟹	(+ 1 2)
'(quote a)	⟹	(quote a)
''a	⟹	(quote a)

As noted in section 5.10, constants are immutable.
Note: Different constants that are the value of a quote expression may share the same locations.

11.4.2 Procedures

(lambda ⟨formals⟩ ⟨body⟩)   syntax
    Syntax: ⟨Formals⟩ must be a formal parameter list as described below, and ⟨body⟩ must be as described in section 11.3.
    Semantics: A lambda expression evaluates to a procedure. The environment in effect when the lambda expression is evaluated is remembered as part of the procedure. When the procedure is later called with some arguments, the environment in which the lambda expression was evaluated is extended by binding the variables in the parameter list to fresh locations, and the resulting argument values are stored in those locations. Then, the expressions in the body of the lambda expression (which may contain definitions and thus represent a letrec* form, see section 11.3) are evaluated sequentially in the extended environment. The results of the last expression in the body are returned as the results of the procedure call.

(lambda (x) (+ x x))	⟹	*a procedure*
((lambda (x) (+ x x)) 4)	⟹	8

```
((lambda (x)
   (define (p y)
      (+ y 1))
   (+ (p x) x))
 5)                                        ⟹  11
```

```
(define reverse-subtract
```

```
   (lambda (x y) (- y x)))
 (reverse-subtract 7 10)                        ⟹   3

 (define add4
   (let ((x 4))
     (lambda (y) (+ x y))))
 (add4 6)                                        ⟹   10
```

⟨Formals⟩ must have one of the following forms:

- (⟨variable₁⟩ ...): The procedure takes a fixed number of arguments; when the procedure is called, the arguments are stored in the bindings of the corresponding variables.
- ⟨variable⟩: The procedure takes any number of arguments; when the procedure is called, the sequence of arguments is converted into a newly allocated list, and the list is stored in the binding of the ⟨variable⟩.
- (⟨variable₁⟩ ... ⟨variableₙ⟩ . ⟨variableₙ₊₁⟩): If a period . precedes the last variable, then the procedure takes n or more arguments, where n is the number of parameters before the period (there must be at least one). The value stored in the binding of the last variable is a newly allocated list of the arguments left over after all the other arguments have been matched up against the other parameters.

```
 ((lambda x x) 3 4 5 6)                          ⟹   (3 4 5 6)
 ((lambda (x y . z) z) 3 4 5 6)                  ⟹   (5 6)
```

Any ⟨variable⟩ must not appear more than once in ⟨formals⟩.

11.4.3 Conditionals

```
(if ⟨test⟩ ⟨consequent⟩ ⟨alternate⟩)                               syntax
(if ⟨test⟩ ⟨consequent⟩)                                           syntax
```
   Syntax: ⟨Test⟩, ⟨consequent⟩, and ⟨alternate⟩ must be expressions.
   Semantics: An if expression is evaluated as follows: first, ⟨test⟩ is evaluated. If it yields a true value (see section 5.7), then ⟨consequent⟩ is evaluated and its values are returned. Otherwise ⟨alternate⟩ is evaluated and its values are returned. If ⟨test⟩ yields #f and no ⟨alternate⟩ is specified, then the result of the expression is unspecified.

```
   (if (> 3 2) 'yes 'no)                         ⟹   yes
   (if (> 2 3) 'yes 'no)                         ⟹   no
   (if (> 3 2)
       (- 3 2)
       (+ 3 2))                                  ⟹   1
   (if #f #f)                                    ⟹   unspecified
```

   The ⟨consequent⟩ and ⟨alternate⟩ expressions are in tail context if the if expression itself is; see section 11.20.

11.4.4 Assignments

(set! ⟨variable⟩ ⟨expression⟩)   syntax
⟨Expression⟩ is evaluated, and the resulting value is stored in the location to which
⟨variable⟩ is bound. ⟨Variable⟩ must be bound either in some region enclosing the
set! expression or at the top level. The result of the set! expression is unspecified.

```
(let ((x 2))
  (+ x 1)
  (set! x 4)
  (+ x 1))                                ⟹  5
```

It is a syntax violation if ⟨variable⟩ refers to an immutable binding.
Note: The identifier set! is exported with level 1 as well. See section 11.19.

11.4.5 Derived conditionals

(cond ⟨cond clause$_1$⟩ ⟨cond clause$_2$⟩ ...)   syntax
=>   auxiliary syntax
else   auxiliary syntax
   Syntax: Each ⟨cond clause⟩ must be of the form

   (⟨test⟩ ⟨expression$_1$⟩ ...)

where ⟨test⟩ is an expression. Alternatively, a ⟨cond clause⟩ may be of the form

   (⟨test⟩ => ⟨expression⟩)

The last ⟨cond clause⟩ may be an "else clause", which has the form

   (else ⟨expression$_1$⟩ ⟨expression$_2$⟩ ...).

Semantics: A cond expression is evaluated by evaluating the ⟨test⟩ expressions of
successive ⟨cond clause⟩s in order until one of them evaluates to a true value (see
section 5.7). When a ⟨test⟩ evaluates to a true value, then the remaining ⟨expression⟩s
in its ⟨cond clause⟩ are evaluated in order, and the results of the last ⟨expression⟩
in the ⟨cond clause⟩ are returned as the results of the entire cond expression. If
the selected ⟨cond clause⟩ contains only the ⟨test⟩ and no ⟨expression⟩s, then the
value of the ⟨test⟩ is returned as the result. If the selected ⟨cond clause⟩ uses the =>
alternate form, then the ⟨expression⟩ is evaluated. Its value must be a procedure.
This procedure should accept one argument; it is called on the value of the ⟨test⟩
and the values returned by this procedure are returned by the cond expression. If all
⟨test⟩s evaluate to #f, and there is no else clause, then the conditional expression
returns unspecified values; if there is an else clause, then its ⟨expression⟩s are
evaluated, and the values of the last one are returned.

```
(cond ((> 3 2) 'greater)
      ((< 3 2) 'less))               ⟹   greater
(cond ((> 3 3) 'greater)
```

```
        ((< 3 3) 'less)
        (else 'equal))                    ⟹  equal
  (cond ('(1 2 3) => cadr)
        (else #f))                        ⟹  2
```

For a ⟨cond clause⟩ of one of the following forms

```
    (⟨test⟩ ⟨expression₁⟩ ...)
    (else ⟨expression₁⟩ ⟨expression₂⟩ ...)
```

the last ⟨expression⟩ is in tail context if the cond form itself is. For a ⟨cond clause⟩ of the form

```
    (⟨test⟩ => ⟨expression⟩)
```

the (implied) call to the procedure that results from the evaluation of ⟨expression⟩ is in a tail context if the cond form itself is. See section 11.20.

A sample definition of cond in terms of simpler forms is in appendix B.

(case ⟨key⟩ ⟨case clause₁⟩ ⟨case clause₂⟩ ...)   syntax

Syntax: ⟨Key⟩ must be an expression. Each ⟨case clause⟩ must have one of the following forms:

```
    (((⟨datum₁⟩ ...) ⟨expression₁⟩ ⟨expression₂⟩ ...)
    (else ⟨expression₁⟩ ⟨expression₂⟩ ...)
```

The second form, which specifies an "else clause", may only appear as the last ⟨case clause⟩. Each ⟨datum⟩ is an external representation of some object. The data represented by the ⟨datum⟩s need not be distinct.

Semantics: A case expression is evaluated as follows. ⟨Key⟩ is evaluated and its result is compared using eqv? (see section 11.5) against the data represented by the ⟨datum⟩s of each ⟨case clause⟩ in turn, proceeding in order from left to right through the set of clauses. If the result of evaluating ⟨key⟩ is equivalent to a datum of a ⟨case clause⟩, the corresponding ⟨expression⟩s are evaluated from left to right and the results of the last expression in the ⟨case clause⟩ are returned as the results of the case expression. Otherwise, the comparison process continues. If the result of evaluating ⟨key⟩ is different from every datum in each set, then if there is an else clause its expressions are evaluated and the results of the last are the results of the case expression; otherwise the case expression returns unspecified values.

```
    (case (* 2 3)
      ((2 3 5 7) 'prime)
      ((1 4 6 8 9) 'composite))          ⟹  composite
    (case (car '(c d))
      ((a) 'a)
      ((b) 'b))                          ⟹  unspecified
    (case (car '(c d))
      ((a e i o u) 'vowel)
      ((w y) 'semivowel)
      (else 'consonant))                 ⟹  consonant
```

The last ⟨expression⟩ of a ⟨case clause⟩ is in tail context if the case expression itself is; see section 11.20.

(and ⟨test₁⟩ ...)   syntax

Syntax: The ⟨test⟩s must be expressions.

Semantics: If there are no ⟨test⟩s, #t is returned. Otherwise, the ⟨test⟩ expressions are evaluated from left to right until a ⟨test⟩ returns #f or the last ⟨test⟩ is reached. In the former case, the and expression returns #f without evaluating the remaining expressions. In the latter case, the last expression is evaluated and its values are returned.

```
(and (= 2 2) (> 2 1))        ⟹    #t
(and (= 2 2) (< 2 1))        ⟹    #f
(and 1 2 'c '(f g))          ⟹    (f g)
(and)                        ⟹    #t
```

The and keyword could be defined in terms of if using syntax-rules (see section 11.19) as follows:

```
(define-syntax and
  (syntax-rules ()
    ((and) #t)
    ((and test) test)
    ((and test1 test2 ...)
     (if test1 (and test2 ...) #f))))
```

The last ⟨test⟩ expression is in tail context if the and expression itself is; see section 11.20.

(or ⟨test₁⟩ ...)   syntax

Syntax: The ⟨test⟩s must be expressions.

Semantics: If there are no ⟨test⟩s, #f is returned. Otherwise, the ⟨test⟩ expressions are evaluated from left to right until a ⟨test⟩ returns a true value *val* (see section 5.7) or the last ⟨test⟩ is reached. In the former case, the or expression returns *val* without evaluating the remaining expressions. In the latter case, the last expression is evaluated and its values are returned.

```
(or (= 2 2) (> 2 1))         ⟹    #t
(or (= 2 2) (< 2 1))         ⟹    #t
(or #f #f #f)                ⟹    #f
(or '(b c) (/ 3 0))          ⟹    (b c)
```

The or keyword could be defined in terms of if using syntax-rules (see section 11.19) as follows:

```
(define-syntax or
  (syntax-rules ()
    ((or) #f)
```

```
((or test) test)
((or test1 test2 ...)
 (let ((x test1))
   (if x x (or test2 ...))))))))
```

The last ⟨test⟩ expression is in tail context if the or expression itself is; see section 11.20.

11.4.6 Binding constructs

The binding constructs described in this section create local bindings for variables that are visible only in a delimited region. The syntax of the constructs let, let*, letrec, and letrec* is identical, but they differ in the regions (see section 5.2) they establish for their variable bindings and in the order in which the values for the bindings are computed. In a let expression, the initial values are computed before any of the variables become bound; in a let* expression, the bindings and evaluations are performed sequentially. In a letrec or letrec* expression, all the bindings are in effect while their initial values are being computed, thus allowing mutually recursive definitions. In a letrec expression, the initial values are computed before being assigned to the variables; in a letrec*, the evaluations and assignments are performed sequentially.

In addition, the binding constructs let-values and let*-values generalize let and let* to allow multiple variables to be bound to the results of expressions that evaluate to multiple values. They are analogous to let and let* in the way they establish regions: in a let-values expression, the initial values are computed before any of the variables become bound; in a let*-values expression, the bindings are performed sequentially.

Sample definitions of all the binding forms of this section in terms of simpler forms are in appendix B.

(let ⟨bindings⟩ ⟨body⟩)   syntax
  Syntax: ⟨Bindings⟩ must have the form

    (((⟨variable$_1$⟩ ⟨init$_1$⟩) ...),

where each ⟨init⟩ is an expression, and ⟨body⟩ is as described in section 11.3. Any variable must not appear more than once in the ⟨variable⟩s.

  Semantics: The ⟨init⟩s are evaluated in the current environment (in some unspecified order), the ⟨variable⟩s are bound to fresh locations holding the results, the ⟨body⟩ is evaluated in the extended environment, and the values of the last expression of ⟨body⟩ are returned. Each binding of a ⟨variable⟩ has ⟨body⟩ as its region.

```
(let ((x 2) (y 3))
  (* x y))                              ⟹  6

(let ((x 2) (y 3))
```

```
    (let ((x 7)
          (z (+ x y)))
      (* z x)))                                    ⟹   35
```

See also named let, section 11.16.

(let* ⟨bindings⟩ ⟨body⟩)   syntax
  Syntax: ⟨Bindings⟩ must have the form

    (((⟨variable₁⟩ ⟨init₁⟩) ...),

where each ⟨init⟩ is an expression, and ⟨body⟩ is as described in section 11.3.
  Semantics: The let* form is similar to let, but the ⟨init⟩s are evaluated and
bindings created sequentially from left to right, with the region of each binding
including the bindings to its right as well as ⟨body⟩. Thus the second ⟨init⟩ is
evaluated in an environment in which the first binding is visible and initialized, and
so on.

```
    (let ((x 2) (y 3))
      (let* ((x 7)
             (z (+ x y)))
        (* z x)))                                  ⟹   70
```

Note: While the variables bound by a let expression must be distinct, the variables
bound by a let* expression need not be distinct.

(letrec ⟨bindings⟩ ⟨body⟩)   syntax
  Syntax: ⟨Bindings⟩ must have the form

    (((⟨variable₁⟩ ⟨init₁⟩) ...),

where each ⟨init⟩ is an expression, and ⟨body⟩ is as described in section 11.3. Any
variable must not appear more than once in the ⟨variable⟩s.
  Semantics: The ⟨variable⟩s are bound to fresh locations, the ⟨init⟩s are evaluated
in the resulting environment (in some unspecified order), each ⟨variable⟩ is assigned
to the result of the corresponding ⟨init⟩, the ⟨body⟩ is evaluated in the resulting
environment, and the values of the last expression in ⟨body⟩ are returned. Each
binding of a ⟨variable⟩ has the entire letrec expression as its region, making it
possible to define mutually recursive procedures.

```
    (letrec ((even?
              (lambda (n)
                (if (zero? n)
                    #t
                    (odd? (- n 1)))))
             (odd?
              (lambda (n)
                (if (zero? n)
                    #f
                    (even? (- n 1))))))
      (even? 88))                                  ⟹   #t
```

It should be possible to evaluate each ⟨init⟩ without assigning or referring to the value of any ⟨variable⟩. In the most common uses of letrec, all the ⟨init⟩s are lambda expressions and the restriction is satisfied automatically. Another restriction is that the continuation of each ⟨init⟩ should not be invoked more than once.

Implementation responsibilities: Implementations must detect any references to a ⟨variable⟩ during the evaluation of the ⟨init⟩ expressions (using one particular evaluation order and order of evaluating the ⟨init⟩ expressions). If an implementation detects such a violation of the restriction, it must raise an exception with condition type &assertion. Implementations may or may not detect that the continuation of each ⟨init⟩ is invoked more than once. However, if the implementation detects this, it must raise an exception with condition type &assertion.

(letrec* ⟨bindings⟩ ⟨body⟩)   syntax

   Syntax: ⟨Bindings⟩ must have the form

     (((⟨variable₁⟩ ⟨init₁⟩) ...),

where each ⟨init⟩ is an expression, and ⟨body⟩ is as described in section 11.3. Any variable must not appear more than once in the ⟨variable⟩s.

Semantics: The ⟨variable⟩s are bound to fresh locations, each ⟨variable⟩ is assigned in left-to-right order to the result of evaluating the corresponding ⟨init⟩, the ⟨body⟩ is evaluated in the resulting environment, and the values of the last expression in ⟨body⟩ are returned. Despite the left-to-right evaluation and assignment order, each binding of a ⟨variable⟩ has the entire letrec* expression as its region, making it possible to define mutually recursive procedures.

```
(letrec* ((p
           (lambda (x)
             (+ 1 (q (- x 1)))))
          (q
           (lambda (y)
             (if (zero? y)
                 0
                 (+ 1 (p (- y 1))))))
          (x (p 5))
          (y x))
  y)                                    ⟹  5
```

It must be possible to evaluate each ⟨init⟩ without assigning or referring to the value of the corresponding ⟨variable⟩ or the ⟨variable⟩ of any of the bindings that follow it in ⟨bindings⟩. Another restriction is that the continuation of each ⟨init⟩ should not be invoked more than once.

Implementation responsibilities: Implementations must, during the evaluation of an ⟨init⟩ expression, detect references to the value of the corresponding ⟨variable⟩ or the ⟨variable⟩ of any of the bindings that follow it in ⟨bindings⟩. If an implementation detects such a violation of the restriction, it must raise an exception with condition type &assertion. Implementations may or may not detect that the continuation of each ⟨init⟩ is invoked more than once. However, if the implementation detects this, it must raise an exception with condition type &assertion.

(let-values ⟨mv-bindings⟩ ⟨body⟩)   syntax
   Syntax: ⟨Mv-bindings⟩ must have the form

     (((⟨formals₁⟩ ⟨init₁⟩) ...),

where each ⟨init⟩ is an expression, and ⟨body⟩ is as described in section 11.3. Any variable must not appear more than once in the set of ⟨formals⟩.

   Semantics: The ⟨init⟩s are evaluated in the current environment (in some unspecified order), and the variables occurring in the ⟨formals⟩ are bound to fresh locations containing the values returned by the ⟨init⟩s, where the ⟨formals⟩ are matched to the return values in the same way that the ⟨formals⟩ in a lambda expression are matched to the arguments in a procedure call. Then, the ⟨body⟩ is evaluated in the extended environment, and the values of the last expression of ⟨body⟩ are returned. Each binding of a variable has ⟨body⟩ as its region. If the ⟨formals⟩ do not match, an exception with condition type &assertion is raised.

```
(let-values (((a b) (values 1 2))
             ((c d) (values 3 4)))
    (list a b c d))                        ⟹ (1 2 3 4)

(let-values (((a b . c) (values 1 2 3 4)))
    (list a b c))                          ⟹ (1 2 (3 4))

(let ((a 'a) (b 'b) (x 'x) (y 'y))
    (let-values (((a b) (values x y))
                 ((x y) (values a b)))
        (list a b x y)))                   ⟹ (x y a b)
```

(let*-values ⟨mv-bindings⟩ ⟨body⟩)   syntax
   Syntax: ⟨Mv-bindings⟩ must have the form

     (((⟨formals₁⟩ ⟨init₁⟩) ...),

where each ⟨init⟩ is an expression, and ⟨body⟩ is as described in section 11.3. In each ⟨formals⟩, any variable must not appear more than once.

   Semantics: The let*-values form is similar to let-values, but the ⟨init⟩s are evaluated and bindings created sequentially from left to right, with the region of the bindings of each ⟨formals⟩ including the bindings to its right as well as ⟨body⟩. Thus the second ⟨init⟩ is evaluated in an environment in which the bindings of the first ⟨formals⟩ is visible and initialized, and so on.

```
(let ((a 'a) (b 'b) (x 'x) (y 'y))
    (let*-values (((a b) (values x y))
                  ((x y) (values a b)))
        (list a b x y)))                   ⟹ (x y x y)
```

Note: While all of the variables bound by a let-values expression must be distinct, the variables bound by different ⟨formals⟩ of a let*-values expression need not be distinct.

11.4.7 Sequencing

```
(begin ⟨form⟩ ...)                              syntax
(begin ⟨expression⟩ ⟨expression⟩ ...)           syntax
```

The ⟨begin⟩ keyword has two different roles, depending on its context:

- It may appear as a form in a ⟨body⟩ (see section 11.3), ⟨library body⟩ (see section 7.1), or ⟨top-level body⟩ (see chapter 8), or directly nested in a begin form that appears in a body. In this case, the begin form must have the shape specified in the first header line. This use of begin acts as a *splicing* form—the forms inside the ⟨body⟩ are spliced into the surrounding body, as if the begin wrapper were not actually present.

  A begin form in a ⟨body⟩ or ⟨library body⟩ must be non-empty if it appears after the first ⟨expression⟩ within the body.

- It may appear as an ordinary expression and must have the shape specified in the second header line. In this case, the ⟨expression⟩s are evaluated sequentially from left to right, and the values of the last ⟨expression⟩ are returned. This expression type is used to sequence side effects such as assignments or input and output.

```
(define x 0)

(begin (set! x 5)
       (+ x 1))                    ⟹  6

(begin (display "4 plus 1 equals ")
       (display (+ 4 1)))          ⟹  unspecified
         and prints  4 plus 1 equals 5
```

11.5 Equivalence predicates

A *predicate* is a procedure that always returns a boolean value (#t or #f). An *equivalence predicate* is the computational analogue of a mathematical equivalence relation (it is symmetric, reflexive, and transitive). Of the equivalence predicates described in this section, eq? is the finest or most discriminating, and equal? is the coarsest. The eqv? predicate is slightly less discriminating than eq?.

```
(eqv? obj₁ obj₂)                                procedure
```

The eqv? procedure defines a useful equivalence relation on objects. Briefly, it returns #t if obj_1 and obj_2 should normally be regarded as the same object and #f otherwise. This relation is left slightly open to interpretation, but the following partial specification of eqv? must hold for all implementations.

The eqv? procedure returns #t if one of the following holds:

- Obj_1 and obj_2 are both booleans and are the same according to the `boolean=?` procedure (section 11.8).
- Obj_1 and obj_2 are both symbols and are the same according to the `symbol=?` procedure (section 11.10).
- Obj_1 and obj_2 are both exact number objects and are numerically equal (see =, section 11.7).
- Obj_1 and obj_2 are both inexact number objects, are numerically equal (see =, section 11.7), and yield the same results (in the sense of eqv?) when passed as arguments to any other procedure that can be defined as a finite composition of Scheme's standard arithmetic procedures.
- Obj_1 and obj_2 are both characters and are the same character according to the `char=?` procedure (section 11.11).
- Both obj_1 and obj_2 are the empty list.
- Obj_1 and obj_2 are objects such as pairs, vectors, bytevectors (library chapter 2), strings, records (library chapter 6), ports (library section 8.2), or hashtables (library chapter 13) that refer to the same locations in the store (section 5.10).
- Obj_1 and obj_2 are record-type descriptors that are specified to be eqv? in library section 6.3.

The eqv? procedure returns #f if one of the following holds:

- Obj_1 and obj_2 are of different types (section 11.1).
- Obj_1 and obj_2 are booleans for which the `boolean=?` procedure returns #f.
- Obj_1 and obj_2 are symbols for which the `symbol=?` procedure returns #f.
- One of obj_1 and obj_2 is an exact number object but the other is an inexact number object.
- Obj_1 and obj_2 are rational number objects for which the = procedure returns #f.
- Obj_1 and obj_2 yield different results (in the sense of eqv?) when passed as arguments to any other procedure that can be defined as a finite composition of Scheme's standard arithmetic procedures.
- Obj_1 and obj_2 are characters for which the `char=?` procedure returns #f.
- One of obj_1 and obj_2 is the empty list, but the other is not.
- Obj_1 and obj_2 are objects such as pairs, vectors, bytevectors (library chapter 2), strings, records (library chapter 6), ports (library section 8.2), or hashtables (library chapter 13) that refer to distinct locations.
- Obj_1 and obj_2 are pairs, vectors, strings, or records, or hashtables, where the applying the same accessor (i.e. `car`, `cdr`, `vector-ref`, `string-ref`, or record accessors) to both yields results for which eqv? returns #f.
- Obj_1 and obj_2 are procedures that would behave differently (return different values or have different side effects) for some arguments.

Note: The eqv? procedure returning #t when obj_1 and obj_2 are number objects does not imply that = would also return #t when called with obj_1 and obj_2 as arguments.

```
(eqv? 'a 'a)        ⟹   #t
(eqv? 'a 'b)        ⟹   #f
```

```
(eqv? 2 2)                              ⟹   #t
(eqv? '() '())                          ⟹   #t
(eqv? 100000000 100000000)              ⟹   #t
(eqv? (cons 1 2) (cons 1 2))            ⟹   #f
(eqv? (lambda () 1)
      (lambda () 2))                    ⟹   #f
(eqv? #f 'nil)                          ⟹   #f
```

The following examples illustrate cases in which the above rules do not fully specify the behavior of eqv?. All that can be said about such cases is that the value returned by eqv? must be a boolean.

```
(let ((p (lambda (x) x)))
  (eqv? p p))                           ⟹   unspecified
(eqv? "" "")                            ⟹   unspecified
(eqv? '#() '#())                        ⟹   unspecified
(eqv? (lambda (x) x)
      (lambda (x) x))                   ⟹   unspecified
(eqv? (lambda (x) x)
      (lambda (y) y))                   ⟹   unspecified
(eqv? +nan.0 +nan.0)                    ⟹   unspecified
```

The next set of examples shows the use of eqv? with procedures that have local state. Calls to gen-counter must return a distinct procedure every time, since each procedure has its own internal counter. Calls to gen-loser return procedures that behave equivalently when called. However, eqv? may not detect this equivalence.

```
(define gen-counter
  (lambda ()
    (let ((n 0))
      (lambda () (set! n (+ n 1)) n))))
(let ((g (gen-counter)))
  (eqv? g g))                           ⟹   unspecified
(eqv? (gen-counter) (gen-counter))
                                        ⟹   #f
(define gen-loser
  (lambda ()
    (let ((n 0))
      (lambda () (set! n (+ n 1)) 27))))
(let ((g (gen-loser)))
  (eqv? g g))                           ⟹   unspecified
(eqv? (gen-loser) (gen-loser))
                                        ⟹   unspecified

(letrec ((f (lambda () (if (eqv? f g) 'both 'f)))
         (g (lambda () (if (eqv? f g) 'both 'g))))
  (eqv? f g))                           ⟹   unspecified
```

```
(letrec ((f (lambda () (if (eqv? f g) 'f 'both)))
         (g (lambda () (if (eqv? f g) 'g 'both))))
  (eqv? f g))                           ⟹   #f
```

Implementations may share structure between constants where appropriate. Furthermore, a constant may be copied at any time by the implementation so as to exist simultaneously in different sets of locations, as noted in section 11.4.1. Thus the value of eqv? on constants is sometimes implementation-dependent.

```
(eqv? '(a) '(a))                        ⟹   unspecified
(eqv? "a" "a")                          ⟹   unspecified
(eqv? '(b) (cdr '(a b)))                ⟹   unspecified
(let ((x '(a)))
  (eqv? x x))                           ⟹   #t
```

(eq? obj_1 obj_2)   procedure

The eq? predicate is similar to eqv? except that in some cases it is capable of discerning distinctions finer than those detectable by eqv?.

The eq? and eqv? predicates are guaranteed to have the same behavior on symbols, booleans, the empty list, pairs, procedures, non-empty strings, bytevectors, and vectors, and records. The behavior of eq? on number objects and characters is implementation-dependent, but it always returns either #t or #f, and returns #t only when eqv? would also return #t. The eq? predicate may also behave differently from eqv? on empty vectors, empty bytevectors, and empty strings.

```
(eq? 'a 'a)                             ⟹   #t
(eq? '(a) '(a))                         ⟹   unspecified
(eq? (list 'a) (list 'a))               ⟹   #f
(eq? "a" "a")                           ⟹   unspecified
(eq? "" "")                             ⟹   unspecified
(eq? '() '())                           ⟹   #t
(eq? 2 2)                               ⟹   unspecified
(eq? #\A #\A)                           ⟹   unspecified
(eq? car car)                           ⟹   #t
(let ((n (+ 2 3)))
  (eq? n n))                            ⟹   unspecified
(let ((x '(a)))
  (eq? x x))                            ⟹   #t
(let ((x '#()))
  (eq? x x))                            ⟹   unspecified
(let ((p (lambda (x) x)))
  (eq? p p))                            ⟹   unspecified
```

(equal? obj_1 obj_2)   procedure

The equal? predicate returns #t if and only if the (possibly infinite) unfoldings of its arguments into regular trees are equal as ordered trees.

The equal? predicate treats pairs and vectors as nodes with outgoing edges, uses string=? to compare strings, uses bytevector=? to compare bytevectors (see library chapter 2), and uses eqv? to compare other nodes.

```
(equal? 'a 'a)                        ⟹   #t
(equal? '(a) '(a))                    ⟹   #t
(equal? '(a (b) c)
        '(a (b) c))                   ⟹   #t
(equal? "abc" "abc")                  ⟹   #t
(equal? 2 2)                          ⟹   #t
(equal? (make-vector 5 'a)
        (make-vector 5 'a))           ⟹   #t
(equal? '#vu8(1 2 3 4 5)
        (u8-list->bytevector
          '(1 2 3 4 5))               ⟹   #t
(equal? (lambda (x) x)
        (lambda (y) y))               ⟹   unspecified


(let* ((x (list 'a))
       (y (list 'a))
       (z (list x y)))
   (list (equal? z (list y x))
         (equal? z (list x x))))      ⟹   (#t #t)
```

Note: The equal? procedure must always terminate, even if its arguments contain cycles.

11.6 Procedure predicate

(procedure? *obj*)   procedure

Returns #t if *obj* is a procedure, otherwise returns #f.

```
(procedure? car)                     ⟹   #t
(procedure? 'car)                    ⟹   #f
(procedure? (lambda (x) (* x x)))    ⟹   #t
(procedure? '(lambda (x) (* x x)))   ⟹   #f
```

11.7 Arithmetic

The procedures described here implement arithmetic that is generic over the numerical tower described in chapter 3. The generic procedures described in this section accept both exact and inexact number objects as arguments, performing coercions and selecting the appropriate operations as determined by the numeric subtypes of their arguments.

Library chapter 11 describes libraries that define other numerical procedures.

11.7.1 Propagation of exactness and inexactness

The procedures listed below must return the mathematically correct exact result
provided all their arguments are exact:

```
+                  -                  *

max                min                abs
numerator          denominator        gcd
lcm                floor              ceiling
truncate           round              rationalize
real-part          imag-part          make-rectangular
```

The procedures listed below must return the correct exact result provided all their
arguments are exact, and no divisors are zero:

```
/

div                mod                div-and-mod
div0               mod0               div0-and-mod0
```

Moreover, the procedure expt must return the correct exact result provided its
first argument is an exact real number object and its second argument is an exact
integer object.

The general rule is that the generic operations return the correct exact result when
all of their arguments are exact and the result is mathematically well-defined, but
return an inexact result when any argument is inexact. Exceptions to this rule include
sqrt, exp, log, sin, cos, tan, asin, acos, atan, expt, make-polar, magnitude, and
angle, which may (but are not required to) return inexact results even when given
exact arguments, as indicated in the specification of these procedures.

One general exception to the rule above is that an implementation may return an
exact result despite inexact arguments if that exact result would be the correct result
for all possible substitutions of exact arguments for the inexact ones. An example is
(* 1.0 0) which may return either 0 (exact) or 0.0 (inexact).

11.7.2 Representability of infinities and NaNs

The specification of the numerical operations is written as though infinities and
NaNs are representable, and specifies many operations with respect to these number
objects in ways that are consistent with the IEEE-754 standard for binary floating-
point arithmetic. An implementation of Scheme may or may not represent infinities
and NaNs; however, an implementation must raise a continuable exception with
condition type &no-infinities or &no-nans (respectively; see library section 11.3)
whenever it is unable to represent an infinity or NaN as specified. In this case, the
continuation of the exception handler is the continuation that otherwise would have
received the infinity or NaN value. This requirement also applies to conversions
between number objects and external representations, including the reading of
program source code.

11.7.3 Semantics of common operations

Some operations are the semantic basis for several arithmetic procedures. The behavior of these operations is described in this section for later reference.

11.7.4 Integer division

Scheme's operations for performing integer division rely on mathematical operations div, mod, div_0, and mod_0, that are defined as follows:

div, mod, div_0, and mod_0 each accept two real numbers x_1 and x_2 as operands, where x_2 must be nonzero.

div returns an integer, and mod returns a real. Their results are specified by

$$x_1 \text{ div } x_2 = n_d$$
$$x_1 \text{ mod } x_2 = x_m$$

where

$$x_1 = n_d \cdot x_2 + x_m$$
$$0 \leqslant x_m < |x_2|$$

Examples:

$$123 \text{ div } 10 = 12$$
$$123 \text{ mod } 10 = 3$$
$$123 \text{ div } -10 = -12$$
$$123 \text{ mod } -10 = 3$$
$$-123 \text{ div } 10 = -13$$
$$-123 \text{ mod } 10 = 7$$
$$-123 \text{ div } -10 = 13$$
$$-123 \text{ mod } -10 = 7$$

div_0 and mod_0 are like div and mod, except the result of mod_0 lies within a half-open interval centered on zero. The results are specified by

$$x_1 \text{ div}_0 x_2 = n_d$$
$$x_1 \text{ mod}_0 x_2 = x_m$$

where:

$$x_1 = n_d \cdot x_2 + x_m$$
$$-|\tfrac{x_2}{2}| \leqslant x_m < |\tfrac{x_2}{2}|$$

Examples:

$$123 \text{ div}_0 10 = 12$$
$$123 \text{ mod}_0 10 = 3$$
$$123 \text{ div}_0 -10 = -12$$
$$123 \text{ mod}_0 -10 = 3$$
$$-123 \text{ div}_0 10 = -12$$

$$-123 \bmod_0 10 = -3$$
$$-123 \text{ div}_0 -10 = 12$$
$$-123 \bmod_0 -10 = -3$$

11.7.5 Transcendental functions

In general, the transcendental functions log, $\sin^{-1}$ (arcsine), $\cos^{-1}$ (arccosine), and $\tan^{-1}$ are multiply defined. The value of $\log z$ is defined to be the one whose imaginary part lies in the range from $-\pi$ (inclusive if -0.0 is distinguished, exclusive otherwise) to π (inclusive). $\log 0$ is undefined.

The value of $\log z$ for non-real z is defined in terms of log on real numbers as

$$\log z = \log |z| + (\text{angle } z)i$$

where angle z is the angle of $z = a \cdot e^{ib}$ specified as:

$$\text{angle } z = b + 2\pi n$$

with $-\pi \leqslant \text{angle } z \leqslant \pi$ and angle $z = b + 2\pi n$ for some integer n.

With the one-argument version of log defined this way, the values of the two-argument-version of log, $\sin^{-1} z$, $\cos^{-1} z$, $\tan^{-1} z$, and the two-argument version of $\tan^{-1}$ are according to the following formulæ:

$$\log z \ b = \frac{\log z}{\log b}$$
$$\sin^{-1} z = -i \log(iz + \sqrt{1 - z^2})$$
$$\cos^{-1} z = \pi/2 - \sin^{-1} z$$
$$\tan^{-1} z = (\log(1 + iz) - \log(1 - iz))/(2i)$$
$$\tan^{-1} x \ y = \text{angle}(x + yi)$$

The range of $\tan^{-1} x \ y$ is as in the following table. The asterisk (*) indicates that the entry applies to implementations that distinguish minus zero.

	y condition	x condition	range of result r
	$y = 0.0$	$x > 0.0$	0.0
*	$y = +0.0$	$x > 0.0$	$+0.0$
*	$y = -0.0$	$x > 0.0$	-0.0
	$y > 0.0$	$x > 0.0$	$0.0 < r < \frac{\pi}{2}$
	$y > 0.0$	$x = 0.0$	$\frac{\pi}{2}$
	$y > 0.0$	$x < 0.0$	$\frac{\pi}{2} < r < \pi$
	$y = 0.0$	$x < 0$	π
*	$y = +0.0$	$x < 0.0$	π
*	$y = -0.0$	$x < 0.0$	$-\pi$
	$y < 0.0$	$x < 0.0$	$-\pi < r < -\frac{\pi}{2}$
	$y < 0.0$	$x = 0.0$	$-\frac{\pi}{2}$
	$y < 0.0$	$x > 0.0$	$-\frac{\pi}{2} < r < 0.0$
	$y = 0.0$	$x = 0.0$	undefined
*	$y = +0.0$	$x = +0.0$	$+0.0$
*	$y = -0.0$	$x = +0.0$	-0.0
*	$y = +0.0$	$x = -0.0$	π
*	$y = -0.0$	$x = -0.0$	$-\pi$
*	$y = +0.0$	$x = 0$	$\frac{\pi}{2}$
*	$y = -0.0$	$x = 0$	$-\frac{\pi}{2}$

11.7.6 Numerical operations

11.7.7 Numerical type predicates

(number? *obj*)	procedure
(complex? *obj*)	procedure
(real? *obj*)	procedure
(rational? *obj*)	procedure
(integer? *obj*)	procedure

These numerical type predicates can be applied to any kind of argument. They return #t if the object is a number object of the named type, and #f otherwise. In general, if a type predicate is true of a number object then all higher type predicates are also true of that number object. Consequently, if a type predicate is false of a number object, then all lower type predicates are also false of that number object.

If z is a complex number object, then (real? z) is true if and only if (zero? (imag-part z)) and (exact? (imag-part z)) are both true.

If x is a real number object, then (rational? x) is true if and only if there exist exact integer objects k_1 and k_2 such that (= x (/ k_1 k_2)) and (= (numerator x) k_1) and (= (denominator x) k_2) are all true. Thus infinities and NaNs are not rational number objects.

If q is a rational number objects, then (integer? q) is true if and only if (= (denominator q) 1) is true. If q is not a rational number object, then (integer? q) is #f.

```
(complex? 3+4i)                    ⟹    #t
(complex? 3)                       ⟹    #t
(real? 3)                          ⟹    #t
(real? -2.5+0.0i)                  ⟹    #f
(real? -2.5+0i)                    ⟹    #t
(real? -2.5)                       ⟹    #t
(real? #e1e10)                     ⟹    #t
(rational? 6/10)                   ⟹    #t
(rational? 6/3)                    ⟹    #t
(rational? 2)                      ⟹    #t
(integer? 3+0i)                    ⟹    #t
(integer? 3.0)                     ⟹    #t
(integer? 8/4)                     ⟹    #t


(number? +nan.0)                   ⟹    #t
(complex? +nan.0)                  ⟹    #t
(real? +nan.0)                     ⟹    #t
(rational? +nan.0)                 ⟹    #f
(complex? +inf.0)                  ⟹    #t
(real? -inf.0)                     ⟹    #t
(rational? -inf.0)                 ⟹    #f
(integer? -inf.0)                  ⟹    #f
```

Note: Except for number?, the behavior of these type predicates on inexact number objects is unreliable, because any inaccuracy may affect the result.

(real-valued? *obj*)   procedure
(rational-valued? *obj*)   procedure
(integer-valued? *obj*)   procedure

These numerical type predicates can be applied to any kind of argument. The real-valued? procedure returns #t if the object is a number object and is equal in the sense of = to some real number object, or if the object is a NaN, or a complex number object whose real part is a NaN and whose imaginary part is zero in the sense of zero?. The rational-valued? and integer-valued? procedures return #t if the object is a number object and is equal in the sense of = to some object of the named type, and otherwise they return #f.

```
(real-valued? +nan.0)              ⟹    #t
(real-valued? +nan.0+0i)           ⟹    #t
(real-valued? -inf.0)              ⟹    #t
(real-valued? 3)                   ⟹    #t
(real-valued? -2.5+0.0i)           ⟹    #t
(real-valued? -2.5+0i)             ⟹    #t
(real-valued? -2.5)                ⟹    #t
(real-valued? #e1e10)              ⟹    #t
```

```
(rational-valued? +nan.0)        ⟹   #f
(rational-valued? -inf.0)        ⟹   #f
(rational-valued? 6/10)          ⟹   #t
(rational-valued? 6/10+0.0i)     ⟹   #t
(rational-valued? 6/10+0i)       ⟹   #t
(rational-valued? 6/3)           ⟹   #t

(integer-valued? 3+0i)           ⟹   #t
(integer-valued? 3+0.0i)         ⟹   #t
(integer-valued? 3.0)            ⟹   #t
(integer-valued? 3.0+0.0i)       ⟹   #t
(integer-valued? 8/4)            ⟹   #t
```

Note: These procedures test whether a given number object can be coerced to the specified type without loss of numerical accuracy. Specifically, the behavior of these predicates differs from the behavior of `real?`, `rational?`, and `integer?` on complex number objects whose imaginary part is inexact zero.

Note: The behavior of these type predicates on inexact number objects is unreliable, because any inaccuracy may affect the result.

`(exact? z)`   procedure

`(inexact? z)`   procedure

These numerical predicates provide tests for the exactness of a quantity. For any number object, precisely one of these predicates is true.

```
(exact? 5)                       ⟹   #t
(inexact? +inf.0)                ⟹   #t
```

11.7.8 Generic conversions

`(inexact z)`   procedure

`(exact z)`   procedure

The `inexact` procedure returns an inexact representation of *z*. If inexact number objects of the appropriate type have bounded precision, then the value returned is an inexact number object that is nearest to the argument. If an exact argument has no reasonably close inexact equivalent, an exception with condition type `&implementation-restriction` may be raised.

Note: For a real number object whose magnitude is finite but so large that it has no reasonable finite approximation as an inexact number, a reasonably close inexact equivalent may be `+inf.0` or `-inf.0`. Similarly, the inexact representation of a complex number object whose components are finite may have infinite components.

The `exact` procedure returns an exact representation of *z*. The value returned is the exact number object that is numerically closest to the argument; in most cases, the result of this procedure should be numerically equal to its argument. If an inexact argument has no reasonably close exact equivalent, an exception with condition type &implementation-restriction may be raised.

These procedures implement the natural one-to-one correspondence between exact and inexact integer objects throughout an implementation-dependent range.

The inexact and exact procedures are idempotent.

11.7.9 Arithmetic operations

$(= z_1\ z_2\ z_3\ ...)$	procedure
$(<\ x_1\ x_2\ x_3\ ...)$	procedure
$(>\ x_1\ x_2\ x_3\ ...)$	procedure
$(<=\ x_1\ x_2\ x_3\ ...)$	procedure
$(>=\ x_1\ x_2\ x_3\ ...)$	procedure

These procedures return #t if their arguments are (respectively): equal, monotonically increasing, monotonically decreasing, monotonically nondecreasing, or monotonically nonincreasing, and #f otherwise.

(= +inf.0 +inf.0)	$\Longrightarrow$	#t
(= -inf.0 +inf.0)	$\Longrightarrow$	#f
(= -inf.0 -inf.0)	$\Longrightarrow$	#t

For any real number object x that is neither infinite nor NaN:

(< -inf.0 x +inf.0)	$\Longrightarrow$	#t
(> +inf.0 x -inf.0)	$\Longrightarrow$	#t

For any number object z:

(= +nan.0 z)	$\Longrightarrow$	#f

For any real number object x:

(< +nan.0 x)	$\Longrightarrow$	#f
(> +nan.0 x)	$\Longrightarrow$	#f

These predicates must be transitive.

Note: The traditional implementations of these predicates in Lisp-like languages are not transitive.

Note: While it is possible to compare inexact number objects using these predicates, the results may be unreliable because a small inaccuracy may affect the result; this is especially true of = and zero? (below).

When in doubt, consult a numerical analyst.

(zero? z)	procedure
(positive? x)	procedure
(negative? x)	procedure
(odd? n)	procedure
(even? n)	procedure

```
(finite? x)                                                 procedure
(infinite? x)                                               procedure
(nan? x)                                                    procedure
```

These numerical predicates test a number object for a particular property, return-ing #t or #f. The zero? procedure tests if the number object is = to zero, positive? tests whether it is greater than zero, negative? tests whether it is less than zero, odd? tests whether it is odd, even? tests whether it is even, finite? tests whether it is not an infinity and not a NaN, infinite? tests whether it is an infinity, nan? tests whether it is a NaN.

```
(zero? +0.0)                    ⟹    #t
(zero? -0.0)                    ⟹    #t
(zero? +nan.0)                  ⟹    #f
(positive? +inf.0)             ⟹    #t
(negative? -inf.0)             ⟹    #t
(positive? +nan.0)             ⟹    #f
(negative? +nan.0)             ⟹    #f
(finite? +inf.0)               ⟹    #f
(finite? 5)                     ⟹    #t
(finite? 5.0)                   ⟹    #t
(infinite? 5.0)                ⟹    #f
(infinite? +inf.0)             ⟹    #t
```

Note: As with the predicates above, the results may be unreliable because a small inaccuracy may affect the result.

```
(max x₁ x₂ ...)                                             procedure
(min x₁ x₂ ...)                                             procedure
```

These procedures return the maximum or minimum of their arguments.

```
(max 3 4)                       ⟹    4
(max 3.9 4)                     ⟹    4.0
```

For any real number object x that is not a NaN:

```
(max +inf.0 x)                  ⟹    +inf.0
(min -inf.0 x)                  ⟹    -inf.0
```

Note: If any argument is inexact, then the result is also inexact (unless the procedure can prove that the inaccuracy is not large enough to affect the result, which is possible only in unusual implementations). If min or max is used to compare number objects of mixed exactness, and the numerical value of the result cannot be represented as an inexact number object without loss of accuracy, then the procedure may raise an exception with condition type &implementation-restriction.

```
(+ z₁ ...)                                                  procedure
(* z₁ ...)                                                  procedure
```

These procedures return the sum or product of their arguments.

```
(+ 3 4)                        ⟹   7
(+ 3)                          ⟹   3
(+)                            ⟹   0
(+ +inf.0 +inf.0)              ⟹   +inf.0
(+ +inf.0 -inf.0)              ⟹   +nan.0


(* 4)                          ⟹   4
(*)                            ⟹   1
(* 5 +inf.0)                   ⟹   +inf.0
(* -5 +inf.0)                  ⟹   -inf.0
(* +inf.0 +inf.0)              ⟹   +inf.0
(* +inf.0 -inf.0)              ⟹   -inf.0
(* 0 +inf.0)                   ⟹   0 or +nan.0
(* 0 +nan.0)                   ⟹   0 or +nan.0
(* 1.0 0)                      ⟹   0 or 0.0
```

For any real number object x that is neither infinite nor NaN:

```
(+ +inf.0 x)                   ⟹   +inf.0
(+ -inf.0 x)                   ⟹   -inf.0
```

For any real number object x:

```
(+ +nan.0 x)                   ⟹   +nan.0
```

For any real number object x that is not an exact 0:

```
(* +nan.0 x)                   ⟹   +nan.0
```

If any of these procedures are applied to mixed non-rational real and non-real complex arguments, they either raise an exception with condition type &implementation-restriction or return an unspecified number object.

Implementations that distinguish −0.0 should adopt behavior consistent with the following examples:

```
(+ 0.0 -0.0)                   ⟹   0.0
(+ -0.0 0.0)                   ⟹   0.0
(+ 0.0 0.0)                    ⟹   0.0
(+ -0.0 -0.0)                  ⟹   -0.0
```

$(- z)$ procedure
$(- z_1 \ z_2 \ z_3 \ ...)$ procedure

With two or more arguments, this procedures returns the difference of its arguments, associating to the left. With one argument, however, it returns the additive inverse of its argument.

```
(- 3 4)                        ⟹   -1
(- 3 4 5)                      ⟹   -6
(- 3)                          ⟹   -3
(- +inf.0 +inf.0)              ⟹   +nan.0
```

   If this procedure is applied to mixed non-rational real and non-real complex arguments, it either raises an exception with condition type `&implementation-restriction`
or returns an unspecified number object.

   Implementations that distinguish −0.0 should adopt behavior consistent with the
following examples:

(- 0.0)	⟹ -0.0
(- -0.0)	⟹ 0.0
(- 0.0 -0.0)	⟹ 0.0
(- -0.0 0.0)	⟹ -0.0
(- 0.0 0.0)	⟹ 0.0
(- -0.0 -0.0)	⟹ 0.0

(/ z)	procedure
(/ z₁ z₂ z₃ ...)	procedure

   If all of the arguments are exact, then the divisors must all be nonzero. With two
or more arguments, this procedure returns the quotient of its arguments, associating
to the left. With one argument, however, it returns the multiplicative inverse of its
argument.

(/ 3 4 5)	⟹ 3/20
(/ 3)	⟹ 1/3
(/ 0.0)	⟹ +inf.0
(/ 1.0 0)	⟹ +inf.0
(/ -1 0.0)	⟹ -inf.0
(/ +inf.0)	⟹ 0.0
(/ 0 0)	⟹ &assertion *exception*
(/ 3 0)	⟹ &assertion *exception*
(/ 0 3.5)	⟹ 0.0
(/ 0 0.0)	⟹ +nan.0
(/ 0.0 0)	⟹ +nan.0
(/ 0.0 0.0)	⟹ +nan.0

   If this procedure is applied to mixed non-rational real and non-real complex
arguments, it either raises an exception with condition type `&implementation-`
`restriction` or returns an unspecified number object.

(abs x)	procedure

   Returns the absolute value of its argument.

(abs -7)	⟹ 7
(abs -inf.0)	⟹ +inf.0

(div-and-mod x₁ x₂)	procedure
(div x₁ x₂)	procedure
(mod x₁ x₂)	procedure

(div0-and-mod0 x_1 x_2)	procedure
(div0 x_1 x_2)	procedure
(mod0 x_1 x_2)	procedure

These procedures implement number-theoretic integer division and return the results of the corresponding mathematical operations specified in section 11.7.4. If x_1 and x_2 are exact, x_2 must be nonzero. In the cases where the mathematical requirements in section 11.7.4 cannot be satisfied by any number object, either an exception is raised with condition type &implementation-restriction, or unspecified number objects (one for div mod, div0 and mod0, two for div-and-mod and div0-and-mod0) are returned.

$$
\begin{array}{lll}
\text{(div } x_1 \ x_2) & \Longrightarrow & x_1 \ \text{div} \ x_2 \\
\text{(mod } x_1 \ x_2) & \Longrightarrow & x_1 \ \text{mod} \ x_2 \\
\text{(div-and-mod } x_1 \ x_2) & \Longrightarrow & x_1 \ \text{div} \ x_2, \ x_1 \ \text{mod} \ x_2 \\
& & ; \ \text{two return values} \\
\text{(div0 } x_1 \ x_2) & \Longrightarrow & x_1 \ \text{div}_0 \ x_2 \\
\text{(mod0 } x_1 \ x_2) & \Longrightarrow & x_1 \ \text{mod}_0 \ x_2 \\
\text{(div0-and-mod0 } x_1 \ x_2) & \Longrightarrow & x_1 \ \text{div}_0 \ x_2, \ x_1 \ \text{mod}_0 \ x_2 \\
& & ; \ \text{two return values}
\end{array}
$$

(gcd n_1 ...)	procedure
(lcm n_1 ...)	procedure

These procedures return the greatest common divisor or least common multiple of their arguments. The result is always non-negative.

$$
\begin{array}{lll}
\text{(gcd 32 -36)} & \Longrightarrow & 4 \\
\text{(gcd)} & \Longrightarrow & 0 \\
\text{(lcm 32 -36)} & \Longrightarrow & 288 \\
\text{(lcm 32.0 -36)} & \Longrightarrow & 288.0 \\
\text{(lcm)} & \Longrightarrow & 1
\end{array}
$$

(numerator q)	procedure
(denominator q)	procedure

These procedures return the numerator or denominator of their argument; the result is computed as if the argument was represented as a fraction in lowest terms. The denominator is always positive. The denominator of 0 is defined to be 1.

$$
\begin{array}{lll}
\text{(numerator (/ 6 4))} & \Longrightarrow & 3 \\
\text{(denominator (/ 6 4))} & \Longrightarrow & 2 \\
\text{(denominator} & & \\
\quad \text{(inexact (/ 6 4)))} & \Longrightarrow & 2.0
\end{array}
$$

(floor x)	procedure
(ceiling x)	procedure

(truncate x)   procedure
(round x)   procedure

These procedures return inexact integer objects for inexact arguments that are not infinities or NaNs, and exact integer objects for exact rational arguments. For such arguments, floor returns the largest integer object not larger than x. The ceiling procedure returns the smallest integer object not smaller than x. The truncate procedure returns the integer object closest to x whose absolute value is not larger than the absolute value of x. The round procedure returns the closest integer object to x, rounding to even when x represents a number halfway between two integers. *Note:* If the argument to one of these procedures is inexact, then the result is also inexact. If an exact value is needed, the result should be passed to the exact procedure.

Although infinities and NaNs are not integer objects, these procedures return an infinity when given an infinity as an argument, and a NaN when given a NaN.

```
(floor -4.3)                    ⟹    -5.0
(ceiling -4.3)                  ⟹    -4.0
(truncate -4.3)                 ⟹    -4.0
(round -4.3)                    ⟹    -4.0

(floor 3.5)                     ⟹    3.0
(ceiling 3.5)                   ⟹    4.0
(truncate 3.5)                  ⟹    3.0
(round 3.5)                     ⟹    4.0

(round 7/2)                     ⟹    4
(round 7)                       ⟹    7

(floor +inf.0)                  ⟹    +inf.0
(ceiling -inf.0)                ⟹    -inf.0
(round +nan.0)                  ⟹    +nan.0
```

(rationalize x_1 x_2)   procedure

The rationalize procedure returns the a number object representing the *simplest* rational number differing from x_1 by no more than x_2. A rational number r_1 is *simpler* than another rational number r_2 if $r_1 = p_1/q_1$ and $r_2 = p_2/q_2$ (in lowest terms) and $|p_1| \leq |p_2|$ and $|q_1| \leq |q_2|$. Thus 3/5 is simpler than 4/7. Although not all rationals are comparable in this ordering (consider 2/7 and 3/5) any interval contains a rational number that is simpler than every other rational number in that interval (the simpler 2/5 lies between 2/7 and 3/5). Note that $0 = 0/1$ is the simplest rational of all.

```
(rationalize (exact .3) 1/10)   ⟹    1/3
(rationalize .3 1/10)           ⟹    #i1/3  ; approximately
```

```
(rationalize +inf.0 3)              ⟹  +inf.0
(rationalize +inf.0 +inf.0)         ⟹  +nan.0
(rationalize 3 +inf.0)              ⟹  0.0
```

The first two examples hold only in implementations whose inexact real number objects have sufficient precision.

(exp z)	procedure
(log z)	procedure
(log z_1 z_2)	procedure
(sin z)	procedure
(cos z)	procedure
(tan z)	procedure
(asin z)	procedure
(acos z)	procedure
(atan z)	procedure
(atan x_1 x_2)	procedure

These procedures compute the usual transcendental functions. The exp procedure computes the base-*e* exponential of z. The log procedure with a single argument computes the natural logarithm of z (not the base-ten logarithm); (log z_1 z_2) computes the base-z_2 logarithm of z_1. The asin, acos, and atan procedures compute arcsine, arccosine, and arctangent, respectively. The two-argument variant of atan computes (angle (make-rectangular x_2 x_1)).

See section 11.7.5 for the underlying mathematical operations. These procedures may return inexact results even when given exact arguments.

```
(exp +inf.0)        ⟹  +inf.0
(exp -inf.0)        ⟹  0.0
(log +inf.0)        ⟹  +inf.0
(log 0.0)           ⟹  -inf.0
(log 0)             ⟹  &assertion exception
(log -inf.0)        ⟹  +inf.0+3.1415926535589793i
                       ; approximately
(atan -inf.0)     ⟹  -1.5707963267948965 ; approximately
(atan +inf.0)     ⟹  1.5707963267948965 ; approximately
(log -1.0+0.0i)   ⟹  0.0+3.1415926535589793i ; approximately
(log -1.0-0.0i)   ⟹  0.0-3.1415926535589793i ; approximately
                     ; if -0.0 is distinguished
```

(sqrt z)	procedure

Returns the principal square root of z. For rational z, the result has either positive real part, or zero real part and non-negative imaginary part. With log defined as in section 11.7.5, the value of (sqrt z) could be expressed as $e^{\frac{\log z}{2}}$.

The sqrt procedure may return an inexact result even when given an exact argument.

```
(sqrt -5)                  ⟹   0.0+2.236067977499979i ; approximately
(sqrt +inf.0)              ⟹   +inf.0
(sqrt -inf.0)              ⟹   +inf.0i
```

(exact-integer-sqrt k)   procedure

The exact-integer-sqrt procedure returns two non-negative exact integer objects s and r where $k = s^2 + r$ and $k < (s+1)^2$.

```
(exact-integer-sqrt 4)              ⟹  2 0
                                       ; two return values
(exact-integer-sqrt 5)              ⟹  2 1
                                       ; two return values
```

(expt z_1 z_2)   procedure

Returns z_1 raised to the power z_2. For nonzero z_1, this is $e^{z_2 \log z_1}$. 0.0^z is 1.0 if $z = 0.0$, and 0.0 if (real-part z) is positive. For other cases in which the first argument is zero, either an exception is raised with condition type &implementation-restriction, or an unspecified number object is returned.

For an exact real number object z_1 and an exact integer object z_2, (expt z_1 z_2) must return an exact result. For all other values of z_1 and z_2, (expt z_1 z_2) may return an inexact result, even when both z_1 and z_2 are exact.

```
(expt 5 3)                  ⟹   125
(expt 5 -3)                 ⟹   1/125
(expt 5 0)                  ⟹   1
(expt 0 5)                  ⟹   0
(expt 0 5+.0000312i)        ⟹   0.0
(expt 0 -5)                 ⟹   unspecified
(expt 0 -5+.0000312i)       ⟹   unspecified
(expt 0 0)                  ⟹   1
(expt 0.0 0.0)              ⟹   1.0
```

(make-rectangular x_1 x_2)   procedure
(make-polar x_3 x_4)   procedure
(real-part z)   procedure
(imag-part z)   procedure
(magnitude z)   procedure
(angle z)   procedure

Suppose a_1, a_2, a_3, and a_4 are real numbers, and c is a complex number such that the following holds:

$$c = a_1 + a_2 i = a_3 e^{i a_4}$$

Then, if x_1, x_2, x_3, and x_4 are number objects representing a_1, a_2, a_3, and a_4, respectively, (make-rectangular x_1 x_2) returns c, and (make-polar x_3 x_4) returns c.

```
(make-rectangular 1.1 2.2)          ⟹ 1.1+2.2i ; approximately
(make-polar 1.1 2.2)                ⟹ 1.1@2.2 ; approximately
```

Conversely, if $-\pi \leqslant a_4 \leqslant \pi$, and if z is a number object representing c, then (real-part z) returns a_1 (imag-part z) returns a_2, (magnitude z) returns a_3, and (angle z) returns a_4.

```
(real-part 1.1+2.2i)                ⟹ 1.1 ; approximately
(imag-part 1.1+2.2i)                ⟹ 2.2 ; approximately
(magnitude 1.1@2.2)                 ⟹ 1.1 ; approximately
(angle 1.1@2.2)                     ⟹ 2.2 ; approximately

(angle -1.0)                        ⟹ 3.141592653589793 ; approximately
(angle -1.0+0.0i)                   ⟹ 3.141592653589793 ; approximately
(angle -1.0-0.0i)                   ⟹ -3.141592653589793 ; approximately
                                    ; if -0.0 is distinguished
(angle +inf.0)                      ⟹ 0.0
(angle -inf.0)                      ⟹ 3.141592653589793 ; approximately
```

Moreover, suppose x_1, x_2 are such that either x_1 or x_2 is an infinity, then

```
(make-rectangular x₁ x₂)            ⟹ z
(magnitude z)                       ⟹ +inf.0
```

The make-polar, magnitude, and angle procedures may return inexact results even when given exact arguments.

```
(angle -1)                          ⟹ 3.141592653589793 ; approximately
```

11.7.10 Numerical Input and Output

```
(number->string z)                                              procedure
(number->string z radix)                                        procedure
(number->string z radix precision)                              procedure
```
Radix must be an exact integer object, either 2, 8, 10, or 16. If omitted, *radix* defaults to 10. If a *precision* is specified, then z must be an inexact complex number object, *precision* must be an exact positive integer object, and *radix* must be 10. The number->string procedure takes a number object and a radix and returns as a string an external representation of the given number object in the given radix such that

```
(let ((number z) (radix radix))
  (eqv? (string->number
          (number->string number radix)
        radix)
      number))
```

is true. If no possible result makes this expression true, an exception with condition type `&implementation-restriction` is raised.

Note: The error case can occur only when *z* is not a complex number object or is a complex number object with a non-rational real or imaginary part.

If a *precision* is specified, then the representations of the inexact real components of the result, unless they are infinite or NaN, specify an explicit ⟨mantissa width⟩ *p*, and *p* is the least $p \geqslant precision$ for which the above expression is true.

If *z* is inexact, the radix is 10, and the above expression and condition can be satisfied by a result that contains a decimal point, then the result contains a decimal point and is expressed using the minimum number of digits (exclusive of exponent, trailing zeroes, and mantissa width) needed to make the above expression and condition true (Burger & Dybvig, 1996; Clinger, 1990); otherwise the format of the result is unspecified.

The result returned by `number->string` never contains an explicit radix prefix.

(`string->number` *string*)   procedure
(`string->number` *string radix*)   procedure

Returns a number object with maximally precise representation expressed by the given *string*. *Radix* must be an exact integer object, either 2, 8, 10, or 16. If supplied, *radix* is a default radix that may be overridden by an explicit radix prefix in *string* (e.g., `"#o177"`). If *radix* is not supplied, then the default radix is 10. If *string* is not a syntactically valid notation for a number object or a notation for a rational number object with a zero denominator, then `string->number` returns `#f`.

(`string->number` `"100"`)	⟹	100
(`string->number` `"100"` 16)	⟹	256
(`string->number` `"1e2"`)	⟹	100.0
(`string->number` `"0/0"`)	⟹	#f
(`string->number` `"+inf.0"`)	⟹	+inf.0
(`string->number` `"-inf.0"`)	⟹	-inf.0
(`string->number` `"+nan.0"`)	⟹	+nan.0

Note: The `string->number` procedure always returns a number object or `#f`; it never raises an exception.

11.8 Booleans

The standard boolean objects for true and false have external representations `#t` and `#f`. However, of all objects, only `#f` counts as false in conditional expressions. See section 5.7.

Note: Programmers accustomed to other dialects of Lisp should be aware that Scheme distinguishes both `#f` and the empty list from each other and from the symbol nil.

(`not` *obj*)   procedure

Returns `#t` if *obj* is `#f`, and returns `#f` otherwise.

```
(not #t)                          ⟹  #f
(not 3)                           ⟹  #f
(not (list 3))                    ⟹  #f
(not #f)                          ⟹  #t
(not '())                         ⟹  #f
(not (list))                      ⟹  #f
(not 'nil)                        ⟹  #f
```

(boolean? *obj*)   procedure

    Returns #t if *obj* is either #t or #f and returns #f otherwise.

```
(boolean? #f)                     ⟹  #t
(boolean? 0)                      ⟹  #f
(boolean? '())                    ⟹  #f
```

(boolean=? *bool$_1$ bool$_2$ bool$_3$* ...)   procedure

    Returns #t if the booleans are the same.

11.9 Pairs and lists

A *pair* is a compound structure with two fields called the car and cdr fields (for historical reasons). Pairs are created by the procedure cons. The car and cdr fields are accessed by the procedures car and cdr.

Pairs are used primarily to represent lists. A list can be defined recursively as either the empty list or a pair whose cdr is a list. More precisely, the set of lists is defined as the smallest set X such that

- The empty list is in X.
- If *list* is in X, then any pair whose cdr field contains *list* is also in X.

The objects in the car fields of successive pairs of a list are the elements of the list. For example, a two-element list is a pair whose car is the first element and whose cdr is a pair whose car is the second element and whose cdr is the empty list. The length of a list is the number of elements, which is the same as the number of pairs.

The empty list is a special object of its own type. It is not a pair. It has no elements and its length is zero.

Note: The above definitions imply that all lists have finite length and are terminated by the empty list.

A chain of pairs not ending in the empty list is called an *improper list*. Note that an improper list is not a list. The list and dotted notations can be combined to represent improper lists:

```
(a b c . d)
```

is equivalent to

```
(a . (b . (c . d)))
```

Whether a given pair is a list depends upon what is stored in the cdr field.

(pair? *obj*)   procedure

Returns #t if *obj* is a pair, and otherwise returns #f.

```
(pair? '(a . b))        ⟹   #t
(pair? '(a b c))        ⟹   #t
(pair? '())             ⟹   #f
(pair? '#(a b))         ⟹   #f
```

(cons *obj₁* *obj₂*)   procedure

Returns a newly allocated pair whose car is *obj₁* and whose cdr is *obj₂*. The pair is guaranteed to be different (in the sense of eqv?) from every existing object.

```
(cons 'a '())           ⟹   (a)
(cons '(a) '(b c d))    ⟹   ((a) b c d)
(cons "a" '(b c))       ⟹   ("a" b c)
(cons 'a 3)             ⟹   (a . 3)
(cons '(a b) 'c)        ⟹   ((a b) . c)
```

(car *pair*)   procedure

Returns the contents of the car field of *pair*.

```
(car '(a b c))          ⟹   a
(car '((a) b c d))      ⟹   (a)
(car '(1 . 2))          ⟹   1
(car '())               ⟹   &assertion exception
```

(cdr *pair*)   procedure

Returns the contents of the cdr field of *pair*.

```
(cdr '((a) b c d))      ⟹   (b c d)
(cdr '(1 . 2))          ⟹   2
(cdr '())               ⟹   &assertion exception
```

(caar *pair*)   procedure
(cadr *pair*)   procedure
     ⋮
(cdddar *pair*)   procedure
(cddddr *pair*)   procedure

These procedures are compositions of car and cdr, where for example caddr could be defined by

```
(define caddr (lambda (x) (car (cdr (cdr x))))).
```

Arbitrary compositions, up to four deep, are provided. There are twenty-eight of these procedures in all.

(null? *obj*)   procedure
   Returns #t if *obj* is the empty list, #f otherwise.

(list? *obj*)   procedure
   Returns #t if *obj* is a list, #f otherwise. By definition, all lists are chains of pairs that have finite length and are terminated by the empty list.

```
(list? '(a b c))                    ⟹    #t
(list? '())                         ⟹    #t
(list? '(a . b))                    ⟹    #f
```

(list *obj* ...)   procedure
   Returns a newly allocated list of its arguments.

```
(list 'a (+ 3 4) 'c)                ⟹    (a 7 c)
(list)                              ⟹    ()
```

(length *list*)   procedure
   Returns the length of *list*.

```
(length '(a b c))                   ⟹    3
(length '(a (b) (c d e)))           ⟹    3
(length '())                        ⟹    0
```

(append *list* ... *obj*)   procedure
(append)   procedure
   Returns a possibly improper list consisting of the elements of the first *list* followed by the elements of the other *list*s, with *obj* as the cdr of the final pair. An improper list results if *obj* is not a list. The append procedure returns the empty list if called with no arguments.

```
(append '(x) '(y))                  ⟹    (x y)
(append '(a) '(b c d))              ⟹    (a b c d)
(append '(a (b)) '((c)))            ⟹    (a (b) (c))
(append '(a b) '(c . d))            ⟹    (a b c . d)
(append '() 'a)                     ⟹    a
(append)                            ⟹    ()
(append 'a)                         ⟹    a
```

   If append constructs a nonempty chain of pairs, it is always newly allocated. If no pairs are allocated, *obj* is returned.

(reverse *list*)   procedure
   Returns a newly allocated list consisting of the elements of *list* in reverse order.

```
(reverse '(a b c))                    ⟹   (c b a)
(reverse '(a (b c) d (e (f))))        ⟹   ((e (f)) d (b c) a)
```

(list-tail *list* *k*)   procedure

List should be a list of size at least *k*. The list-tail procedure returns the subchain of pairs of *list* obtained by omitting the first *k* elements.

```
(list-tail '(a b c d) 2)          ⟹   (c d)
```

Implementation responsibilities: The implementation must check that *list* is a chain of pairs whose length is at least *k*. It should not check that it is a chain of pairs beyond this length.

(list-ref *list* *k*)   procedure

List must be a list whose length is at least $k + 1$. The list-tail procedure returns the *k*th element of *list*.

```
(list-ref '(a b c d) 2)           ⟹   c
```

Implementation responsibilities: The implementation must check that *list* is a chain of pairs whose length is at least $k + 1$. It should not check that it is a list of pairs beyond this length.

(map *proc* *list$_1$* *list$_2$* ...)   procedure

The *list*s should all have the same length. *Proc* should accept as many arguments as there are *list*s and return a single value. *Proc* should not mutate any of the *list*s.

The map procedure applies *proc* element-wise to the elements of the *list*s and returns a list of the results, in order. *Proc* is always called in the same dynamic environment as map itself. The order in which *proc* is applied to the elements of the *list*s is unspecified. If multiple returns occur from map, the values returned by earlier returns are not mutated.

```
(map cadr '((a b) (d e) (g h)))   ⟹   (b e h)

(map (lambda (n) (expt n n))
     '(1 2 3 4 5))                ⟹   (1 4 27 256 3125)

(map + '(1 2 3) '(4 5 6))         ⟹   (5 7 9)

(let ((count 0))
  (map (lambda (ignored)
         (set! count (+ count 1))
         count)
       '(a b)))                   ⟹   (1 2) or (2 1)
```

Implementation responsibilities: The implementation should check that the *list*s all have the same length. The implementation must check the restrictions on *proc* to the extent performed by applying it as described. An implementation may check whether *proc* is an appropriate argument before applying it.

(for-each *proc list₁ list₂* ...)   procedure
The *list*s should all have the same length. *Proc* should accept as many arguments as there are *list*s. *Proc* should not mutate any of the *list*s.

The for-each procedure applies *proc* element-wise to the elements of the *list*s for its side effects, in order from the first elements to the last. *Proc* is always called in the same dynamic environment as for-each itself. The return values of for-each are unspecified.

```
(let ((v (make-vector 5)))
  (for-each (lambda (i)
              (vector-set! v i (* i i)))
            '(0 1 2 3 4))
  v)                                          ⟹    #(0 1 4 9 16)

(for-each (lambda (x) x) '(1 2 3 4))          ⟹  unspecified

(for-each even? '())                          ⟹  unspecified
```

Implementation responsibilities: The implementation should check that the *list*s all have the same length. The implementation must check the restrictions on *proc* to the extent performed by applying it as described. An implementation may check whether *proc* is an appropriate argument before applying it.
Note: Implementations of for-each may or may not tail-call *proc* on the last elements.

11.10 Symbols

Symbols are objects whose usefulness rests on the fact that two symbols are identical (in the sense of eq?, eqv? and equal?) if and only if their names are spelled the same way. A symbol literal is formed using quote.

(symbol? *obj*)   procedure
Returns #t if *obj* is a symbol, otherwise returns #f.

```
(symbol? 'foo)          ⟹    #t
(symbol? (car '(a b)))  ⟹    #t
(symbol? "bar")         ⟹    #f
(symbol? 'nil)          ⟹    #t
(symbol? '())           ⟹    #f
(symbol? #f)            ⟹    #f
```

(symbol->string *symbol*) procedure

Returns the name of *symbol* as an immutable string.

```
(symbol->string 'flying-fish)
                                    ⟹  "flying-fish"
(symbol->string 'Martin)            ⟹  "Martin"
(symbol->string
   (string->symbol "Malvina"))
                                    ⟹  "Malvina"
```

(symbol=? *symbol₁* *symbol₂* *symbol₃* ...) procedure

Returns #t if the symbols are the same, i.e., if their names are spelled the same.

(string->symbol *string*) procedure

Returns the symbol whose name is *string*.

```
(eq? 'mISSISSIppi 'mississippi)
        ⟹  #f
(string->symbol "mISSISSIppi")
        ⟹  the symbol with name "mISSISSIppi"
(eq? 'bitBlt (string->symbol "bitBlt"))
        ⟹  #t
(eq? 'JollyWog
     (string->symbol
       (symbol->string 'JollyWog)))
        ⟹  #t
(string=? "K. Harper, M.D."
          (symbol->string
            (string->symbol "K. Harper, M.D.")))
        ⟹  #t
```

11.11 Characters

Characters are objects that represent Unicode scalar values (Unicode Consortium, 2007).

Note: Unicode defines a standard mapping between sequences of *Unicode scalar values* (integers in the range 0 to #x10FFFF, excluding the range #xD800 to #xDFFF) in the latest version of the standard and human-readable "characters". More precisely, Unicode distinguishes between glyphs, which are printed for humans to read, and characters, which are abstract entities that map to glyphs (sometimes in a way that's sensitive to surrounding characters). Furthermore, different sequences of scalar values sometimes correspond to the same character. The relationships among scalar, characters, and glyphs are subtle and complex.

Despite this complexity, most things that a literate human would call a "character" can be represented by a single Unicode scalar value (although several sequences of

Unicode scalar values may represent that same character). For example, Roman letters, Cyrillic letters, Hebrew consonants, and most Chinese characters fall into this category.

Unicode scalar values exclude the range #xD800 to #xDFFF, which are part of the range of Unicode *code points*. However, the Unicode code points in this range, the so-called *surrogates*, are an artifact of the UTF-16 encoding, and can only appear in specific Unicode encodings, and even then only in pairs that encode scalar values. Consequently, all characters represent code points, but the surrogate code points do not have representations as characters.

(char? *obj*)   procedure
    Returns #t if *obj* is a character, otherwise returns #f.

(char->integer *char*)   procedure
(integer->char *sv*)   procedure
Sv must be a Unicode scalar value, i.e., a non-negative exact integer object in $[0, \#xD7FF] \cup [\#xE000, \#x10FFFF]$.

    Given a character, char->integer returns its Unicode scalar value as an exact integer object. For a Unicode scalar value *sv*, integer->char returns its associated character.

    (integer->char 32) $\Longrightarrow$ #\space
    (char->integer (integer->char 5000))
                                                              $\Longrightarrow$ 5000
    (integer->char #\xD800) $\Longrightarrow$ &assertion *exception*

(char=? $char_1$ $char_2$ $char_3$ ...)   procedure
(char<? $char_1$ $char_2$ $char_3$ ...)   procedure
(char>? $char_1$ $char_2$ $char_3$ ...)   procedure
(char<=? $char_1$ $char_2$ $char_3$ ...)   procedure
(char>=? $char_1$ $char_2$ $char_3$ ...)   procedure
    These procedures impose a total ordering on the set of characters according to their Unicode scalar values.

    (char<? #\z #\ß) $\Longrightarrow$ #t
    (char<? #\z #\Z) $\Longrightarrow$ #f

11.12 Strings

Strings are sequences of characters.

    The *length* of a string is the number of characters that it contains. This number is fixed when the string is created. The *valid indices* of a string are the integers less than the length of the string. The first character of a string has index 0, the second has index 1, and so on.

(string? *obj*)   procedure

Returns #t if *obj* is a string, otherwise returns #f.

(make-string *k*)   procedure
(make-string *k char*)   procedure

Returns a newly allocated string of length *k*. If *char* is given, then all elements of
the string are initialized to *char*, otherwise the contents of the *string* are unspecified.

(string *char* ...)   procedure

Returns a newly allocated string composed of the arguments.

(string-length *string*)   procedure

Returns the number of characters in the given *string* as an exact integer object.

(string-ref *string k*)   procedure

K must be a valid index of *string*. The string-ref procedure returns character *k*
of *string* using zero-origin indexing.
Note: Implementors should make string-ref run in constant time.

(string=? *string$_1$ string$_2$ string$_3$* ...)   procedure

Returns #t if the strings are the same length and contain the same characters in
the same positions. Otherwise, the string=? procedure returns #f.

   (string=? "Straße" "Strasse") $\Longrightarrow$ #f

(string<? *string$_1$ string$_2$ string$_3$* ...)   procedure
(string>? *string$_1$ string$_2$ string$_3$* ...)   procedure
(string<=? *string$_1$ string$_2$ string$_3$* ...)   procedure
(string>=? *string$_1$ string$_2$ string$_3$* ...)   procedure

These procedures are the lexicographic extensions to strings of the corresponding
orderings on characters. For example, string<? is the lexicographic ordering on
strings induced by the ordering char<? on characters. If two strings differ in length
but are the same up to the length of the shorter string, the shorter string is considered
to be lexicographically less than the longer string.

   (string<? "z" "ß") $\Longrightarrow$ #t
   (string<? "z" "zz") $\Longrightarrow$ #t
   (string<? "z" "Z") $\Longrightarrow$ #f

(substring *string start end*)   procedure

String must be a string, and *start* and *end* must be exact integer objects satisfying

$$0 \leqslant start \leqslant end \leqslant (\text{string-length } string).$$

The substring procedure returns a newly allocated string formed from the characters of *string* beginning with index *start* (inclusive) and ending with index *end*
(exclusive).

(string-append *string* ...)   procedure
   Returns a newly allocated string whose characters form the concatenation of the
given strings.

(string->list *string*)   procedure
(list->string *list*)   procedure
List must be a list of characters. The string->list procedure returns a newly
allocated list of the characters that make up the given string. The list->string
procedure returns a newly allocated string formed from the characters in *list*. The
string->list and list->string procedures are inverses so far as equal? is
concerned.

(string-for-each *proc* *string*$_1$ *string*$_2$ ...)   procedure
   The *string*s must all have the same length. *Proc* should accept as many arguments
as there are *string*s. The string-for-each procedure applies *proc* element-wise to
the characters of the *string*s for its side effects, in order from the first characters to
the last. *Proc* is always called in the same dynamic environment as string-for-each
itself. The return values of string-for-each are unspecified.
   Analogous to for-each.
   Implementation responsibilities: The implementation must check the restrictions on
proc to the extent performed by applying it as described. An implementation may
check whether *proc* is an appropriate argument before applying it.

(string-copy *string*)   procedure
   Returns a newly allocated copy of the given *string*.

11.13 Vectors

Vectors are heterogeneous structures whose elements are indexed by integers. A
vector typically occupies less space than a list of the same length, and the average
time needed to access a randomly chosen element is typically less for the vector than
for the list.
   The *length* of a vector is the number of elements that it contains. This number is
a non-negative integer that is fixed when the vector is created. The *valid indices* of a
vector are the exact non-negative integer objects less than the length of the vector.
The first element in a vector is indexed by zero, and the last element is indexed by
one less than the length of the vector.
   Like list constants, vector constants must be quoted:

   '#(0 (2 2 2 2) "Anna") $\implies$ #(0 (2 2 2 2) "Anna")

(vector? *obj*)   procedure
   Returns #t if *obj* is a vector. Otherwise the procedure returns #f.

```
(make-vector k)                                          procedure
(make-vector k fill)                                     procedure
```
Returns a newly allocated vector of *k* elements. If a second argument is given, then each element is initialized to *fill*. Otherwise the initial contents of each element is unspecified.

```
(vector obj ...)                                          procedure
```
Returns a newly allocated vector whose elements contain the given arguments. Analogous to list.

```
(vector 'a 'b 'c)            ⟹  #(a b c)
```

```
(vector-length vector)                                    procedure
```
Returns the number of elements in *vector* as an exact integer object.

```
(vector-ref vector k)                                     procedure
```
K must be a valid index of *vector*. The vector-ref procedure returns the contents of element *k* of *vector*.

```
(vector-ref '#(1 1 2 3 5 8 13 21) 5)    ⟹  8
```

```
(vector-set! vector k obj)                                procedure
```
K must be a valid index of *vector*. The vector-set! procedure stores *obj* in element *k* of *vector*, and returns unspecified values.

Passing an immutable vector to vector-set! should cause an exception with condition type &assertion to be raised.

```
(let ((vec (vector 0 '(2 2 2 2) "Anna")))
  (vector-set! vec 1 '("Sue" "Sue"))
  vec)                          ⟹  #(0 ("Sue" "Sue") "Anna")

(vector-set! '#(0 1 2) 1 "doe")    ⟹  unspecified
            ; constant vector
            ; should raise &assertion exception
```

```
(vector->list vector)                                     procedure
(list->vector list)                                       procedure
```
The vector->list procedure returns a newly allocated list of the objects contained in the elements of *vector*. The list->vector procedure returns a newly created vector initialized to the elements of the list *list*.

```
(vector->list '#(dah dah didah))    ⟹  (dah dah didah)
(list->vector '(dididit dah))       ⟹  #(dididit dah)
```

(vector-fill! *vector fill*)   procedure
Stores *fill* in every element of *vector* and returns unspecified values.

(vector-map *proc vector₁ vector₂* ...)   procedure
The *vector*s must all have the same length. *Proc* should accept as many arguments
as there are *vector*s and return a single value.

The vector-map procedure applies *proc* element-wise to the elements of the
*vector*s and returns a vector of the results, in order. *Proc* is always called in the same
dynamic environment as vector-map itself. The order in which *proc* is applied to the
elements of the *vector*s is unspecified. If multiple returns occur from vector-map,
the return values returned by earlier returns are not mutated.

Analogous to map.

Implementation responsibilities: The implementation must check the restrictions on
proc to the extent performed by applying it as described. An implementation may
check whether *proc* is an appropriate argument before applying it.

(vector-for-each *proc vector₁ vector₂* ...)   procedure
The *vector*s must all have the same length. *Proc* should accept as many arguments
as there are *vector*s. The vector-for-each procedure applies *proc* element-wise to
the elements of the *vector*s for its side effects, in order from the first elements to the
last. *Proc* is always called in the same dynamic environment as vector-for-each
itself. The return values of vector-for-each are unspecified.

Analogous to for-each.

Implementation responsibilities: The implementation must check the restrictions on
proc to the extent performed by applying it as described. An implementation may
check whether *proc* is an appropriate argument before applying it.

11.14 Errors and violations

(error *who message irritant₁* ...)   procedure
(assertion-violation *who message irritant₁* ...)   procedure
Who must be a string or a symbol or #f. *Message* must be a string. The *irritant*s
are arbitrary objects.

These procedures raise an exception. The error procedure should be called
when an error has occurred, typically caused by something that has gone wrong
in the interaction of the program with the external world or the user. The
assertion-violation procedure should be called when an invalid call to a procedure was made, either passing an invalid number of arguments, or passing an
argument that it is not specified to handle.

The *who* argument should describe the procedure or operation that detected the
exception. The *message* argument should describe the exceptional situation. The
*irritant*s should be the arguments to the operation that detected the operation.

The condition object provided with the exception (see library chapter 7) has the
following condition types:

- If *who* is not #f, the condition has condition type &who, with *who* as the value of its field. In that case, *who* should be the name of the procedure or entity that detected the exception. If it is #f, the condition does not have condition type &who.
- The condition has condition type &message, with *message* as the value of its field.
- The condition has condition type &irritants, and its field has as its value a list of the *irritant*s.

Moreover, the condition created by error has condition type &error, and the condition created by assertion-violation has condition type &assertion.

```
(define (fac n)
  (if (not (integer-valued? n))
      (assertion-violation
        'fac "non-integral argument" n))
  (if (negative? n)
      (assertion-violation
        'fac "negative argument" n))
  (letrec
    ((loop (lambda (n r)
             (if (zero? n)
                 r
                 (loop (- n 1) (* r n)))))))
    (loop n 1)))

(fac 5)                                 ⟹ 120
(fac 4.5)                               ⟹ &assertion exception
(fac -3)                                ⟹ &assertion exception
```

(assert ⟨expression⟩)   syntax

An assert form is evaluated by evaluating ⟨expression⟩. If ⟨expression⟩ returns a true value, that value is returned from the assert expression. If ⟨expression⟩ returns #f, an exception with condition types &assertion and &message is raised. The message provided in the condition object is implementation-dependent.

Note: Implementations should exploit the fact that assert is syntax to provide as much information as possible about the location of the assertion failure.

11.15 Control features

This chapter describes various primitive procedures which control the flow of program execution in special ways.

(apply *proc arg₁ ... rest-args*)   procedure

Rest-args must be a list. *Proc* should accept n arguments, where n is number of

*arg*s plus the length of *rest-args*. The apply procedure calls *proc* with the elements
of the list (append (list *arg*₁ ...) *rest-args*) as the actual arguments.

If a call to apply occurs in a tail context, the call to *proc* is also in a tail context.

```
(apply + (list 3 4))                    ⟹   7


(define compose
   (lambda (f g)
      (lambda args
         (f (apply g args)))))

((compose sqrt *) 12 75)                ⟹   30
```

(call-with-current-continuation *proc*)   procedure
(call/cc *proc*)   procedure

Proc should accept one argument. The procedure call-with-current-continuation (which is the same as the procedure call/cc) packages the current continuation
as an "escape procedure" and passes it as an argument to *proc*. The escape procedure
is a Scheme procedure that, if it is later called, will abandon whatever continuation
is in effect at that later time and will instead reinstate the continuation that was
in effect when the escape procedure was created. Calling the escape procedure may
cause the invocation of *before* and *after* procedures installed using dynamic-wind.

The escape procedure accepts the same number of arguments as the continuation
of the original call to call-with-current-continuation.

The escape procedure that is passed to *proc* has unlimited extent just like any
other procedure in Scheme. It may be stored in variables or data structures and may
be called as many times as desired.

If a call to call-with-current-continuation occurs in a tail context, the call
to *proc* is also in a tail context.

The following examples show only some ways in which call-with-current-
continuation is used. If all real uses were as simple as these examples, there would
be no need for a procedure with the power of call-with-current-continuation.

```
(call-with-current-continuation
   (lambda (exit)
      (for-each (lambda (x)
                   (if (negative? x)
                       (exit x)))
                '(54 0 37 -3 245 19))
      #t))                              ⟹   -3

(define list-length
   (lambda (obj)
      (call-with-current-continuation
         (lambda (return)
```

```
           (letrec ((r
                      (lambda (obj)
                        (cond ((null? obj) 0)
                              ((pair? obj)
                               (+ (r (cdr obj)) 1))
                              (else (return #f))))))
                 (r obj))))))

(list-length '(1 2 3 4))                    ⟹  4

(list-length '(a b . c))                    ⟹  #f
(call-with-current-continuation procedure?)  ⟹  #t
```

Note: Calling an escape procedure reenters the dynamic extent of the call to call-with-current-continuation, and thus restores its dynamic environment; see section 5.12.

(values *obj* ...)   procedure
   Delivers all of its arguments to its continuation. The values procedure might be defined as follows:

```
    (define (values . things)
      (call-with-current-continuation
        (lambda (cont) (apply cont things))))
```

The continuations of all non-final expressions within a sequence of expressions, such as in lambda, begin, let, let*, letrec, letrec*, let-values, let*-values, case, and cond forms, usually take an arbitrary number of values.
   Except for these and the continuations created by call-with-values, let-values, and let*-values, continuations implicitly accepting a single value, such as the continuations of ⟨operator⟩ and ⟨operand⟩s of procedure calls or the ⟨test⟩ expressions in conditionals, take exactly one value. The effect of passing an inappropriate number of values to such a continuation is undefined.

(call-with-values *producer consumer*)   procedure
Producer must be a procedure and should accept zero arguments. *Consumer* must be a procedure and should accept as many values as *producer* returns. The call-with-values procedure calls *producer* with no arguments and a continuation that, when passed some values, calls the *consumer* procedure with those values as arguments. The continuation for the call to *consumer* is the continuation of the call to call-with-values.

```
    (call-with-values (lambda () (values 4 5))
                      (lambda (a b) b)) ⟹  5

(call-with-values * -)                      ⟹  -1
```

If a call to `call-with-values` occurs in a tail context, the call to *consumer* is also in a tail context.

Implementation responsibilities: After *producer* returns, the implementation must check that *consumer* accepts as many values as *consumer* has returned.

(`dynamic-wind` *before thunk after*)   procedure
Before, *thunk*, and *after* must be procedures, and each should accept zero arguments. These procedures may return any number of values. The `dynamic-wind` procedure calls *thunk* without arguments, returning the results of this call. Moreover, `dynamic-wind` calls *before* without arguments whenever the dynamic extent of the call to *thunk* is entered, and *after* without arguments whenever the dynamic extent of the call to *thunk* is exited. Thus, in the absence of calls to escape procedures created by `call-with-current-continuation`, `dynamic-wind` calls *before*, *thunk*, and *after*, in that order.

While the calls to *before* and *after* are not considered to be within the dynamic extent of the call to *thunk*, calls to the *before* and *after* procedures of any other calls to `dynamic-wind` that occur within the dynamic extent of the call to *thunk* are considered to be within the dynamic extent of the call to *thunk*.

More precisely, an escape procedure transfers control out of the dynamic extent of a set of zero or more active `dynamic-wind` calls x ... and transfer control into the dynamic extent of a set of zero or more active `dynamic-wind` calls y .... It leaves the dynamic extent of the most recent x and calls without arguments the corresponding *after* procedure. If the *after* procedure returns, the escape procedure proceeds to the next most recent x, and so on. Once each x has been handled in this manner, the escape procedure calls without arguments the *before* procedure corresponding to the least recent y. If the *before* procedure returns, the escape procedure reenters the dynamic extent of the least recent y and proceeds with the next least recent y, and so on. Once each y has been handled in this manner, control is transferred to the continuation packaged in the escape procedure.

Implementation responsibilities: The implementation must check the restrictions on *thunk* and *after* only if they are actually called.

```
(let ((path '())
      (c #f))
  (let ((add (lambda (s)
              (set! path (cons s path)))))
    (dynamic-wind
      (lambda () (add 'connect))
      (lambda ()
        (add (call-with-current-continuation
              (lambda (c0)
                (set! c c0)
                'talk1))))
      (lambda () (add 'disconnect)))
    (if (< (length path) 4)
```

```
      (c 'talk2)
      (reverse path))))
    ⟹ (connect talk1 disconnect connect talk2 disconnect)


  (let ((n 0))
    (call-with-current-continuation
      (lambda (k)
        (dynamic-wind
          (lambda ()
            (set! n (+ n 1))
            (k))
          (lambda ()
            (set! n (+ n 2)))
          (lambda ()
            (set! n (+ n 4)))))))
    n)                                          ⟹ 1


  (let ((n 0))
    (call-with-current-continuation
      (lambda (k)
        (dynamic-wind
          values
          (lambda ()
            (dynamic-wind
              values
              (lambda ()
                (set! n (+ n 1))
                (k))
              (lambda ()
                (set! n (+ n 2))
                (k))))
          (lambda ()
            (set! n (+ n 4)))))))
    n)                                          ⟹ 7
```

Note: Entering a dynamic extent restores its dynamic environment; see section 5.12.

11.16 Iteration

(let ⟨variable⟩ ⟨bindings⟩ ⟨body⟩)   syntax

"Named let" is a variant on the syntax of let that provides a general looping construct and may also be used to express recursion. It has the same syntax and semantics as ordinary let except that ⟨variable⟩ is bound within ⟨body⟩ to a procedure whose parameters are the bound variables and whose body is ⟨body⟩.

Thus the execution of ⟨body⟩ may be repeated by invoking the procedure named by ⟨variable⟩.

```
(let loop ((numbers '(3 -2 1 6 -5))
           (nonneg '())
           (neg '()))
  (cond ((null? numbers) (list nonneg neg))
        ((>= (car numbers) 0)
         (loop (cdr numbers)
               (cons (car numbers) nonneg)
               neg))
        ((< (car numbers) 0)
         (loop (cdr numbers)
               nonneg
               (cons (car numbers) neg)))))
      ⟹    ((6 1 3) (-5 -2))
```

11.17 *Quasiquotation*

(quasiquote ⟨qq template⟩)   syntax
unquote   auxiliary syntax
unquote-splicing   auxiliary syntax

"Backquote" or "quasiquote" expressions are useful for constructing a list or vector structure when some but not all of the desired structure is known in advance.

Syntax: ⟨Qq template⟩ should be as specified by the grammar at the end of this entry.

Semantics: If no unquote or unquote-splicing forms appear within subform ⟨qq template⟩, the result of evaluating (quasiquote ⟨qq template⟩) is equivalent to the result of evaluating (quote ⟨qq template⟩).

If an (unquote ⟨expression⟩ ...) form appears inside a ⟨qq template⟩, however, the ⟨expression⟩s are evaluated ("unquoted") and their results are inserted into the structure instead of the unquote form.

If an (unquote-splicing ⟨expression⟩ ...) form appears inside a ⟨qq template⟩, then the ⟨expression⟩s must evaluate to lists; the opening and closing parentheses of the lists are then "stripped away" and the elements of the lists are inserted in place of the unquote-splicing form.

Any unquote-splicing or multi-operand unquote form must appear only within a list or vector ⟨qq template⟩.

As noted in section 4.3.5, (quasiquote ⟨qq template⟩) may be abbreviated `⟨qq template⟩, (unquote ⟨expression⟩) may be abbreviated ,⟨expression⟩, and (unquote-splicing ⟨expression⟩) may be abbreviated ,@⟨expression⟩.

```
`(list ,(+ 1 2) 4)                         ⟹    (list 3 4)
(let ((name 'a)) `(list ,name ',name))
        ⟹    (list a (quote a))
```

```
`(a ,(+ 1 2) ,@(map abs '(4 -5 6)) b)
        ⟹  (a 3 4 5 6 b)
`(( foo ,(- 10 3)) ,@(cdr '(c)) . ,(car '(cons)))
        ⟹  ((foo 7) . cons)
`#(10 5 ,(- 4) ,@(map - '(16 9)) 8)
        ⟹  #(10 5 -4 -16 -9 8)
(let ((name 'foo))
  `((unquote name name name)))    ⟹  (foo foo foo)
(let ((name '(foo)))
  `((unquote-splicing name name name)))
        ⟹  (foo foo foo)
(let ((q '((append x y) (sqrt 9))))
  ``(foo ,,@q))                           ⟹  `(foo
                (unquote (append x y) (sqrt 9)))
(let ((x '(2 3))
      (y '(4 5)))
  `(foo (unquote (append x y) (- 9))))
        ⟹  (foo (2 3 4 5) -9)
```

Quasiquote forms may be nested. Substitutions are made only for unquoted components appearing at the same nesting level as the outermost quasiquote. The nesting level increases by one inside each successive quasiquotation, and decreases by one inside each unquotation.

```
`(a `(b ,(+ 1 2) ,(foo ,(+ 1 3) d) e) f)
        ⟹  (a `(b ,(+ 1 2) ,(foo 4 d) e) f)
(let ((name1 'x)
      (name2 'y))
  `(a `(b ,,name1 ,',name2 d) e)) ⟹  (a `(b ,x ,'y d) e)
```

A quasiquote expression may return either fresh, mutable objects or literal structure for any structure that is constructed at run time during the evaluation of the expression. Portions that do not need to be rebuilt are always literal. Thus,

```
(let ((a 3)) `((1 2) ,a ,4 ,'five 6))
```

may be equivalent to either of the following expressions:

```
'((1 2) 3 4 five 6)
(let ((a 3))
  (cons '(1 2)
        (cons a (cons 4 (cons 'five '(6))))))
```

However, it is not equivalent to this expression:

```
(let ((a 3)) (list (list 1 2) a 4 'five 6))
```

It is a syntax violation if any of the identifiers quasiquote, unquote, or unquote-splicing appear in positions within a ⟨qq template⟩ otherwise than as described above.

The following grammar for quasiquote expressions is not context-free. It is presented as a recipe for generating an infinite number of production rules. Imagine a copy of the following rules for $D = 1, 2, 3, \ldots$. D keeps track of the nesting depth.

⟨qq template⟩ $\longrightarrow$ ⟨qq template 1⟩
⟨qq template 0⟩ $\longrightarrow$ ⟨expression⟩
⟨quasiquotation D⟩ $\longrightarrow$ (quasiquote ⟨qq template D⟩)
⟨qq template D⟩ $\longrightarrow$ ⟨lexeme datum⟩
  | ⟨list qq template D⟩
  | ⟨vector qq template D⟩
  | ⟨unquotation D⟩
⟨list qq template D⟩ $\longrightarrow$ (⟨qq template or splice D⟩*)
  | (⟨qq template or splice D⟩$^{+}$. ⟨qq template D⟩)
  | ⟨quasiquotation $D + 1$⟩
⟨vector qq template D⟩ $\longrightarrow$ #(⟨qq template or splice D⟩*)
⟨unquotation D⟩ $\longrightarrow$ (unquote ⟨qq template $D - 1$⟩)
⟨qq template or splice D⟩ $\longrightarrow$ ⟨qq template D⟩
  | ⟨splicing unquotation D⟩
⟨splicing unquotation D⟩ $\longrightarrow$
   (unquote-splicing ⟨qq template $D - 1$⟩*)
  | (unquote ⟨qq template $D - 1$⟩*)

In ⟨quasiquotation⟩s, a ⟨list qq template D⟩ can sometimes be confused with either an ⟨unquotation D⟩ or a ⟨splicing unquotation D⟩. The interpretation as an ⟨unquotation⟩ or ⟨splicing unquotation D⟩ takes precedence.

11.18 Binding constructs for syntactic keywords

The let-syntax and letrec-syntax forms bind keywords. Like a begin form, a let-syntax or letrec-syntax form may appear in a definition context, in which case it is treated as a definition, and the forms in the body must also be definitions. A let-syntax or letrec-syntax form may also appear in an expression context, in which case the forms within their bodies must be expressions.

(let-syntax ⟨bindings⟩ ⟨form⟩ ...)   syntax
 Syntax: ⟨Bindings⟩ must have the form

  (((⟨keyword⟩ ⟨expression⟩)) ...)

Each ⟨keyword⟩ is an identifier, and each ⟨expression⟩ is an expression that evaluates, at macro-expansion time, to a *transformer*. Transformers may be created by syntax-rules or identifier-syntax (see section 11.19) or by one of the other mechanisms described in library chapter 12. It is a syntax violation for ⟨keyword⟩ to appear more than once in the list of keywords being bound.

 Semantics: The ⟨form⟩s are expanded in the syntactic environment obtained by extending the syntactic environment of the let-syntax form with macros whose keywords are the ⟨keyword⟩s, bound to the specified transformers. Each binding of a ⟨keyword⟩ has the ⟨form⟩s as its region.

The ⟨form⟩s of a `let-syntax` form are treated, whether in definition or expression context, as if wrapped in an implicit `begin`; see section 11.4.7. Thus definitions in the result of expanding the ⟨form⟩s have the same region as any definition appearing in place of the `let-syntax` form would have.

Implementation responsibilities: The implementation should detect if the value of ⟨expression⟩ cannot possibly be a transformer.

```
(let-syntax ((when (syntax-rules ()
                     ((when test stmt1 stmt2 ...)
                      (if test
                          (begin stmt1
                                 stmt2 ...))))))
  (let ((if #t))
    (when if (set! if 'now))
    if))                                  ⟹   now


(let ((x 'outer))
  (let-syntax ((m (syntax-rules () ((m) x))))
    (let ((x 'inner))
      (m))))                              ⟹   outer
(let ()
  (let-syntax
    ((def (syntax-rules ()
            ((def stuff ...) (define stuff ...)))))
    (def foo 42))
  foo)                                    ⟹  42


(let ()
  (let-syntax ())
  5)                                      ⟹  5
```

`(letrec-syntax ⟨bindings⟩ ⟨form⟩ ...)`   syntax

Syntax: Same as for `let-syntax`.

Semantics: The ⟨form⟩s are expanded in the syntactic environment obtained by extending the syntactic environment of the `letrec-syntax` form with macros whose keywords are the ⟨keyword⟩s, bound to the specified transformers. Each binding of a ⟨keyword⟩ has the ⟨bindings⟩ as well as the ⟨form⟩s within its region, so the transformers can transcribe forms into uses of the macros introduced by the `letrec-syntax` form.

The ⟨form⟩s of a `letrec-syntax` form are treated, whether in definition or expression context, as if wrapped in an implicit `begin`; see section 11.4.7. Thus definitions in the result of expanding the ⟨form⟩s have the same region as any definition appearing in place of the `letrec-syntax` form would have.

Implementation responsibilities: The implementation should detect if the value of ⟨expression⟩ cannot possibly be a transformer.

```
(letrec-syntax
   ((my-or (syntax-rules ()
              ((my-or) #f)
              ((my-or e) e)
              ((my-or e1 e2 ...)
               (let ((temp e1))
                 (if temp
                     temp
                     (my-or e2 ...)))))))
   (let ((x #f)
         (y 7)
         (temp 8)
         (let odd?)
         (if even?))
     (my-or x
            (let temp)
            (if y)
            y)))                              ⟹  7
```

The following example highlights how `let-syntax` and `letrec-syntax` differ.

```
(let ((f (lambda (x) (+ x 1))))
   (let-syntax ((f (syntax-rules ()
                      ((f x) x)))
                (g (syntax-rules ()
                      ((g x) (f x)))))
      (list (f 1) (g 1))))          ⟹ (1 2)

(let ((f (lambda (x) (+ x 1))))
   (letrec-syntax ((f (syntax-rules ()
                         ((f x) x)))
                   (g (syntax-rules ()
                         ((g x) (f x)))))
      (list (f 1) (g 1))))          ⟹ (1 1)
```

The two expressions are identical except that the `let-syntax` form in the first expression is a `letrec-syntax` form in the second. In the first expression, the f occurring in g refers to the `let`-bound variable f, whereas in the second it refers to the keyword f whose binding is established by the `letrec-syntax` form.

11.19 Macro transformers

```
(syntax-rules (⟨literal⟩ ...) ⟨syntax rule⟩ ...)              syntax (expand)
_                                                  auxiliary syntax (expand)
...                                                auxiliary syntax (expand)
```
    Syntax: Each ⟨literal⟩ must be an identifier. Each ⟨syntax rule⟩ must have the following form:

    (⟨srpattern⟩ ⟨template⟩)

    An ⟨srpattern⟩ is a restricted form of ⟨pattern⟩, namely, a nonempty ⟨pattern⟩ in one of four parenthesized forms below whose first subform is an identifier or an underscore _. A ⟨pattern⟩ is an identifier, constant, or one of the following.

```
(⟨pattern⟩ ...)
(⟨pattern⟩ ⟨pattern⟩ ... . ⟨pattern⟩)
(⟨pattern⟩ ... ⟨pattern⟩ ⟨ellipsis⟩ ⟨pattern⟩ ...)
(⟨pattern⟩ ... ⟨pattern⟩ ⟨ellipsis⟩ ⟨pattern⟩ ... . ⟨pattern⟩)
#(⟨pattern⟩ ...)
#(⟨pattern⟩ ... ⟨pattern⟩ ⟨ellipsis⟩ ⟨pattern⟩ ...)
```

    An ⟨ellipsis⟩ is the identifier "..." (three periods).
    A ⟨template⟩ is a pattern variable, an identifier that is not a pattern variable, a pattern datum, or one of the following.

```
(⟨subtemplate⟩ ...)
(⟨subtemplate⟩ ... . ⟨template⟩)
#(⟨subtemplate⟩ ...)
```

    A ⟨subtemplate⟩ is a ⟨template⟩ followed by zero or more ellipses.
    Semantics: An instance of `syntax-rules` evaluates, at macro-expansion time, to a new macro transformer by specifying a sequence of hygienic rewrite rules. A use of a macro whose keyword is associated with a transformer specified by `syntax-rules` is matched against the patterns contained in the ⟨syntax rule⟩s, beginning with the leftmost ⟨syntax rule⟩. When a match is found, the macro use is transcribed hygienically according to the template. It is a syntax violation when no match is found.
    An identifier appearing within a ⟨pattern⟩ may be an underscore (_), a literal identifier listed in the list of literals (⟨literal⟩ ...), or an ellipsis (...). All other identifiers appearing within a ⟨pattern⟩ are *pattern variables*. It is a syntax violation if an ellipsis or underscore appears in (⟨literal⟩ ...).
    While the first subform of ⟨srpattern⟩ may be an identifier, the identifier is not involved in the matching and is not considered a pattern variable or literal identifier.
    Pattern variables match arbitrary input subforms and are used to refer to elements of the input. It is a syntax violation if the same pattern variable appears more than once in a ⟨pattern⟩.

Underscores also match arbitrary input subforms but are not pattern variables and so cannot be used to refer to those elements. Multiple underscores may appear in a ⟨pattern⟩.

A literal identifier matches an input subform if and only if the input subform is an identifier and either both its occurrence in the input expression and its occurrence in the list of literals have the same lexical binding, or the two identifiers have the same name and both have no lexical binding.

A subpattern followed by an ellipsis can match zero or more elements of the input.

More formally, an input form F matches a pattern P if and only if one of the following holds:

- P is an underscore (_).
- P is a pattern variable.
- P is a literal identifier and F is an identifier such that both P and F would refer to the same binding if both were to appear in the output of the macro outside of any bindings inserted into the output of the macro. (If neither of two like-named identifiers refers to any binding, i.e., both are undefined, they are considered to refer to the same binding.)
- P is of the form $(P_1 \ldots P_n)$ and F is a list of n elements that match P_1 through P_n.
- P is of the form $(P_1 \ldots P_n . P_x)$ and F is a list or improper list of n or more elements whose first n elements match P_1 through P_n and whose nth cdr matches P_x.
- P is of the form $(P_1 \ldots P_k \ P_e \ \langle ellipsis \rangle \ P_{m+1} \ldots P_n)$, where ⟨ellipsis⟩ is the identifier $\ldots$ and F is a list of n elements whose first k elements match P_1 through P_k, whose next $m - k$ elements each match P_e, and whose remaining $n - m$ elements match P_{m+1} through P_n.
- P is of the form $(P_1 \ldots P_k \ P_e \ \langle ellipsis \rangle \ P_{m+1} \ldots P_n . P_x)$, where ⟨ellipsis⟩ is the identifier $\ldots$ and F is a list or improper list of n elements whose first k elements match P_1 through P_k, whose next $m - k$ elements each match P_e, whose next $n - m$ elements match P_{m+1} through P_n, and whose nth and final cdr matches P_x.
- P is of the form $\#(P_1 \ldots P_n)$ and F is a vector of n elements that match P_1 through P_n.
- P is of the form $\#(P_1 \ldots P_k \ P_e \ \langle ellipsis \rangle \ P_{m+1} \ldots P_n)$, where ⟨ellipsis⟩ is the identifier $\ldots$ and F is a vector of n or more elements whose first k elements match P_1 through P_k, whose next $m - k$ elements each match P_e, and whose remaining $n - m$ elements match P_{m+1} through P_n.
- P is a pattern datum (any nonlist, nonvector, nonsymbol datum) and F is equal to P in the sense of the equal? procedure.

When a macro use is transcribed according to the template of the matching ⟨syntax rule⟩, pattern variables that occur in the template are replaced by the subforms they match in the input.

Pattern data and identifiers that are not pattern variables or ellipses are copied into the output. A subtemplate followed by an ellipsis expands into zero or more occurrences of the subtemplate. Pattern variables that occur in subpatterns followed by one or more ellipses may occur only in subtemplates that are followed by (at least) as many ellipses. These pattern variables are replaced in the output by the input subforms to which they are bound, distributed as specified. If a pattern variable is followed by more ellipses in the subtemplate than in the associated subpattern, the input form is replicated as necessary. The subtemplate must contain at least one pattern variable from a subpattern followed by an ellipsis, and for at least one such pattern variable, the subtemplate must be followed by exactly as many ellipses as the subpattern in which the pattern variable appears. (Otherwise, the expander would not be able to determine how many times the subform should be repeated in the output.) It is a syntax violation if the constraints of this paragraph are not met.

A template of the form (⟨ellipsis⟩ ⟨template⟩) is identical to ⟨template⟩, except that ellipses within the template have no special meaning. That is, any ellipses contained within ⟨template⟩ are treated as ordinary identifiers. In particular, the template (... ...) produces a single ellipsis, ... This allows syntactic abstractions to expand into forms containing ellipses.

```
(define-syntax be-like-begin
  (syntax-rules ()
    ((be-like-begin name)
     (define-syntax name
       (syntax-rules ()
         ((name expr (... ...))
          (begin expr (... ...))))))))


(be-like-begin sequence)
(sequence 1 2 3 4)                      ⟹ 4
```

As an example for hygienic use of auxiliary identifier, if let and cond are defined as in section 11.4.6 and appendix B then they are hygienic (as required) and the following is not an error.

```
(let ((=> #f))
  (cond (#t => 'ok)))                    ⟹ ok
```

The macro transformer for cond recognizes => as a local variable, and hence an expression, and not as the identifier =>, which the macro transformer treats as a syntactic keyword. Thus the example expands into

```
(let ((=> #f))
  (if #t (begin => 'ok)))
```

instead of

```
(let ((=> #f))
  (let ((temp #t))
    (if temp ('ok temp))))
```

which would result in an assertion violation.

```
(identifier-syntax ⟨template⟩)                              syntax (expand)
(identifier-syntax                                          syntax (expand)
  (⟨id₁⟩ ⟨template₁⟩)
  ((set! ⟨id₂⟩ ⟨pattern⟩)
   ⟨template₂⟩))
set!                                            auxiliary syntax (expand)
```

Syntax: The ⟨id⟩s must be identifiers. The ⟨template⟩s must be as for `syntax-rules`.

Semantics: When a keyword is bound to a transformer produced by the first form of `identifier-syntax`, references to the keyword within the scope of the binding are replaced by ⟨template⟩.

```
(define p (cons 4 5))
(define-syntax p.car (identifier-syntax (car p)))
p.car                             ⟹ 4
(set! p.car 15)                   ⟹ &syntax exception
```

The second, more general, form of `identifier-syntax` permits the transformer to determine what happens when `set!` is used. In this case, uses of the identifier by itself are replaced by ⟨template₁⟩, and uses of `set!` with the identifier are replaced by ⟨template₂⟩.

```
(define p (cons 4 5))
(define-syntax p.car
  (identifier-syntax
    (_ (car p))
    ((set! _ e) (set-car! p e))))
(set! p.car 15)
p.car                                    ⟹ 15
p                                        ⟹ (15 . 5)
```

11.20 Tail calls and tail contexts

A *tail call* is a procedure call that occurs in a *tail context*. Tail contexts are defined inductively. Note that a tail context is always determined with respect to a particular lambda expression.

- The last expression within the body of a lambda expression, shown as ⟨tail expression⟩ below, occurs in a tail context.

```
(lambda ⟨formals⟩
  ⟨definition⟩*
  ⟨expression⟩* ⟨tail expression⟩)
```

- If one of the following expressions is in a tail context, then the subexpressions shown as ⟨tail expression⟩ are in a tail context. These were derived from specifications of the syntax of the forms described in this chapter by replacing some occurrences of ⟨expression⟩ with ⟨tail expression⟩. Only those rules that contain tail contexts are shown here.

```
(if ⟨expression⟩ ⟨tail expression⟩ ⟨tail expression⟩)
(if ⟨expression⟩ ⟨tail expression⟩)

(cond ⟨cond clause⟩+)
(cond ⟨cond clause⟩* (else ⟨tail sequence⟩))

(case ⟨expression⟩
  ⟨case clause⟩+)
(case ⟨expression⟩
  ⟨case clause⟩*
  (else ⟨tail sequence⟩))

(and ⟨expression⟩* ⟨tail expression⟩)
(or ⟨expression⟩* ⟨tail expression⟩)

(let ⟨bindings⟩ ⟨tail body⟩)
(let ⟨variable⟩ ⟨bindings⟩ ⟨tail body⟩)
(let* ⟨bindings⟩ ⟨tail body⟩)
(letrec* ⟨bindings⟩ ⟨tail body⟩)
(letrec ⟨bindings⟩ ⟨tail body⟩)
(let-values ⟨mv-bindings⟩ ⟨tail body⟩)
(let*-values ⟨mv-bindings⟩ ⟨tail body⟩)

(let-syntax ⟨bindings⟩ ⟨tail body⟩)
(letrec-syntax ⟨bindings⟩ ⟨tail body⟩)

(begin ⟨tail sequence⟩)
```

A ⟨cond clause⟩ is

  (⟨test⟩ ⟨tail sequence⟩),

a ⟨case clause⟩ is

  ((⟨datum⟩*) ⟨tail sequence⟩),

a ⟨tail body⟩ is

  ⟨definition⟩* ⟨tail sequence⟩,

and a ⟨tail sequence⟩ is

  ⟨expression⟩* ⟨tail expression⟩.

- If a cond expression is in a tail context, and has a clause of the form ($\langle$expression$_1\rangle$ => $\langle$expression$_2\rangle$) then the (implied) call to the procedure that results from the evaluation of $\langle$expression$_2\rangle$ is in a tail context. $\langle$Expression$_2\rangle$ itself is not in a tail context.

Certain built-in procedures must also perform tail calls. The first argument passed to apply and to call-with-current-continuation, and the second argument passed to call-with-values, must be called via a tail call.

In the following example the only tail call is the call to f. None of the calls to g or h are tail calls. The reference to x is in a tail context, but it is not a call and thus is not a tail call.

```
(lambda ()
  (if (g)
      (let ((x (h)))
        x)
      (and (g) (f))))
```

Note: Implementations may recognize that some non-tail calls, such as the call to h above, can be evaluated as though they were tail calls. In the example above, the let expression could be compiled as a tail call to h. (The possibility of h returning an unexpected number of values can be ignored, because in that case the effect of the let is explicitly unspecified and implementation-dependent.)

APPENDICES

A Formal semantics

This appendix presents a non-normative, formal, operational semantics for Scheme, that is based on an earlier semantics (Matthews & Findler, 2007). It does not cover the entire language. The notable missing features are the macro system, I/O, and the numerical tower. The precise list of features included is given in section A.2.

The core of the specification is a single-step term rewriting relation that indicates how an (abstract) machine behaves. In general, the report is not a complete specification, giving implementations freedom to behave differently, typically to allow optimizations. This underspecification shows up in two ways in the semantics.

The first is reduction rules that reduce to special "**unknown:** *string*" states (where the string provides a description of the unknown state). The intention is that rules that reduce to such states can be replaced with arbitrary reduction rules. The precise specification of how to replace those rules is given in section A.12.

The other is that the single-step relation relates one program to multiple different programs, each corresponding to a legal transition that an abstract machine might take. Accordingly we use the transitive closure of the single step relation $\rightarrow^*$ to define the semantics, $\mathcal{S}$, as a function from programs ($\mathcal{P}$) to sets of observable results ($\mathcal{R}$):

$$\mathcal{S} : \mathcal{P} \longrightarrow 2^{\mathcal{R}}$$
$$\mathcal{S}(\mathcal{P}) = \{\mathcal{O}(\mathcal{A}) \mid \mathcal{P} \rightarrow^* \mathcal{A}\}$$

where the function $\mathcal{O}$ turns an answer ($\mathcal{A}$) from the semantics into an observable result. Roughly, $\mathcal{O}$ is the identity function on simple base values, and returns a special tag for more complex values, like procedure and pairs.

So, an implementation conforms to the semantics if, for every program $\mathcal{P}$, the implementation produces one of the results in $\mathcal{S}(\mathcal{P})$ or, if the implementation loops forever, then there is an infinite reduction sequence starting at $\mathcal{P}$, assuming that the reduction relation $\rightarrow$ has been adjusted to replace the **unknown:** states.

The precise definitions of $\mathcal{P}$, $\mathcal{A}$, $\mathcal{R}$, and $\mathcal{O}$ are also given in section A.2.

To help understand the semantics and how it behaves, we have implemented it in PLT Redex. The implementation is available at the report's website: `http://www.r6rs.org/`. All of the reduction rules and the metafunctions shown in the figures in this semantics were generated automatically from the source code.

A.1 Background

We assume the reader has a basic familiarity with context-sensitive reduction semantics. Readers unfamiliar with this system may wish to consult Felleisen and Flatt's monograph (Felleisen & Flatt, 2003) or Wright and Felleisen (Wright & Felleisen, 1994) for a thorough introduction, including the relevant technical background, or an introduction to PLT Redex (Matthews *et al.*, 2004) for a somewhat lighter one.

As a rough guide, we define the operational semantics of a language via a relation on program terms, where the relation corresponds to a single step of an abstract machine. The relation is defined using evaluation contexts, namely terms with a distinguished place in them, called *holes*, where the next step of evaluation occurs. We say that a term e decomposes into an evaluation context E and another term e' if e is the same as E but with the hole replaced by e'. We write $E[e']$ to indicate the term obtained by replacing the hole in E with e'.

For example, assuming that we have defined a grammar containing non-terminals for evaluation contexts (E), expressions (e), variables (x), and values (v), we would write:

$$E_1[((\texttt{lambda } (x_1 \cdots) \ e_1) \ v_1 \ \cdots)] \rightarrow$$
$$E_1[\{x_1 \cdots \mapsto v_1 \cdots\}e_1] \qquad (\#x_1 = \#v_1)$$

to define the β_v rewriting rule (as a part of the $\rightarrow$ single step relation). We use the names of the non-terminals (possibly with subscripts) in a rewriting rule to restrict the application of the rule, so it applies only when some term produced by that grammar appears in the corresponding position in the term. If the same non-terminal with an identical subscript appears multiple times, the rule only applies when the corresponding terms are structurally identical (nonterminals without subscripts are not constrained to match each other). Thus, the occurrence of E_1 on both the left-hand and right-hand side of the rule above means that the context of the application expression does not change when using this rule. The ellipses are a form of Kleene star, meaning that zero or more occurrences of terms matching the pattern proceeding the ellipsis may appear in place of the the ellipsis and the pattern preceding it. We use the notation $\{x_1 \cdots \mapsto v_1 \cdots\}e_1$ for capture-avoiding substitution; in this case it means that each x_1 is replaced with the corresponding v_1 in e_1. Finally, we write side-conditions in parentheses beside a rule; the side-condition in the above rule indicates that the number of x_1s must be the same as the number of v_1s. Sometimes we use equality in the side-conditions; when we do it merely means simple term equality, i.e., the two terms must have the same syntactic shape.

Making the evaluation context E explicit in the rule allows us to define relations that manipulate their context. As a simple example, we can add another rule that signals a violation when a procedure is applied to the wrong number of arguments by discarding the evaluation context on the right-hand side of a rule:

$$E[((\texttt{lambda } (x_1 \cdots) \ e) \ v_1 \ \cdots)] \rightarrow$$
violation: wrong argument count $\qquad (\#x_1 \neq \#v_1)$

Later we take advantage of the explicit evaluation context in more sophisticated ways.

A.2 Grammar

Figure A.2a shows the grammar for the subset of the report this semantics models. Non-terminals are written in *italics* or in a calligraphic font ($\mathscr{P}$ $\mathscr{A}$, $\mathscr{R}$, and $\mathscr{R}_v$) and literals are written in a monospaced font.

$\mathcal{P}$	::=	(store (sf $\cdots$) es) | **uncaught exception:** v | **unknown:** *description*
$\mathcal{A}$	::=	(store (sf $\cdots$) (values v $\cdots$)) | **uncaught exception:** v
	|	**unknown:** *description*
$\mathcal{R}$	::=	(values $\mathcal{R}_v$ $\cdots$) | exception | unknown
$\mathcal{R}_v$	::=	pair | null | 'sym | sqv | condition
	|	procedure
sf	::=	(x v) | (x bh) | (pp (cons v v))
es	::=	'seq | 'sqv | '() | (begin es es $\cdots$)
	|	(begin0 es es $\cdots$) | (es es $\cdots$) | (if es es es) | (set! x es)
	|	x | $nonproc$ | $pproc$ | (lambda f es es $\cdots$)
	|	(letrec ((x es) $\cdots$) es es $\cdots$) | (letrec* ((x es) $\cdots$) es es $\cdots$)
	|	(dw x es es es) | (throw x es) | unspecified
	|	(handlers es $\cdots$ es) | (l! x es) | (reinit x)
f	::=	(x $\cdots$) | (x x $\cdots$ dot x) | x
s	::=	seq | () | sqv | sym
seq	::=	(s s $\cdots$) | (s s $\cdots$ dot sqv) | (s s $\cdots$ dot sym)
sqv	::=	n | #t | #f
p	::=	(store (sf $\cdots$) e)
e	::=	(begin e e $\cdots$) | (begin0 e e $\cdots$) | (e e $\cdots$) | (if e e e)
	|	(set! x e) | (handlers e $\cdots$ e) | x | $nonproc$ | $proc$
	|	(dw x e e e) | unspecified | (letrec ((x e) $\cdots$) e e $\cdots$)
	|	(letrec* ((x e) $\cdots$) e e $\cdots$) | (l! x es) | (reinit x)
v	::=	$nonproc$ | $proc$
$nonproc$	::=	pp | null | 'sym | sqv | (make-cond $string$)
$proc$	::=	(lambda f e e $\cdots$) | $pproc$ | (throw x e)
$pproc$	::=	$aproc$ | $proc1$ | $proc2$ | list | dynamic-wind
	|	apply | values
$proc1$	::=	null? | pair? | car | cdr | call/cc
	|	procedure? | condition? | $raise*$
$proc2$	::=	cons | consi | set-car! | set-cdr! | eqv?
	|	call-with-values | with-exception-handler
$aproc$	::=	+ | - | / | *
$raise*$	::=	raise-continuable | raise
pp	::=	ip | mp
ip	::=	[immutable pair pointers]
mp	::=	[mutable pair pointers]
sym	::=	[variables except dot]
x	::=	[variables except dot and keywords]
n	::=	[numbers]

Fig. A.2a. Grammar for programs and observables

The $\mathcal{P}$ non-terminal represents possible program states. The first alternative is a program with a store and an expression. The second alternative is an uncaught exception, and the third is used to indicate a place where the model does not completely specify the behavior of the primitives it models (see section A.12 for details of those situations). The $\mathscr{A}$ non-terminal represents a final result of a program. It is just like $\mathscr{P}$ except that expression has been reduced to some sequence of values.

The $\mathscr{R}$ and $\mathscr{R}_v$ non-terminals specify the observable results of a program. Each $\mathscr{R}$ is either a sequence of values that correspond to the values produced by the program that terminates normally, or a tag indicating an uncaught exception was raised, or unknown if the program encounters a situation the semantics does not cover. The $\mathscr{R}_v$ non-terminal specifies what the observable results are for a particular value: a pair, the empty list, a symbol, a self-quoting value (#t, #f, and numbers), a condition, or a procedure.

The *sf* non-terminal generates individual elements of the store. The store holds all of the mutable state of a program. It is explained in more detail along with the rules that manipulate it.

Expressions (*es*) include quoted data, begin expressions, begin0 expressions[1], application expressions, if expressions, set! expressions, variables, non-procedure values (*nonproc*), primitive procedures (*pproc*), lambda expressions, letrec and letrec* expressions.

The last few expression forms are only generated for intermediate states (dw for dynamic-wind, throw for continuations, unspecified for the result of the assignment operators, handlers for exception handlers, and l! and reinit for letrec), and should not appear in an initial program. Their use is described in the relevant sections of this appendix.

The *f* non-terminal describes the formals for lambda expressions. (The dot is used instead of a period for procedures that accept an arbitrary number of arguments, in order to avoid meta-circular confusion in our PLT Redex model.)

The *s* non-terminal covers all datums, which can be either non-empty sequences (*seq*), the empty sequence, self-quoting values (*sqv*), or symbols. Non-empty sequences are either just a sequence of datums, or they are terminated with a dot followed by either a symbol or a self-quoting value. Finally the self-quoting values are numbers and the booleans #t and #f.

The *p* non-terminal represents programs that have no quoted data. Most of the reduction rules rewrite *p* to *p*, rather than $\mathscr{P}$ to $\mathscr{P}$, since quoted data is first rewritten into calls to the list construction functions before ordinary evaluation proceeds. In parallel to *es*, *e* represents expressions that have no quoted expressions.

The values (*v*) are divided into four categories:

---

[1] begin0 is not part of the standard, but we include it to make the rules for dynamic-wind and letrec easier to read. Although we model it directly, it can be defined in terms of other forms we model here that do come from the standard:

$$(\text{begin0 } e_1\ e_2\ \cdots) \quad = \quad \begin{array}{l} \texttt{(call-with-values} \\ \texttt{(lambda ()}\ e_1) \\ \texttt{(lambda}\ x \\ \quad e_2\ \cdots \\ \texttt{(apply values}\ x)))\end{array}$$

- Non-procedures (*nonproc*) include pair pointers (pp), the empty list (null), symbols, self-quoting values (*sqv*), and conditions. Conditions represent the report's condition values, but here just contain a message and are otherwise inert.

- User procedures ((lambda f e e $\cdots$)) include multi-arity lambda expressions and lambda expressions with dotted parameter lists,

- Primitive procedures (*pproc*) include

  — arithmetic procedures (*aproc*): +, -, /, and *,
  — procedures of one argument (*proc1*): null?, pair?, car, cdr, call/cc, procedure?, condition?, unspecified?, raise, and raise-continuable,
  — procedures of two arguments (*proc2*): cons, set-car!, set-cdr!, eqv?, and call-with-values,
  — as well as list, dynamic-wind, apply, values, and with-exception-handler.

- Finally, continuations are represented as throw expressions whose body consists of the context where the continuation was grabbed.

The next three set of non-terminals in figure A.2a represent pairs (*pp*), which are divided into immutable pairs (*ip*) and mutable pairs (*mp*). The final set of non-terminals in figure A.2a, *sym*, *x*, and *n* represent symbols, variables, and numbers respectively. The non-terminals *ip*, *mp*, and *sym* are all assumed to all be disjoint. Additionally, the variables x are assumed not to include any keywords or primitive operations, so any program variables whose names coincide with them must be renamed before the semantics can give the meaning of that program.

The set of non-terminals for evaluation contexts is shown in figure A.2b. The P non-terminal controls where evaluation happens in a program that does not contain any quoted data. The E and F evaluation contexts are for expressions. They are factored in that manner so that the PG, G, and H evaluation contexts can re-use F and have fine-grained control over the context to support exceptions and dynamic-wind. The starred and circled variants, E^*, E°, F^*, and F° dictate where a single value is promoted to multiple values and where multiple values are demoted to a single value. The U context is used to manage the report's underspecification of the results of set!, set-car!, and set-cdr! (see section A.12 for details). Finally, the S context is where quoted expressions can be simplified. The precise use of the evaluation contexts is explained along with the relevant rules.

Although it is not written in the grammar figure, variable sequences bound in the store, and in lambda, letrec, and letrec* must not contain any duplicates.

To convert the answers ($\mathscr{A}$) of the semantics into observable results, we use these

$$P \quad ::= \quad (\texttt{store}\ (sf\ \cdots)\ E^{\star})$$

$$
\begin{aligned}
E \quad &::= \quad F[(\texttt{handlers}\ proc\ \cdots\ E^{\star})] \quad | \quad F[(\texttt{dw}\ x\ e\ E^{\star}\ e)] \quad | \quad F \\
E^{\star} \quad &::= \quad [\,]_{\star} \quad | \quad E \\
E^{\circ} \quad &::= \quad [\,]_{\circ} \quad | \quad E
\end{aligned}
$$

$$
\begin{aligned}
F \quad ::= \quad & [\,] \quad | \quad (v\ \cdots\ F^{\circ}\ v\ \cdots) \quad | \quad (\texttt{if}\ F^{\circ}\ e\ e) \quad | \quad (\texttt{set!}\ x\ F^{\circ}) \\
& | \quad (\texttt{begin}\ F^{\star}\ e\ e\ \cdots) \quad | \quad (\texttt{begin0}\ F^{\star}\ e\ e\ \cdots) \\
& | \quad (\texttt{begin0}\ (\texttt{values}\ v\ \cdots)\ F^{\star}\ e\ \cdots) \quad | \quad (\texttt{begin0}\ \texttt{unspecified}\ F^{\star}\ e\ \cdots) \\
& | \quad (\texttt{call-with-values}\ (\texttt{lambda}\ ()\ F^{\star}\ e\ \cdots)\ v) \quad | \quad (\texttt{l!}\ x\ F^{\circ}) \\
F^{\star} \quad ::= \quad & [\,]_{\star} \quad | \quad F \\
F^{\circ} \quad ::= \quad & [\,]_{\circ} \quad | \quad F \\
U \quad ::= \quad & (v\ \cdots\ [\,]\ v\ \cdots) \quad | \quad (\texttt{if}\ [\,]\ e\ e) \quad | \quad (\texttt{set!}\ x\ [\,]) \quad | \quad (\texttt{l!}\ x\ [\,]) \\
& | \quad (\texttt{call-with-values}\ (\texttt{lambda}\ ()\ [\,])\ v)
\end{aligned}
$$

$$
\begin{aligned}
PG \quad &::= \quad (\texttt{store}\ (sf\ \cdots)\ G) \\
G \quad &::= \quad F[(\texttt{dw}\ x\ e\ G\ e)] \quad | \quad F \\
H \quad &::= \quad F[(\texttt{handlers}\ proc\ \cdots\ H)] \quad | \quad F
\end{aligned}
$$

$$
\begin{aligned}
S \quad ::= \quad & [\,] \quad | \quad (\texttt{begin}\ e\ e\ \cdots\ S\ es\ \cdots) \quad | \quad (\texttt{begin}\ S\ es\ \cdots) \\
& | \quad (\texttt{begin0}\ e\ e\ \cdots\ S\ es\ \cdots) \quad | \quad (\texttt{begin0}\ S\ es\ \cdots) \quad | \quad (e\ \cdots\ S\ es\ \cdots) \\
& | \quad (\texttt{if}\ S\ es\ es) \quad | \quad (\texttt{if}\ e\ S\ es) \quad | \quad (\texttt{if}\ e\ e\ S) \quad | \quad (\texttt{set!}\ x\ S) \\
& | \quad (\texttt{handlers}\ s\ \cdots\ S\ es\ \cdots\ es) \quad | \quad (\texttt{handlers}\ s\ \cdots\ S) \quad | \quad (\texttt{throw}\ x\ e) \\
& | \quad (\texttt{lambda}\ f\ S\ es\ \cdots) \quad | \quad (\texttt{lambda}\ f\ e\ e\ \cdots\ S\ es\ \cdots) \\
& | \quad (\texttt{letrec}\ ((x\ e)\ \cdots\ (x\ S)\ (x\ es)\ \cdots)\ es\ es\ \cdots) \\
& | \quad (\texttt{letrec}\ ((x\ e)\ \cdots)\ S\ es\ \cdots) \quad | \quad (\texttt{letrec}\ ((x\ e)\ \cdots)\ e\ e\ \cdots\ S\ es\ \cdots) \\
& | \quad (\texttt{letrec*}\ ((x\ e)\ \cdots\ (x\ S)\ (x\ es)\ \cdots)\ es\ es\ \cdots) \\
& | \quad (\texttt{letrec*}\ ((x\ e)\ \cdots)\ S\ es\ \cdots) \quad | \quad (\texttt{letrec*}\ ((x\ e)\ \cdots)\ e\ e\ \cdots\ S\ es\ \cdots)
\end{aligned}
$$

Fig. A.2b. Grammar for evaluation contexts

two functions:

$$
\begin{aligned}
& \mathcal{O} : \mathcal{A} \rightarrow \mathcal{R} \\
& \mathcal{O}[\![(\texttt{store}\ (sf\ \cdots)\ (\texttt{values}\ v_1\ \cdots))]\!] = \\
& \qquad (\texttt{values}\ \mathcal{O}_v[\![v_1]\!]\ \cdots)
\end{aligned}
$$

$$
\begin{aligned}
& \mathcal{O}[\![\textbf{uncaught exception:}\ v]\!] = \\
& \qquad \texttt{exception}
\end{aligned}
$$

$$
\begin{aligned}
& \mathcal{O}[\![\textbf{unknown:}\ description]\!] = \\
& \qquad \texttt{unknown}
\end{aligned}
$$

$$\text{(store } (\mathit{sf}_1 \ \cdots) \ S_1['\mathit{sqv}_1]) \rightarrow \qquad\qquad\qquad [\text{6sqv}]$$
$$\text{(store } (\mathit{sf}_1 \ \cdots) \ S_1[\mathit{sqv}_1])$$

$$\text{(store } (\mathit{sf}_1 \ \cdots) \ S_1['()]) \rightarrow \qquad\qquad\qquad [\text{6eseq}]$$
$$\text{(store } (\mathit{sf}_1 \ \cdots) \ S_1[\texttt{null}])$$

$$\text{(store } (\mathit{sf}_1 \ \cdots) \ S_1['\mathit{seq}_1]) \rightarrow \qquad\qquad\qquad [\text{6qcons}]$$
$$\text{(store } (\mathit{sf}_1 \ \cdots) \ ((\texttt{lambda } (\mathit{qp}) \ S_1[\mathit{qp}]) \ \mathscr{Q}_i[\![\mathit{seq}_1]\!])) \quad (\mathit{qp} \text{ fresh})$$

$$\text{(store } (\mathit{sf}_1 \ \cdots) \ S_1['\mathit{seq}_1]) \rightarrow \qquad\qquad\qquad [\text{6qconsi}]$$
$$\text{(store } (\mathit{sf}_1 \ \cdots) \ ((\texttt{lambda } (\mathit{qp}) \ S_1[\mathit{qp}]) \ \mathscr{Q}_m[\![\mathit{seq}_1]\!])) \quad (\mathit{qp} \text{ fresh})$$

$\mathscr{Q}_i : \mathit{seq} \rightarrow e$		
$\mathscr{Q}_i[\![()]\!]$	$=$	$\texttt{null}$
$\mathscr{Q}_i[\![(s_1 \ s_2 \ \cdots)]\!]$	$=$	$(\texttt{cons } \mathscr{Q}_i[\![s_1]\!] \ \mathscr{Q}_i[\![(s_2 \ \cdots)]\!])$
$\mathscr{Q}_i[\![(s_1 \ \texttt{dot} \ \mathit{sqv}_1)]\!]$	$=$	$(\texttt{cons } \mathscr{Q}_i[\![s_1]\!] \ \mathit{sqv}_1)$
$\mathscr{Q}_i[\![(s_1 \ s_2 \ s_3 \ \cdots \ \texttt{dot} \ \mathit{sqv}_1)]\!]$	$=$	$(\texttt{cons } \mathscr{Q}_i[\![s_1]\!] \ \mathscr{Q}_i[\![(s_2 \ s_3 \ \cdots \ \texttt{dot} \ \mathit{sqv}_1)]\!])$
$\mathscr{Q}_i[\![(s_1 \ \texttt{dot} \ \mathit{sym}_1)]\!]$	$=$	$(\texttt{cons } \mathscr{Q}_i[\![s_1]\!] \ '\mathit{sym}_1)$
$\mathscr{Q}_i[\![(s_1 \ s_2 \ s_3 \ \cdots \ \texttt{dot} \ \mathit{sym}_1)]\!]$	$=$	$(\texttt{cons } \mathscr{Q}_i[\![s_1]\!] \ \mathscr{Q}_i[\![(s_2 \ s_3 \ \cdots \ \texttt{dot} \ \mathit{sym}_1)]\!])$
$\mathscr{Q}_i[\![\mathit{sym}_1]\!]$	$=$	$'\mathit{sym}_1$
$\mathscr{Q}_i[\![\mathit{sqv}_1]\!]$	$=$	sqv_1

$\mathscr{Q}_m : \mathit{seq} \rightarrow e$		
$\mathscr{Q}_m[\![()]\!]$	$=$	$\texttt{null}$
$\mathscr{Q}_m[\![(s_1 \ s_2 \ \cdots)]\!]$	$=$	$(\texttt{consi } \mathscr{Q}_m[\![s_1]\!] \ \mathscr{Q}_m[\![(s_2 \ \cdots)]\!])$
$\mathscr{Q}_m[\![(s_1 \ \texttt{dot} \ \mathit{sqv}_1)]\!]$	$=$	$(\texttt{consi } \mathscr{Q}_m[\![s_1]\!] \ \mathit{sqv}_1)$
$\mathscr{Q}_m[\![(s_1 \ s_2 \ s_3 \ \cdots \ \texttt{dot} \ \mathit{sqv}_1)]\!]$	$=$	$(\texttt{consi } \mathscr{Q}_m[\![s_1]\!] \ \mathscr{Q}_m[\![(s_2 \ s_3 \ \cdots \ \texttt{dot} \ \mathit{sqv}_1)]\!])$
$\mathscr{Q}_m[\![(s_1 \ \texttt{dot} \ \mathit{sym}_1)]\!]$	$=$	$(\texttt{consi } \mathscr{Q}_m[\![s_1]\!] \ '\mathit{sym}_1)$
$\mathscr{Q}_m[\![(s_1 \ s_2 \ s_3 \ \cdots \ \texttt{dot} \ \mathit{sym}_1)]\!]$	$=$	$(\texttt{consi } \mathscr{Q}_m[\![s_1]\!] \ \mathscr{Q}_m[\![(s_2 \ s_3 \ \cdots \ \texttt{dot} \ \mathit{sym}_1)]\!])$
$\mathscr{Q}_m[\![\mathit{sym}_1]\!]$	$=$	$'\mathit{sym}_1$
$\mathscr{Q}_m[\![\mathit{sqv}_1]\!]$	$=$	sqv_1

Fig. A.3. Quote

$\mathscr{O}_v : v \rightarrow \mathscr{R}_v$		
$\mathscr{O}_v[\![\mathit{pp}_1]\!]$	$=$	$\texttt{pair}$
$\mathscr{O}_v[\![\texttt{null}]\!]$	$=$	$\texttt{null}$
$\mathscr{O}_v[\!['\mathit{sym}_1]\!]$	$=$	$'\mathit{sym}_1$
$\mathscr{O}_v[\![\mathit{sqv}_1]\!]$	$=$	sqv_1
$\mathscr{O}_v[\![(\texttt{make-cond } \mathit{string})]\!]$	$=$	$\texttt{condition}$
$\mathscr{O}_v[\![\mathit{proc}]\!]$	$=$	$\texttt{procedure}$

They eliminate the store, and replace complex values with simple tags that indicate only the kind of value that was produced or, if no values were produced, indicates that either an uncaught exception was raised, or that the program reached a state that is not specified by the semantics.

A.3 Quote

The first reduction rules that apply to any program is the rules in figure A.3 that eliminate quoted expressions. The first two rules erase the quote for quoted expressions that do not introduce any pairs. The last two rules lift quoted datums to the top of the expression so they are evaluated only once, and turn the datums into calls to either cons or consi, via the metafunctions $\mathcal{Q}_i$ and $\mathcal{Q}_m$.

Note that the left-hand side of the [6qcons] and [6qconsi] rules are identical, meaning that if one rule applies to a term, so does the other rule. Accordingly, a quoted expression may be lifted out into a sequence of cons expressions, which create mutable pairs, or into a sequence of consi expressions, which create immutable pairs (see section A.7 for the rules on how that happens).

These rules apply before any other because of the contexts in which they, and all of the other rules, apply. In particular, these rule applies in the S context. Figure A.2b shows that the S context allows this reduction to apply in any subexpression of an e, as long as all of the subexpressions to the left have no quoted expressions in them, although expressions to the right may have quoted expressions. Accordingly, this rule applies once for each quoted expression in the program, moving out to the beginning of the program. The rest of the rules apply in contexts that do not contain any quoted expressions, ensuring that these rules convert all quoted data into lists before those rules apply.

Although the identifier qp does not have a subscript, the semantics of PLT Redex's "fresh" declaration takes special care to ensures that the qp on the right-hand side of the rule is indeed the same as the one in the side-condition.

A.4 Multiple values

The basic strategy for multiple values is to add a rule that demotes (values v) to v and another rule that promotes v to (values v). If we allowed these rules to apply in an arbitrary evaluation context, however, we would get infinite reduction sequences of endless alternation between promotion and demotion. So, the semantics allows demotion only in a context expecting a single value and allows promotion only in a context expecting multiple values. We obtain this behavior with a small extension to the Felleisen-Hieb framework (also present in the operational model for R^5RS (Matthews & Findler, 2005)). We extend the notation so that holes have names (written with a subscript), and the context-matching syntax may also demand a hole of a particular name (also written with a subscript, for instance $E[e]_\star$). The extension allows us to give different names to the holes in which multiple values are expected and those in which single values are expected, and structure the grammar of contexts accordingly.

To exploit this extension, we use three kinds of holes in the evaluation context grammar in figure A.2b. The ordinary hole [ ] appears where the usual kinds of evaluation can occur. The hole [ ]$_\star$ appears in contexts that allow multiple values and [ ]$_\circ$ appears in contexts that expect a single value. Accordingly, the rule [6promote] only applies in [ ]$_\star$ contexts, and [6demote] only applies in [ ]$_\circ$ contexts.

$$P_1[v_1]_\star \rightarrow \qquad\qquad\qquad\qquad\qquad\qquad \text{[6promote]}$$
$$P_1[(\texttt{values } v_1)]$$

$$P_1[(\texttt{values } v_1)]_\circ \rightarrow \qquad\qquad\qquad\qquad\qquad \text{[6demote]}$$
$$P_1[v_1]$$

$$P_1[(\texttt{call-with-values (lambda () (values } v_2 \ \cdots \texttt{)) } v_1)] \rightarrow \qquad \text{[6cwvd]}$$
$$P_1[(v_1 \ v_2 \ \cdots)]$$

$$P_1[(\texttt{call-with-values } v_1 \ v_2)] \rightarrow \qquad\qquad\qquad\qquad \text{[6cwvw]}$$
$$P_1[(\texttt{call-with-values (lambda () } (v_1)) \ v_2)] \quad (v_1 \neq (\texttt{lambda () } e))$$

Fig. A.4. Multiple values and call-with-values

To see how the evaluation contexts are organized to ensure that promotion and demotion occur in the right places, consider the F, $F^\star$ and F° evaluation contexts. The $F^\star$ and F° evaluation contexts are just the same as F, except that they allow promotion to multiple values and demotion to a single value, respectively. So, the F evaluation context, rather than being defined in terms of itself, exploits $F^\star$ and F° to dictate where promotion and demotion can occur. For example, F can be (if F° e e) meaning that demotion from (values v) to v can occur in the test of an if expression. Similarly, F can be (begin $F^\star$ e e $\cdots$) meaning that v can be promoted to (values v) in the first subexpression of a begin.

In general, the promotion and demotion rules simplify the definitions of the other rules. For instance, the rule for if does not need to consider multiple values in its first subexpression. Similarly, the rule for begin does not need to consider the case of a single value as its first subexpression.

The other two rules in figure A.4 handle call-with-values. The evaluation contexts for call-with-values (in the F non-terminal) allow evaluation in the body of a procedure that has been passed as the first argument to call-with-values, as long as the second argument has been reduced to a value. Once evaluation inside that procedure completes, it will produce multiple values (since it is an $F^\star$ position), and the entire call-with-values expression reduces to an application of its second argument to those values, via the rule [6cwvd]. Finally, in the case that the first argument to call-with-values is a value, but is not of the form (lambda () e), the rule [6cwvw] wraps it in a thunk to trigger evaluation.

A.5 Exceptions

The workhorses for the exception system are

$$(\texttt{handlers } proc \ \cdots \ e)$$

expressions and the G and PG evaluation contexts (shown in figure A.2b). The handlers expression records the active exception handlers ($proc$ $\cdots$) in some expression (e). The intention is that only the nearest enclosing handlers expression is relevant to raised exceptions, and the G and PG evaluation contexts help achieve

$PG\,[(raise*v_1)] \rightarrow$ [6xunee]
uncaught exception: v_1

$P\,[(\texttt{handlers}\ G\,[(raise*v_1)])] \rightarrow$ [6xuneh]
uncaught exception: v_1

$PG_1[(\texttt{with-exception-handler}\ proc_1\ proc_2)] \rightarrow$ [6xwh1]
$PG_1[(\texttt{handlers}\ proc_1\ (proc_2))]$

$P_1[(\texttt{handlers}\ proc_1\ \cdots\ G_1[(\texttt{with-exception-handler}\ proc_2\ proc_3)])] \rightarrow$ [6xwhn]
$P_1[(\texttt{handlers}\ proc_1\ \cdots\ G_1[(\texttt{handlers}\ proc_1\ \cdots\ proc_2\ (proc_3))])]$

$P_1[(\texttt{handlers}\ proc_1\ \cdots\ G_1[(\texttt{with-exception-handler}\ v_1\ v_2)])] \rightarrow$ [6xwhne]
$P_1[(\texttt{handlers}\ proc_1\ \cdots$
    $G_1[(\texttt{raise}\ (\texttt{make-cond}\ \text{"with-exception-handler expects procs"}))])]$
  $(v_1 \notin proc\ \text{or}\ v_2 \notin proc)$

$P_1[(\texttt{handlers}\ proc_1\ \cdots\ proc_2\ G_1[(\texttt{raise-continuable}\ v_1)])] \rightarrow$ [6xrc]
$P_1[(\texttt{handlers}\ proc_1\ \cdots\ proc_2\ G_1[(\texttt{handlers}\ proc_1\ \cdots\ (proc_2\ v_1))])]$

$P_1[(\texttt{handlers}\ proc_1\ \cdots\ proc_2\ G_1[(\texttt{raise}\ v_1)])] \rightarrow$ [6xr]
$P_1[(\texttt{handlers}\ proc_1\ \cdots\ proc_2$
    $G_1[(\texttt{handlers}\ proc_1\ \cdots$
        $(\texttt{begin}\ ((proc_2\ v_1)\ (\texttt{raise}\ (\texttt{make-cond}\ \text{"handler returned"})))\ \cdots))]$

$P_1[(\texttt{condition?}\ (\texttt{make-cond}\ string))] \rightarrow$ [6ct]
$P_1[\texttt{\#t}]$

$P_1[(\texttt{condition?}\ v_1)] \rightarrow$ [6cf]
$P_1[\texttt{\#f}]$ $(v_1 \neq (\texttt{make-cond}\ string))$

$P_1[(\texttt{handlers}\ proc_1\ \cdots\ (\texttt{values}\ v_1\ \cdots))] \rightarrow$ [6xdone]
$P_1[(\texttt{values}\ v_1\ \cdots)]$

$PG_1[(\texttt{with-exception-handler}\ v_1\ v_2)] \rightarrow$ [6weherr]
$PG_1[(\texttt{raise}\ (\texttt{make-cond}\ \text{"with-exception-handler expects procs"}))]$
  $(v_1 \notin proc\ \text{or}\ v_2 \notin proc)$

Fig. A.5. Exceptions

---

that goal. They are just like their counterparts E and P, except that handlers expressions cannot occur on the path to the hole, and the exception system rules take advantage of that context to find the closest enclosing handler.

To see how the contexts work together with handler expressions, consider the left-hand side of the [6xunee] rule in figure A.5. It matches expressions that have a call to raise or raise-continuable (the non-terminal *raise** matches both exception-raising procedures) in a PG evaluation context. Since the PG context does not contain any handlers expressions, this exception cannot be caught, so this expression reduces to a final state indicating the uncaught exception. The rule [6xuneh] also signals an uncaught exception, but it covers the case where a handlers expression has exhausted all of the handlers available to it. The rule applies to expressions that have a handlers expression (with no exception handlers) in an arbitrary evaluation context where a call to one of the exception-raising functions is nested in the `handlers` expression. The use of the *G* evaluation context ensures that there are no other `handler` expressions between this one and the raise.

The next two rules cover call to the procedure `with-exception-handler`. The [6xwh1] rule applies when there are no handler expressions. It constructs a new one and applies v_2 as a thunk in the handler body. If there already is a handler expression, the [6xwhn] applies. It collects the current handlers and adds the new one into a new `handlers` expression and, as with the previous rule, invokes the second argument to `with-exception-handlers`.

The next two rules cover exceptions that are raised in the context of a `handlers` expression. If a continuable exception is raised, [6xrc] applies. It takes the most recently installed handler from the nearest enclosing `handlers` expression and applies it to the argument to `raise-continuable`, but in a context where the exception handlers do not include that latest handler. The [6xr] rule behaves similarly, except it raises a new exception if the handler returns. The new exception is created with the `make-cond` special form.

The `make-cond` special form is a stand-in for the report's conditions. It does not evaluate its argument (note its absence from the *E* grammar in figure A.2b). That argument is just a literal string describing the context in which the exception was raised. The only operation on conditions is `condition?`, whose semantics are given by the two rules [6ct] and [6cf].

Finally, the rule [6xdone] drops a `handlers` expression when its body is fully evaluated, and the rule [6weherr] raises an exception when `with-exception-handler` is supplied with incorrect arguments.

A.6 Arithmetic and basic forms

This model does not include the report's arithmetic, but does include an idealized form in order to make experimentation with other features and writing test suites for the model simpler. Figure A.6 shows the reduction rules for the primitive procedures that implement addition, subtraction, multiplication, and division. They defer to their mathematical analogues. In addition, when the subtraction or divison operator are applied to no arguments, or when division receives a zero as a divisor, or when any of the arithmetic operations receive a non-number, an exception is raised.

The bottom half of figure A.6 shows the rules for `if`, `begin`, and `begin0`. The relevant evaluation contexts are given by the *F* non-terminal.

The evaluation contexts for `if` only allow evaluation in its test expression. Once that is a value, the rules reduce an `if` expression to its consequent if the test is not `#f`, and to its alternative if it is `#f`.

The `begin` evaluation contexts allow evaluation in the first subexpression of a begin, but only if there are two or more subexpressions. In that case, once the first expression has been fully simplified, the reduction rules drop its value. If there is only a single subexpression, the `begin` itself is dropped.

Like the begin evaluation contexts, the `begin0` evaluation contexts allow evaluation of the first subexpression of a `begin0` expression when there are two or more

$$P_1[(+)] \qquad\qquad\qquad\qquad \to P_1[0] \qquad\qquad\qquad\qquad\qquad\qquad\qquad \text{[6+0]}$$

$$P_1[(+\ n_1\ n_2\ \cdots)] \qquad\qquad \to P_1[^\lceil\Sigma\{n_1, n_2\cdots\}^\rceil] \qquad\qquad\qquad\qquad \text{[6+]}$$

$$P_1[(-\ n_1)] \qquad\qquad\qquad \to P_1[^\lceil-n_1^\rceil] \qquad\qquad\qquad\qquad\qquad \text{[6u-]}$$

$$P_1[(-\ n_1\ n_2\ n_3\ \cdots)] \qquad \to P_1[^\lceil n_1 - \Sigma\{n_2, n_3\cdots\}^\rceil] \qquad\qquad\qquad \text{[6-]}$$

$$P_1[(-)] \qquad\qquad\qquad\quad \to P_1[(\text{raise (make-cond "arity mismatch"}))] \quad \text{[6-arity]}$$

$$P_1[(*)] \qquad\qquad\qquad\quad \to P_1[1] \qquad\qquad\qquad\qquad\qquad\qquad\quad \text{[6*1]}$$

$$P_1[(*\ n_1\ n_2\ \cdots)] \qquad\quad \to P_1[^\lceil\Pi\{n_1, n_2\cdots\}^\rceil] \qquad\qquad\qquad\qquad \text{[6*]}$$

$$P_1[(/\ n_1)] \qquad\qquad\qquad \to P_1[(/\ 1\ n_1)] \qquad\qquad\qquad\qquad\qquad \text{[6u/]}$$

$$P_1[(/\ n_1\ n_2\ n_3\ \cdots)] \qquad \to P_1[^\lceil n_1/\Pi\{n_2, n_3\cdots\}^\rceil] \qquad\qquad\qquad \text{[6/]}$$
$$(0 \notin \{n_2, n_3, \ldots\})$$

$$P_1[(/\ n_1\ n_2\ \cdots\ 0\ n_3\ \cdots)] \to P_1[(\text{raise (make-cond "divison by zero"}))] \qquad \text{[6/0]}$$

$$P_1[(/)] \qquad\qquad\qquad\quad \to P_1[(\text{raise (make-cond "arity mismatch"}))] \quad \text{[6/arity]}$$

$$P_1[(aproc\ v_1\ \cdots)] \to \qquad\qquad\qquad\qquad\qquad\qquad\qquad\qquad\qquad \text{[6ae]}$$
$$P_1[(\text{raise (make-cond "arith-op applied to non-number"}))]$$
$$(\exists v \in v_1\ \cdots\ \text{s.t. } v \text{ is not a number})$$

$$P_1[(\text{if } v_1\ e_1\ e_2)] \to \qquad\qquad\qquad\qquad\qquad\qquad\qquad\qquad \text{[6if3t]}$$
$$P_1[e_1] \quad (v_1 \neq \#f)$$

$$P_1[(\text{if } \#f\ e_1\ e_2)] \to \qquad\qquad\qquad\qquad\qquad\qquad\qquad\qquad \text{[6if3f]}$$
$$P_1[e_2]$$

$$P_1[(\text{begin (values } v\ \cdots)\ e_1\ e_2\ \cdots)] \to \qquad\qquad\qquad\qquad\qquad \text{[6beginc]}$$
$$P_1[(\text{begin } e_1\ e_2\ \cdots)]$$

$$P_1[(\text{begin } e_1)] \to \qquad\qquad\qquad\qquad\qquad\qquad\qquad\qquad \text{[6begind]}$$
$$P_1[e_1]$$

$$P_1[(\text{begin0 (values } v_1\ \cdots)\ (\text{values } v_2\ \cdots)\ e_2\ \cdots)] \to \quad \text{[6begin0n]}$$
$$P_1[(\text{begin0 (values } v_1\ \cdots)\ e_2\ \cdots)]$$

$$P_1[(\text{begin0 } e_1)] \to \qquad\qquad\qquad\qquad\qquad\qquad\qquad\qquad \text{[6begin01]}$$
$$P_1[e_1]$$

Fig. A.6. Arithmetic and basic forms

---

subexpressions. The begin0 evaluation contexts also allow evaluation in the second subexpression of a begin0 expression, as long as the first subexpression has been fully simplified. The [6begin0n] rule for begin0 then drops a fully simplified second subexpression. Eventually, there is only a single expression in the begin0, at which point the [begin01] rule fires, and removes the begin0 expression.

$P_1[(\text{list } v_1\ v_2\ \cdots)] \rightarrow$ [6listc]
$P_1[(\text{cons } v_1\ (\text{list } v_2\ \cdots))]$

$P_1[(\text{list})] \rightarrow$ [6listn]
$P_1[\text{null}]$

$(\text{store } (sf_1\ \cdots)\ E_1[(\text{cons } v_1\ v_2)]) \rightarrow$ [6cons]
$(\text{store } (sf_1\ \cdots\ (mp\ (\text{cons } v_1\ v_2)))\ E_1[mp])$ (mp fresh)

$(\text{store } (sf_1\ \cdots)\ E_1[(\text{consi } v_1\ v_2)]) \rightarrow$ [6consi]
$(\text{store } (sf_1\ \cdots\ (ip\ (\text{cons } v_1\ v_2)))\ E_1[ip])$ (ip fresh)

$(\text{store } (sf_1\ \cdots\ (pp_i\ (\text{cons } v_1\ v_2))\ sf_2\ \cdots)\ E_1[(\text{car } pp_i)]) \rightarrow$ [6car]
$(\text{store } (sf_1\ \cdots\ (pp_i\ (\text{cons } v_1\ v_2))\ sf_2\ \cdots)\ E_1[v_1])$

$(\text{store } (sf_1\ \cdots\ (pp_i\ (\text{cons } v_1\ v_2))\ sf_2\ \cdots)\ E_1[(\text{cdr } pp_i)]) \rightarrow$ [6cdr]
$(\text{store } (sf_1\ \cdots\ (pp_i\ (\text{cons } v_1\ v_2))\ sf_2\ \cdots)\ E_1[v_2])$

$(\text{store } (sf_1\ \cdots\ (mp_1\ (\text{cons } v_1\ v_2))\ sf_2\ \cdots)\ E_1[(\text{set-car! } mp_1\ v_3)]) \rightarrow$ [6setcar]
$(\text{store } (sf_1\ \cdots\ (mp_1\ (\text{cons } v_3\ v_2))\ sf_2\ \cdots)\ E_1[\text{unspecified}])$

$(\text{store } (sf_1\ \cdots\ (mp_1\ (\text{cons } v_1\ v_2))\ sf_2\ \cdots)\ E_1[(\text{set-cdr! } mp_1\ v_3)]) \rightarrow$ [6setcdr]
$(\text{store } (sf_1\ \cdots\ (mp_1\ (\text{cons } v_1\ v_3))\ sf_2\ \cdots)\ E_1[\text{unspecified}])$

$P_1[(\text{null? null})] \rightarrow$ [6null?t]
$P_1[\text{\#t}]$

$P_1[(\text{null? } v_1)] \rightarrow$ [6null?f]
$P_1[\text{\#f}]$ ($v_1 \neq \text{null}$)

$P_1[(\text{pair? } pp)] \rightarrow$ [6pair?t]
$P_1[\text{\#t}]$

$P_1[(\text{pair? } v_1)] \rightarrow$ [6pair?f]
$P_1[\text{\#f}]$ ($v_1 \notin pp$)

$P_1[(\text{car } v_i)] \rightarrow$ [6care]
$P_1[(\text{raise (make-cond "can't take car of non-pair"))}]$ ($v_i \notin pp$)

$P_1[(\text{cdr } v_i)] \rightarrow$ [6cdre]
$P_1[(\text{raise (make-cond "can't take cdr of non-pair"))}]$ ($v_i \notin pp$)

$P_1[(\text{set-car! } v_1\ v_2)] \rightarrow$ [6scare]
$P_1[(\text{raise (make-cond "can't set-car! on a non-pair or an immutable pair"))}]$ ($v_1 \notin mp$)

$P_1[(\text{set-cdr! } v_1\ v_2)] \rightarrow$ [6scdre]
$P_1[(\text{raise (make-cond "can't set-cdr! on a non-pair or an immutable pair"))}]$ ($v_1 \notin mp$)

Fig. A.7. Lists

A.7 Lists

The rules in figure A.7 handle lists. The first two rules handle list by reducing it to a succession of calls to cons, followed by null.

The next two rules, [6cons] and [6consi], allocate new cons cells. They both move (cons v_1 v_2) into the store, bound to a fresh pair pointer (see also section A.3 for

$P_1[(\texttt{eqv? } v_1 \ v_1)] \rightarrow$ [6eqt]
$P_1[\texttt{\#t}]$ $(v_1 \notin proc, v_1 \neq (\texttt{make-cond } string))$

$P_1[(\texttt{eqv? } v_1 \ v_2)] \rightarrow$ [6eqf]
$P_1[\texttt{\#f}]$
     $(v_1 \neq v_2, v_1 \notin proc$ or $v_2 \notin proc, v_1 \neq (\texttt{make-cond } string)$ or $v_2 \neq (\texttt{make-cond } string))$

$P_1[(\texttt{eqv? } (\texttt{make-cond } string_1) \ (\texttt{make-cond } string_2))] \rightarrow$ [6eqct]
$P_1[\texttt{\#t}]$

$P_1[(\texttt{eqv? } (\texttt{make-cond } string_1) \ (\texttt{make-cond } string_2))] \rightarrow$ [6eqcf]
$P_1[\texttt{\#f}]$

Fig. A.8. Eqv

---

a description of "fresh"). The [6cons] uses a *mp* variable, to indicate the pair is mutable, and the [6consi] uses a *ip* variable to indicate the pair is immutable.

The rules [6car] and [6cdr] extract the components of a pair from the store when presented with a pair pointer (the *pp* can be either *mp* or *ip*, as shown in figure A.2a).

The rules [6setcar] and [6setcdr] handle assignment of mutable pairs. They replace the contents of the appropriate location in the store with the new value, and reduce to unspecified. See section A.12 for an explanation of how unspecified reduces.

The next four rules handle the null? predicate and the pair? predicate, and the final four rules raise exceptions when car, cdr, set-car! or set-cdr! receive non pairs.

A.8 Eqv

The rules for eqv? are shown in figure A.8. The first two rules cover most of the behavior of eqv?. The first says that when the two arguments to eqv? are syntactically identical, then eqv? produces #t and the second says that when the arguments are not syntactically identical, then eqv? produces #f. The structure of *v* has been carefully designed so that simple term equality corresponds closely to eqv?'s behavior. For example, pairs are represented as pointers into the store and eqv? only compares those pointers.

The side-conditions on those first two rules ensure that they do not apply when simple term equality does not match the behavior of eqv?. There are two situations where it does not match: comparing two conditions and comparing two procedures. For the first, the report does not specify eqv?'s behavior, except to say that it must return a boolean, so the remaining two rules ([6eqct], and [6eqcf]) allow such comparisons to return #t or #f. Comparing two procedures is covered in section A.12.

$P_1[(e_1 \cdots e_i \, e_{i+1} \cdots)] \rightarrow$ [6mark]
$P_1[((\text{lambda } (x) \ (e_1 \cdots x \ e_{i+1} \cdots)) \ e_i)]$
  $(x \text{ fresh}, e_i \notin v, \exists e \in e_1 \cdots e_{i+1} \cdots \text{ s.t. } e \notin v)$

$(\text{store } (sf_1 \cdots) \ E_1[((\text{lambda } (x_1 \ x_2 \cdots) \ e_1 \ e_2 \cdots) \ v_1 \ v_2 \cdots)]) \rightarrow$ [6appN!]
$(\text{store } (sf_1 \cdots \ (bp \ v_1)) \ E_1[(\{x_1 \mapsto bp\}(\text{lambda } (x_2 \cdots) \ e_1 \ e_2 \cdots) \ v_2 \cdots)])$
  $(bp \text{ fresh}, \#x_2 = \#v_2, \mathscr{V}[\![x_1, (\text{lambda } (x_2 \cdots) \ e_1 \ e_2 \cdots)]\!])$

$P_1[((\text{lambda } (x_1 \ x_2 \cdots) \ e_1 \ e_2 \cdots) \ v_1 \ v_2 \cdots)] \rightarrow$ [6appN]
$P_1[(\{x_1 \mapsto v_1\}(\text{lambda } (x_2 \cdots) \ e_1 \ e_2 \cdots) \ v_2 \cdots)]$
  $(\#x_2 = \#v_2, \neg\mathscr{V}[\![x_1, (\text{lambda } (x_2 \cdots) \ e_1 \ e_2 \cdots)]\!])$

$P_1[((\text{lambda } () \ e_1 \ e_2 \cdots))] \rightarrow$ [6app0]
$P_1[(\text{begin } e_1 \ e_2 \cdots)]$

$P_1[((\text{lambda } (x_1 \ x_2 \cdots \text{ dot } x_r) \ e_1 \ e_2 \cdots) \ v_1 \ v_2 \cdots v_3 \cdots)] \rightarrow$ [6μapp]
$P_1[((\text{lambda } (x_1 \ x_2 \cdots x_r) \ e_1 \ e_2 \cdots) \ v_1 \ v_2 \cdots (\text{list } v_3 \cdots))]$
  $(\#x_2 = \#v_2)$

$P_1[((\text{lambda } x_1 \ e_1 \ e_2 \cdots) \ v_1 \cdots)] \rightarrow$ [6μapp1]
$P_1[((\text{lambda } (x_1) \ e_1 \ e_2 \cdots) \ (\text{list } v_1 \cdots))]$

$(\text{store } (sf_1 \cdots \ (x_1 \ v_1) \ sf_2 \cdots) \ E_1[x_1]) \rightarrow$ [6var]
$(\text{store } (sf_1 \cdots \ (x_1 \ v_1) \ sf_2 \cdots) \ E_1[v_1])$

$(\text{store } (sf_1 \cdots \ (x_1 \ v_1) \ sf_2 \cdots) \ E_1[(\text{set! } x_1 \ v_2)]) \rightarrow$ [6set]
$(\text{store } (sf_1 \cdots \ (x_1 \ v_2) \ sf_2 \cdots) \ E_1[\text{unspecified}])$

$P_1[(\text{procedure? } proc)] \rightarrow$ [6proct]
$P_1[\#t]$

$P_1[(\text{procedure? } nonproc)] \rightarrow$ [6procf]
$P_1[\#f]$

$P_1[((\text{lambda } (x_1 \cdots) \ e_1 \ e_2 \cdots) \ v_1 \cdots)] \rightarrow$ [6arity]
$P_1[(\text{raise } (\text{make-cond "arity mismatch"}))]$ $(\#x_1 \neq \#v_1)$

$P_1[((\text{lambda } (x_1 \ x_2 \cdots \text{ dot } x) \ e_1 \ e_2 \cdots) \ v_1 \cdots)] \rightarrow$ [6μarity]
$P_1[(\text{raise } (\text{make-cond "arity mismatch"}))]$ $(\#v_1 < \#x_2 + 1)$

$P_1[(nonproc \ v \cdots)] \rightarrow$ [6appe]
$P_1[(\text{raise } (\text{make-cond "can't call non-procedure"}))]$

$P_1[(proc1 \ v_1 \cdots)] \rightarrow$ [61arity]
$P_1[(\text{raise } (\text{make-cond "arity mismatch"}))]$ $(\#v_1 \neq 1)$

$P_1[(proc2 \ v_1 \cdots)] \rightarrow$ [62arity]
$P_1[(\text{raise } (\text{make-cond "arity mismatch"}))]$ $(\#v_1 \neq 2)$

Fig. A.9a. Procedures & application

A.9 Procedures and application

In evaluating a procedure call, the report leaves unspecified the order in which arguments are evaluated. So, our reduction system allows multiple, different reductions to occur, one for each possible order of evaluation.

$\mathscr{V} \in 2^{X \times e}$

$\mathscr{V}[\![x_1, (\texttt{set!}\ x_2\ e_1)]\!]$ if $x_1 = x_2$

$\mathscr{V}[\![x_1, (\texttt{set!}\ x_2\ e_1)]\!]$ if $\mathscr{V}[\![x_1, e_1]\!]$ and $x_1 \neq x_2$

$\mathscr{V}[\![x_1, (\texttt{begin}\ e_1\ e_2\ e_3\ \cdots)]\!]$ if $\mathscr{V}[\![x_1, e_1]\!]$ or $\mathscr{V}[\![x_1, (\texttt{begin}\ e_2\ e_3\ \cdots)]\!]$

$\mathscr{V}[\![x_1, (\texttt{begin}\ e_1)]\!]$ if $\mathscr{V}[\![x_1, e_1]\!]$

$\mathscr{V}[\![x_1, (e_1\ e_2\ \cdots)]\!]$ if $\mathscr{V}[\![x_1, (\texttt{begin}\ e_1\ e_2\ \cdots)]\!]$

$\mathscr{V}[\![x_1, (\texttt{if}\ e_1\ e_2\ e_3)]\!]$ if $\mathscr{V}[\![x_1, e_1]\!]$ or $\mathscr{V}[\![x_1, e_2]\!]$ or $\mathscr{V}[\![x_1, e_3]\!]$

$\mathscr{V}[\![x_1, (\texttt{begin0}\ e_1\ e_2\ \cdots)]\!]$ if $\mathscr{V}[\![x_1, (\texttt{begin}\ e_1\ e_2\ \cdots)]\!]$

$\mathscr{V}[\![x_1, (\texttt{lambda}\ (x_2\ \cdots)\ e_1\ e_2\ \cdots)]\!]$ if $\mathscr{V}[\![x_1, (\texttt{begin}\ e_1\ e_2\ \cdots)]\!]$ and $x_1 \notin \{x_2 \cdots\}$

$\mathscr{V}[\![x_1, (\texttt{lambda}\ (x_2\ \cdots\ \texttt{dot}\ x_3)\ e_1\ e_2\ \cdots)]\!]$

                                if $\mathscr{V}[\![x_1, (\texttt{begin}\ e_1\ e_2\ \cdots)]\!]$ and $x_1 \notin \{x_2 \cdots x_3\}$

$\mathscr{V}[\![x_1, (\texttt{lambda}\ x_2\ e_1\ e_2\ \cdots)]\!]$ if $\mathscr{V}[\![x_1, (\texttt{begin}\ e_1\ e_2\ \cdots)]\!]$ and $x_1 \neq x_2$

$\mathscr{V}[\![x_1, (\texttt{letrec}\ ((x_2\ e_1)\ \cdots)\ e_2\ e_3\ \cdots)]\!]$

                                if $\mathscr{V}[\![x_1, (\texttt{begin}\ e_1\ \cdots\ e_2\ e_3\ \cdots)]\!]$ and $x_1 \notin \{x_2 \cdots\}$

$\mathscr{V}[\![x_1, (\texttt{letrec*}\ ((x_2\ e_1)\ \cdots)\ e_2\ e_3\ \cdots)]\!]$

                                if $\mathscr{V}[\![x_1, (\texttt{begin}\ e_1\ \cdots\ e_2\ e_3\ \cdots)]\!]$ and $x_1 \notin \{x_2 \cdots\}$

$\mathscr{V}[\![x_1, (\texttt{l!}\ x_2\ e_1)]\!]$ if $\mathscr{V}[\![x_1, (\texttt{set!}\ x_2\ e_1)]\!]$

$\mathscr{V}[\![x_1, (\texttt{reinit}\ x_2\ e_1)]\!]$ if $\mathscr{V}[\![x_1, (\texttt{set!}\ x_2\ e_1)]\!]$

$\mathscr{V}[\![x_1, (\texttt{dw}\ x_2\ e_1\ e_2\ e_3)]\!]$ if $\mathscr{V}[\![x_1, e_1]\!]$ or $\mathscr{V}[\![x_1, e_2]\!]$ or $\mathscr{V}[\![x_1, e_3]\!]$

Fig. A.9b. Variable-assignment relation

To capture unspecified evaluation order but allow only evaluation that is consistent with some sequential ordering of the evaluation of an application's subexpressions, we use non-deterministic choice to first pick a subexpression to reduce only when we have not already committed to reducing some other subexpression. To achieve that effect, we limit the evaluation of application expressions to only those that have a single expression that is not fully reduced, as shown in the non-terminal F, in figure A.2b. To evaluate application expressions that have more than two arguments to evaluate, the rule [6mark] picks one of the subexpressions of an application that is not fully simplified and lifts it out in its own application, allowing it to be evaluated. Once one of the lifted expressions is evaluated, the [6appN] substitutes its value back into the original application.

The [6appN] rule also handles other applications whose arguments are finished by substituting the first argument for the first formal parameter in the expression. Its side-condition uses the relation in figure A.9b to ensure that there are no set! expressions with the parameter x_1 as a target. If there is such an assignment, the [6appN!] rule applies (see also section A.3 for a description of "fresh"). Instead of directly substituting the actual parameter for the formal parameter, it creates a new location in the store, initially bound the actual parameter, and substitutes a variable standing for that location in place of the formal parameter. The store, then, handles any eventual assignment to the parameter. Once all of the parameters have been substituted away, the rule [6app0] applies and evaluation of the body of the procedure begins.

At first glance, the rule [6appN] appears superfluous, since it seems like the rules could just reduce first by [6appN!] and then look up the variable when it is

$P_1[(\texttt{apply } proc_1 \ v_1 \ \cdots \ \texttt{null})] \rightarrow$ [6applyf]
$P_1[(proc_1 \ v_1 \ \cdots)]$

$(\texttt{store } (sf_1 \ \cdots \ (pp_1 \ (\texttt{cons } v_2 \ v_3)) \ sf_2 \ \cdots)$ [6applyc]
    $E_1[(\texttt{apply } proc_1 \ v_1 \ \cdots \ pp_1)]) \ \rightarrow$
$(\texttt{store } (sf_1 \ \cdots \ (pp_1 \ (\texttt{cons } v_2 \ v_3)) \ sf_2 \ \cdots) \ E_1[(\texttt{apply } proc_1 \ v_1 \ \cdots \ v_2 \ v_3)])$
   $(\neg\mathscr{C}[\![pp_1, v_3, (sf_1 \ \cdots \ (pp_1 \ (\texttt{cons } v_2 \ v_3)) \ sf_2 \ \cdots)]\!])$

$(\texttt{store } (sf_1 \ \cdots \ (pp_1 \ (\texttt{cons } v_2 \ v_3)) \ sf_2 \ \cdots)$ [6applyce]
    $E_1[(\texttt{apply } proc_1 \ v_1 \ \cdots \ pp_1)]) \ \rightarrow$
$(\texttt{store } (sf_1 \ \cdots \ (pp_1 \ (\texttt{cons } v_2 \ v_3)) \ sf_2 \ \cdots)$
    $E_1[(\texttt{raise (make-cond "apply called on circular list")})])$
   $(\mathscr{C}[\![pp_1, v_3, (sf_1 \ \cdots \ (pp_1 \ (\texttt{cons } v_2 \ v_3)) \ sf_2 \ \cdots)]\!])$

$P_1[(\texttt{apply } nonproc \ v \ \cdots)] \rightarrow$ [6applynf]
$P_1[(\texttt{raise (make-cond "can't apply non-procedure")})]$

$P_1[(\texttt{apply } proc \ v_1 \ \cdots \ v_2)] \rightarrow$ [6applye]
$P_1[(\texttt{raise (make-cond "apply's last argument non-list")})]$ $(v_2 \notin list\text{-}v)$

$P_1[(\texttt{apply})] \rightarrow$ [6apparity0]
$P_1[(\texttt{raise (make-cond "arity mismatch")})]$

$P_1[(\texttt{apply } v)] \rightarrow$ [6apparity1]
$P_1[(\texttt{raise (make-cond "arity mismatch")})]$

$\mathscr{C} \in 2^{pp \times val \times (sf \ \cdots)}$
$\mathscr{C}[\![pp_1, pp_2, (sf_1 \ \cdots \ (pp_2 \ (\texttt{cons } v_1 \ v_2)) \ sf_2 \ \cdots)]\!]$ if $pp_1 = v_2$
$\mathscr{C}[\![pp_1, pp_2, (sf_1 \ \cdots \ (pp_2 \ (\texttt{cons } v_1 \ v_2)) \ sf_2 \ \cdots)]\!]$
    if $\mathscr{C}[\![pp_1, v_2, (sf_1 \ \cdots \ (pp_2 \ (\texttt{cons } v_1 \ v_2)) \ sf_2 \ \cdots)]\!]$ and $pp_1 \neq v_2$

Fig. A.9c. Apply

---

evaluated. There are two reasons why we keep the [6appN], however. The first is purely conventional: reducing applications via substitution is taught to us at an early age and is commonly used in rewriting systems in the literature. The second reason is more technical: the [6mark] rule requires that [6appN] be applied once e_i has been reduced to a value. [6appN!] would lift the value into the store and put a variable reference into the application, leading to another use of [6mark], and another use of [6appN!], which continues forever.

The rule [6μapp] handles a well-formed application of a function with a dotted parameter lists. It such an application into an application of an ordinary procedure by constructing a list of the extra arguments. Similarly, the rule [6μapp1] handles an application of a procedure that has a single variable as its parameter list.

The rule [6var] handles variable lookup in the store and [6set] handles variable assignment.

The next two rules [6proct] and [6procf] handle applications of `procedure?`, and the remaining rules cover applications of non-procedures and arity violations.

The rules in figure A.9c cover `apply`. The first rule, [6applyf], covers the case

$P_1[(\text{dynamic-wind } proc_1\ proc_2\ proc_3)] \rightarrow$ [6wind]
$P_1[(\text{begin } (proc_1)\ (\text{begin0 } (\text{dw } x\ (proc_1)\ (proc_2)\ (proc_3))\ (proc_3)))]$ $(x\ \text{fresh})$

$P_1[(\text{dynamic-wind } v_1\ v_2\ v_3)] \rightarrow$ [6winde]
$P_1[(\text{raise } (\text{make-cond "dynamic-wind expects procs"}))]$
    $(v_1 \notin proc\ \text{or } v_2 \notin proc\ \text{or } v_3 \notin proc)$

$P_1[(\text{dynamic-wind } v_1\ \cdots)] \rightarrow$ [6dwarity]
$P_1[(\text{raise } (\text{make-cond "arity mismatch"}))]$ $(\#v_1 \neq 3)$

$P_1[(\text{dw } x\ e_1\ (\text{values } v_1\ \cdots)\ e_2)] \rightarrow$ [6dwdone]
$P_1[(\text{values } v_1\ \cdots)]$

$(\text{store } (sf_1\ \cdots)\ E_1[(\text{call/cc } v_1)]) \rightarrow$ [6call/cc]
$(\text{store } (sf_1\ \cdots)\ E_1[(v_1\ (\text{throw } x\ E_1[x]))])$ $(x\ \text{fresh})$

$(\text{store } (sf_1\ \cdots)\ E_1[((\text{throw } x_1\ E_2[x_1])\ v_1\ \cdots)]) \rightarrow$ [6throw]
$(\text{store } (sf_1\ \cdots)\ \mathcal{T}[\![E_1, E_2]\!][(\text{values } v_1\ \cdots)])$

$\mathcal{T} : E \times E \rightarrow E$
$\mathcal{T}[\![H_1[(\text{dw } x_1\ e_1\ E_1\ e_2)], H_2[(\text{dw } x_1\ e_3\ E_2\ e_4)]]\!]$ $=$ $H_2[(\text{dw } x_1\ e_3\ \mathcal{T}[\![E_1, E_2]\!]\ e_4)]$
$\mathcal{T}[\![E_1, E_2]\!]$ $=$ $(\text{begin } \mathcal{S}[\![E_1]\!][1]\ \mathcal{R}[\![E_2]\!])$
                                                                                                                       (otherwise)

$\mathcal{R} : E \rightarrow E$
$\mathcal{R}[\![H_1[(\text{dw } x_1\ e_1\ E_1\ e_2)]]\!]$ $=$ $H_1[(\text{begin } e_1\ (\text{dw } x_1\ e_1\ \mathcal{R}[\![E_1]\!]\ e_2))]$
$\mathcal{R}[\![H_1]\!]$ $=$ H_1 (otherwise)

$\mathcal{S} : E \rightarrow E$
$\mathcal{S}[\![E_1[(\text{dw } x_1\ e_1\ H_2\ e_2)]]\!]$ $=$ $\mathcal{S}[\![E_1]\!][(\text{begin0 } (\text{dw } x_1\ e_1\ [\ ]\ e_2)\ e_2)]$
$\mathcal{S}[\![H_1]\!]$ $=$ $[\ ]$ (otherwise)

Fig. A.10. Call/cc and dynamic wind

where the last argument to `apply` is the empty list, and simply reduces by erasing the empty list and the `apply`. The second rule, [6applyc] covers a well-formed application of `apply` where `apply`'s final argument is a pair. It reduces by extracting the components of the pair from the store and putting them into the application of `apply`. Repeated application of this rule thus extracts all of the list elements passed to `apply` out of the store.

The remaining five rules cover the various violations that can occur when using `apply`. The first one covers the case where `apply` is supplied with a cyclic list. The next four cover applying a non-procedure, passing a non-list as the last argument, and supplying too few arguments to `apply`.

A.10 Call/cc and dynamic wind

The specification of `dynamic-wind` uses (dw *x e e e*) expressions to record which dynamic-wind *thunk*s are active at each point in the computation. Its first argument is an identifier that is globally unique and serves to identify invocations of dynamic-wind, in order to avoid exiting and re-entering the same dynamic context during a continuation switch. The second, third, and fourth arguments are calls to some *before*, *thunk*, and *after* procedures from a call to dynamic-wind. Evaluation only occurs in the middle expression; the dw expression only serves to record which *before* and *after* procedures need to be run during a continuation switch. Accordingly, the reduction rule for an application of dynamic-wind reduces to a call to the *before* procedure, a dw expression and a call to the *after* procedure, as shown in rule [6wind] in figure A.10. The next two rules cover abuses of the dynamic-wind procedure: calling it with non-procedures, and calling it with the wrong number of arguments. The [6dwdone] rule erases a dw expression when its second argument has finished evaluating.

The next two rules cover call/cc. The rule [6call/cc] creates a new continuation. It takes the context of the call/cc expression and packages it up into a throw expression that represents the continuation. The throw expression uses the fresh variable x to record where the application of call/cc occurred in the context for use in the [6throw] rule when the continuation is applied. That rule takes the arguments of the continuation, wraps them with a call to values, and puts them back into the place where the original call to call/cc occurred, replacing the current context with the context returned by the $\mathcal{T}$ metafunction.

The $\mathcal{T}$ (for "trim") metafunction accepts two D contexts and builds a context that matches its second argument, the destination context, except that additional calls to the *before* and *after* procedures from dw expressions in the context have been added.

The first clause of the $\mathcal{T}$ metafunction exploits the H context, a context that contains everything except dw expressions. It ensures that shared parts of the dynamic-wind context are ignored, recurring deeper into the two expression contexts as long as the first dw expression in each have matching identifiers (x_1). The final rule is a catchall; it only applies when all the others fail and thus applies either when there are no dws in the context, or when the dw expressions do not match. It calls the two other metafunctions defined in figure A.10 and puts their results together into a begin expression.

The $\mathcal{R}$ metafunction extracts all of the *before* procedures from its argument and the $\mathcal{S}$ metafunction extracts all of the *after* procedures from its argument. They each construct new contexts and exploit H to work through their arguments, one dw at a time. In each case, the metafunctions are careful to keep the right dw context around each of the procedures in case a continuation jump occurs during one of their evaluations. Since $\mathcal{R}$, receives the destination context, it keeps the intermediate parts of the context in its result. In contrast $\mathcal{S}$ discards all of the context except the dws, since that was the context where the call to the continuation occurred.

A.11 Letrec

Figre A.11 shows the rules that handle letrec and letrec* and the supplementary expressions that they produce, 1! and reinit. As a first approximation, both letrec and letrec* reduce by allocating locations in the store to hold the values of the init

(store $(sf_1 \cdots (x_1 \text{ bh}) sf_2 \cdots)$ $E_1[(\text{l! } x_1 v_2)])] \rightarrow$ [6initdt]
(store $(sf_1 \cdots (x_1 v_2) sf_2 \cdots)$ $E_1[\text{unspecified}])$

(store $(sf_1 \cdots (x_1 v_1) sf_2 \cdots)$ $E_1[(\text{l! } x_1 v_2)])] \rightarrow$ [6initv]
(store $(sf_1 \cdots (x_1 v_2) sf_2 \cdots)$ $E_1[\text{unspecified}])$

(store $(sf_1 \cdots (x_1 \text{ bh}) sf_2 \cdots)$ $E_1[(\text{set! } x_1 v_1)])] \rightarrow$ [6setdt]
(store $(sf_1 \cdots (x_1 v_1) sf_2 \cdots)$ $E_1[\text{unspecified}])$

(store $(sf_1 \cdots (x_1 \text{ bh}) sf_2 \cdots)$ $E_1[(\text{set! } x_1 v_1)])] \rightarrow$ [6setdte]
(store $(sf_1 \cdots (x_1 \text{ bh}) sf_2 \cdots)$
     $E_1[(\text{raise (make-cond "letrec variable touched")})])$

(store $(sf_1 \cdots (x_1 \text{ bh}) sf_2 \cdots)$ $E_1[x_1]) \rightarrow$ [6dt]
(store $(sf_1 \cdots (x_1 \text{ bh}) sf_2 \cdots)$
     $E_1[(\text{raise (make-cond "letrec variable touched")})])$

(store $(sf_1 \cdots (x_1 \text{ \#f}) sf_2 \cdots)$ $E_1[(\text{reinit } x_1)])] \rightarrow$ [6init]
(store $(sf_1 \cdots (x_1 \text{ \#t}) sf_2 \cdots)$ $E_1['ignore])$

(store $(sf_1 \cdots (x_1 \text{ \#t}) sf_2 \cdots)$ $E_1[(\text{reinit } x_1)])] \rightarrow$ [6reinit]
(store $(sf_1 \cdots (x_1 \text{ \#t}) sf_2 \cdots)$ $E_1['ignore])$

(store $(sf_1 \cdots (x_1 \text{ \#t}) sf_2 \cdots)$ $E_1[(\text{reinit } x_1)])] \rightarrow$ [6reinite]
(store $(sf_1 \cdots (x_1 \text{ \#t}) sf_2 \cdots)$
     $E_1[(\text{raise (make-cond "reinvoked continuation of letrec init")})])$

(store $(sf_1 \cdots)$ $E_1[(\text{letrec } ((x_1 e_1) \cdots) e_2 e_3 \cdots)])] \rightarrow$ [6letrec]
(store $(sf_1 \cdots (lx \text{ bh}) \cdots (ri \text{ \#f}) \cdots)$
  $E_1[((\text{lambda } (x_1 \cdots) (\text{l! } lx x_1) \cdots \{x_1 \mapsto lx \cdots\}e_2 \{x_1 \mapsto lx \cdots\}e_3 \cdots)$
     $(\text{begin0 } \{x_1 \mapsto lx \cdots\}e_1 (\text{reinit } ri)) \cdots)])$
$(lx \cdots \text{ fresh}, ri \cdots \text{ fresh})$

(store $(sf_1 \cdots)$ $E_1[(\text{letrec* } ((x_1 e_1) \cdots) e_2 e_3 \cdots)])] \rightarrow$ [6letrec*]
(store $(sf_1 \cdots (lx \text{ bh}) \cdots (ri \text{ \#f}) \cdots)$
$E_1[\{x_1 \mapsto lx \cdots\}(\text{begin (begin (l! } lx e_1) (\text{reinit } ri)) \cdots e_2 e_3 \cdots)])$
$(lx \cdots \text{ fresh}, ri \cdots \text{ fresh})$

Fig. A.11. Letrec and letrec*

---

expressions, initializing those locations to bh (for "black hole"), evaluating the init expressions, and then using l! to update the locations in the store with the value of the init expressions. They also use reinit to detect when an init expression in a letrec is reentered via a continuation.

Before considering how letrec and letrec* use l! and reinit, first consider how l! and reinit behave. The first two rules in figure A.11 cover l!. It behaves very much like set!, but it initializes both ordinary variables, and variables that are current bound to the black hole (bh).

The next two rules cover ordinary set! when applied to a variable that is currently bound to a black hole. This situation can arise when the program assigns to a variable before letrec initializes it, eg (letrec ((x (set! x 5))) x). The report specifies that either an implementation should perform the assignment, as reflected in the [6setdt] rule or it raise an exception, as reflected in the [6setdte] rule.

The [6dt] rule covers the case where a variable is referred to before the value of a init expression is filled in, which must always raise an exception.

A reinit expression is used to detect a program that captures a continuation in an initialization expression and returns to it, as shown in the three rules [6init], [6reinit], and [6reinite]. The reinit form accepts an identifier that is bound in the store to a boolean as its argument. Those are identifiers are initially #f. When reinit is evaluated, it checks the value of the variable and, if it is still #f, it changes it to #t. If it is already #t, then reinit either just does nothing, or it raises an exception, in keeping with the two legal behaviors of letrec and letrec*.

The last two rules in figure A.11 put together 1! and reinit. The [6letrec] rule reduces a letrec expression to an application expression, in order to capture the unspecified order of evaluation of the init expressions. Each init expression is wrapped in a begin0 that records the value of the init and then uses reinit to detect continuations that return to the init expression. Once all of the init expressions have been evaluated, the procedure on the right-hand side of the rule is invoked, causing the value of the init expression to be filled in the store, and evaluation continues with the body of the original letrec expression.

The [6letrec*] rule behaves similarly, but uses a begin expression rather than an application, since the init expressions are evaluated from left to right. Moreover, each init expression is filled into the store as it is evaluated, so that subsequent init expressions can refer to its value.

A.12 Underspecification

The rules in figure A.12 cover aspects of the semantics that are explicitly unspecified. Implementations can replace the rules [6ueqv], [6uval] and with different rules that cover the left-hand sides and, as long as they follow the informal specification, any replacement is valid. Those three situations correspond to the case when eqv? applied to two procedures and when multiple values are used in a single-value context.

The remaining rules in figure A.12 cover the results from the assignment operations, set!, set-car!, and set-cdr!. An implementation does not adjust those rules, but instead renders them useless by adjusting the rules that insert unspecified: [6setcar], [6setcdr], [6set], and [6setd]. Those rules can be adjusted by replacing unspecified with any number of values in those rules.

So, the remaining rules just specify the minimal behavior that we know that a value or values must have and otherwise reduce to an **unknown:** state. The rule [6udemand] drops unspecified in the U context. See figure A.2b for the precise definition of U, but intuitively it is a context that is only a single expression layer deep that contains expressions whose value depends on the value of their subexpressions, like the first subexpression of a if. Following that are rules that discard unspecified in expressions that discard the results of some of their subexpressions. The [6ubegin] shows how begin discards its first expression when there are more expressions to

$P[(\text{eqv? } proc_1 \; proc_2)] \rightarrow$ [6ueqv]
unknown: equivalence of procedures

$P[(\text{values } v_1 \; \cdots)]_\circ \rightarrow$ [6uval]
unknown: context expected one value, received $\#v_1$ $(\#v_1 \neq 1)$

$P[U[\text{unspecified}]] \rightarrow$ [6udemand]
unknown: unspecified result

$(\text{store } (sf \; \cdots) \; \text{unspecified}) \rightarrow$ [6udemandtl]
unknown: unspecified result

$P_1[(\text{begin unspecified } e_1 \; e_2 \; \cdots)] \rightarrow$ [6ubegin]
$P_1[(\text{begin } e_1 \; e_2 \; \cdots)]$

$P_1[(\text{handlers } v \; \cdots \; \text{unspecified})] \rightarrow$ [6uhandlers]
$P_1[\text{unspecified}]$

$P_1[(\text{dw } x \; e_1 \; \text{unspecified } e_2)] \rightarrow$ [6udw]
$P_1[\text{unspecified}]$

$P_1[(\text{begin0 (values } v_1 \; \cdots) \; \text{unspecified } e_1 \; \cdots)] \rightarrow$ [6ubegin0]
$P_1[(\text{begin0 (values } v_1 \; \cdots) \; e_1 \; \cdots)]$

$P_1[(\text{begin0 unspecified (values } v_2 \; \cdots) \; e_2 \; \cdots)] \rightarrow$ [6ubegin0u]
$P_1[(\text{begin0 unspecified } e_2 \; \cdots)]$

$P_1[(\text{begin0 unspecified unspecified } e_2 \; \cdots)] \rightarrow$ [6ubegin0uu]
$P_1[(\text{begin0 unspecified } e_2 \; \cdots)]$

Fig. A.12. Explicitly unspecified behavior

---

evaluate. The next two rules, [6uhandlers] and [6udw] propagate unspecified to
their context, since they also return any number of values to their context. Finally,
the two begin0 rules preserve unspecified until the rule [6begin01] can return it
to its context.

B Sample definitions for derived forms

This appendix contains sample definitions for some of the keywords described in
this report in terms of simpler forms:

cond

The cond keyword (section 11.4.5) could be defined in terms of if, let and begin
using syntax-rules as follows:

```
(define-syntax cond
  (syntax-rules (else =>)
    ((cond (else result1 result2 ...))
     (begin result1 result2 ...))
```

```
((cond (test => result))
 (let ((temp test))
   (if temp (result temp))))
((cond (test => result) clause1 clause2 ...)
 (let ((temp test))
   (if temp
       (result temp)
       (cond clause1 clause2 ...))))
((cond (test)) test)
((cond (test) clause1 clause2 ...)
 (let ((temp test))
   (if temp
       temp
       (cond clause1 clause2 ...))))
((cond (test result1 result2 ...))
 (if test (begin result1 result2 ...)))
((cond (test result1 result2 ...)
       clause1 clause2 ...)
 (if test
     (begin result1 result2 ...)
     (cond clause1 clause2 ...)))))
```

case

The case keyword (section 11.4.5) could be defined in terms of let, cond, and memv
(see library chapter 3) using syntax-rules as follows:

```
(define-syntax case
  (syntax-rules (else)
    ((case expr0
       ((key ...) res1 res2 ...)
       ...
       (else else-res1 else-res2 ...))
     (let ((tmp expr0))
       (cond
         ((memv tmp '(key ...)) res1 res2 ...)
         ...
         (else else-res1 else-res2 ...))))
    ((case expr0
       ((keya ...) res1a res2a ...)
       ((keyb ...) res1b res2b ...)
       ...)
     (let ((tmp expr0))
       (cond
         ((memv tmp '(keya ...)) res1a res2a ...)
```

```
((memv tmp '(keyb ...)) res1b res2b ...)
...)))))
```

let*

The let* keyword (section 11.4.6) could be defined in terms of let using syntax-rules as follows:

```
(define-syntax let*
  (syntax-rules ()
    ((let* () body1 body2 ...)
     (let () body1 body2 ...))
    ((let* ((name1 expr1) (name2 expr2) ...)
       body1 body2 ...)
     (let ((name1 expr1))
       (let* ((name2 expr2) ...)
         body1 body2 ...)))))
```

letrec

The letrec keyword (section 11.4.6) could be defined approximately in terms of let and set! using syntax-rules, using a helper to generate the temporary variables needed to hold the values before the assignments are made, as follows:

```
(define-syntax letrec
  (syntax-rules ()
    ((letrec () body1 body2 ...)
     (let () body1 body2 ...))
    ((letrec ((var init) ...) body1 body2 ...)
     (letrec-helper
       (var ...)
       ()
       ((var init) ...)
       body1 body2 ...))))

(define-syntax letrec-helper
  (syntax-rules ()
    ((letrec-helper
       ()
       (temp ...)
       ((var init) ...)
       body1 body2 ...)
     (let ((var <undefined>) ...)
       (let ((temp init) ...)
         (set! var temp)
         ...)
```

```
          (let () body1 body2 ...)))
      ((letrec-helper
        (x y ...)
        (temp ...)
        ((var init) ...)
        body1 body2 ...)
      (letrec-helper
        (y ...)
        (newtemp temp ...)
        ((var init) ...)
        body1 body2 ...)))))
```

The syntax <undefined> represents an expression that returns something that, when stored in a location, causes an exception with condition type &assertion to be raised if an attempt to read from or write to the location occurs before the assignments generated by the letrec transformation take place. (No such expression is defined in Scheme.)

A simpler definition using syntax-case and generate-temporaries is given in library chapter 12.

letrec*

The letrec* keyword could be defined approximately in terms of let and set! using syntax-rules as follows:

```
(define-syntax letrec*
  (syntax-rules ()
    ((letrec* ((var1 init1) ...) body1 body2 ...)
     (let ((var1 <undefined>) ...)
       (set! var1 init1)
       ...
       (let () body1 body2 ...)))))
```

The syntax <undefined> is as in the definition of letrec above.

let-values

The following definition of let-values (section 11.4.6) using syntax-rules employs a pair of helpers to create temporary names for the formals.

```
(define-syntax let-values
  (syntax-rules ()
    ((let-values (binding ...) body1 body2 ...)
     (let-values-helper1
       ()
       (binding ...)
       body1 body2 ...))))
```

```scheme
(define-syntax let-values-helper1
  ;; map over the bindings
  (syntax-rules ()
    ((let-values
       ((id temp) ...)
       ()
       body1 body2 ...)
     (let ((id temp) ...) body1 body2 ...))
    ((let-values
       assocs
       ((formals1 expr1) (formals2 expr2) ...)
       body1 body2 ...)
     (let-values-helper2
       formals1
       ()
       expr1
       assocs
       ((formals2 expr2) ...)
       body1 body2 ...))))

(define-syntax let-values-helper2
  ;; create temporaries for the formals
  (syntax-rules ()
    ((let-values-helper2
       ()
       temp-formals
       expr1
       assocs
       bindings
       body1 body2 ...)
     (call-with-values
       (lambda () expr1)
       (lambda temp-formals
         (let-values-helper1
           assocs
           bindings
           body1 body2 ...))))
    ((let-values-helper2
       (first . rest)
       (temp ...)
       expr1
       (assoc ...)
       bindings
       body1 body2 ...)
```

```
    (let-values-helper2
      rest
      (temp ... newtemp)
      expr1
      (assoc ... (first newtemp))
      bindings
      body1 body2 ...))
  ((let-values-helper2
     rest-formal
     (temp ...)
     expr1
     (assoc ...)
     bindings
     body1 body2 ...)
   (call-with-values
     (lambda () expr1)
     (lambda (temp ... . newtemp)
       (let-values-helper1
         (assoc ... (rest-formal newtemp))
         bindings
         body1 body2 ...))))))
```

let*-values

The following macro defines `let*-values` in terms of `let` and `let-values` using `syntax-rules`:

```
(define-syntax let*-values
  (syntax-rules ()
    ((let*-values () body1 body2 ...)
     (let () body1 body2 ...))
    ((let*-values (binding1 binding2 ...)
       body1 body2 ...)
     (let-values (binding1)
       (let*-values (binding2 ...)
         body1 body2 ...)))))
```

let

The `let` keyword could be defined in terms of `lambda` and `letrec` using `syntax-rules` as follows:

```
(define-syntax let
  (syntax-rules ()
    ((let ((name val) ...) body1 body2 ...)
     ((lambda (name ...) body1 body2 ...)
```

```
     val ...))
   ((let tag ((name val) ...) body1 body2 ...)
   ((letrec ((tag (lambda (name ...)
                    body1 body2 ...)))
       tag)
   val ...))))
```

C Additional material

This report itself, as well as more material related to this report such as reference implementations of some parts of Scheme and archives of mailing lists discussing this report is at

http://www.r6rs.org/

The Schemers web site at

http://www.schemers.org/

as well as the Readscheme site at

http://library.readscheme.org/

contain extensive Scheme bibliographies, as well as papers, programs, implementations, and other material related to Scheme.

D Example

This section describes an example consisting of the (runge-kutta) library, which provides an integrate-system procedure that integrates the system

$$y'_k = f_k(y_1, y_2, \ldots, y_n), \ k = 1, \ldots, n$$

of differential equations with the method of Runge-Kutta.

As the (runge-kutta) library makes use of the (rnrs base (6)) library, its skeleton is as follows:

```
#!r6rs
(library (runge-kutta)
  (export integrate-system
          head tail)
  (import (rnrs base))
  ⟨library body⟩)
```

The procedure definitions described below go in the place of ⟨library body⟩.

The parameter system-derivative is a function that takes a system state (a vector of values for the state variables $y_1, \ldots, y_n$) and produces a system derivative (the values $y'_1, \ldots, y'_n$). The parameter initial-state provides an initial system state, and h is an initial guess for the length of the integration step.

The value returned by integrate-system is an infinite stream of system states.

```
(define integrate-system
  (lambda (system-derivative initial-state h)
    (let ((next (runge-kutta-4 system-derivative h)))
      (letrec ((states
                 (cons initial-state
                       (lambda ()
                         (map-streams next states)))))
        states))))
```

The `runge-kutta-4` procedure takes a function, `f`, that produces a system derivative from a system state. The `runge-kutta-4` procedure produces a function that
takes a system state and produces a new system state.

```
(define runge-kutta-4
  (lambda (f h)
    (let ((*h (scale-vector h))
          (*2 (scale-vector 2))
          (*1/2 (scale-vector (/ 1 2)))
          (*1/6 (scale-vector (/ 1 6))))
      (lambda (y)
        ;; y is a system state
        (let* ((k0 (*h (f y)))
               (k1 (*h (f (add-vectors y (*1/2 k0)))))
               (k2 (*h (f (add-vectors y (*1/2 k1)))))
               (k3 (*h (f (add-vectors y k2)))))
          (add-vectors y
            (*1/6 (add-vectors k0
                               (*2 k1)
                               (*2 k2)
                               k3)))))))))


(define elementwise
  (lambda (f)
    (lambda vectors
      (generate-vector
        (vector-length (car vectors))
        (lambda (i)
          (apply f
                 (map (lambda (v) (vector-ref  v i))
                      vectors)))))))

(define generate-vector
  (lambda (size proc)
    (let ((ans (make-vector size)))
      (letrec ((loop
                 (lambda (i)
```

```
                    (cond ((= i size) ans)
                          (else
                           (vector-set! ans i (proc i))
                           (loop (+ i 1)))))))))
        (loop 0)))))

(define add-vectors (elementwise +))

(define scale-vector
  (lambda (s)
    (elementwise (lambda (x) (* x s)))))
```

The map-streams procedure is analogous to map: it applies its first argument (a procedure) to all the elements of its second argument (a stream).

```
(define map-streams
  (lambda (f s)
    (cons (f (head s))
          (lambda () (map-streams f (tail s)))))))
```

Infinite streams are implemented as pairs whose car holds the first element of the stream and whose cdr holds a procedure that delivers the rest of the stream.

```
(define head car)
(define tail
  (lambda (stream) ((cdr stream))))
```

The following program illustrates the use of integrate-system in integrating the system

$$C\frac{dv_C}{dt} = -i_L - \frac{v_C}{R}$$

$$L\frac{di_L}{dt} = v_C$$

which models a damped oscillator.

```
#!r6rs
(import (rnrs base)
        (rnrs io simple)
        (runge-kutta))

(define damped-oscillator
  (lambda (R L C)
    (lambda (state)
      (let ((Vc (vector-ref state 0))
            (Il (vector-ref state 1)))
        (vector (- 0 (+ (/ Vc (* R C)) (/ Il C)))
                (/ Vc L))))))
```

```
(define the-states
  (integrate-system
    (damped-oscillator 10000 1000 .001)
    '#(1 0)
    .01))

(letrec ((loop (lambda (s)
                 (newline)
                 (write (head s))
                 (loop (tail s)))))
  (loop the-states))

(close-output-port (current-output-port))
```

This prints output like the following:

```
#(1 0)
#(0.99895054 9.994835e-6)
#(0.99780226 1.9978681e-5)
#(0.9965554 2.9950552e-5)
#(0.9952102 3.990946e-5)
#(0.99376684 4.985443e-5)
#(0.99222565 5.9784474e-5)
#(0.9905868 6.969862e-5)
#(0.9888506 7.9595884e-5)
#(0.9870173 8.94753e-5)
```

E Language changes

This chapter describes most of the changes that have been made to Scheme since the "Revised⁵ Report" (Kelsey *et al.*, 1998) was published:

- Scheme source code now uses the Unicode character set. Specifically, the character set that can be used for identifiers has been greatly expanded.
- Identifiers can now start with the characters ->.
- Identifiers and symbol literals are now case-sensitive.
- Identifiers and representations of characters, booleans, number objects, and . must be explicitly delimited.
- # is now a delimiter.
- Bytevector literal syntax has been added.
- Matched square brackets can be used synonymously with parentheses.
- The read-syntax abbreviations #' (for syntax), #` (for quasisyntax), #, (for unsyntax), and #,@ (for unsyntax-splicing have been added; see section 4.3.5.)

identifier	moved to	identifier	moved to
assoc	lists	inexact->exact	r5rs
assv	lists	member	lists
assq	lists	memv	lists
call-with-input-file	io simple	memq	lists
call-with-output-file	io simple	modulo	r5rs
char-upcase	unicode	newline	io simple
char-downcase	unicode	null-environment	r5rs
char-ci=?	unicode	open-input-file	io simple
char-ci<?	unicode	open-output-file	io simple
char-ci>?	unicode	peek-char	io simple
char-ci<=?	unicode	quotient	r5rs
char-ci>=?	unicode	read	io simple
char-alphabetic?	unicode	read-char	io simple
char-numeric?	unicode	remainder	r5rs
char-whitespace?	unicode	scheme-report-environment	r5rs
char-upper-case?	unicode	set-car!	mutable-pairs
char-lower-case?	unicode	set-cdr!	mutable-pairs
close-input-port	io simple	string-ci=?	unicode
close-output-port	io simple	string-ci<?	unicode
current-input-port	io simple	string-ci>?	unicode
current-output-port	io simple	string-ci<=?	unicode
display	io simple	string-ci>=?	unicode
do	control	string-set!	mutable-strings
eof-object?	io simple	string-fill!	mutable-strings
eval	eval	with-input-from-file	io simple
delay	r5rs	with-output-to-file	io simple
exact->inexact	r5rs	write	io simple
force	r5rs	write-char	io simple

Fig. A.1. Identifiers moved to libraries

- # can no longer be used in place of digits in number representations.
- The external representation of number objects can now include a mantissa width.
- Literals for NaNs and infinities were added.
- String and character literals can now use a variety of escape sequences.
- Block and datum comments have been added.
- The #!r6rs comment for marking report-compliant lexical syntax has been added.
- Characters are now specified to correspond to Unicode scalar values.
- Many of the procedures and syntactic forms of the language are now part of the (rnrs base (6)) library. Some procedures and syntactic forms have been moved to other libraries; see figure A.1. In the "moved to" column, an entry x means that the identifier has moved to (rnrs x (6)).
- The base language has the following new procedures and syntactic forms: letrec*, let-values, let*-values, real-valued?, rational-valued?, integer-valued?, exact, inexact, finite?, infinite?, nan?, div, mod, div-and-mod, div0, mod0, div0-and-mod0, exact-integer-sqrt, boolean=?, symbol=?, string-for-each, vector-map, vector-for-each, error, assertion-violation, assert, call/cc, identifier-syntax.
- The following procedures have been removed: char-ready?, transcript-on, transcript-off, load.
- The case-insensitive string comparisons (string-ci=?, string-ci<?, string-

`ci>?`, `string-ci<=?`, `string-ci>=?`) operate on the case-folded versions of the strings rather than as the simple lexicographic ordering induced by the corresponding character comparison procedures.

- Libraries have been added to the language.
- A number of standard libraries are described in a separate report (Sperber *et al.*, 2007a).
- Many situations that "were an error" now have defined or constrained behavior. In particular, many are now specified in terms of the exception system.
- The full numerical tower is now required.
- The semantics for the transcendental functions has been specified more fully.
- The semantics of `expt` for zero bases has been refined.
- In `syntax-rules` forms, a _ may be used in place of the keyword.
- The `let-syntax` and `letrec-syntax` no longer introduce a new environment for their bodies.
- For implementations that support NaNs or infinities, many arithmetic operations have been specified on these values consistently with IEEE 754.
- For implementations that support a distinct -0.0, the semantics of many arithmetic operations with regard to -0.0 has been specified consistently with IEEE 754.
- Scheme's real number objects now have an exact zero as their imaginary part.
- The specification of `quasiquote` has been extended. Nested quasiquotations work correctly now, and `unquote` and `unquote-splicing` have been extended to several operands.
- Procedures now may or may not refer to locations. Consequently, `eqv?` is now unspecified in a few cases where it was specified before.
- The mutability of the values of `quasiquote` structures has been specified to some degree.
- The dynamic environment of the *before* and *after* procedures of `dynamic-wind` is now specified.
- Various expressions that have only side effects are now allowed to return an arbitrary number of values.
- The order and semantics for macro expansion has been more fully specified.
- Internal definitions are now defined in terms of `letrec*`.
- The old notion of program structure and Scheme's top-level environment has been replaced by top-level programs and libraries.
- The denotational semantics has been replaced by an operational semantics based on an earlier semantics for the language of the "Revised[5] Report" (Kelsey *et al.*, 1998; Matthews & Findler, 2007).

PART TWO
Standard Libraries

Abstract
The report gives a defining description of the standard libraries of the programming language Scheme.

This report frequently refers back to the *Revised*[6] *Report on the Algorithmic Language Scheme*; references to the report are identified by designations such as "report section" or "report chapter".

---

1 Unicode

The procedures exported by the (rnrs unicode (6)) library provide access to some aspects of the Unicode semantics for characters and strings: category information, case-independent comparisons, case mappings, and normalization (Unicode Consortium, 2007).

Some of the procedures that operate on characters or strings ignore the difference between upper case and lower case. These procedures have "-ci" (for "case insensitive") embedded in their names.

1.1 Characters

(char-upcase *char*)	procedure
(char-downcase *char*)	procedure
(char-titlecase *char*)	procedure
(char-foldcase *char*)	procedure

These procedures take a character argument and return a character result. If the argument is an upper-case or title-case character, and if there is a single character that is its lower-case form, then char-downcase returns that character. If the argument is a lower-case or title-case character, and there is a single character that is its upper-case form, then char-upcase returns that character. If the argument is a lower-case or upper-case character, and there is a single character that is its title-case form, then char-titlecase returns that character. If the argument is not a title-case character and there is no single character that is its title-case form, then char-titlecase returns the upper-case form of the argument. Finally, if the character has a case-folded character, then char-foldcase returns that character. Otherwise the character returned is the same as the argument. For Turkic characters İ (#\x130) and ı (#\x131), char-foldcase behaves as the identity function; otherwise char-foldcase is the same as char-downcase composed with char-upcase.

```
(char-upcase #\i)        ⟹ #\I
(char-downcase #\i)      ⟹ #\i
(char-titlecase #\i)     ⟹ #\I
```

```
(char-foldcase #\i)                    ⟹ #\i

(char-upcase #\ß)                       ⟹ #\ß
(char-downcase #\ß)                     ⟹ #\ß
(char-titlecase #\ß)                    ⟹ #\ß
(char-foldcase #\ß)                     ⟹ #\ß

(char-upcase #\Σ)                       ⟹ #\Σ
(char-downcase #\Σ)                     ⟹ #\σ
(char-titlecase #\Σ)                    ⟹ #\Σ
(char-foldcase #\Σ)                     ⟹ #\σ

(char-upcase #\ς)                       ⟹ #\Σ
(char-downcase #\ς)                     ⟹ #\ς
(char-titlecase #\ς)                    ⟹ #\Σ
(char-foldcase #\ς)                     ⟹ #\σ
```

Note: Note that char-titlecase does not always return a title-case character.

Note: These procedures are consistent with Unicode's locale-independent mappings from scalar values to scalar values for upcase, downcase, titlecase, and case-folding operations. These mappings can be extracted from UnicodeData.txt and CaseFolding.txt from the Unicode Consortium, ignoring Turkic mappings in the latter.

Note that these character-based procedures are an incomplete approximation to case conversion, even ignoring the user's locale. In general, case mappings require the context of a string, both in arguments and in result. The string-upcase, string-downcase, string-titlecase, and string-foldcase procedures (section 1.2) perform more general case conversion.

(char-ci=? *char₁* *char₂* *char₃* ...)   procedure
(char-ci<? *char₁* *char₂* *char₃* ...)   procedure
(char-ci>? *char₁* *char₂* *char₃* ...)   procedure
(char-ci<=? *char₁* *char₂* *char₃* ...)   procedure
(char-ci>=? *char₁* *char₂* *char₃* ...)   procedure

These procedures are similar to char=?, etc., but operate on the case-folded versions of the characters.

```
(char-ci<? #\z #\Z)                     ⟹ #f
(char-ci=? #\z #\Z)                     ⟹ #t
(char-ci=? #\ς #\σ)                     ⟹ #t
```

(char-alphabetic? *char*)   procedure
(char-numeric? *char*)   procedure
(char-whitespace? *char*)   procedure

(char-upper-case? *char*)   procedure
(char-lower-case? *char*)   procedure
(char-title-case? *char*)   procedure

These procedures return #t if their arguments are alphabetic, numeric, whitespace, upper-case, lower-case, or title-case characters, respectively; otherwise they return #f.

A character is alphabetic if it has the Unicode "Alphabetic" property. A character is numeric if it has the Unicode "Numeric" property. A character is whitespace if has the Unicode "White_Space" property. A character is upper case if it has the Unicode "Uppercase" property, lower case if it has the "Lowercase" property, and title case if it is in the Lt general category.

```
(char-alphabetic? #\a)          ⟹ #t
(char-numeric? #\1)             ⟹ #t
(char-whitespace? #\space)      ⟹ #t
(char-whitespace? #\x00A0)      ⟹ #t
(char-upper-case? #\Σ)          ⟹ #t
(char-lower-case? #\σ)          ⟹ #t
(char-lower-case? #\x00AA)      ⟹ #t
(char-title-case? #\I)          ⟹ #f
(char-title-case? #\x01C5)      ⟹ #t
```

(char-general-category *char*)   procedure

Returns a symbol representing the Unicode general category of *char*, one of Lu, Ll, Lt, Lm, Lo, Mn, Mc, Me, Nd, Nl, No, Ps, Pe, Pi, Pf, Pd, Pc, Po, Sc, Sm, Sk, So, Zs, Zp, Zl, Cc, Cf, Cs, Co, or Cn.

```
(char-general-category #\a)     ⟹ Ll
(char-general-category #\space) ⟹ Zs
(char-general-category #\x10FFFF) ⟹ Cn
```

1.2 Strings

(string-upcase *string*)   procedure
(string-downcase *string*)   procedure
(string-titlecase *string*)   procedure
(string-foldcase *string*)   procedure

These procedures take a string argument and return a string result. They are defined in terms of Unicode's locale-independent case mappings from Unicode scalar-value sequences to scalar-value sequences. In particular, the length of the result string can be different from the length of the input string. When the specified result is equal in the sense of string=? to the argument, these procedures may return the argument instead of a newly allocated string.

The `string-upcase` procedure converts a string to upper case; `string-downcase` converts a string to lower case. The `string-foldcase` procedure converts the string to its case-folded counterpart, using the full case-folding mapping, but without the special mappings for Turkic languages. The `string-titlecase` procedure converts the first cased character of each word, and downcases all other cased characters.

```
(string-upcase "Hi")            ⟹ "HI"
(string-downcase "Hi")          ⟹ "hi"
(string-foldcase "Hi")          ⟹ "hi"

(string-upcase "Straße")        ⟹ "STRASSE"
(string-downcase "Straße")      ⟹ "straße"
(string-foldcase "Straße")      ⟹ "strasse"
(string-downcase "STRASSE")     ⟹ "strasse"

(string-downcase "Σ")           ⟹ "σ"

; Chi Alpha Omicron Sigma:
(string-upcase "ΧΑΟΣ")          ⟹ "ΧΑΟΣ"
(string-downcase "ΧΑΟΣ")        ⟹ "χαος"
(string-downcase "ΧΑΟΣΣ")       ⟹ "χαοσς"
(string-downcase "ΧΑΟΣ Σ")      ⟹ "χαος σ"
(string-foldcase "ΧΑΟΣΣ")       ⟹ "χαοσσ"
(string-upcase "χαος")          ⟹ "ΧΑΟΣ"
(string-upcase "χαοσ")          ⟹ "ΧΑΟΣ"

(string-titlecase "kNock KNoCK")
                                ⟹ "Knock Knock"
(string-titlecase "who's there?")
                                ⟹ "Who's There?"
(string-titlecase "r6rs")       ⟹ "R6rs"
(string-titlecase "r6rs")       ⟹ "R6rs"
```

Note: The case mappings needed for implementing these procedures can be extracted from `UnicodeData.txt`, `SpecialCasing.txt`, `WordBreakProperty.txt`, and `CaseFolding.txt` from the Unicode Consortium.

Since these procedures are locale-independent, they may not be appropriate for some locales.

Note: Word breaking, as needed for the correct casing of Σ and for `string-titlecase`, is specified in Unicode Standard Annex #29 (Davis, 2006).

```
(string-ci=? string₁ string₂ string₃ ...)                    procedure
(string-ci<? string₁ string₂ string₃ ...)                    procedure
(string-ci>? string₁ string₂ string₃ ...)                    procedure
```

```
(string-ci<=? string₁ string₂ string₃ ...)                    procedure
(string-ci>=? string₁ string₂ string₃ ...)                    procedure
```

These procedures are similar to `string=?`, etc., but operate on the case-folded versions of the strings.

```
(string-ci<? "z" "Z")                    ⟹ #f
(string-ci=? "z" "Z")                    ⟹ #t
(string-ci=? "Straße" "Strasse")
                                         ⟹ #t
(string-ci=? "Straße" "STRASSE")
                                         ⟹ #t
(string-ci=? "ΧΑΟΣ" "χαοσ")
                                         ⟹ #t
```

```
(string-normalize-nfd string)                                 procedure
(string-normalize-nfkd string)                                procedure
(string-normalize-nfc string)                                 procedure
(string-normalize-nfkc string)                                procedure
```

These procedures take a string argument and return a string result, which is the input string normalized to Unicode normalization form D, KD, C, or KC, respectively. When the specified result is equal in the sense of `string=?` to the argument, these procedures may return the argument instead of a newly allocated string.

```
(string-normalize-nfd "\xE9;")
                                    ⟹ "\x65;\x301;"
(string-normalize-nfc "\xE9;")
                                    ⟹ "\xE9;"
(string-normalize-nfd "\x65;\x301;")
                                    ⟹ "\x65;\x301;"
(string-normalize-nfc "\x65;\x301;")
                                    ⟹ "\xE9;"
```

2 Bytevectors

Many applications deal with blocks of binary data by accessing them in various ways—extracting signed or unsigned numbers of various sizes. Therefore, the (`rnrs bytevectors (6)`) library provides a single type for blocks of binary data with multiple ways to access that data. It deals with integers and floating-point representations in various sizes with specified endianness.

Bytevectors are objects of a disjoint type. Conceptually, a bytevector represents a sequence of 8-bit bytes. The description of bytevectors uses the term *byte* for an exact integer object in the interval $\{-128, \ldots, 127\}$ and the term *octet* for an exact integer object in the interval $\{0, \ldots, 255\}$. A byte corresponds to its two's complement representation as an octet.

The length of a bytevector is the number of bytes it contains. This number is fixed. A valid index into a bytevector is an exact, non-negative integer object less than the length of the bytevector. The first byte of a bytevector has index 0; the last byte has an index one less than the length of the bytevector.

Generally, the access procedures come in different flavors according to the size of the represented integer and the endianness of the representation. The procedures also distinguish signed and unsigned representations. The signed representations all use two's complement.

Like string literals, literals representing bytevectors do not need to be quoted:

    #vu8(12 23 123)   ⟹ #vu8(12 23 123)

2.1 Endianness

Many operations described in this chapter accept an *endianness* argument. Endianness describes the encoding of exact integer objects as several contiguous bytes in a bytevector (Cohen, 1980). For this purpose, the binary representation of the integer object is split into consecutive bytes. The little-endian encoding places the least significant byte of an integer first, with the other bytes following in increasing order of significance. The big-endian encoding places the most significant byte of an integer first, with the other bytes following in decreasing order of significance.

This terminology also applies to IEEE-754 numbers: IEEE 754 describes how to represent a floating-point number as an exact integer object, and endianness describes how the bytes of such an integer are laid out in a bytevector.
Note: Little- and big-endianness are only the most common kinds of endianness. Some architectures distinguish between the endianness at different levels of a binary representation.

2.2 General operations

(endianness ⟨endianness symbol⟩)   syntax
The name of ⟨endianness symbol⟩ must be a symbol describing an endianness. An implementation must support at least the symbols big and little, but may support other endianness symbols. (endianness ⟨endianness symbol⟩) evaluates to the symbol named ⟨endianness symbol⟩. Whenever one of the procedures operating on bytevectors accepts an endianness as an argument, that argument must be one of these symbols. It is a syntax violation for ⟨endianness symbol⟩ to be anything other than an endianness symbol supported by the implementation.
Note: Implementors should use widely accepted designations for endianness symbols other than big and little.
Note: Only the name of ⟨endianness symbol⟩ is significant.

(native-endianness)   procedure
Returns the endianness symbol associated implementation's preferred endian-

ness (usually that of the underlying machine architecture). This may be any ⟨endianness symbol⟩, including a symbol other than big and little.

(bytevector? *obj*)   procedure
    Returns #t if *obj* is a bytevector, otherwise returns #f.

(make-bytevector *k*)   procedure
(make-bytevector *k* *fill*)   procedure
    Returns a newly allocated bytevector of *k* bytes.

    If the *fill* argument is missing, the initial contents of the returned bytevector are unspecified.

    If the *fill* argument is present, it must be an exact integer object in the interval $\{-128, \ldots 255\}$ that specifies the initial value for the bytes of the bytevector: If *fill* is positive, it is interpreted as an octet; if it is negative, it is interpreted as a byte.

(bytevector-length *bytevector*)   procedure
    Returns, as an exact integer object, the number of bytes in *bytevector*.

(bytevector=? *bytevector₁* *bytevector₂*)   procedure
    Returns #t if *bytevector₁* and *bytevector₂* are equal—that is, if they have the same length and equal bytes at all valid indices. It returns #f otherwise.

(bytevector-fill! *bytevector* *fill*)   procedure
    The *fill* argument is as in the description of the make-bytevector procedure. The bytevector-fill! procedure stores *fill* in every element of *bytevector* and returns unspecified values. Analogous to vector-fill!.

(bytevector-copy! *source* *source-start*   procedure
     target *target-start* *k*)
Source and *target* must be bytevectors. *Source-start*, *target-start*, and *k* must be non-negative exact integer objects that satisfy

$$0 \leq \textit{source-start} \leq \textit{source-start} + k \leq l_{source}$$
$$0 \leq \textit{target-start} \leq \textit{target-start} + k \leq l_{target}$$

where l_{source} is the length of *source* and l_{target} is the length of *target*.

    The bytevector-copy! procedure copies the bytes from *source* at indices

$$\textit{source-start}, \ldots, \textit{source-start} + k - 1$$

to consecutive indices in *target* starting at *target-index*.

    This must work even if the memory regions for the source and the target overlap, i.e., the bytes at the target location after the copy must be equal to the bytes at the source location before the copy.

    This returns unspecified values.

```
(let ((b (u8-list->bytevector '(1 2 3 4 5 6 7 8))))
    (bytevector-copy! b 0 b 3 4)
    (bytevector->u8-list b))        ⟹  (1 2 3 1 2 3 4 8)
```

(bytevector-copy *bytevector*) procedure

Returns a newly allocated copy of *bytevector*.

2.3 Operations on bytes and octets

(bytevector-u8-ref *bytevector k*) procedure
(bytevector-s8-ref *bytevector k*) procedure
K must be a valid index of *bytevector*.

The bytevector-u8-ref procedure returns the byte at index *k* of *bytevector*, as an octet.

The bytevector-s8-ref procedure returns the byte at index *k* of *bytevector*, as a (signed) byte.

```
(let ((b1 (make-bytevector 16 -127))
      (b2 (make-bytevector 16 255)))
  (list
    (bytevector-s8-ref b1 0)
    (bytevector-u8-ref b1 0)
    (bytevector-s8-ref b2 0)
    (bytevector-u8-ref b2 0)))     ⟹ (-127 129 -1 255)
```

(bytevector-u8-set! *bytevector k octet*) procedure
(bytevector-s8-set! *bytevector k byte*) procedure
K must be a valid index of *bytevector*.

The bytevector-u8-set! procedure stores *octet* in element *k* of *bytevector*.

The bytevector-s8-set! procedure stores the two's-complement representation of *byte* in element *k* of *bytevector*.

Both procedures return unspecified values.

```
(let ((b (make-bytevector 16 -127)))

  (bytevector-s8-set! b 0 -126)
  (bytevector-u8-set! b 1 246)

  (list
    (bytevector-s8-ref b 0)
    (bytevector-u8-ref b 0)
    (bytevector-s8-ref b 1)
    (bytevector-u8-ref b 1)))     ⟹ (-126 130 -10 246)
```

(bytevector->u8-list *bytevector*) procedure
(u8-list->bytevector *list*) procedure
List must be a list of octets.

The `bytevector->u8-list` procedure returns a newly allocated list of the octets of *bytevector* in the same order.

The `u8-list->bytevector` procedure returns a newly allocated bytevector whose elements are the elements of list *list*, in the same order. It is analogous to `list->vector`.

2.4 Operations on integers of arbitrary size

(`bytevector-uint-ref` *bytevector k endianness size*)   procedure
(`bytevector-sint-ref` *bytevector k endianness size*)   procedure
(`bytevector-uint-set!` *bytevector k n endianness size*)   procedure
(`bytevector-sint-set!` *bytevector k n endianness size*)   procedure

Size must be a positive exact integer object. $K,\ldots,k+size-1$ must be valid indices of *bytevector*.

The `bytevector-uint-ref` procedure retrieves the exact integer object corresponding to the unsigned representation of size *size* and specified by *endianness* at indices $k,\ldots,k+size-1$.

The `bytevector-sint-ref` procedure retrieves the exact integer object corresponding to the two's-complement representation of size *size* and specified by *endianness* at indices $k,\ldots,k+size-1$.

For `bytevector-uint-set!`, *n* must be an exact integer object in the interval $\{0,\ldots,256^{size}-1\}$.

The `bytevector-uint-set!` procedure stores the unsigned representation of size *size* and specified by *endianness* into *bytevector* at indices $k,\ldots,k+size-1$.

For `bytevector-sint-set!`, *n* must be an exact integer object in the interval $\{-256^{size}/2,\ldots,256^{size}/2-1\}$. `bytevector-sint-set!` stores the two's-complement representation of size *size* and specified by *endianness* into *bytevector* at indices $k,\ldots,k+size-1$.

The `...-set!` procedures return unspecified values.

```
(define b (make-bytevector 16 -127))

(bytevector-uint-set! b 0 (- (expt 2 128) 3)
                      (endianness little) 16)

(bytevector-uint-ref b 0 (endianness little) 16)
    ⟹ #xfffffffffffffffffffffffffffffffd

(bytevector-sint-ref b 0 (endianness little) 16)
    ⟹ -3

(bytevector->u8-list b)
    ⟹ (253 255 255 255 255 255 255 255
        255 255 255 255 255 255 255 255)
```

```
(bytevector-uint-set! b 0 (- (expt 2 128) 3)
                      (endianness big) 16)
(bytevector-uint-ref b 0 (endianness big) 16)
        ⟹ #xfffffffffffffffffffffffffffffffffffd
```

```
(bytevector-sint-ref b 0 (endianness big) 16)
        ⟹ -3
```

```
(bytevector->u8-list b)
        ⟹ (255 255 255 255 255 255 255 255
           255 255 255 255 255 255 255 253))
```

(bytevector->uint-list *bytevector endianness size*)   procedure
(bytevector->sint-list *bytevector endianness size*)   procedure
(uint-list->bytevector *list endianness size*)   procedure
(sint-list->bytevector *list endianness size*)   procedure

Size must be a positive exact integer object. For uint-list->bytevector, *list* must be a list of exact integer objects in the interval $\{0, \ldots, 256^{size} - 1\}$. For sint-list->bytevector, *list* must be a list of exact integer objects in the interval $\{-256^{size}/2, \ldots, 256^{size}/2 - 1\}$. The length of *bytevector* must be divisible by *size*.

These procedures convert between lists of integer objects and their consecutive representations according to *size* and *endianness* in the *bytevector* objects in the same way as bytevector->u8-list and u8-list->bytevector do for one-byte representations.

```
(let ((b (u8-list->bytevector '(1 2 3 255 1 2 1 2))))
    (bytevector->sint-list b (endianness little) 2))
        ⟹ (513 -253 513 513)
```

```
(let ((b (u8-list->bytevector '(1 2 3 255 1 2 1 2))))
    (bytevector->uint-list b (endianness little) 2))
        ⟹ (513 65283 513 513)
```

2.5 Operations on 16-bit integers

(bytevector-u16-ref *bytevector k endianness*)   procedure
(bytevector-s16-ref *bytevector k endianness*)   procedure
(bytevector-u16-native-ref *bytevector k*)   procedure
(bytevector-s16-native-ref *bytevector k*)   procedure
(bytevector-u16-set! *bytevector k n endianness*)   procedure
(bytevector-s16-set! *bytevector k n endianness*)   procedure

(bytevector-u16-native-set! *bytevector* *k* *n*)   procedure
(bytevector-s16-native-set! *bytevector* *k* *n*)   procedure

K must be a valid index of *bytevector*; so must $k + 1$. For bytevector-u16-set!
and bytevector-u16-native-set!, *n* must be an exact integer object in the interval
$\{0, \ldots, 2^{16} - 1\}$. For bytevector-s16-set! and bytevector-s16-native-set!, *n*
must be an exact integer object in the interval $\{-2^{15}, \ldots, 2^{15} - 1\}$.

These retrieve and set two-byte representations of numbers at indices k and $k + 1$,
according to the endianness specified by *endianness*. The procedures with u16 in
their names deal with the unsigned representation; those with s16 in their names
deal with the two's-complement representation.

The procedures with native in their names employ the native endianness, and
work only at aligned indices: k must be a multiple of 2.

The ...-set! procedures return unspecified values.

```
(define b
  (u8-list->bytevector
    '(255 255 255 255 255 255 255 255
      255 255 255 255 255 255 255 253)))

(bytevector-u16-ref b 14 (endianness little))
        ⟹ 65023
(bytevector-s16-ref b 14 (endianness little))
        ⟹ -513
(bytevector-u16-ref b 14 (endianness big))
        ⟹ 65533
(bytevector-s16-ref b 14 (endianness big))
        ⟹ -3

(bytevector-u16-set! b 0 12345 (endianness little))
(bytevector-u16-ref b 0 (endianness little))
        ⟹ 12345

(bytevector-u16-native-set! b 0 12345)
(bytevector-u16-native-ref b 0)    ⟹ 12345

(bytevector-u16-ref b 0 (endianness little))
        ⟹ unspecified
```

2.6 Operations on 32-bit integers

(bytevector-u32-ref *bytevector* *k* *endianness*)   procedure
(bytevector-s32-ref *bytevector* *k* *endianness*)   procedure
(bytevector-u32-native-ref *bytevector* *k*)   procedure
(bytevector-s32-native-ref *bytevector* *k*)   procedure

(bytevector-u32-set! *bytevector k n endianness*)   procedure
(bytevector-s32-set! *bytevector k n endianness*)   procedure
(bytevector-u32-native-set! *bytevector k n*)   procedure
(bytevector-s32-native-set! *bytevector k n*)   procedure

$K, \ldots, k+3$ must be valid indices of *bytevector*. For bytevector-u32-set! and bytevector-u32-native-set!, n must be an exact integer object in the interval $\{0, \ldots, 2^{32} - 1\}$. For bytevector-s32-set! and bytevector-s32-native-set!, n must be an exact integer object in the interval $\{-2^{31}, \ldots, 2^{32} - 1\}$.

These retrieve and set four-byte representations of numbers at indices $k, \ldots, k+3$, according to the endianness specified by *endianness*. The procedures with u32 in their names deal with the unsigned representation; those with s32 with the two's-complement representation.

The procedures with native in their names employ the native endianness, and work only at aligned indices: k must be a multiple of 4.

The ... -set! procedures return unspecified values.

```
(define b
  (u8-list->bytevector
    '(255 255 255 255 255 255 255 255
      255 255 255 255 255 255 255 253)))
```

(bytevector-u32-ref b 12 (endianness little))
       $\Longrightarrow$ 4261412863
(bytevector-s32-ref b 12 (endianness little))
       $\Longrightarrow$ -33554433
(bytevector-u32-ref b 12 (endianness big))
       $\Longrightarrow$ 4294967293
(bytevector-s32-ref b 12 (endianness big))
       $\Longrightarrow$ -3

2.7 Operations on 64-bit integers

(bytevector-u64-ref *bytevector k endianness*)   procedure
(bytevector-s64-ref *bytevector k endianness*)   procedure
(bytevector-u64-native-ref *bytevector k*)   procedure
(bytevector-s64-native-ref *bytevector k*)   procedure
(bytevector-u64-set! *bytevector k n endianness*)   procedure
(bytevector-s64-set! *bytevector k n endianness*)   procedure
(bytevector-u64-native-set! *bytevector k n*)   procedure
(bytevector-s64-native-set! *bytevector k n*)   procedure

$K, \ldots, k+7$ must be valid indices of *bytevector*. For bytevector-u64-set! and bytevector-u64-native-set!, n must be an exact integer object in the interval $\{0, \ldots, 2^{64} - 1\}$. For bytevector-s64-set! and bytevector-s64-native-set!, n must be an exact integer object in the interval $\{-2^{63}, \ldots, 2^{64} - 1\}$.

These retrieve and set eight-byte representations of numbers at indices $k, \ldots, k+7$, according to the endianness specified by *endianness*. The procedures with u64 in their names deal with the unsigned representation; those with s64 with the two's-complement representation.

The procedures with native in their names employ the native endianness, and work only at aligned indices: k must be a multiple of 8.

The ...-set! procedures return unspecified values.

```
(define b
  (u8-list->bytevector
    '(255 255 255 255 255 255 255 255
      255 255 255 255 255 255 255 253)))

(bytevector-u64-ref b 8 (endianness little))
         ⟹ 18302628885633695743
(bytevector-s64-ref b 8 (endianness little))
         ⟹ -144115188075855873
(bytevector-u64-ref b 8 (endianness big))
         ⟹ 18446744073709551613
(bytevector-s64-ref b 8 (endianness big))
         ⟹ -3
```

2.8 Operations on IEEE-754 representations

```
(bytevector-ieee-single-native-ref bytevector k)          procedure
(bytevector-ieee-single-ref bytevector k endianness)      procedure
```
$K, \ldots, k+3$ must be valid indices of *bytevector*. For bytevector-ieee-single-native-ref, k must be a multiple of 4.

These procedures return the inexact real number object that best represents the IEEE-754 single-precision number represented by the four bytes beginning at index k.

```
(bytevector-ieee-double-native-ref bytevector k)          procedure
(bytevector-ieee-double-ref bytevector k endianness)      procedure
```
$K, \ldots, k+7$ must be valid indices of *bytevector*. For bytevector-ieee-double-native-ref, k must be a multiple of 8.

These procedures return the inexact real number object that best represents the IEEE-754 double-precision number represented by the eight bytes beginning at index k.

```
(bytevector-ieee-single-native-set! bytevector k x)       procedure
(bytevector-ieee-single-set! bytevector                   procedure
    k x endianness)
```

$K,\ldots,k+3$ must be valid indices of *bytevector*. For `bytevector-ieee-single-set!`, k must be a multiple of 4.

These procedures store an IEEE-754 single-precision representation of x into elements k through $k+3$ of *bytevector*, and return unspecified values.

(`bytevector-ieee-double-native-set!` *bytevector k x*)	procedure
(`bytevector-ieee-double-set!` *bytevector*	procedure
k x endianness)	

$K,\ldots,k+7$ must be valid indices of *bytevector*. For `bytevector-ieee-double-set!`, k must be a multiple of 8.

These procedures store an IEEE-754 double-precision representation of x into elements k through $k+7$ of *bytevector*, and return unspecified values.

2.9 Operations on strings

This section describes procedures that convert between strings and bytevectors containing Unicode encodings of those strings. When decoding bytevectors, encoding errors are handled as with the `replace` semantics of textual I/O (see section 8.2.4): If an invalid or incomplete character encoding is encountered, then the replacement character U+FFFD is appended to the string being generated, an appropriate number of bytes are ignored, and decoding continues with the following bytes.

(`string->utf8` *string*)	procedure

Returns a newly allocated (unless empty) bytevector that contains the UTF-8 encoding of the given string.

(`string->utf16` *string*)	procedure
(`string->utf16` *string endianness*)	procedure

If *endianness* is specified, it must be the symbol `big` or the symbol `little`. The `string->utf16` procedure returns a newly allocated (unless empty) bytevector that contains the UTF-16BE or UTF-16LE encoding of the given string (with no byte-order mark). If endianness is not specified or is `big`, then UTF-16BE is used. If endianness is `little`, then UTF-16LE is used.

(`string->utf32` *string*)	procedure
(`string->utf32` *string endianness*)	procedure

If *endianness* is specified, it must be the symbol `big` or the symbol `little`. The `string->utf32` procedure returns a newly allocated (unless empty) bytevector that contains the UTF-32BE or UTF-32LE encoding of the given string (with no byte mark). If endianness is not specified or is `big`, then UTF-32BE is used. If endianness is `little`, then UTF-32LE is used.

(`utf8->string` *bytevector*)	procedure

Returns a newly allocated (unless empty) string whose character sequence is encoded by the given bytevector.

(utf16->string *bytevector* *endianness*) procedure
(utf16->string *bytevector* procedure
    endianness *endianness-mandatory*)

Endianness must be the symbol big or the symbol little. The utf16->string procedure returns a newly allocated (unless empty) string whose character sequence is encoded by the given bytevector. *Bytevector* is decoded according to UTF-16, UTF-16BE, UTF-16LE, or a fourth encoding scheme that differs from all three of those as follows: If *endianness-mandatory?* is absent or #f, utf16->string determines the endianness according to a UTF-16 BOM at the beginning of *bytevector* if a BOM is present; in this case, the BOM is not decoded as a character. Also in this case, if no UTF-16 BOM is present, *endianness* specifies the endianness of the encoding. If *endianness-mandatory?* is a true value, *endianness* specifies the endianness of the encoding, and any UTF-16 BOM in the encoding is decoded as a regular character. *Note:* A UTF-16 BOM is either a sequence of bytes #xFE, #xFF specifying big and UTF-16BE, or #xFF, #xFE specifying little and UTF-16LE.

(utf32->string *bytevector* *endianness*) procedure
(utf32->string *bytevector* procedure
    endianness *endianness-mandatory*)

Endianness must be the symbol big or the symbol little. The utf32->string procedure returns a newly allocated (unless empty) string whose character sequence is encoded by the given bytevector. *Bytevector* is decoded according to UTF-32, UTF-32BE, UTF-32LE, or a fourth encoding scheme that differs from all three of those as follows: If *endianness-mandatory?* is absent or #f, utf32->string determines the endianness according to a UTF-32 BOM at the beginning of *bytevector* if a BOM is present; in this case, the BOM is not decoded as a character. Also in this case, if no UTF-32 BOM is present, *endianness* specifies the endianness of the encoding. If *endianness-mandatory?* is a true value, *endianness* specifies the endianness of the encoding, and any UTF-32 BOM in the encoding is decoded as a regular character. *Note:* A UTF-32 BOM is either a sequence of bytes #x00, #x00, #xFE, #xFF specifying big and UTF-32BE, or #xFF, #xFE, #x00, #x00, specifying little and UTF-32LE.

3 List utilities

This chapter describes the (rnrs lists (6)) library, which contains various useful procedures that operate on lists.

(find *proc* *list*) procedure

Proc should accept one argument and return a single value. *Proc* should not mutate *list*. The find procedure applies *proc* to the elements of *list* in order. If *proc* returns a true value for an element, find immediately returns that element. If *proc* returns #f for all elements of the list, find returns #f. *Proc* is always called in the same dynamic environment as find itself.

```
(find even? '(3 1 4 1 5 9))          ⟹ 4
(find even? '(3 1 5 1 5 9))          ⟹ #f
```

Implementation responsibilities: The implementation must check that *list* is a chain of pairs up to the found element, or that it is indeed a list if no element is found. It should not check that it is a chain of pairs beyond the found element. The implementation must check the restrictions on *proc* to the extent performed by applying it as described. An implementation may check whether *proc* is an appropriate argument before applying it.

(for-all *proc list$_1$ list$_2$ ... list$_n$*)   procedure
(exists *proc list$_1$ list$_2$ ... list$_n$*)   procedure

The *list*s should all have the same length, and *proc* should accept *n* arguments and return a single value. *Proc* should not mutate the *list* arguments.

For natural numbers $i = 0, 1, \ldots$, the for-all procedure successively applies *proc* to arguments $x_i^1 \ldots x_i^n$, where x_i^j is the *i*th element of *list$_j$*, until #f is returned. If *proc* returns true values for all but the last element of *list$_1$*, for-all performs a tail call of *proc* on the *k*th elements, where *k* is the length of *list$_1$*. If *proc* returns #f on any set of elements, for-all returns #f after the first such application of *proc*. If the *list*s are all empty, for-all returns #t.

For natural numbers $i = 0, 1, \ldots$, the exists procedure applies *proc* successively to arguments $x_i^1 \ldots x_i^n$, where x_i^j is the *i*th element of *list$_j$*, until a true value is returned. If *proc* returns #f for all but the last elements of the *list*s, exists performs a tail call of *proc* on the *k*th elements, where *k* is the length of *list$_1$*. If *proc* returns a true value on any set of elements, exists returns that value after the first such application of *proc*. If the *list*s are all empty, exists returns #f.

Proc is always called in the same dynamic environment as for-all or, respectively, exists itself.

```
(for-all even? '(3 1 4 1 5 9))       ⟹ #f
(for-all even? '(2 4 14))            ⟹ #t
(for-all even? '(2 4 14 . 9))        ⟹ &assertion exception
(for-all (lambda (n) (and (even? n) n))
         '(2 4 14))                  ⟹ 14
(for-all < '(1 2 3) '(2 3 4))        ⟹ #t
(for-all < '(1 2 4) '(2 3 4))        ⟹ #f

(exists even? '(3 1 4 1 5 9))        ⟹ #t
(exists even? '(3 1 1 5 9))          ⟹ #f
(exists even? '(3 1 1 5 9 . 2))      ⟹ &assertion exception
(exists (lambda (n) (and (even? n) n)) '(2 1 4 14))
         ⟹ 2
(exists < '(1 2 4) '(2 3 4))         ⟹ #t
(exists > '(1 2 3) '(2 3 4))         ⟹ #f
```

Implementation responsibilities: The implementation must check that the *list*s are chains of pairs to the extent necessary to determine the return value. If this requires traversing the lists entirely, the implementation should check that the *list*s all have the same length. If not, it should not check that the *list*s are chains of pairs beyond the traversal. The implementation must check the restrictions on *proc* to the extent performed by applying it as described. An implementation may check whether *proc* is an appropriate argument before applying it.

`(filter `*`proc`*` `*`list`*`)`   procedure
`(partition `*`proc`*` `*`list`*`)`   procedure

Proc should accept one argument and return a single value. *Proc* should not mutate *list*.

The `filter` procedure applies *proc* to each element of *list* and returns a list of the elements of *list* for which *proc* returned a true value. The `partition` procedure also applies *proc* to each element of *list*, but returns two values, the first one a list of the elements of *list* for which *proc* returned a true value, and the second a list of the elements of *list* for which *proc* returned #f. In both cases, the elements of the result list(s) are in the same order as they appear in the input list. *Proc* is always called in the same dynamic environment as `filter` or, respectively, `partition` itself. If multiple returns occur from `filter` or `partitions`, the return values returned by earlier returns are not mutated.

```
(filter even? '(3 1 4 1 5 9 2 6)) ⟹ (4 2 6)

(partition even? '(3 1 4 1 5 9 2 6))
          ⟹ (4 2 6) (3 1 1 5 9) ; two values
```

Implementation responsibilities: The implementation must check the restrictions on *proc* to the extent performed by applying it as described. An implementation may check whether *proc* is an appropriate argument before applying it.

`(fold-left `*`combine`*` `*`nil`*` `*`list`*`₁ `*`list`*`₂ ... `*`list`*`ₙ)`   procedure

The *list*s should all have the same length. *Combine* must be a procedure. It should accept one more argument than there are *list*s and return a single value. It should not mutate the *list* arguments. The `fold-left` procedure iterates the *combine* procedure over an accumulator value and the elements of the *list*s from left to right, starting with an accumulator value of *nil*. More specifically, `fold-left` returns *nil* if the *list*s are empty. If they are not empty, *combine* is first applied to *nil* and the respective first elements of the *list*s in order. The result becomes the new accumulator value, and *combine* is applied to the new accumulator value and the respective next elements of the *list*. This step is repeated until the end of the list is reached; then the accumulator value is returned. *Combine* is always called in the same dynamic environment as `fold-left` itself.

```
(fold-left + 0 '(1 2 3 4 5))              ⟹ 15

(fold-left (lambda (a e) (cons e a)) '()
           '(1 2 3 4 5))                  ⟹ (5 4 3 2 1)

(fold-left (lambda (count x)
              (if (odd? x) (+ count 1) count))
           0
           '(3 1 4 1 5 9 2 6 5 3)) ⟹ 7

(fold-left (lambda (max-len s)
              (max max-len (string-length s)))
           0
           '("longest" "long" "longer"))
           ⟹ 7

(fold-left cons '(q) '(a b c))     ⟹ ((((q) . a) . b) . c)

(fold-left + 0 '(1 2 3) '(4 5 6)) ⟹ 21
```

Implementation responsibilities: The implementation should check that the *list*s all have the same length. The implementation must check the restrictions on *combine* to the extent performed by applying it as described. An implementation may check whether *combine* is an appropriate argument before applying it.

(fold-right *combine nil list₁ list₂ ...listₙ*)   procedure
   The *list*s should all have the same length. *Combine* must be a procedure. It should accept one more argument than there are *list*s and return a single value. *Combine* should not mutate the *list* arguments. The fold-right procedure iterates the *combine* procedure over the elements of the *list*s from right to left and an accumulator value, starting with an accumulator value of *nil*. More specifically, fold-right returns *nil* if the *list*s are empty. If they are not empty, *combine* is first applied to the respective last elements of the *list*s in order and *nil*. The result becomes the new accumulator value, and *combine* is applied to the respective previous elements of the *list*s and the new accumulator value. This step is repeated until the beginning of the list is reached; then the accumulator value is returned. *Proc* is always called in the same dynamic environment as fold-right itself.

```
(fold-right + 0 '(1 2 3 4 5))             ⟹ 15

(fold-right cons '() '(1 2 3 4 5)) ⟹ (1 2 3 4 5)

(fold-right (lambda (x l)
              (if (odd? x) (cons x l) l))
           '()
```

```
          ’(3 1 4 1 5 9 2 6 5))  ⟹  (3 1 1 5 9 5)

   (fold-right cons ’(q) ’(a b c))      ⟹  (a b c q)

   (fold-right + 0 ’(1 2 3) ’(4 5 6))⟹  21
```

Implementation responsibilities: The implementation should check that the *list*s all have the same length. The implementation must check the restrictions on *combine* to the extent performed by applying it as described. An implementation may check whether *combine* is an appropriate argument before applying it.

(remp *proc list*)	procedure
(remove *obj list*)	procedure
(remv *obj list*)	procedure
(remq *obj list*)	procedure

Proc should accept one argument and return a single value. *Proc* should not mutate *list*.

Each of these procedures returns a list of the elements of *list* that do not satisfy a given condition. The remp procedure applies *proc* to each element of *list* and returns a list of the elements of *list* for which *proc* returned #f. *Proc* is always called in the same dynamic environment as remp itself. The remove, remv, and remq procedures return a list of the elements that are not *obj*. The remq procedure uses eq? to compare *obj* with the elements of *list*, while remv uses eqv? and remove uses equal?. The elements of the result list are in the same order as they appear in the input list. If multiple returns occur from remp, the return values returned by earlier returns are not mutated.

```
   (remp even? ’(3 1 4 1 5 9 2 6 5))  ⟹  (3 1 1 5 9 5)

   (remove 1 ’(3 1 4 1 5 9 2 6 5))     ⟹  (3 4 5 9 2 6 5)

   (remv 1 ’(3 1 4 1 5 9 2 6 5))       ⟹  (3 4 5 9 2 6 5)

   (remq ’foo ’(bar foo baz))          ⟹  (bar baz)
```

Implementation responsibilities: The implementation must check the restrictions on *proc* to the extent performed by applying it as described. An implementation may check whether *proc* is an appropriate argument before applying it.

(memp *proc list*)	procedure
(member *obj list*)	procedure
(memv *obj list*)	procedure
(memq *obj list*)	procedure

Proc should accept one argument and return a single value. *Proc* should not mutate *list*.

These procedures return the first sublist of *list* whose car satisfies a given condition, where the sublists of *lists* are the lists returned by (list-tail *list k*) for *k* less than the length of *list*. The memp procedure applies *proc* to the cars of the sublists of *list* until it finds one for which *proc* returns a true value. *Proc* is always called in the same dynamic environment as memp itself. The member, memv, and memq procedures look for the first occurrence of *obj*. If *list* does not contain an element satisfying the condition, then #f (not the empty list) is returned. The member procedure uses equal? to compare *obj* with the elements of *list*, while memv uses eqv? and memq uses eq?.

    (memp even? '(3 1 4 1 5 9 2 6 5)) ⟹ (4 1 5 9 2 6 5)

    (memq 'a '(a b c))   ⟹ (a b c)
    (memq 'b '(a b c))   ⟹ (b c)
    (memq 'a '(b c d))   ⟹ #f
    (memq (list 'a) '(b (a) c))   ⟹ #f
    (member (list 'a)
            '(b (a) c))   ⟹ ((a) c)
    (memq 101 '(100 101 102))   ⟹ *unspecified*
    (memv 101 '(100 101 102))   ⟹ (101 102)

Implementation responsibilities: The implementation must check that *list* is a chain of pairs up to the found element, or that it is indeed a list if no element is found. It should not check that it is a chain of pairs beyond the found element. The implementation must check the restrictions on *proc* to the extent performed by applying it as described. An implementation may check whether *proc* is an appropriate argument before applying it.

(assp *proc alist*)   procedure
(assoc *obj alist*)   procedure
(assv *obj alist*)   procedure
(assq *obj alist*)   procedure

Alist (for "association list") should be a list of pairs. *Proc* should accept one argument and return a single value. *Proc* should not mutate *alist*.

These procedures find the first pair in *alist* whose car field satisfies a given condition, and returns that pair without traversing *alist* further. If no pair in *alist* satisfies the condition, then #f is returned. The assp procedure successively applies *proc* to the car fields of *alist* and looks for a pair for which it returns a true value. *Proc* is always called in the same dynamic environment as assp itself. The assoc, assv, and assq procedures look for a pair that has *obj* as its car. The assoc procedure uses equal? to compare *obj* with the car fields of the pairs in *alist*, while assv uses eqv? and assq uses eq?.

Implementation responsibilities: The implementation must check that *alist* is a chain of pairs containing pairs up to the found pair, or that it is indeed a list of pairs if no element is found. It should not check that it is a chain of pairs beyond the found element. The implementation must check the restrictions on *proc* to the extent

performed by applying it as described. An implementation may check whether *proc*
is an appropriate argument before applying it.

```
(define d '((3 a) (1 b) (4 c)))

(assp even? d)                              ⟹ (4 c)
(assp odd? d)                               ⟹ (3 a)

(define e '((a 1) (b 2) (c 3)))
(assq 'a e)                                 ⟹ (a 1)
(assq 'b e)                                 ⟹ (b 2)
(assq 'd e)                                 ⟹ #f
(assq (list 'a) '(((a)) ((b)) ((c))))
                                            ⟹ #f
(assoc (list 'a) '(((a)) ((b)) ((c))))
                                            ⟹ ((a))
(assq 5 '((2 3) (5 7) (11 13)))
                                            ⟹ unspecified
(assv 5 '((2 3) (5 7) (11 13)))
                                            ⟹ (5 7)
```

(cons* *obj₁* ... *objₙ* *obj*)   procedure
(cons* *obj*)   procedure
 If called with at least two arguments, cons* returns a freshly allocated chain of
pairs whose cars are *obj₁*, ..., *objₙ*, and whose last cdr is *obj*. If called with only one
argument, cons* returns that argument.

```
(cons* 1 2 '(3 4 5))                        ⟹ (1 2 3 4 5)
(cons* 1 2 3)                               ⟹ (1 2 . 3)
(cons* 1)                                   ⟹ 1
```

4 Sorting

This chapter describes the (rnrs sorting (6)) library for sorting lists and vectors.

(list-sort *proc list*)   procedure
(vector-sort *proc vector*)   procedure
Proc should accept any two elements of *list* or *vector*, and should not have any side
effects. *Proc* should return a true value when its first argument is strictly less than
its second, and #f otherwise.
 The list-sort and vector-sort procedures perform a stable sort of *list* or
vector in ascending order according to *proc*, without changing *list* or *vector* in any
way. The list-sort procedure returns a list, and vector-sort returns a vector.
The results may be eq? to the argument when the argument is already sorted, and
the result of list-sort may share structure with a tail of the original list. The

sorting algorithm performs $O(n \lg n)$ calls to *proc* where n is the length of *list* or *vector*, and all arguments passed to *proc* are elements of the list or vector being sorted, but the pairing of arguments and the sequencing of calls to *proc* are not specified. If multiple returns occur from `list-sort` or `vector-sort`, the return values returned by earlier returns are not mutated.

```
(list-sort < '(3 5 2 1))            ⟹ (1 2 3 5)
(vector-sort < '#(3 5 2 1))         ⟹ #(1 2 3 5)
```

Implementation responsibilities: The implementation must check the restrictions on *proc* to the extent performed by applying it as described. An implementation may check whether *proc* is an appropriate argument before applying it.

(vector-sort! *proc vector*)   procedure
Proc should accept any two elements of the vector, and should not have any side effects. *Proc* should return a true value when its first argument is strictly less than its second, and #f otherwise. The `vector-sort!` procedure destructively sorts *vector* in ascending order according to *proc*. The sorting algorithm performs $O(n^2)$ calls to *proc* where n is the length of *vector*, and all arguments passed to *proc* are elements of the vector being sorted, but the pairing of arguments and the sequencing of calls to *proc* are not specified. The sorting algorithm may be unstable. The procedure returns unspecified values.

```
(define v (vector 3 5 2 1))
(vector-sort! < v)                  ⟹ unspecified
v                                   ⟹ #(1 2 3 5)
```

Implementation responsibilities: The implementation must check the restrictions on *proc* to the extent performed by applying it as described. An implementation may check whether *proc* is an appropriate argument before applying it.

5 Control structures

This chapter describes the (rnrs control (6)) library, which provides useful control structures.

(when ⟨test⟩ ⟨expression₁⟩ ⟨expression₂⟩ ...)   syntax
(unless ⟨test⟩ ⟨expression₁⟩ ⟨expression₂⟩ ...)   syntax
    Syntax: ⟨Test⟩ must be an expression.
    Semantics: A when expression is evaluated by evaluating the ⟨test⟩ expression. If ⟨test⟩ evaluates to a true value, the remaining ⟨expression⟩s are evaluated in order, and the results of the last ⟨expression⟩ are returned as the results of the entire when expression. Otherwise, the when expression returns unspecified values. An unless expression is evaluated by evaluating the ⟨test⟩ expression. If ⟨test⟩ evaluates to #f, the remaining ⟨expression⟩s are evaluated in order, and the results of the last

⟨expression⟩ are returned as the results of the entire `unless` expression. Otherwise, the `unless` expression returns unspecified values.

The final ⟨expression⟩ is in tail context if the `when` or `unless` form is itself in tail context.

```
(when (> 3 2) 'greater)           ⟹ greater
(when (< 3 2) 'greater)           ⟹ unspecified
(unless (> 3 2) 'less)            ⟹ unspecified
(unless (< 3 2) 'less)            ⟹ less
```

The `when` and `unless` expressions are derived forms. They could be defined by the following macros:

```
(define-syntax when
  (syntax-rules ()
    ((when test result1 result2 ...)
     (if test
         (begin result1 result2 ...)))))

(define-syntax unless
  (syntax-rules ()
    ((unless test result1 result2 ...)
     (if (not test)
         (begin result1 result2 ...)))))
```

(do ((⟨variable₁⟩ ⟨init₁⟩ ⟨step₁⟩)   syntax
     ...)
    (⟨test⟩ ⟨expression⟩ ...)
  ⟨command⟩ ...)

Syntax: The ⟨init⟩s, ⟨step⟩s, ⟨test⟩s, and ⟨command⟩s must be expressions. The ⟨variable⟩s must be pairwise distinct variables.

Semantics: The do expression is an iteration construct. It specifies a set of variables to be bound, how they are to be initialized at the start, and how they are to be updated on each iteration.

A do expression is evaluated as follows: The ⟨init⟩ expressions are evaluated (in some unspecified order), the ⟨variable⟩s are bound to fresh locations, the results of the ⟨init⟩ expressions are stored in the bindings of the ⟨variable⟩s, and then the iteration phase begins.

Each iteration begins by evaluating ⟨test⟩; if the result is #f, then the ⟨command⟩s are evaluated in order for effect, the ⟨step⟩ expressions are evaluated in some unspecified order, the ⟨variable⟩s are bound to fresh locations holding the results, and the next iteration begins.

If ⟨test⟩ evaluates to a true value, the ⟨expression⟩s are evaluated from left to right and the values of the last ⟨expression⟩ are returned. If no ⟨expression⟩s are present, then the do expression returns unspecified values.

The region of the binding of a ⟨variable⟩ consists of the entire do expression except for the ⟨init⟩s.

A ⟨step⟩ may be omitted, in which case the effect is the same as if (⟨variable⟩ ⟨init⟩ ⟨variable⟩) had been written instead of (⟨variable⟩ ⟨init⟩).

If a do expression appears in a tail context, the ⟨expression⟩s are a ⟨tail sequence⟩ in the sense of report section 11.20, i.e., the last ⟨expression⟩ is also in a tail context.

```
(do ((vec (make-vector 5))
     (i 0 (+ i 1)))
    ((= i 5) vec)
  (vector-set! vec i i))            ⟹  #(0 1 2 3 4)


(let ((x '(1 3 5 7 9)))
  (do ((x x (cdr x))
       (sum 0 (+ sum (car x))))
      ((null? x) sum)))            ⟹  25
```

The following definition of do uses a trick to expand the variable clauses.

```
(define-syntax do
  (syntax-rules ()
    ((do ((var init step ...) ...)
         (test expr ...)
       command ...)
     (letrec
       ((loop
         (lambda (var ...)
           (if test
               (begin
                 #f ; avoid empty begin
                 expr ...)
               (begin
                 command
                 ...
                 (loop (do "step" var step ...)
                   ...))))))
       (loop init ...)))
    ((do "step" x)
     x)
    ((do "step" x y)
     y)))
```

(case-lambda ⟨case-lambda clause⟩ ...)   syntax
   Syntax: Each ⟨case-lambda clause⟩ must be of the form

```
((formals) (body))
```

⟨Formals⟩ must be as in a lambda form (report section 11.4.2), and ⟨body⟩ is as described in report section 11.3.

Semantics: A case-lambda expression evaluates to a procedure. This procedure, when applied, tries to match its arguments to the ⟨case-lambda clause⟩s in order. The arguments match a clause if one of the following conditions is fulfilled:

- ⟨Formals⟩ has the form (⟨variable⟩ ...) and the number of arguments is the same as the number of formal parameters in ⟨formals⟩.
- ⟨Formals⟩ has the form
  (⟨variable$_1$⟩ ... ⟨variable$_n$⟩ . ⟨variable$_{n+1}$⟩)
  and the number of arguments is at least n.
- ⟨Formals⟩ has the form ⟨variable⟩.

For the first clause matched by the arguments, the variables of the ⟨formals⟩ are bound to fresh locations containing the argument values in the same arrangement as with lambda.

The last expression of a ⟨body⟩ in a case-lambda expression is in tail context.

If the arguments match none of the clauses, an exception with condition type &assertion is raised.

```
(define foo
  (case-lambda
    (() 'zero)
    ((x) (list 'one x))
    ((x y) (list 'two x y))
    ((a b c d . e) (list 'four a b c d e))
    (rest (list 'rest rest))))
```

```
(foo)          ⟹ zero
(foo 1)        ⟹ (one 1)
(foo 1 2)      ⟹ (two 1 2)
(foo 1 2 3)    ⟹ (rest (1 2 3))
(foo 1 2 3 4)  ⟹ (four 1 2 3 4 ())
```

The case-lambda keyword can be defined in terms of lambda by the following macros:

```
(define-syntax case-lambda
  (syntax-rules ()
    ((_ (fmls b1 b2 ...))
     (lambda fmls b1 b2 ...))
    ((_ (fmls b1 b2 ...) ...)
     (lambda args
       (let ((n (length args)))
         (case-lambda-help args n
           (fmls b1 b2 ...) ...))))))
```

```
(define-syntax case-lambda-help
  (syntax-rules ()
    ((_ args n)
     (assertion-violation #f
       "unexpected number of arguments"))
    ((_ args n ((x ...) b1 b2 ...) more ...)
     (if (= n (length '(x ...)))
         (apply (lambda (x ...) b1 b2 ...) args)
         (case-lambda-help args n more ...)))
    ((_ args n ((x1 x2 ... . r) b1 b2 ...) more ...)
     (if (>= n (length '(x1 x2 ...)))
         (apply (lambda (x1 x2 ... . r) b1 b2 ...)
                args)
         (case-lambda-help args n more ...)))
    ((_ args n (r b1 b2 ...) more ...)
     (apply (lambda r b1 b2 ...) args)))))
```

6 Records

This section describes abstractions for creating new data types representing records.

A record is a compound data structure with a fixed number of components, called *fields*. Each record has an associated type specified by a *record-type descriptor*, which is an object that specifies the fields of the record and various other properties that all records of that type share. Record objects are created by a *record constructor*, a procedure that creates a fresh record object and initializes its fields to values. Records of different types can be distinguished from each other and from other types of objects by *record predicates*. A record predicate returns #t when passed a record of the type specified by the record-type descriptor and #f otherwise. An *accessor* extracts from a record the component associated with a field, and a *mutator* changes the component to a different value.

Record types can be extended via single inheritance, allowing record types to model hierarchies that occur in applications like algebraic data types as well as single-inheritance class systems. If a record type t extends another record type p, each record of type t is also a record of type p, and the predicate, accessors, and mutators applicable to a record of type p are also applicable to a record of type t. The extension relationship is transitive in the sense that a type extends its parent's parent, if any, and so on. A record type that does not extend another record type is called a *base record type*.

A record type can be *sealed* to prevent it from being extended. Moreover, a record type can be *nongenerative*, i.e., it is globally identified by a "uid", and new, compatible definitions of a nongenerative record type with the same uid as a previous always yield the same record type.

The record mechanism spans three libraries:

- the (rnrs records syntactic (6)) library, a syntactic layer for defining a record type and associated constructor, predicate, accessor, and mutators,
- the (rnrs records procedural (6)) library, a procedural layer for creating and manipulating record types and creating constructors, predicates, accessors, and mutators;
- the (rnrs records inspection (6)) library, a set of inspection procedures.

The inspection procedures allow programs to obtain from a record instance a descriptor for the type and from there obtain access to the fields of the record instance. This facility allows the creation of portable printers and inspectors. A program may prevent access to a record's type—and thereby protect the information stored in the record from the inspection mechanism—by declaring the type opaque. Thus, opacity as presented here can be used to enforce abstraction barriers.

Any of the standard types mentioned in this report may or may not be implemented as an opaque record type. Thus, it may be possible to use inspection on objects of the standard types.

The procedural layer is particularly useful for writing interpreters that construct host-compatible record types. It may also serve as a target for expansion of the syntactic layers. The record operations provided through the procedural layer may, however, be less efficient than the operations provided through the syntactic layer, which is designed to allow expand-time determination of record-instance sizes and field offsets. Therefore, alternative implementations of syntactic record-type definition should, when possible, expand into the syntactic layer rather than the procedural layer.

The syntactic layer is used more commonly and therefore described first. This chapter uses the *rtd* and *constructor-descriptor* parameter names for arguments that must be record-type descriptors and constructor descriptors, respectively (see section 6.3).

6.1 Mutability and equivalence of records

The fields of a record type are designated *mutable* or *immutable*. Correspondingly, a record type with no mutable field is called *immutable*, and all records of that type are immutable objects. All other record types are *mutable*, and so are their records.

Each call to a record constructor returns a new record with a fresh location (see report section 5.10). Consequently, for two records obj_1 and obj_2, the return value of (eqv? obj_1 obj_2), as well as the return value of (eq? obj_1 obj_2), adheres to the following criteria (see report section 11.5):

- If obj_1 and obj_2 have different record types (i.e., their record-type descriptors are not eqv?), eqv? returns #f.
- If obj_1 and obj_2 are both records of the same record type, and are the results of two separate calls to record constructors, then eqv? returns #f.
- If obj_1 and obj_2 are both the result of a single call to a record constructor, then eqv? returns #t.

- If obj_1 and obj_2 are both records of the same record type, where applying an accessor to both yields results for which eqv? returns #f, then eqv? returns #f.

6.2 Syntactic layer

The syntactic layer is provided by the (rnrs records syntactic (6)) library. Some details of the specification are explained in terms of the specification of the procedural layer below.

The record-type-defining form define-record-type is a definition and can appear anywhere any other ⟨definition⟩ can appear.

(define-record-type ⟨name spec⟩ ⟨record clause⟩*)	syntax
fields	auxiliary syntax
mutable	auxiliary syntax
immutable	auxiliary syntax
parent	auxiliary syntax
protocol	auxiliary syntax
sealed	auxiliary syntax
opaque	auxiliary syntax
nongenerative	auxiliary syntax
parent-rtd	auxiliary syntax

A define-record-type form defines a record type along with associated constructor descriptor and constructor, predicate, field accessors, and field mutators. The define-record-type form expands into a set of definitions in the environment where define-record-type appears; hence, it is possible to refer to the bindings (except for that of the record type itself) recursively.

The ⟨name spec⟩ specifies the names of the record type, constructor, and predicate. It must take one of the following forms:

> (⟨record name⟩ ⟨constructor name⟩ ⟨predicate name⟩)
> ⟨record name⟩

⟨Record name⟩, ⟨constructor name⟩, and ⟨predicate name⟩ must all be identifiers.
⟨Record name⟩, taken as a symbol, becomes the name of the record type. (See the description of make-record-type-descriptor below.) Additionally, it is bound by this definition to an expand-time or run-time representation of the record type and can be used as parent name in syntactic record-type definitions that extend this definition. It can also be used as a handle to gain access to the underlying record-type descriptor and constructor descriptor (see record-type-descriptor and record-constructor-descriptor below).
⟨Constructor name⟩ is defined by this definition to be a constructor for the defined record type, with a protocol specified by the protocol clause, or, in its absence, using a default protocol. For details, see the description of the protocol clause below.

⟨Predicate name⟩ is defined by this definition to a predicate for the defined record type.

The second form of ⟨name spec⟩ is an abbreviation for the first form, where the name of the constructor is generated by prefixing the record name with `make-`, and the predicate name is generated by adding a question mark (?) to the end of the record name. For example, if the record name is `frob`, the name of the constructor is `make-frob`, and the predicate name is `frob?`.

Each ⟨record clause⟩ must take one of the following forms; it is a syntax violation if multiple ⟨record clause⟩s of the same kind appear in a `define-record-type` form.

`(fields ⟨field spec⟩*)`

Each ⟨field spec⟩ has one of the following forms

```
(immutable ⟨field name⟩ ⟨accessor name⟩)
(mutable ⟨field name⟩
         ⟨accessor name⟩ ⟨mutator name⟩)
(immutable ⟨field name⟩)
(mutable ⟨field name⟩)
⟨field name⟩
```

⟨Field name⟩, ⟨accessor name⟩, and ⟨mutator name⟩ must all be identifiers. The first form declares an immutable field called ⟨field name⟩, with the corresponding accessor named ⟨accessor name⟩. The second form declares a mutable field called ⟨field name⟩, with the corresponding accessor named ⟨accessor name⟩, and with the corresponding mutator named ⟨mutator name⟩.

If ⟨field spec⟩ takes the third or fourth form, the accessor name is generated by appending the record name and field name with a hyphen separator, and the mutator name (for a mutable field) is generated by adding a `-set!` suffix to the accessor name. For example, if the record name is `frob` and the field name is `widget`, the accessor name is `frob-widget` and the mutator name is `frob-widget-set!`.

If ⟨field spec⟩ is just a ⟨field name⟩ form, it is an abbreviation for `(immutable ⟨field name⟩)`.

The ⟨field name⟩s become, as symbols, the names of the fields in the record-type descriptor being created, in the same order.

The `fields` clause may be absent; this is equivalent to an empty `fields` clause.

`(parent ⟨parent name⟩)`

Specifies that the record type is to have parent type ⟨parent name⟩, where ⟨parent name⟩ is the ⟨record name⟩ of a record type previously defined using `define-record-type`. The record-type definition associated with ⟨parent name⟩ must not be sealed.

`(protocol ⟨expression⟩)`

⟨Expression⟩ is evaluated in the same environment as the `define-record-type` form. It must evaluate to a procedure, and this procedure should be a protocol appropriate for the record type being defined.

The protocol is used to create a record-constructor descriptor as described below. If no `protocol` clause is specified, a constructor descriptor is still created using a default protocol. The clause can be absent only if the record type being defined has no parent type, or if the parent definition does not specify a protocol.

```
(sealed #t)
(sealed #f)
```

If this option is specified with operand #t, the defined record type is sealed, i.e., no extensions of the record type can be created. If this option is specified with operand #f, or is absent, the defined record type is not sealed.

```
(opaque #t)
(opaque #f)
```

If this option is specified with operand #t, or if an opaque parent record type is specified, the defined record type is opaque. Otherwise, the defined record type is not opaque. See the specification of record-rtd below for details.

```
(nongenerative ⟨uid⟩)
(nongenerative)
```

This specifies that the record type is nongenerative with uid ⟨uid⟩, which must be an ⟨identifier⟩. If ⟨uid⟩ is absent, a unique uid is generated at macro-expansion time. If two record-type definitions specify the same *uid*, then the record-type definitions should be equivalent, i.e., the implied arguments to make-record-type-descriptor must be equivalent as described under make-record-type-descriptor. See section 6.3. If this condition is not met, it is either considered a syntax violation or an exception with condition type &assertion is raised. If the condition is met, a single record type is generated for both definitions.

In the absence of a nongenerative clause, a new record type is generated every time a define-record-type form is evaluated:

```
(let ((f (lambda (x)
           (define-record-type r ...)
           (if x r? (make-r ...)))))
  ((f #t) (f #f)))                    ⟹ #f
```

```
(parent-rtd ⟨parent rtd⟩ ⟨parent cd⟩)
```

Specifies that the record type is to have its parent type specified by ⟨parent rtd⟩, which should be an expression evaluating to a record-type descriptor or #f, and ⟨parent cd⟩, which should be an expression evaluating to a constructor descriptor (see below) or #f.

If ⟨parent rtd⟩ evaluates to #f, then if ⟨parent cd⟩ evaluates to a value, that value must be #f.

If ⟨parent rtd⟩ evaluates to a record-type descriptor, the record type must not be sealed. Moreover, a record-type definition must not have both a parent and a parent-rtd clause.

Note: The syntactic layer is designed to allow record-instance sizes and field offsets to be determined at expand time, i.e., by a macro definition of define-record-type, as long as the parent (if any) is known. Implementations that take advantage of this may generate less efficient constructor, accessor, and mutator code when the parent-rtd clause is used, since the type of the parent is generally not known until run time. The parent clause should therefore be used instead when possible.

All bindings created by define-record-type (for the record type, the constructor, the predicate, the accessors, and the mutators) must have names that are pairwise distinct.

If no parent clause is present, no parent-rtd clause is present, or a parent-rtd clause is present but ⟨parent rtd⟩ evaluates to #f, the record type is a base type.

The constructor created by a define-record-type form is a procedure as follows:

- If the record type is a base type and no protocol clause is present, the constructor accepts as many arguments as there are fields, in the same order as they appear in the fields clause, and returns a record object with the fields initialized to the corresponding arguments.

- If the record type is a base type and a protocol clause is present, the protocol expression, if it evaluates to a value, must evaluate to a procedure, and this procedure should accept a single argument. The protocol procedure is called once during the evaluation of the define-record-type form with a procedure p as its argument. It should return a procedure, which will become the constructor bound to ⟨constructor name⟩. The procedure p accepts as many arguments as there are fields, in the same order as they appear in the fields clause, and returns a record object with the fields initialized to the corresponding arguments.

  The constructor returned by the protocol procedure can accept an arbitrary number of arguments, and should call p once to construct a record object, and return that record object.

  For example, the following protocol expression for a record-type definition with three fields creates a constructor that accepts values for all fields, and initialized them in the reverse order of the arguments:

  ```
  (lambda (p)
    (lambda (v1 v2 v3)
      (p v3 v2 v1)))
  ```

- If the record type is not a base type and a protocol clause is present, then the protocol procedure is called once with a procedure n as its argument. As in the previous case, the protocol procedure should return a procedure, which will become the constructor bound to ⟨constructor name⟩. However, n is different from p in the previous case: It accepts arguments corresponding to the arguments of the constructor of the parent type. It then returns a procedure p that accepts as many arguments as there are (additional) fields in this type, in the same order as in the fields clause, and returns a record object with the fields of the parent record types initialized according to their constructors and the arguments to n, and the fields of this record type initialized to its arguments of p.

  The constructor returned by the protocol procedure can accept an arbitrary number of arguments, and should call n once to construct the procedure p, and call *p* once to create the record object, and finally return that record object.

For example, the following protocol expression assumes that the constructor of the parent type takes three arguments:

```
(lambda (n)
  (lambda (v1 v2 v3 x1 x2 x3 x4)
    (let ((p (n v1 v2 v3)))
      (p x1 x2 x3 x4))))
```

The resulting constructor accepts seven arguments, and initializes the fields of the parent types according to the constructor of the parent type, with v1, v2, and v3 as arguments. It also initializes the fields of this record type to the values of x1, . . . , x4.

- If there is a parent clause, but no protocol clause, then the parent type must not have a protocol clause itself. Similarly, if there is a parent-rtd clause whose ⟨parent rtd⟩ evaluates to a record-type descriptor, but no protocol clause, then the ⟨parent cd⟩ expression, if it evaluates to a value, must evaluate to #f. The constructor bound to ⟨constructor name⟩ is a procedure that accepts arguments corresponding to the parent types' constructor first, and then one argument for each field in the same order as in the fields clause. The constructor returns a record object with the fields initialized to the corresponding arguments.

A protocol may perform other actions consistent with the requirements described above, including mutation of the new record or other side effects, before returning the record.

Any definition that takes advantage of implicit naming for the constructor, predicate, accessor, and mutator names can be rewritten trivially to a definition that specifies all names explicitly. For example, the implicit-naming record definition:

```
(define-record-type frob
  (fields (mutable widget))
  (protocol
    (lambda (p)
      (lambda (n) (p (make-widget n))))))
```

is equivalent to the following explicit-naming record definition.

```
(define-record-type (frob make-frob frob?)
  (fields (mutable widget
                   frob-widget
                   frob-widget-set!))
  (protocol
    (lambda (p)
      (lambda (n) (p (make-widget n))))))
```

Also, the implicit-naming record definition:

```
(define-record-type point (fields x y))
```

is equivalent to the following explicit-naming record definition:

```
(define-record-type (point make-point point?)
  (fields
    (immutable x point-x)
    (immutable y point-y)))
```

With implicit naming, it is still possible to specify some of the names explicitly; for example, the following overrides the choice of accessor and mutator names for the widget field.

```
(define-record-type frob
  (fields (mutable widget getwid setwid!))
  (protocol
    (lambda (p)
      (lambda (n) (p (make-widget n))))))
```

(record-type-descriptor ⟨record name⟩)   syntax

Evaluates to the record-type descriptor (see below) associated with the type specified by ⟨record name⟩.

Note: The record-type-descriptor procedure works on both opaque and non-opaque record types.

(record-constructor-descriptor ⟨record name⟩)   syntax

Evaluates to the record-constructor descriptor (see below) associated with ⟨record name⟩.

The following example uses the record? procedure from the (rnrs records inspection (6)) library (section 6.4):

```
(define-record-type (point make-point point?)
  (fields (immutable x point-x)
          (mutable y point-y set-point-y!))
  (nongenerative
    point-4893d957-e00b-11d9-817f-00111175eb9e))

(define-record-type (cpoint make-cpoint cpoint?)
  (parent point)
  (protocol
   (lambda (n)
     (lambda (x y c)
       ((n x y) (color->rgb c)))))
  (fields
    (mutable rgb cpoint-rgb cpoint-rgb-set!)))

(define (color->rgb c)
```

```
    (cons 'rgb c))

(define p1 (make-point 1 2))
(define p2 (make-cpoint 3 4 'red))

(point? p1)                          ⟹ #t
(point? p2)                          ⟹ #t
(point? (vector))                    ⟹ #f
(point? (cons 'a 'b))                ⟹ #f
(cpoint? p1)                         ⟹ #f
(cpoint? p2)                         ⟹ #t
(point-x p1)                         ⟹ 1
(point-y p1)                         ⟹ 2
(point-x p2)                         ⟹ 3
(point-y p2)                         ⟹ 4
(cpoint-rgb p2)                      ⟹ (rgb . red)

(set-point-y! p1 17)                 ⟹ unspecified
(point-y p1)                         ⟹ 17)

(record-rtd p1)
          ⟹ (record-type-descriptor point)

(define-record-type (ex1 make-ex1 ex1?)
  (protocol (lambda (p) (lambda a (p a))))
  (fields (immutable f ex1-f)))

(define ex1-i1 (make-ex1 1 2 3))
(ex1-f ex1-i1)                       ⟹ (1 2 3)

(define-record-type (ex2 make-ex2 ex2?)
  (protocol
    (lambda (p) (lambda (a . b) (p a b))))
  (fields (immutable a ex2-a)
          (immutable b ex2-b)))

(define ex2-i1 (make-ex2 1 2 3))
(ex2-a ex2-i1)                       ⟹ 1
(ex2-b ex2-i1)                       ⟹ (2 3)

(define-record-type (unit-vector
                      make-unit-vector
                      unit-vector?)
  (protocol
    (lambda (p)
```

```scheme
(lambda (x y z)
  (let ((length
         (sqrt (+ (* x x)
                  (* y y)
                  (* z z)))))
    (p (/ x length)
       (/ y length)
       (/ z length)))))))
(fields (immutable x unit-vector-x)
        (immutable y unit-vector-y)
        (immutable z unit-vector-z)))

(define *ex3-instance* #f)

(define-record-type ex3
  (parent cpoint)
  (protocol
   (lambda (n)
     (lambda (x y t)
       (let ((r ((n x y 'red) t)))
         (set! *ex3-instance* r)
         r))))
  (fields
   (mutable thickness))
  (sealed #t) (opaque #t))

(define ex3-i1 (make-ex3 1 2 17))
(ex3? ex3-i1)                        ⟹ #t
(cpoint-rgb ex3-i1)                  ⟹ (rgb . red)
(ex3-thickness ex3-i1)              ⟹ 17
(ex3-thickness-set! ex3-i1 18)       ⟹ unspecified
(ex3-thickness ex3-i1)              ⟹ 18
*ex3-instance*                       ⟹ ex3-i1

(record? ex3-i1)                     ⟹ #f
```

6.3 Procedural layer

The procedural layer is provided by the (rnrs records procedural (6)) library.

(make-record-type-descriptor *name*   procedure
    parent uid sealed? opaque? fields)

Returns a *record-type descriptor*, or *rtd*, representing a record type distinct from all built-in types and other record types.

The *name* argument must be a symbol. It names the record type, and is intended purely for informational purposes and may be used for printing by the underlying Scheme system.

The *parent* argument must be either #f or an rtd. If it is an rtd, the returned record type, *t*, extends the record type *p* represented by *parent*. An exception with condition type &assertion is raised if *parent* is sealed (see below).

The *uid* argument must be either #f or a symbol. If *uid* is a symbol, the record-creation operation is *nongenerative* i.e., a new record type is created only if no previous call to make-record-type-descriptor was made with the *uid*. If *uid* is #f, the record-creation operation is *generative*, i.e., a new record type is created even if a previous call to make-record-type-descriptor was made with the same arguments.

If make-record-type-descriptor is called twice with the same *uid* symbol, the parent arguments in the two calls must be eqv?, the *fields* arguments equal?, the *sealed?* arguments boolean-equivalent (both #f or both true), and the *opaque?* arguments boolean-equivalent if the parents are not opaque. If these conditions are not met, an exception with condition type &assertion is raised when the second call occurs. If they are met, the second call returns, without creating a new record type, the same record-type descriptor (in the sense of eqv?) as the first call.

Note: Users are encouraged to use symbol names constructed using the UUID namespace (Leach *et al.*, 2005) (for example, using the record-type name as a prefix) for the uid argument.

The *sealed?* flag must be a boolean. If true, the returned record type is sealed, i.e., it cannot be extended.

The *opaque?* flag must be a boolean. If true, the record type is opaque. If passed an instance of the record type, record? returns #f. Moreover, if record-rtd (see "Inspection" below) is called with an instance of the record type, an exception with condition type &assertion is raised. The record type is also opaque if an opaque parent is supplied. If *opaque?* is #f and an opaque parent is not supplied, the record is not opaque.

The *fields* argument must be a vector of field specifiers. Each field specifier must be a list of the form (mutable *name*) or a list of the form (immutable *name*). Each name must be a symbol and names the corresponding field of the record type; the names need not be distinct. A field identified as mutable may be modified, whereas, when a program attempts to obtain a mutator for a field identified as immutable, an exception with condition type &assertion is raised. Where field order is relevant, e.g., for record construction and field access, the fields are considered to be ordered as specified, although no particular order is required for the actual representation of a record instance.

The specified fields are added to the parent fields, if any, to determine the complete set of fields of the returned record type. If *fields* is modified after make-record-type-descriptor has been called, the effect on the returned rtd is unspecified.

A generative record-type descriptor created by a call to make-record-type-descriptor is not eqv? to any record-type descriptor (generative or nongenerative) created by another call to make-record-type-descriptor. A generative record-type descriptor is eqv? only to itself, i.e., (eqv? rtd_1 rtd_2) iff (eq? rtd_1 rtd_2). Also, two nongenerative record-type descriptors are eqv? iff they were created by calls to make-record-type-descriptor with the same uid arguments.

(record-type-descriptor? *obj*)   procedure
    Returns #t if the argument is a record-type descriptor, #f otherwise.

(make-record-constructor-descriptor *rtd*   procedure
         parent-constructor-descriptor protocol)
Returns a *record-constructor descriptor* (or *constructor descriptor* for short) that specifies a *record constructor* (or *constructor* for short), that can be used to construct record values of the type specified by *rtd*, and which can be obtained via record-constructor. A constructor descriptor can also be used to create other constructor descriptors for subtypes of its own record type. *Rtd* must be a record-type descriptor. *Protocol* must be a procedure or #f. If it is #f, a default *protocol* procedure is supplied.

If *protocol* is a procedure, it is handled analogously to the protocol expression in a define-record-type form.

If *rtd* is a base record type *parent-constructor-descriptor* must be #f. In this case, *protocol* is called by record-constructor with a single argument *p*. *P* is a procedure that expects one argument for every field of *rtd* and returns a record with the fields of *rtd* initialized to these arguments. The procedure returned by *protocol* should call *p* once with the number of arguments *p* expects and return the resulting record as shown in the simple example below:

```
(lambda (p)
  (lambda (v1 v2 v3)
    (p v1 v2 v3)))
```

Here, the call to p returns a record whose fields are initialized with the values of v1, v2, and v3. The expression above is equivalent to (lambda (p) p). Note that the procedure returned by *protocol* is otherwise unconstrained; specifically, it can take any number of arguments.

If *rtd* is an extension of another record type *parent-rtd* and *protocol* is a procedure, *parent-constructor-descriptor* must be a constructor descriptor of *parent-rtd* or #f. If *parent-constructor-descriptor* is a constructor descriptor, *protocol* is called by record-constructor with a single argument *n*, which is a procedure that accepts the same number of arguments as the constructor of *parent-constructor-descriptor* and returns a procedure *p* that, when called, constructs the record itself. The *p* procedure expects one argument for every field of *rtd* (not including parent fields) and returns a record with the fields of *rtd* initialized to these arguments, and the fields of *parent-rtd* and its parents initialized as specified by *parent-constructor-descriptor*.

The procedure returned by *protocol* should call *n* once with the number of arguments *n* expects, call the procedure *p* it returns once with the number of arguments *p* expects and return the resulting record. A simple *protocol* in this case might be written as follows:

```
(lambda (n)
  (lambda (v1 v2 v3 x1 x2 x3 x4)
    (let ((p (n v1 v2 v3)))
      (p x1 x2 x3 x4))))
```

This passes arguments v1, v2, v3 to *n* for *parent-constructor-descriptor* and calls p with x1, ..., x4 to initialize the fields of *rtd* itself.

Thus, the constructor descriptors for a record type form a sequence of protocols parallel to the sequence of record-type parents. Each constructor descriptor in the chain determines the field values for the associated record type. Child record constructors need not know the number or contents of parent fields, only the number of arguments accepted by the parent constructor.

Protocol may be #f, specifying a default constructor that accepts one argument for each field of *rtd* (including the fields of its parent type, if any). Specifically, if *rtd* is a base type, the default *protocol* procedure behaves as if it were (lambda (p) p). If *rtd* is an extension of another type, then *parent-constructor-descriptor* must be either #f or itself specify a default constructor, and the default *protocol* procedure behaves as if it were:

```
(lambda (n)
  (lambda (v₁ ... vⱼ x₁ ... xₖ)
    (let ((p (n v₁ ... vⱼ)))
      (p x₁ ... xₖ))))
```

The resulting constructor accepts one argument for each of the record type's complete set of fields (including those of the parent record type, the parent's parent record type, etc.) and returns a record with the fields initialized to those arguments, with the field values for the parent coming before those of the extension in the argument list. (In the example, j is the complete number of fields of the parent type, and k is the number of fields of *rtd* itself.)

If *rtd* is an extension of another record type and *parent-constructor-descriptor* is #f, *parent-constructor-descriptor* is treated as if it were a constructor descriptor for the parent rtd of *rtd* with a default protocol.

Implementation responsibilities: If *protocol* is a procedure, the implementation must check the restrictions on it to the extent performed by applying it as described when the constructor is called. An implementation may check whether *protocol* is an appropriate argument before applying it.

```
(define rtd1
  (make-record-type-descriptor
    'rtd1 #f #f #f #f
    '#((immutable x1) (immutable x2))))

(define rtd2
  (make-record-type-descriptor
    'rtd2 rtd1 #f #f #f
    '#((immutable x3) (immutable x4))))
```

```
(define rtd3
  (make-record-type-descriptor
   'rtd3 rtd2 #f #f #f
   '#((immutable x5) (immutable x6))))

(define protocol1
  (lambda (p)
    (lambda (a b c)
      (p (+ a b) (+ b c)))))

(define protocol2
  (lambda (n)
    (lambda (a b c d e f)
      (let ((p (n a b c)))
        (p (+ d e) (+ e f))))))

(define protocol3
  (lambda (n)
    (lambda (a b c d e f g h i)
      (let ((p (n a b c d e f)))
        (p (+ g h) (+ h i))))))

(define cd1
  (make-record-constructor-descriptor
    rtd1 #f protocol1))

(define cd2
  (make-record-constructor-descriptor
    rtd2 cd1 protocol2))

(define cd3
  (make-record-constructor-descriptor
    rtd3 cd2 protocol3))

(define make-rtd1 (record-constructor cd1))

(define make-rtd2 (record-constructor cd2))

(define make-rtd3 (record-constructor cd3))

(make-rtd3 1 2 3 4 5 6 7 8 9)      ⟹
  ⟨record with fields initialized to 3, 5, 9, 11, 15, 17⟩
```

(record-constructor *constructor-descriptor*)   procedure
   Calls the *protocol* of *constructor-descriptor* (as described for make-record-constructor-descriptor) and returns the resulting constructor *constructor* for records
of the record type associated with *constructor-descriptor*.

(record-predicate *rtd*)   procedure
   Returns a procedure that, given an object *obj*, returns #t if *obj* is a record of the
type represented by *rtd*, and #f otherwise.

(record-accessor *rtd k*)   procedure
K must be a valid field index of *rtd*. The record-accessor procedure returns a
one-argument procedure whose argument must be a record of the type represented
by *rtd*. This procedure returns the value of the selected field of that record.
   The field selected corresponds to the *k*th element (0-based) of the *fields* argument
to the invocation of make-record-type-descriptor that created *rtd*. Note that *k*
cannot be used to specify a field of any type *rtd* extends.

(record-mutator *rtd k*)   procedure
K must be a valid field index of *rtd*. The record-mutator procedure returns a
two-argument procedure whose arguments must be a record record *r* of the type
represented by *rtd* and an object *obj*. This procedure stores *obj* within the field
of *r* specified by *k*. The *k* argument is as in record-accessor. If *k* specifies an
immutable field, an exception with condition type &assertion is raised. The mutator
returns unspecified values.

```
(define :point
  (make-record-type-descriptor
    'point #f
    #f #f #f
    '#((mutable x) (mutable y))))

(define :point-cd
  (make-record-constructor-descriptor :point #f #f))

(define make-point (record-constructor :point-cd))

(define point? (record-predicate :point))
(define point-x (record-accessor :point 0))
(define point-y (record-accessor :point 1))
(define point-x-set! (record-mutator :point 0))
(define point-y-set! (record-mutator :point 1))

(define p1 (make-point 1 2))
(point? p1)                            ⟹ #t
(point-x p1)                           ⟹ 1
```

```
(point-y p1)                              ⟹ 2
(point-x-set! p1 5)                       ⟹ unspecified
(point-x p1)                              ⟹ 5

(define :point2
  (make-record-type-descriptor
    'point2 :point
    #f #f #f '#((mutable x) (mutable y))))

(define make-point2
  (record-constructor
    (make-record-constructor-descriptor :point2
      #f #f)))
(define point2? (record-predicate :point2))
(define point2-xx (record-accessor :point2 0))
(define point2-yy (record-accessor :point2 1))

(define p2 (make-point2 1 2 3 4))
(point? p2)                               ⟹ #t
(point-x p2)                              ⟹ 1
(point-y p2)                              ⟹ 2
(point2-xx p2)                            ⟹ 3
(point2-yy p2)                            ⟹ 4

(define :point-cd/abs
  (make-record-constructor-descriptor
    :point #f
    (lambda (new)
      (lambda (x y)
        (new (abs x) (abs y))))))

(define make-point/abs
  (record-constructor :point-cd/abs))

(point-x (make-point/abs -1 -2))   ⟹ 1
(point-y (make-point/abs -1 -2))   ⟹ 2

(define :cpoint
  (make-record-type-descriptor
    'cpoint :point
    #f #f #f
    '#((mutable rgb))))

(define make-cpoint
  (record-constructor
```

```
      (make-record-constructor-descriptor
       :cpoint :point-cd
       (lambda (p)
         (lambda (x y c)
((p x y) (color->rgb c)))))))))

    (define make-cpoint/abs
      (record-constructor
       (make-record-constructor-descriptor
        :cpoint :point-cd/abs
        (lambda (p)
          (lambda (x y c)
((p x y) (color->rgb c)))))))))

    (define cpoint-rgb
      (record-accessor :cpoint 0))

    (define (color->rgb c)
      (cons 'rgb c))

    (cpoint-rgb (make-cpoint -1 -3 'red))
              ⟹ (rgb . red)
    (point-x (make-cpoint -1 -3 'red))
              ⟹ -1
    (point-x (make-cpoint/abs -1 -3 'red))
              ⟹ 1
```

6.4 Inspection

The (rnrs records inspection (6)) library provides procedures for inspecting
records and their record-type descriptors. These procedures are designed to allow
the writing of portable printers and inspectors.

On the one hand, record? and record-rtd treat records of opaque record types
as if they were not records. On the other hand, the inspection procedures that
operate on record-type descriptors themselves are not affected by opacity. In other
words, opacity controls whether a program can obtain an rtd from a record. If
the program has access to the original rtd via make-record-type-descriptor or
record-type-descriptor, it can still make use of the inspection procedures.

(record? *obj*)   procedure
    Returns #t if *obj* is a record, and its record type is not opaque, and returns #f
otherwise.

(record-rtd *record*)   procedure
    Returns the rtd representing the type of *record* if the type is not opaque. The rtd

of the most precise type is returned; that is, the type t such that *record* is of type t but not of any type that extends t. If the type is opaque, an exception is raised with condition type &assertion.

(record-type-name *rtd*)   procedure
    Returns the name of the record-type descriptor *rtd*.

(record-type-parent *rtd*)   procedure
    Returns the parent of the record-type descriptor *rtd*, or #f if it has none.

(record-type-uid *rtd*)   procedure
    Returns the uid of the record-type descriptor rtd, or #f if it has none. (An implementation may assign a generated uid to a record type even if the type is generative, so the return of a uid does not necessarily imply that the type is nongenerative.)

(record-type-generative? *rtd*)   procedure
    Returns #t if *rtd* is generative, and #f if not.

(record-type-sealed? *rtd*)   procedure
    Returns #t if the record-type descriptor is sealed, and #f if not.

(record-type-opaque? *rtd*)   procedure
    Returns #t if the the record-type descriptor is opaque, and #f if not.

(record-type-field-names *rtd*)   procedure
    Returns a vector of symbols naming the fields of the type represented by *rtd* (not including the fields of parent types) where the fields are ordered as described under make-record-type-descriptor. The returned vector may be immutable. If the returned vector is modified, the effect on *rtd* is unspecified.

(record-field-mutable? *rtd k*)   procedure
    Returns #t if the field specified by k of the type represented by *rtd* is mutable, and #f if not. K is as in record-accessor.

7 Exceptions and conditions

Scheme allows programs to deal with exceptional situations using two cooperating facilities: the exception system for raising and handling exceptional situations, and the condition system for describing these situations.

    The exception system allows the program, when it detects an exceptional situation, to pass control to an exception handler, and to dynamically establish such exception handlers. Exception handlers are always invoked with an object describing the exceptional situation. Scheme's condition system provides a standardized taxonomy of such descriptive objects, as well as a facility for extending the taxonomy.

7.1 Exceptions

This section describes Scheme's exception-handling and exception-raising constructs provided by the ⟨rnrs exceptions (6)⟩ library.

Exception handlers are one-argument procedures that determine the action the program takes when an exceptional situation is signalled. The system implicitly maintains a current exception handler.

The program raises an exception by invoking the current exception handler, passing it an object encapsulating information about the exception. Any procedure accepting one argument may serve as an exception handler and any object may be used to represent an exception.

The system maintains the current exception handler as part of the dynamic environment of the program; see report section 5.12.

When a program begins its execution, the current exception handler is expected to handle all &serious conditions by interrupting execution, reporting that an exception has been raised, and displaying information about the condition object that was provided. The handler may then exit, or may provide a choice of other options. Moreover, the exception handler is expected to return when passed any other non-&serious condition. Interpretation of these expectations necessarily depends upon the nature of the system in which programs are executed, but the intent is that users perceive the raising of an exception as a controlled escape from the situation that raised the exception, not as a crash.

(with-exception-handler *handler thunk*)   procedure
Handler must be a procedure and should accept one argument. *Thunk* must be a procedure and should accept zero arguments. The with-exception-handler procedure returns the results of invoking *thunk* without arguments. *Handler* is installed as the current exception handler for the dynamic extent (as determined by dynamic-wind) of the invocation of *thunk*.

Implementation responsibilities: The implementation must check the restrictions on *thunk* to the extent performed by applying it as described above. The implementation must check the restrictions on *handler* to the extent performed by applying it as described when it is called as a result of a call to raise or raise-continuable. An implementation may check whether *handler* is an appropriate argument before applying it.

(guard (⟨variable⟩   syntax
   ⟨cond clause₁⟩ ⟨cond clause₂⟩ ...)
  ⟨body⟩)
=>   auxiliary syntax
else   auxiliary syntax
 Syntax: Each ⟨cond clause⟩ is as in the specification of cond. (See report section 11.4.5.) => and else are the same as in the ⟨rnrs base (6)⟩ library.

 Semantics: Evaluating a guard form evaluates ⟨body⟩ with an exception handler that binds the raised object to ⟨variable⟩ and within the scope of that binding evaluates the clauses as if they were the clauses of a cond expression. That implicit cond expression is evaluated with the continuation and dynamic environment of the guard expression. If every ⟨cond clause⟩'s ⟨test⟩ evaluates to #f and there is no else clause, then raise-continuable is invoked on the raised object within the dynamic environment of the original call to raise except that the current exception handler is that of the guard expression.

The final expression in a ⟨cond clause⟩ is in a tail context if the guard expression itself is.

(raise *obj*)   procedure

Raises a non-continuable exception by invoking the current exception handler on *obj*. The handler is called with a continuation whose dynamic environment is that of the call to raise, except that the current exception handler is the one that was in place when the handler being called was installed. When the handler returns, a non-continuable exception with condition type &non-continuable is raised in the same dynamic environment as the handler.

(raise-continuable *obj*)   procedure

Raises a *continuable exception* by invoking the current exception handler on *obj*. The handler is called with a continuation that is equivalent to the continuation of the call to raise-continuable, with these two exceptions: (1) the current exception handler is the one that was in place when the handler being called was installed, and (2) if the handler being called returns, then it will again become the current exception handler. If the handler returns, the values it returns become the values returned by the call to raise-continuable.

```
    (guard (con
             ((error? con)
              (if (message-condition? con)
                  (display (condition-message con))
                  (display "an error has occurred"))
              'error)
             ((violation? con)
              (if (message-condition? con)
                  (display (condition-message con))
                  (display "the program has a bug"))
              'violation))
      (raise
        (condition
          (make-error)
          (make-message-condition "I am an error"))))
        prints: I am an error
                                                  ⟹ error
      (guard (con
               ((error? con)
```

```
            (if (message-condition? con)
                (display (condition-message con))
                (display "an error has occurred"))
            'error))
    (raise
      (condition
        (make-violation)
        (make-message-condition "I am an error"))))
                                          ⟹ &violation exception


    (guard (con
             ((error? con)
              (display "error opening file")
              #f))
      (call-with-input-file "foo.scm" read))
        prints: error opening file
                                          ⟹ #f


    (with-exception-handler
      (lambda (con)
        (cond
          ((not (warning? con))
           (raise con))
          ((message-condition? con)
           (display (condition-message con)))
          (else
           (display "a warning has been issued")))
        42)
      (lambda ()
        (+ (raise-continuable
             (condition
               (make-warning)
               (make-message-condition
                 "should be a number")))
           23)))
        prints: should be a number
                                          ⟹ 65
```

7.2 Conditions

The section describes Scheme's (rnrs conditions (6)) library for creating and inspecting condition types and values. A condition value encapsulates information about an exceptional situation. Scheme also defines a number of basic condition types.

Scheme conditions provides two mechanisms to enable communication about an exceptional situation: subtyping among condition types allows handling code to determine the general nature of an exception even though it does not anticipate its exact nature, and compound conditions allow an exceptional situation to be described in multiple ways.

7.2.1 Condition objects

Conceptually, there are two different kinds of condition objects: *simple conditions* and *compound conditions*. An object that is either a simple condition or a compound condition is simply a *condition*. Compound conditions form a type disjoint from the base types described in report section 11.1. A simple condition describes a single aspect of an exceptional situation. A compound condition represents multiple aspects of an exceptional situation as a list of simple conditions, its *components*. Most of the operations described in this section treat a simple condition identically to a compound condition with itself as its own sole component. For a subtype *t* of &condition, a *condition of type t* is either a record of type *t* or a compound condition containing a component of type *t*.

&condition   condition type

Simple conditions are records of subtypes of the &condition record type. The &condition type has no fields and is neither sealed nor opaque.

(condition *condition*₁ ...)   procedure

The condition procedure returns a condition object with the components of the *condition*s as its components, in the same order, i.e., with the components of *condition*₁ appearing first in the same order as in *condition*₁, then with the components of *condition*₂, and so on. The returned condition is compound if the total number of components is zero or greater than one. Otherwise, it may be compound or simple.

(simple-conditions *condition*)   procedure

The simple-conditions procedure returns a list of the components of *condition*, in the same order as they appeared in the construction of *condition*. The returned list is immutable. If the returned list is modified, the effect on *condition* is unspecified. *Note:* Because condition decomposes its arguments into simple conditions, simple-conditions always returns a "flattened" list of simple conditions.

(condition? *obj*)   procedure

Returns #t if *obj* is a (simple or compound) condition, otherwise returns #f.

(condition-predicate *rtd*)   procedure

Rtd must be a record-type descriptor of a subtype of &condition. The condition-predicate procedure returns a procedure that takes one argument. This procedure returns #t if its argument is a condition of the condition type represented by *rtd*, i.e., if it is either a simple condition of that record type (or one of its subtypes) or a

compound condittion with such a simple condition as one of its components, and
#f otherwise.

(condition-accessor *rtd proc*)   procedure
Rtd must be a record-type descriptor of a subtype of &condition. *Proc* should
accept one argument, a record of the record type of *rtd*. The condition-accessor
procedure returns a procedure that accepts a single argument, which must be a
condition of the type represented by *rtd*. This procedure extracts the first component
of the condition of the type represented by *rtd*, and returns the result of applying
proc to that component.

```
(define-record-type (&cond1 make-cond1 real-cond1?)
  (parent &condition)
  (fields
   (immutable x real-cond1-x)))

(define cond1?
  (condition-predicate
   (record-type-descriptor &cond1)))
(define cond1-x
  (condition-accessor
    (record-type-descriptor &cond1)
    real-cond1-x))

(define foo (make-cond1 'foo))

(condition? foo)                    ⟹ #t
(cond1? foo)                        ⟹ #t
(cond1-x foo)                       ⟹ foo

(define-record-type (&cond2 make-cond2 real-cond2?)
  (parent &condition)
  (fields
   (immutable y real-cond2-y)))

(define cond2?
  (condition-predicate
   (record-type-descriptor &cond2)))
(define cond2-y
  (condition-accessor
     (record-type-descriptor &cond2)
     real-cond2-y))

(define bar (make-cond2 'bar))
```

```
(condition? (condition foo bar))    ⟹ #t
(cond1? (condition foo bar))         ⟹ #t
(cond2? (condition foo bar))         ⟹ #t
(cond1? (condition foo))             ⟹ #t
(real-cond1? (condition foo))        ⟹ unspecified
(real-cond1? (condition foo bar))    ⟹ #f
(cond1-x (condition foo bar))        ⟹ foo
(cond2-y (condition foo bar))        ⟹ bar


(equal? (simple-conditions (condition foo bar))
        (list foo bar))              ⟹ #t


(equal? (simple-conditions
            (condition foo (condition bar)))
        (list foo bar))              ⟹ #t
```

(define-condition-type ⟨condition-type⟩   syntax
    ⟨supertype⟩
  ⟨constructor⟩ ⟨predicate⟩
  ⟨field-spec$_1$⟩ ...)

Syntax: ⟨Condition-type⟩, ⟨supertype⟩, ⟨constructor⟩, and ⟨predicate⟩ must all be identifiers. Each ⟨field-spec⟩ must be of the form

    (⟨field⟩ ⟨accessor⟩)

where both ⟨field⟩ and ⟨accessor⟩ must be identifiers.

Semantics: The define-condition-type form expands into a record-type definition for a record type ⟨condition-type⟩ (see section 6.2). The record type will be non-opaque, non-sealed, and its fields will be immutable. It will have ⟨supertype⟩ has its parent type. The remaining identifiers will be bound as follows:

- ⟨Constructor⟩ is bound to a default constructor for the type (see section 6.3): It accepts one argument for each of the record type's complete set of fields (including parent types, with the fields of the parent coming before those of the extension in the arguments) and returns a condition object initialized to those arguments.
- ⟨Predicate⟩ is bound to a predicate that identifies conditions of type ⟨condition-type⟩ or any of its subtypes.
- Each ⟨accessor⟩ is bound to a procedure that extracts the corresponding field from a condition of type ⟨condition-type⟩.

```
(define-condition-type &c &condition
  make-c c?
  (x c-x))


(define-condition-type &c1 &c
```

```
    make-c1 c1?
    (a c1-a))

(define-condition-type &c2 &c
  make-c2 c2?
  (b c2-b))

(define v1 (make-c1 "V1" "a1"))
```

`(c? v1)`	$\Longrightarrow$ #t
`(c1? v1)`	$\Longrightarrow$ #t
`(c2? v1)`	$\Longrightarrow$ #f
`(c-x v1)`	$\Longrightarrow$ "V1"
`(c1-a v1)`	$\Longrightarrow$ "a1"

```
(define v2 (make-c2 "V2" "b2"))
```

`(c? v2)`	$\Longrightarrow$ #t
`(c1? v2)`	$\Longrightarrow$ #f
`(c2? v2)`	$\Longrightarrow$ #t
`(c-x v2)`	$\Longrightarrow$ "V2"
`(c2-b v2)`	$\Longrightarrow$ "b2"

```
(define v3 (condition
              (make-c1 "V3/1" "a3")
              (make-c2 "V3/2" "b3")))
```

`(c? v3)`	$\Longrightarrow$ #t
`(c1? v3)`	$\Longrightarrow$ #t
`(c2? v3)`	$\Longrightarrow$ #t
`(c-x v3)`	$\Longrightarrow$ "V3/1"
`(c1-a v3)`	$\Longrightarrow$ "a3"
`(c2-b v3)`	$\Longrightarrow$ "b3"

```
(define v4 (condition v1 v2))
```

`(c? v4)`	$\Longrightarrow$ #t
`(c1? v4)`	$\Longrightarrow$ #t
`(c2? v4)`	$\Longrightarrow$ #t
`(c-x v4)`	$\Longrightarrow$ "V1"
`(c1-a v4)`	$\Longrightarrow$ "a1"
`(c2-b v4)`	$\Longrightarrow$ "b2"

```
(define v5 (condition v2 v3))
```

`(c? v5)`	$\Longrightarrow$ #t
`(c1? v5)`	$\Longrightarrow$ #t

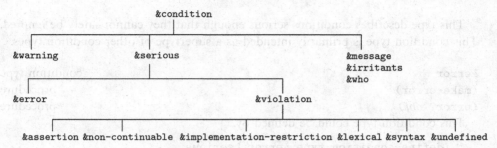

Fig. 1. Hierarchy of standard condition types

```
(c2? v5)                           ⟹ #t
(c-x v5)                           ⟹ "V2"
(c1-a v5)                          ⟹ "a3"
(c2-b v5)                          ⟹ "b2"
```

7.3 Standard condition types

&message	condition type
(make-message-condition *message*)	procedure
(message-condition? *obj*)	procedure
(condition-message *condition*)	procedure

This condition type could be defined by

```
(define-condition-type &message &condition
  make-message-condition message-condition?
  (message condition-message))
```

It carries a message further describing the nature of the condition to humans.

&warning	condition type
(make-warning)	procedure
(warning? *obj*)	procedure

This condition type could be defined by

```
(define-condition-type &warning &condition
  make-warning warning?)
```

This type describes conditions that do not, in principle, prohibit immediate continued execution of the program, but may interfere with the program's execution later.

&serious	condition type
(make-serious-condition)	procedure
(serious-condition? *obj*)	procedure

This condition type could be defined by

```
(define-condition-type &serious &condition
  make-serious-condition serious-condition?)
```

This type describes conditions serious enough that they cannot safely be ignored. This condition type is primarily intended as a supertype of other condition types.

`&error`	condition type
`(make-error)`	procedure
`(error? obj)`	procedure

This condition type could be defined by

```
(define-condition-type &error &serious
   make-error error?)
```

This type describes errors, typically caused by something that has gone wrong in the interaction of the program with the external world or the user.

`&violation`	condition type
`(make-violation)`	procedure
`(violation? obj)`	procedure

This condition type could be defined by

```
(define-condition-type &violation &serious
   make-violation violation?)
```

This type describes violations of the language standard or a library standard, typically caused by a programming error.

`&assertion`	condition type
`(make-assertion-violation)`	procedure
`(assertion-violation? obj)`	procedure

This condition type could be defined by

```
(define-condition-type &assertion &violation
   make-assertion-violation assertion-violation?)
```

This type describes an invalid call to a procedure, either passing an invalid number of arguments, or passing an argument of the wrong type.

`&irritants`	condition type
`(make-irritants-condition irritants)`	procedure
`(irritants-condition? obj)`	procedure
`(condition-irritants condition)`	procedure

This condition type could be defined by

```
(define-condition-type &irritants &condition
   make-irritants-condition irritants-condition?
   (irritants condition-irritants))
```

Irritants should be a list of objects. This condition provides additional information about a condition, typically the argument list of a procedure that detected an exception. Conditions of this type are created by the `error` and `assertion-violation` procedures of report section 11.14.

```
&who                                                      condition type
(make-who-condition who)                                      procedure
(who-condition? obj)                                          procedure
(condition-who condition)                                     procedure
```
This condition type could be defined by

```
    (define-condition-type &who &condition
       make-who-condition who-condition?
       (who condition-who))
```

Who should be a symbol or string identifying the entity reporting the exception. Conditions of this type are created by the error and assertion-violation procedures (report section 11.14), and the syntax-violation procedure (section 12.9).

```
&non-continuable                                          condition type
(make-non-continuable-violation)                              procedure
(non-continuable-violation? obj)                             procedure
```
This condition type could be defined by

```
    (define-condition-type &non-continuable &violation
       make-non-continuable-violation
       non-continuable-violation?)
```

This type indicates that an exception handler invoked via raise has returned.

```
&implementation-restriction                              condition type
(make-implementation-restriction-violation)                 procedure
(implementation-restriction-violation? obj)                 procedure
```
This condition type could be defined by

```
    (define-condition-type &implementation-restriction
         &violation
       make-implementation-restriction-violation
       implementation-restriction-violation?)
```

This type describes a violation of an implementation restriction allowed by the specification, such as the absence of representations for NaNs and infinities. (See section 11.3.)

```
&lexical                                                 condition type
(make-lexical-violation)                                     procedure
(lexical-violation? obj)                                     procedure
```
This condition type could be defined by

```
    (define-condition-type &lexical &violation
       make-lexical-violation lexical-violation?)
```

This type describes syntax violations at the level of the datum syntax.

&syntax   condition type
(make-syntax-violation *form subform*)   procedure
(syntax-violation? *obj*)   procedure
(syntax-violation-form *condition*)   procedure
(syntax-violation-subform *condition*)   procedure

This condition type could be defined by

```
(define-condition-type &syntax &violation
  make-syntax-violation syntax-violation?
  (form syntax-violation-form)
  (subform syntax-violation-subform))
```

This type describes syntax violations. *Form* should be the erroneous syntax object or a datum representing the code of the erroneous form. *Subform* should be an optional syntax object or datum within the erroneous form that more precisely locates the violation. It can be #f to indicate the absence of more precise information.

&undefined   condition type
(make-undefined-violation)   procedure
(undefined-violation? *obj*)   procedure

This condition type could be defined by

```
(define-condition-type &undefined &violation
  make-undefined-violation undefined-violation?)
```

This type describes unbound identifiers in the program.

8 I/O

This chapter describes Scheme's libraries for performing input and output:

- The (rnrs io ports (6)) library (section 8.2) is an I/O layer for conventional, imperative buffered input and output with text and binary data.
- The (rnrs io simple (6)) library (section 8.3) is a convenience library atop the (rnrs io ports (6)) library for textual I/O, compatible with the traditional Scheme I/O procedures (Kelsey *et al.*, 1998).

Section 8.1 defines a condition-type hierarchy that is exported by both the (rnrs io ports (6)) and (rnrs io simple (6)) libraries.

8.1 Condition types

The procedures described in this chapter, when they detect an exceptional situation that arises from an "I/O errors", raise an exception with condition type &i/o.

The condition types and corresponding predicates and accessors are exported by both the (rnrs io ports (6)) and (rnrs io simple (6)) libraries. They are also exported by the (rnrs files (6)) library described in chapter 9.

&i/o   condition type
(make-i/o-error)   procedure
(i/o-error? *obj*)   procedure
    This condition type could be defined by

        (define-condition-type &i/o &error
          make-i/o-error i/o-error?)

This is a supertype for a set of more specific I/O errors.

&i/o-read   condition type
(make-i/o-read-error)   procedure
(i/o-read-error? *obj*)   procedure
    This condition type could be defined by

        (define-condition-type &i/o-read &i/o
          make-i/o-read-error i/o-read-error?)

This condition type describes read errors that occurred during an I/O operation.

&i/o-write   condition type
(make-i/o-write-error)   procedure
(i/o-write-error? *obj*)   procedure
    This condition type could be defined by

        (define-condition-type &i/o-write &i/o
          make-i/o-write-error i/o-write-error?)

This condition type describes write errors that occurred during an I/O operation.

&i/o-invalid-position   condition type
(make-i/o-invalid-position-error *position*)   procedure
(i/o-invalid-position-error? *obj*)   procedure
(i/o-error-position *condition*)   procedure
    This condition type could be defined by

        (define-condition-type &i/o-invalid-position &i/o
          make-i/o-invalid-position-error
          i/o-invalid-position-error?
          (position i/o-error-position))

This condition type describes attempts to set the file position to an invalid position. *Position* should be the file position that the program intended to set. This condition describes a range error, but not an assertion violation.

&i/o-filename   condition type

```
(make-i/o-filename-error filename)                          procedure
(i/o-filename-error? obj)                                   procedure
(i/o-error-filename condition)                              procedure
```
   This condition type could be defined by

```
    (define-condition-type &i/o-filename &i/o
       make-i/o-filename-error i/o-filename-error?
       (filename i/o-error-filename))
```

   This condition type describes an I/O error that occurred during an operation on
a named file. *Filename* should be the name of the file.

```
&i/o-file-protection                                    condition type
(make-i/o-file-protection-error filename)                  procedure
(i/o-file-protection-error? obj)                           procedure
```
   This condition type could be defined by

```
    (define-condition-type &i/o-file-protection
        &i/o-filename
      make-i/o-file-protection-error
      i/o-file-protection-error?)
```

   A condition of this type specifies that an operation tried to operate on a named
file with insufficient access rights.

```
&i/o-file-is-read-only                                  condition type
(make-i/o-file-is-read-only-error filename)                procedure
(i/o-file-is-read-only-error? obj)                         procedure
```
   This condition type could be defined by

```
    (define-condition-type &i/o-file-is-read-only
        &i/o-file-protection
      make-i/o-file-is-read-only-error
      i/o-file-is-read-only-error?)
```

   A condition of this type specifies that an operation tried to operate on a named
read-only file under the assumption that it is writeable.

```
&i/o-file-already-exists                                condition type
(make-i/o-file-already-exists-error filename)              procedure
(i/o-file-already-exists-error? obj)                       procedure
```
   This condition type could be defined by

```
    (define-condition-type &i/o-file-already-exists
        &i/o-filename
      make-i/o-file-already-exists-error
      i/o-file-already-exists-error?)
```

A condition of this type specifies that an operation tried to operate on an existing named file under the assumption that it did not exist.

`&i/o-file-does-not-exist`	condition type
`(make-i/o-file-does-not-exist-error` *filename*`)`	procedure
`(i/o-file-does-not-exist-error?` *obj*`)`	procedure

This condition type could be defined by

```
(define-condition-type &i/o-file-does-not-exist
    &i/o-filename
  make-i/o-file-does-not-exist-error
  i/o-file-does-not-exist-error?)
```

A condition of this type specifies that an operation tried to operate on an non-existent named file under the assumption that it existed.

`&i/o-port`	condition type
`(make-i/o-port-error` *pobj*`)`	procedure
`(i/o-port-error?` *obj*`)`	procedure
`(i/o-error-port` *condition*`)`	procedure

This condition type could be defined by

```
(define-condition-type &i/o-port &i/o
  make-i/o-port-error i/o-port-error?
  (pobj i/o-error-port))
```

This condition type specifies the port with which an I/O error is associated. *Pobj* should be the port. Conditions raised by procedures accepting a port as an argument should include an `&i/o-port-error` condition.

8.2 Port I/O

The `(rnrs io ports (6))` library defines an I/O layer for conventional, imperative buffered input and output. A *port* represents a buffered access object for a data sink or source or both simultaneously. The library allows ports to be created from arbitrary data sources and sinks.

The `(rnrs io ports (6))` library distinguishes between *input ports* and *output ports*. An input port is a source for data, whereas an output port is a sink for data. A port may be both an input port and an output port; such a port typically provides simultaneous read and write access to a file or other data.

The `(rnrs io ports (6))` library also distinguishes between *binary ports*, which are sources or sinks for uninterpreted bytes, and *textual ports*, which are sources or sinks for characters and strings.

This section uses *input-port, output-port, binary-port, textual-port, binary-input-port, textual-input-port, binary-output-port, textual-output-port,* and *port* as parameter names for arguments that must be input ports (or combined input/output ports), output ports (or combined input/output ports), binary ports, textual ports, binary input ports, textual input ports, binary output ports, textual output ports, or any kind of port, respectively.

8.2.1 File names

Some of the procedures described in this chapter accept a file name as an argument. Valid values for such a file name include strings that name a file using the native notation of filesystem paths on an implementation's underlying operating system, and may include implementation-dependent values as well.

A *filename* parameter name means that the corresponding argument must be a file name.

8.2.2 File options

When opening a file, the various procedures in this library accept a `file-options` object that encapsulates flags to specify how the file is to be opened. A `file-options` object is an enum-set (see chapter 14) over the symbols constituting valid file options. A *file-options* parameter name means that the corresponding argument must be a file-options object.

(file-options ⟨file-options symbol⟩ ...)   syntax
    Each ⟨file-options symbol⟩ must be a symbol. The `file-options` syntax returns a file-options object that encapsulates the specified options.

    When supplied to an operation that opens a file for output, the file-options object returned by (file-options) specifies that the file is created if it does not exist and an exception with condition type `&i/o-file-already-exists` is raised if it does exist. The following standard options can be included to modify the default behavior.

- no-create If the file does not already exist, it is not created; instead, an exception with condition type `&i/o-file-does-not-exist` is raised. If the file already exists, the exception with condition type `&i/o-file-already-exists` is not raised and the file is truncated to zero length.
- no-fail If the file already exists, the exception with condition type `&i/o-file-already-exists` is not raised, even if `no-create` is not included, and the file is truncated to zero length.
- no-truncate If the file already exists and the exception with condition type `&i/o-file-already-exists` has been inhibited by inclusion of `no-create` or `no-fail`, the file is not truncated, but the port's current position is still set to the beginning of the file.

These options have no effect when a file is opened only for input. Symbols other than those listed above may be used as ⟨file-options symbol⟩s; they have implementation-specific meaning, if any.

Note: Only the name of ⟨file-options symbol⟩ is significant.

8.2.3 Buffer modes

Each port has an associated buffer mode. For an output port, the buffer mode defines when an output operation flushes the buffer associated with the output port. For an input port, the buffer mode defines how much data will be read to satisfy read operations. The possible buffer modes are the symbols none for no buffering, line for flushing upon line endings and reading up to line endings, or other implementation-dependent behavior, and block for arbitrary buffering. This section uses the parameter name *buffer-mode* for arguments that must be buffer-mode symbols.

If two ports are connected to the same mutable source, both ports are unbuffered, and reading a byte or character from that shared source via one of the two ports would change the bytes or characters seen via the other port, a lookahead operation on one port will render the peeked byte or character inaccessible via the other port, while a subsequent read operation on the peeked port will see the peeked byte or character even though the port is otherwise unbuffered.

In other words, the semantics of buffering is defined in terms of side effects on shared mutable sources, and a lookahead operation has the same side effect on the shared source as a read operation.

(buffer-mode ⟨buffer-mode symbol⟩)   syntax
⟨Buffer-mode symbol⟩ must be a symbol whose name is one of none, line, and block. The result is the corresponding symbol, and specifies the associated buffer mode.
Note: Only the name of ⟨buffer-mode symbol⟩ is significant.

(buffer-mode? *obj*)   procedure
Returns #t if the argument is a valid buffer-mode symbol, and returns #f otherwise.

8.2.4 *Transcoders*

Several different Unicode encoding schemes describe standard ways to encode characters and strings as byte sequences and to decode those sequences (Unicode Consortium, 2007). Within this document, a *codec* is an immutable Scheme object that represents a Unicode or similar encoding scheme.

An *end-of-line style* is a symbol that, if it is not none, describes how a textual port transcodes representations of line endings.

A *transcoder* is an immutable Scheme object that combines a codec with an end-of-line style and a method for handling decoding errors. Each transcoder represents some specific bidirectional (but not necessarily lossless), possibly stateful translation between byte sequences and Unicode characters and strings. Every transcoder can operate in the input direction (bytes to characters) or in the output direction (characters to bytes). A *transcoder* parameter name means that the corresponding argument must be a transcoder.

A *binary port* is a port that supports binary I/O, does not have an associated transcoder and does not support textual I/O. A *textual port* is a port that supports textual I/O, and does not support binary I/O. A textual port may or may not have an associated transcoder.

```
(latin-1-codec)                                                    procedure
(utf-8-codec)                                                      procedure
(utf-16-codec)                                                     procedure
```
These are predefined codecs for the ISO 8859-1, UTF-8, and UTF-16 encoding schemes (Unicode Consortium, 2007).

A call to any of these procedures returns a value that is equal in the sense of eqv? to the result of any other call to the same procedure.

```
(eol-style ⟨eol-style symbol⟩)                                        syntax
```
⟨Eol-style symbol⟩ should be a symbol whose name is one of lf, cr, crlf, nel, crnel, ls, and none. The form evaluates to the corresponding symbol. If the name of *eol-style symbol* is not one of these symbols, the effect and result are implementation-dependent; in particular, the result may be an eol-style symbol acceptable as an *eol-style* argument to make-transcoder. Otherwise, an exception is raised.

All eol-style symbols except none describe a specific line-ending encoding:

lf	⟨linefeed⟩
cr	⟨carriage return⟩
crlf	⟨carriage return⟩ ⟨linefeed⟩
nel	⟨next line⟩
crnel	⟨carriage return⟩ ⟨next line⟩
ls	⟨line separator⟩

For a textual port with a transcoder, and whose transcoder has an eol-style symbol none, no conversion occurs. For a textual input port, any eol-style symbol other than none means that all of the above line-ending encodings are recognized and are translated into a single linefeed. For a textual output port, none and lf are equivalent. Linefeed characters are encoded according to the specified eol-style symbol, and all other characters that participate in possible line endings are encoded as is.

Note: Only the name of ⟨eol-style symbol⟩ is significant.

```
(native-eol-style)                                                 procedure
```
Returns the default end-of-line style of the underlying platform, e.g., lf on Unix and crlf on Windows.

```
&i/o-decoding                                                 condition type
(make-i/o-decoding-error pobj)                                     procedure
(i/o-decoding-error? obj)                                          procedure
```
This condition type could be defined by

```
(define-condition-type &i/o-decoding &i/o-port
  make-i/o-decoding-error i/o-decoding-error?)
```

An exception with this type is raised when one of the operations for textual input from a port encounters a sequence of bytes that cannot be translated into a character or string by the input direction of the port's transcoder.

When such an exception is raised, the port's position is past the invalid encoding.

`&i/o-encoding`	condition type
`(make-i/o-encoding-error pobj cobj)`	procedure
`(i/o-encoding-error? obj)`	procedure
`(i/o-encoding-error-char condition)`	procedure

This condition type could be defined by

```
(define-condition-type &i/o-encoding &i/o-port
    make-i/o-encoding-error i/o-encoding-error?
  (cobj i/o-encoding-error-char))
```

An exception with this type is raised when one of the operations for textual output to a port encounters a character that cannot be translated into bytes by the output direction of the port's transcoder. *Cobj* should be the character that could not be encoded.

`(error-handling-mode ⟨error-handling-mode symbol⟩)`   syntax
⟨Error-handling-mode symbol⟩ should be a symbol whose name is one of `ignore`, `raise`, and `replace`. The form evaluates to the corresponding symbol. If ⟨error-handling-mode symbol⟩ is not one of these identifiers, effect and result are implementation-dependent: The result may be an error-handling-mode symbol acceptable as a *handling-mode* argument to `make-transcoder`. If it is not acceptable as a *handling-mode* argument to `make-transcoder`, an exception is raised.
Note: Only the name of ⟨error-handling-style symbol⟩ is significant.

The error-handling mode of a transcoder specifies the behavior of textual I/O operations in the presence of encoding or decoding errors.

If a textual input operation encounters an invalid or incomplete character encoding, and the error-handling mode is `ignore`, an appropriate number of bytes of the invalid encoding are ignored and decoding continues with the following bytes. If the error-handling mode is `replace`, the replacement character U+FFFD is injected into the data stream, an appropriate number of bytes are ignored, and decoding continues with the following bytes. If the error-handling mode is `raise`, an exception with condition type `&i/o-decoding` is raised.

If a textual output operation encounters a character it cannot encode, and the error-handling mode is `ignore`, the character is ignored and encoding continues with the next character. If the error-handling mode is `replace`, a codec-specific replacement character is emitted by the transcoder, and encoding continues with the next character. The replacement character is U+FFFD for transcoders whose codec is one of the Unicode encodings, but is the ? character for the Latin-1 encoding. If the error-handling mode is `raise`, an exception with condition type `&i/o-encoding` is raised.

`(make-transcoder codec)`   procedure

(make-transcoder *codec eol-style*)   procedure
(make-transcoder *codec eol-style handling-mode*)   procedure
Codec must be a codec; *eol-style*, if present, an eol-style symbol; and *handling-mode*,
if present, an error-handling-mode symbol. *Eol-style* may be omitted, in which case
it defaults to the native end-of-line style of the underlying platform. *Handling-mode*
may be omitted, in which case it defaults to replace. The result is a transcoder
with the behavior specified by its arguments.

(native-transcoder)   procedure
    Returns an implementation-dependent transcoder that represents a possibly locale-
dependent "native" transcoding.

(transcoder-codec *transcoder*)   procedure
(transcoder-eol-style *transcoder*)   procedure
(transcoder-error-handling-mode *transcoder*)   procedure
    These are accessors for transcoder objects; when applied to a transcoder returned
by make-transcoder, they return the *codec*, *eol-style*, and *handling-mode* arguments,
respectively.

(bytevector->string *bytevector transcoder*)   procedure
    Returns the string that results from transcoding the *bytevector* according to the
input direction of the transcoder.

(string->bytevector *string transcoder*)   procedure
    Returns the bytevector that results from transcoding the *string* according to the
output direction of the transcoder.

8.2.5 End-of-file object

The end-of-file object is returned by various I/O procedures when they reach end
of file.

(eof-object)   procedure
    Returns the end-of-file object.

        (eqv? (eof-object) (eof-object)) $\implies$ #t
        (eq? (eof-object) (eof-object)) $\implies$ #t

Note: The end-of-file object is not a datum value, and thus has no external
representation.

(eof-object? *obj*)   procedure
    Returns #t if *obj* is the end-of-file object, #f otherwise.

8.2.6 Input and output ports

The operations described in this section are common to input and output ports, both binary and textual. A port may also have an associated *position* that specifies a particular place within its data sink or source, and may also provide operations for inspecting and setting that place.

(port? *obj*) procedure

Returns #t if the argument is a port, and returns #f otherwise.

(port-transcoder *port*) procedure

Returns the transcoder associated with *port* if *port* is textual and has an associated transcoder, and returns #f if *port* is binary or does not have an associated transcoder.

(textual-port? *port*) procedure
(binary-port? *port*) procedure

The textual-port? procedure returns #t if *port* is textual, and returns #f otherwise. The binary-port? procedure returns #t if *port* is binary, and returns #f otherwise.

(transcoded-port *binary-port transcoder*) procedure

The transcoded-port procedure returns a new textual port with the specified *transcoder*. Otherwise the new textual port's state is largely the same as that of *binary-port*. If *binary-port* is an input port, the new textual port will be an input port and will transcode the bytes that have not yet been read from *binary-port*. If *binary-port* is an output port, the new textual port will be an output port and will transcode output characters into bytes that are written to the byte sink represented by *binary-port*.

As a side effect, however, transcoded-port closes *binary-port* in a special way that allows the new textual port to continue to use the byte source or sink represented by *binary-port*, even though *binary-port* itself is closed and cannot be used by the input and output operations described in this chapter.

(port-has-port-position? *port*) procedure
(port-position *port*) procedure

The port-has-port-position? procedure returns #t if the port supports the port-position operation, and #f otherwise.

For a binary port, the port-position procedure returns the index of the position at which the next byte would be read from or written to the port as an exact non-negative integer object. For a textual port, port-position returns a value of some implementation-dependent type representing the port's position; this value may be useful only as the *pos* argument to set-port-position!, if the latter is supported on the port (see below).

If the port does not support the operation, port-position raises an exception with condition type &assertion.

Note: For a textual port, the port position may or may not be an integer object. If it is an integer object, the integer object does not necessarily correspond to a byte or character position.

(port-has-set-port-position!? *port*)   procedure
(set-port-position! *port pos*)   procedure

If *port* is a binary port, *pos* should be a non-negative exact integer object. If *port* is a textual port, *pos* should be the return value of a call to port-position on *port*.

The port-has-set-port-position!? procedure returns #t if the port supports the set-port-position! operation, and #f otherwise.

The set-port-position! procedure raises an exception with condition type &assertion if the port does not support the operation, and an exception with condition type &i/o-invalid-position if *pos* is not in the range of valid positions of *port*. Otherwise, it sets the current position of the port to *pos*. If *port* is an output port, set-port-position! first flushes *port*. (See flush-output-port, section 8.2.10.)

If *port* is a binary output port and the current position is set beyond the current end of the data in the underlying data sink, the object is not extended until new data is written at that position. The contents of any intervening positions are unspecified. Binary ports created by open-file-output-port and open-file-input/output-port can always be extended in this manner within the limits of the underlying operating system. In other cases, attempts to set the port beyond the current end of data in the underlying object may result in an exception with condition type &i/o-invalid-position.

(close-port *port*)   procedure

Closes the port, rendering the port incapable of delivering or accepting data. If *port* is an output port, it is flushed before being closed. This has no effect if the port has already been closed. A closed port is still a port. The close-port procedure returns unspecified values.

(call-with-port *port proc*)   procedure

Proc must accept one argument. The call-with-port procedure calls *proc* with *port* as an argument. If *proc* returns, *port* is closed automatically and the values returned by *proc* are returned. If *proc* does not return, *port* is not closed automatically, except perhaps when it is possible to prove that *port* will never again be used for an input or output operation.

8.2.7 Input ports

An input port allows the reading of an infinite sequence of bytes or characters punctuated by end-of-file objects. An input port connected to a finite data source ends in an infinite sequence of end-of-file objects.

It is unspecified whether a character encoding consisting of several bytes may have an end of file between the bytes. If, for example, get-char raises an &i/o-decoding

exception because the character encoding at the port's position is incomplete up to the next end of file, a subsequent call to get-char may successfully decode a character if bytes completing the encoding are available after the end of file.

(input-port? *obj*) procedure

Returns #t if the argument is an input port (or a combined input and output port), and returns #f otherwise.

(port-eof? *input-port*) procedure

Returns #t if the lookahead-u8 procedure (if *input-port* is a binary port) or the lookahead-char procedure (if *input-port* is a textual port) would return the end-of-file object, and #f otherwise. The operation may block indefinitely if no data is available but the port cannot be determined to be at end of file.

(open-file-input-port *filename*) procedure
(open-file-input-port *filename file-options*) procedure
(open-file-input-port *filename* procedure
    file-options buffer-mode)
(open-file-input-port *filename* procedure
    file-options buffer-mode maybe-transcoder)
Maybe-transcoder must be either a transcoder or #f.

The open-file-input-port procedure returns an input port for the named file. The *file-options* and *maybe-transcoder* arguments are optional.

The *file-options* argument, which may determine various aspects of the returned port (see section 8.2.2), defaults to the value of (file-options).

The *buffer-mode* argument, if supplied, must be one of the symbols that name a buffer mode. The *buffer-mode* argument defaults to block.

If *maybe-transcoder* is a transcoder, it becomes the transcoder associated with the returned port.

If *maybe-transcoder* is #f or absent, the port will be a binary port and will support the port-position and set-port-position! operations. Otherwise the port will be a textual port, and whether it supports the port-position and set-port-position! operations is implementation-dependent (and possibly transcoder-dependent).

(open-bytevector-input-port *bytevector*) procedure
(open-bytevector-input-port *bytevector* procedure
    maybe-transcoder)
Maybe-transcoder must be either a transcoder or #f.

The open-bytevector-input-port procedure returns an input port whose bytes are drawn from *bytevector*. If *transcoder* is specified, it becomes the transcoder associated with the returned port.

If *maybe-transcoder* is #f or absent, the port will be a binary port and will support the port-position and set-port-position! operations. Otherwise the port will be a textual port, and whether it supports the port-position and set-port-position! operations will be implementation-dependent (and possibly transcoder-dependent).

If *bytevector* is modified after open-bytevector-input-port has been called, the effect on the returned port is unspecified.

(open-string-input-port *string*)   procedure

Returns a textual input port whose characters are drawn from *string*. The port may or may not have an associated transcoder; if it does, the transcoder is implementation-dependent. The port should support the port-position and set-port-position! operations.

If *string* is modified after open-string-input-port has been called, the effect on the returned port is unspecified.

(standard-input-port)   procedure

Returns a fresh binary input port connected to standard input. Whether the port supports the port-position and set-port-position! operations is implementation-dependent.

(current-input-port)   procedure

This returns a default textual port for input. Normally, this default port is associated with standard input, but can be dynamically re-assigned using the with-input-from-file procedure from the (rnrs io simple (6)) library (see section 8.3). The port may or may not have an associated transcoder; if it does, the transcoder is implementation-dependent.

(make-custom-binary-input-port *id read!*   procedure
    get-position set-position! close)

Returns a newly created binary input port whose byte source is an arbitrary algorithm represented by the *read!* procedure. *Id* must be a string naming the new port, provided for informational purposes only. *Read!* must be a procedure and should behave as specified below; it will be called by operations that perform binary input.

Each of the remaining arguments may be #f; if any of those arguments is not #f, it must be a procedure and should behave as specified below.

- (*read! bytevector start count*)
  Start will be a non-negative exact integer object, *count* will be a positive exact integer object, and *bytevector* will be a bytevector whose length is at least *start + count*. The *read!* procedure should obtain up to *count* bytes from the byte source, and should write those bytes into *bytevector* starting at index *start*. The *read!* procedure should return an exact integer object. This integer object should represent the number of bytes that it has read. To indicate an end of file, the *read!* procedure should write no bytes and return 0.
- (*get-position*)
  The *get-position* procedure (if supplied) should return an exact integer object representing the current position of the input port. If not supplied, the custom port will not support the port-position operation.

- (*set-position!* *pos*)

  Pos will be a non-negative exact integer object. The *set-position!* procedure (if supplied) should set the position of the input port to *pos*. If not supplied, the custom port will not support the `set-port-position!` operation.

- (*close*)

  The *close* procedure (if supplied) should perform any actions that are necessary when the input port is closed.

Implementation responsibilities: The implementation must check the return values of *read!* and *get-position* only when it actually calls them as part of an I/O operation requested by the program. The implementation is not required to check that these procedures otherwise behave as described. If they do not, however, the behavior of the resulting port is unspecified.

(make-custom-textual-input-port *id read!*   procedure
  get-position set-position! close)

Returns a newly created textual input port whose character source is an arbitrary algorithm represented by the *read!* procedure. *Id* must be a string naming the new port, provided for informational purposes only. *Read!* must be a procedure and should behave as specified below; it will be called by operations that perform textual input.

Each of the remaining arguments may be `#f`; if any of those arguments is not `#f`, it must be a procedure and should behave as specified below.

- (*read!* *string start count*)

  Start will be a non-negative exact integer object, *count* will be a positive exact integer object, and *string* will be a string whose length is at least *start* + *count*. The *read!* procedure should obtain up to *count* characters from the character source, and should write those characters into *string* starting at index *start*. The *read!* procedure should return an exact integer object representing the number of characters that it has written. To indicate an end of file, the *read!* procedure should write no bytes and return 0.

- (*get-position*)

  The *get-position* procedure (if supplied) should return a single value. The return value should represent the current position of the input port. If not supplied, the custom port will not support the `port-position` operation.

- (*set-position!* *pos*)

  The *set-position!* procedure (if supplied) should set the position of the input port to *pos* if *pos* is the return value of a call to *get-position*. If not supplied, the custom port will not support the `set-port-position!` operation.

- (*close*)

  The *close* procedure (if supplied) should perform any actions that are necessary when the input port is closed.

The port may or may not have an an associated transcoder; if it does, the transcoder is implementation-dependent.

Implementation responsibilities: The implementation must check the return values of *read!* and *get-position* only when it actually calls them as part of an I/O operation requested by the program. The implementation is not required to check that these procedures otherwise behave as described. If they do not, however, the behavior of the resulting port is unspecified.

Note: Even when the *get-position* procedure is supplied, the port-position procedure cannot generally return a precise value for a custom textual input port if data has been read from the port. Therefore, it is likely that this entry will change in a future version of the report.

8.2.8 Binary input

(get-u8 *binary-input-port*)   procedure

Reads from *binary-input-port*, blocking as necessary, until a byte is available from *binary-input-port* or until an end of file is reached. If a byte becomes available, get-u8 returns the byte as an octet and updates *binary-input-port* to point just past that byte. If no input byte is seen before an end of file is reached, the end-of-file object is returned.

(lookahead-u8 *binary-input-port*)   procedure

The lookahead-u8 procedure is like get-u8, but it does not update *binary-input-port* to point past the byte.

(get-bytevector-n *binary-input-port count*)   procedure

Count must be an exact, non-negative integer object representing the number of bytes to be read. The get-bytevector-n procedure reads from *binary-input-port*, blocking as necessary, until *count* bytes are available from *binary-input-port* or until an end of file is reached. If *count* bytes are available before an end of file, get-bytevector-n returns a bytevector of size *count*. If fewer bytes are available before an end of file, get-bytevector-n returns a bytevector containing those bytes. In either case, the input port is updated to point just past the bytes read. If an end of file is reached before any bytes are available, get-bytevector-n returns the end-of-file object.

(get-bytevector-n! *binary-input-port*   procedure
    bytevector start count)

Start and *count* must be exact, non-negative integer objects, with *count* representing the number of bytes to be read. *bytevector* must be a bytevector with at least *start + count* elements.

The get-bytevector-n! procedure reads from *binary-input-port*, blocking as necessary, until *count* bytes are available from *binary-input-port* or until an end of file is reached. If *count* bytes are available before an end of file, they are written into *bytevector* starting at index *start*, and the result is *count*. If fewer bytes are available before the next end of file, the available bytes are written into *bytevector* starting at index *start*, and the result is a number object representing the number of bytes actually read. In either case, the input port is updated to point just past the bytes read. If an end of file is reached before any bytes are available, `get-bytevector-n!` returns the end-of-file object.

(`get-bytevector-some` *binary-input-port*)   procedure

Reads from *binary-input-port*, blocking as necessary, until bytes are available from *binary-input-port* or until an end of file is reached. If bytes become available, `get-bytevector-some` returns a freshly allocated bytevector containing the initial available bytes (at least one), and it updates *binary-input-port* to point just past these bytes. If no input bytes are seen before an end of file is reached, the end-of-file object is returned.

(`get-bytevector-all` *binary-input-port*)   procedure

Attempts to read all bytes until the next end of file, blocking as necessary. If one or more bytes are read, `get-bytevector-all` returns a bytevector containing all bytes up to the next end of file and updates *binary-input-port* to point just past these bytes. Otherwise, `get-bytevector-all` returns the end-of-file object. The operation may block indefinitely waiting to see if more bytes will become available, even if some bytes are already available.

8.2.9 *Textual input*

(`get-char` *textual-input-port*)   procedure

Reads from *textual-input-port*, blocking as necessary, until a complete character is available from *textual-input-port*, or until an end of file is reached.

If a complete character is available before the next end of file, `get-char` returns that character and updates the input port to point past the character. If an end of file is reached before any character is read, `get-char` returns the end-of-file object.

(`lookahead-char` *textual-input-port*)   procedure

The `lookahead-char` procedure is like `get-char`, but it does not update the position of *textual-input-port* to point past the character.
Note: With some of the standard transcoders described in this document, up to four bytes of lookahead are needed. Nonstandard transcoders may need even more lookahead.

(`get-string-n` *textual-input-port count*)   procedure
Count must be an exact, non-negative integer object, representing the number of characters to be read.

The `get-string-n` procedure reads from *textual-input-port*, blocking as necessary, until *count* characters are available, or until an end of file is reached.

If *count* characters are available before end of file, `get-string-n` returns a string consisting of those *count* characters. If fewer characters are available before an end of file, but one or more characters can be read, `get-string-n` returns a string containing those characters. In either case, the input port is updated to point just past the characters read. If no characters can be read before an end of file, the end-of-file object is returned.

(get-string-n! *textual-input-port string start count*)   procedure
Start and *count* must be exact, non-negative integer objects, with *count* representing the number of characters to be read. *String* must be a string with at least *start+count* characters.

The get-string-n! procedure reads from *textual-input-port* in the same manner as get-string-n. If *count* characters are available before an end of file, they are written into *string* starting at index *start*, and *count* is returned. If fewer characters are available before an end of file, but one or more can be read, those characters are written into *string* starting at index *start* and the number of characters actually read is returned as an exact integer object. If no characters can be read before an end of file, the end-of-file object is returned.

(get-string-all *textual-input-port*)   procedure
Reads from *textual-input-port* until an end of file, decoding characters in the same manner as get-string-n and get-string-n!.

If characters are available before the end of file, a string containing all the characters decoded from that data are returned. If no character precedes the end of file, the end-of-file object is returned.

(get-line *textual-input-port*)   procedure
Reads from *textual-input-port* up to and including the linefeed character or end of file, decoding characters in the same manner as get-string-n and get-string-n!.

If a linefeed character is read, a string containing all of the text up to (but not including) the linefeed character is returned, and the port is updated to point just past the linefeed character. If an end of file is encountered before any linefeed character is read, but some characters have been read and decoded as characters, a string containing those characters is returned. If an end of file is encountered before any characters are read, the end-of-file object is returned.
Note: The end-of-line style, if not none, will cause all line endings to be read as linefeed characters. See section 8.2.4.

(get-datum *textual-input-port*)   procedure
Reads an external representation from *textual-input-port* and returns the datum it represents. The get-datum procedure returns the next datum that can be parsed from the given *textual-input-port*, updating *textual-input-port* to point exactly past the end of the external representation of the object.

Any ⟨interlexeme space⟩ (see report section 4.2) in the input is first skipped. If an end of file occurs after the ⟨interlexeme space⟩, the end-of-file object (see section 8.2.5) is returned.

If a character inconsistent with an external representation is encountered in the input, an exception with condition types &lexical and &i/o-read is raised. Also, if the end of file is encountered after the beginning of an external representation, but the external representation is incomplete and therefore cannot be parsed, an exception with condition types &lexical and &i/o-read is raised.

8.2.10 Output ports

An output port is a sink to which bytes or characters are written. The written data may control external devices or may produce files and other objects that may subsequently be opened for input.

(output-port? *obj*)   procedure

Returns #t if the argument is an output port (or a combined input and output port), #f otherwise.

(flush-output-port *output-port*)   procedure

Flushes any buffered output from the buffer of *output-port* to the underlying file, device, or object. The flush-output-port procedure returns unspecified values.

(output-port-buffer-mode *output-port*)   procedure

Returns the symbol that represents the buffer mode of *output-port*.

(open-file-output-port *filename*)   procedure
(open-file-output-port *filename file-options*)   procedure
(open-file-output-port *filename file-options buffer-mode*)   procedure
(open-file-output-port *filename file-options buffer-mode*   procedure
    maybe-transcoder)

Maybe-transcoder must be either a transcoder or #f.

The open-file-output-port procedure returns an output port for the named file.

The *file-options* argument, which may determine various aspects of the returned port (see section 8.2.2), defaults to the value of (file-options).

The *buffer-mode* argument, if supplied, must be one of the symbols that name a buffer mode. The *buffer-mode* argument defaults to block.

If *maybe-transcoder* is a transcoder, it becomes the transcoder associated with the port.

If *maybe-transcoder* is #f or absent, the port will be a binary port and will support the port-position and set-port-position! operations. Otherwise the port will be a textual port, and whether it supports the port-position and set-port-position! operations is implementation-dependent (and possibly transcoder-dependent).

(open-bytevector-output-port)   procedure
(open-bytevector-output-port *maybe-transcoder*)   procedure

Maybe-transcoder must be either a transcoder or #f.

The open-bytevector-output-port procedure returns two values: an output port and an extraction procedure. The output port accumulates the bytes written to it for later extraction by the procedure.

If *maybe-transcoder* is a transcoder, it becomes the transcoder associated with the port. If *maybe-transcoder* is #f or absent, the port will be a binary port and will support the `port-position` and `set-port-position!` operations. Otherwise the port will be a textual port, and whether it supports the `port-position` and `set-port-position!` operations is implementation-dependent (and possibly transcoder-dependent).

The extraction procedure takes no arguments. When called, it returns a bytevector consisting of all the port's accumulated bytes (regardless of the port's current position), removes the accumulated bytes from the port, and resets the port's position.

(call-with-bytevector-output-port *proc*)   procedure
(call-with-bytevector-output-port *proc* *maybe-transcoder*)

Proc must accept one argument. *Maybe-transcoder* must be either a transcoder or #f.

The `call-with-bytevector-output-port` procedure creates an output port that accumulates the bytes written to it and calls *proc* with that output port as an argument. Whenever *proc* returns, a bytevector consisting of all of the port's accumulated bytes (regardless of the port's current position) is returned and the port is closed.

The transcoder associated with the output port is determined as for a call to `open-bytevector-output-port`.

(open-string-output-port)   procedure

Returns two values: a textual output port and an extraction procedure. The output port accumulates the characters written to it for later extraction by the procedure.

The port may or may not have an associated transcoder; if it does, the transcoder is implementation-dependent. The port should support the `port-position` and `set-port-position!` operations.

The extraction procedure takes no arguments. When called, it returns a string consisting of all of the port's accumulated characters (regardless of the current position), removes the accumulated characters from the port, and resets the port's position.

(call-with-string-output-port *proc*)   procedure

Proc must accept one argument. The `call-with-string-output-port` procedure creates a textual output port that accumulates the characters written to it and calls *proc* with that output port as an argument. Whenever *proc* returns, a string consisting of all of the port's accumulated characters (regardless of the port's current position) is returned and the port is closed.

The port may or may not have an associated transcoder; if it does, the transcoder is implementation-dependent. The port should support the `port-position` and `set-port-position!` operations.

(standard-output-port)   procedure
(standard-error-port)   procedure

Returns a fresh binary output port connected to the standard output or standard error respectively. Whether the port supports the port-position and set-port-position! operations is implementation-dependent.

(current-output-port)   procedure
(current-error-port)   procedure

These return default textual ports for regular output and error output. Normally, these default ports are associated with standard output, and standard error, respectively. The return value of current-output-port can be dynamically re-assigned using the with-output-to-file procedure from the (rnrs io simple (6)) library (see section 8.3). A port returned by one of these procedures may or may not have an associated transcoder; if it does, the transcoder is implementation-dependent.

(make-custom-binary-output-port id write!   procedure
    get-position set-position! close)

Returns a newly created binary output port whose byte sink is an arbitrary algorithm represented by the *write!* procedure. *Id* must be a string naming the new port, provided for informational purposes only. *Write!* must be a procedure and should behave as specified below; it will be called by operations that perform binary output.

Each of the remaining arguments may be #f; if any of those arguments is not #f, it must be a procedure and should behave as specified in the description of make-custom-binary-input-port.

- (*write! bytevector start count*)
  Start and *count* will be non-negative exact integer objects, and *bytevector* will be a bytevector whose length is at least *start* + *count*. The *write!* procedure should write up to *count* bytes from *bytevector* starting at index *start* to the byte sink. The *write!* procedure should return the number of bytes that it wrote, as an exact integer object.

Implementation responsibilities: The implementation must check the return values of *write!* only when it actually calls *write!* as part of an I/O operation requested by the program. The implementation is not required to check that *write!* otherwise behaves as described. If it does not, however, the behavior of the resulting port is unspecified.

(make-custom-textual-output-port id write!   procedure
    get-position set-position! close)

Returns a newly created textual output port whose byte sink is an arbitrary algorithm represented by the *write!* procedure. *Id* must be a string naming the new port, provided for informational purposes only. *Write!* must be a procedure and should behave as specified below; it will be called by operations that perform textual output.

Each of the remaining arguments may be #f; if any of those arguments is not #f, it must be a procedure and should behave as specified in the description of make-custom-textual-input-port.

- (*write! string start count*)
  Start and *count* will be non-negative exact integer objects, and *string* will be a string whose length is at least *start + count*. The *write!* procedure should write up to *count* characters from *string* starting at index *start* to the character sink. The *write!* procedure should return the number of characters that it wrote, as an exact integer object.

The port may or may not have an associated transcoder; if it does, the transcoder is implementation-dependent.

Implementation responsibilities: The implementation must check the return values of *write!* only when it actually calls *write!* as part of an I/O operation requested by the program. The implementation is not required to check that *write!* otherwise behaves as described. If it does not, however, the behavior of the resulting port is unspecified.

8.2.11 Binary output

(put-u8 *binary-output-port octet*)   procedure
    Writes *octet* to the output port and returns unspecified values.

(put-bytevector *binary-output-port bytevector*)   procedure
(put-bytevector *binary-output-port bytevector start*)   procedure
(put-bytevector *binary-output-port bytevector start count*)

            procedure*Start* and *count* must be non-negative exact integer objects that default to 0 and (bytevector-length *bytevector*) − *start*, respectively. *Bytevector* must have a length of at least *start + count*. The put-bytevector procedure writes the *count* bytes of the bytevector *bytevector* starting at index *start* to the output port. The put-bytevector procedure returns unspecified values.

8.2.12 Textual output

(put-char *textual-output-port char*)   procedure
    Writes *char* to the port. The put-char procedure returns unspecified values.

(put-string *textual-output-port string*)   procedure
(put-string *textual-output-port string start*)   procedure
(put-string *textual-output-port string start count*)   procedure
Start and *count* must be non-negative exact integer objects. *String* must have a length of at least *start + count*. *Start* defaults to 0. *Count* defaults to

(string-length *string*) − *start*.

The put-string procedure writes the *count* characters of *string* starting at index *start* to the port. The put-string procedure returns unspecified values.

(put-datum *textual-output-port datum*) procedure

Datum should be a datum value. The put-datum procedure writes an external representation of *datum* to *textual-output-port*. The specific external representation is implementation-dependent. However, whenever possible, an implementation should produce a representation for which get-datum, when reading the representation, will return an object equal (in the sense of equal?) to *datum*.

Note: Not all datums may allow producing an external representation for which get-datum will produce an object that is equal to the original. Specifically, NaNs contained in *datum* may make this impossible.

Note: The put-datum procedure merely writes the external representation, but no trailing delimiter. If put-datum is used to write several subsequent external representations to an output port, care should be taken to delimit them properly so they can be read back in by subsequent calls to get-datum.

8.2.13 Input/output ports

(open-file-input/output-port *filename*) procedure
(open-file-input/output-port *filename file-options*) procedure
(open-file-input/output-port *filename file-options buffer-mode*) procedure
(open-file-input/output-port *filename file-options buffer-mode* procedure
    transcoder)

Returns a single port that is both an input port and an output port for the named file. The optional arguments default as described in the specification of open-file-output-port. If the input/output port supports port-position and/or set-port-position!, the same port position is used for both input and output.

(make-custom-binary-input/output-port *id read! write!* procedure
    get-position set-position! close)

Returns a newly created binary input/output port whose byte source and sink are arbitrary algorithms represented by the *read!* and *write!* procedures. *Id* must be a string naming the new port, provided for informational purposes only. *Read!* and *write!* must be procedures, and should behave as specified for the make-custom-binary-input-port and make-custom-binary-output-port procedures.

Each of the remaining arguments may be #f; if any of those arguments is not #f, it must be a procedure and should behave as specified in the description of make-custom-binary-input-port.

Note: Unless both *get-position* and *set-position!* procedures are supplied, a put operation cannot precisely position the port for output to a custom binary input/output port after data has been read from the port. Therefore, it is likely that this entry will change in a future version of the report.

(make-custom-textual-input/output-port *id read! write!*   procedure
   get-position set-position! close)

Returns a newly created textual input/output port whose textual source and sink are arbitrary algorithms represented by the *read!* and *write!* procedures. *Id* must be a string naming the new port, provided for informational purposes only. *Read!* and *write!* must be procedures, and should behave as specified for the make-custom-textual-input-port and make-custom-textual-output-port procedures.

Each of the remaining arguments may be #f; if any of those arguments is not #f, it must be a procedure and should behave as specified in the description of make-custom-textual-input-port.

Note: Even when both *get-position* and *set-position!* procedures are supplied, the port-position procedure cannot generally return a precise value for a custom textual input/output port, and a put operation cannot precisely position the port for output, after data has been read from the port. Therefore, it is likely that this entry will change in a future version of the report.

8.3 Simple I/O

This section describes the (rnrs io simple (6)) library, which provides a somewhat more convenient interface for performing textual I/O on ports. This library implements most of the I/O procedures of the previous revision of this report (Kelsey *et al.*, 1998).

The ports created by the procedures of this library are textual ports associated implementation-dependent transcoders.

(eof-object)   procedure
(eof-object? *obj*)   procedure

These are the same as eof-object and eof-object? from the (rnrs io ports (6)) library.

(call-with-input-file *filename proc*)   procedure
(call-with-output-file *filename proc*)   procedure

Proc should accept one argument. These procedures open the file named by *filename* for input or for output, with no specified file options, and call *proc* with the obtained port as an argument. If *proc* returns, the port is closed automatically and the values returned by *proc* are returned. If *proc* does not return, the port is not closed automatically, unless it is possible to prove that the port will never again be used for an I/O operation.

(input-port? *obj*)   procedure
(output-port? *obj*)   procedure

These are the same as the input-port? and output-port? procedures in the (rnrs io ports (6)) library.

```
(current-input-port)                                                   procedure
(current-output-port)                                                  procedure
(current-error-port)                                                   procedure
```
These are the same as the current-input-port, current-output-port, and current-error-port procedures from the (rnrs io ports (6)) library.

```
(with-input-from-file filename thunk)                                  procedure
(with-output-to-file filename thunk)                                   procedure
```
Thunk must be a procedure and must accept zero arguments. The file is opened for input or output using empty file options, and *thunk* is called with no arguments. During the dynamic extent of the call to *thunk*, the obtained port is made the value returned by current-input-port or current-output-port procedures; the previous default values are reinstated when the dynamic extent is exited. When *thunk* returns, the port is closed automatically. The values returned by *thunk* are returned. If an escape procedure is used to escape back into the call to *thunk* after *thunk* is returned, the behavior is unspecified.

```
(open-input-file filename)                                             procedure
```
Opens *filename* for input, with empty file options, and returns the obtained port.

```
(open-output-file filename)                                            procedure
```
Opens *filename* for output, with empty file options, and returns the obtained port.

```
(close-input-port input-port)                                          procedure
(close-output-port output-port)                                        procedure
```
Closes *input-port* or *output-port*, respectively.

```
(read-char)                                                            procedure
(read-char textual-input-port)                                         procedure
```
Reads from *textual-input-port*, blocking as necessary until a character is available from *textual-input-port*, or the data that are available cannot be the prefix of any valid encoding, or an end of file is reached.

If a complete character is available before the next end of file, read-char returns that character, and updates the input port to point past that character. If an end of file is reached before any data are read, read-char returns the end-of-file object.

If *textual-input-port* is omitted, it defaults to the value returned by current-input-port.

```
(peek-char)                                                            procedure
(peek-char textual-input-port)                                         procedure
```
This is the same as read-char, but does not consume any data from the port.

```
(read)                                                                 procedure
(read textual-input-port)                                              procedure
```
Reads an external representation from *textual-input-port* and returns the datum

it represents. The read procedure operates in the same way as get-datum, see
section 8.2.9.

If *textual-input-port* is omitted, it defaults to the value returned by current-input-
port.

(write-char *char*)   procedure
(write-char *char textual-output-port*)   procedure

   Writes an encoding of the character *char* to the *textual-output-port*, and returns
unspecified values.

   If *textual-output-port* is omitted, it defaults to the value returned by current-
output-port.

(newline)   procedure
(newline *textual-output-port*)   procedure

   This is equivalent to using write-char to write #\linefeed to *textual-output-port*.

   If *textual-output-port* is omitted, it defaults to the value returned by current-
output-port.

(display *obj*)   procedure
(display *obj textual-output-port*)   procedure

   Writes a representation of *obj* to the given *textual-output-port*. Strings that appear
in the written representation are not enclosed in doublequotes, and no characters
are escaped within those strings. Character objects appear in the representation
as if written by write-char instead of by write. The display procedure returns
unspecified values. The *textual-output-port* argument may be omitted, in which case
it defaults to the value returned by current-output-port.

(write *obj*)   procedure
(write *obj textual-output-port*)   procedure

   Writes the external representation of *obj* to *textual-output-port*. The write procedure operates in the same way as put-datum; see section 8.2.12.

   If *textual-output-port* is omitted, it defaults to the value returned by current-
output-port.

9 File system

This chapter describes the (rnrs files (6)) library for operations on the file
system. This library, in addition to the procedures described here, also exports the
I/O condition types described in section 8.1.

(file-exists? *filename*)   procedure
Filename must be a file name (see section 8.2.1). The file-exists? procedure
returns #t if the named file exists at the time the procedure is called, #f otherwise.

(delete-file *filename*)   procedure

Filename must be a file name (see section 8.2.1). The delete-file procedure deletes the named file if it exists and can be deleted, and returns unspecified values. If the file does not exist or cannot be deleted, an exception with condition type &i/o-filename is raised.

10 Command-line access and exit values

The procedures described in this section are exported by the (rnrs programs (6)) library.

(command-line)   procedure

Returns a nonempty list of strings. The first element is an implementation-specific name for the running top-level program. The remaining elements are command-line arguments according to the operating system's conventions.

(exit)   procedure
(exit *obj*)   procedure

Exits the running program and communicates an exit value to the operating system. If no argument is supplied, the exit procedure should communicate to the operating system that the program exited normally. If an argument is supplied, the exit procedure should translate the argument into an appropriate exit value for the operating system. If *obj* is #f, the exit is assumed to be abnormal.

11 Arithmetic

This chapter describes Scheme's libraries for more specialized numerical operations: fixnum and flonum arithmetic, as well as bitwise operations on exact integer objects.

11.1 Bitwise operations

A number of procedures operate on the binary two's-complement representations of exact integer objects: Bit positions within an exact integer object are counted from the right, i.e. bit 0 is the least significant bit. Some procedures allow extracting *bit fields*, i.e., number objects representing subsequences of the binary representation of an exact integer object. Bit fields are always positive, and always defined using a finite number of bits.

11.2 Fixnums

Every implementation must define its fixnum range as a closed interval

$$[-2^{w-1}, 2^{w-1} - 1]$$

such that w is a (mathematical) integer $w \geq 24$. Every mathematical integer within an implementation's fixnum range must correspond to an exact integer object that is representable within the implementation. A fixnum is an exact integer object whose value lies within this fixnum range.

This section describes the (rnrs arithmetic fixnums (6)) library, which defines various operations on fixnums. Fixnum operations perform integer arithmetic on their fixnum arguments, but raise an exception with condition type &implementation-restriction if the result is not a fixnum.

This section uses fx, fx_1, fx_2, etc., as parameter names for arguments that must be fixnums.

(fixnum? *obj*)   procedure

Returns #t if *obj* is an exact integer object within the fixnum range, #f otherwise.

(fixnum-width)   procedure
(least-fixnum)   procedure
(greatest-fixnum)   procedure

These procedures return w, -2^{w-1} and $2^{w-1} - 1$: the width, minimum and the maximum value of the fixnum range, respectively.

(fx=? fx_1 fx_2 fx_3 ...)   procedure
(fx>? fx_1 fx_2 fx_3 ...)   procedure
(fx<? fx_1 fx_2 fx_3 ...)   procedure
(fx>=? fx_1 fx_2 fx_3 ...)   procedure
(fx<=? fx_1 fx_2 fx_3 ...)   procedure

These procedures return #t if their arguments are (respectively): equal, monotonically increasing, monotonically decreasing, monotonically nondecreasing, or monotonically nonincreasing, #f otherwise.

(fxzero? fx)   procedure
(fxpositive? fx)   procedure
(fxnegative? fx)   procedure
(fxodd? fx)   procedure
(fxeven? fx)   procedure

These numerical predicates test a fixnum for a particular property, returning #t or #f. The five properties tested by these procedures are: whether the number object is zero, greater than zero, less than zero, odd, or even.

(fxmax fx_1 fx_2 ...)   procedure
(fxmin fx_1 fx_2 ...)   procedure

These procedures return the maximum or minimum of their arguments.

(fx+ fx_1 fx_2)   procedure
(fx* fx_1 fx_2)   procedure

These procedures return the sum or product of their arguments, provided that sum or product is a fixnum. An exception with condition type &implementation-restriction is raised if that sum or product is not a fixnum.

(fx- fx_1 fx_2)   procedure
(fx- fx)   procedure

With two arguments, this procedure returns the difference $fx_1 - fx_2$, provided that difference is a fixnum.

With one argument, this procedure returns the additive inverse of its argument, provided that integer object is a fixnum.

An exception with condition type &implementation-restriction is raised if the mathematically correct result of this procedure is not a fixnum.

> (fx- (least-fixnum)) $\Longrightarrow$ &assertion *exception*

(fxdiv-and-mod fx_1 fx_2)   procedure
(fxdiv fx_1 fx_2)   procedure
(fxmod fx_1 fx_2)   procedure
(fxdiv0-and-mod0 fx_1 fx_2)   procedure
(fxdiv0 fx_1 fx_2)   procedure
(fxmod0 fx_1 fx_2)   procedure

Fx_2 must be nonzero. These procedures implement number-theoretic integer division and return the results of the corresponding mathematical operations specified in report section 11.7.4.

> (fxdiv fx_1 fx_2) $\Longrightarrow$ fx_1 div fx_2
> (fxmod fx_1 fx_2) $\Longrightarrow$ fx_1 mod fx_2
> (fxdiv-and-mod fx_1 fx_2) $\Longrightarrow$ fx_1 div fx_2, fx_1 mod fx_2
>   ; two return values
> (fxdiv0 fx_1 fx_2) $\Longrightarrow$ fx_1 div$_0$ fx_2
> (fxmod0 fx_1 fx_2) $\Longrightarrow$ fx_1 mod$_0$ fx_2
> (fxdiv0-and-mod0 fx_1 fx_2) $\Longrightarrow$ fx_1 fx_1 div$_0$ fx_2, fx_1 mod$_0$ fx_2
>   ; two return values

(fx+/carry fx_1 fx_2 fx_3)   procedure

Returns the two fixnum results of the following computation:

```
(let* ((s (+ fx1 fx2 fx3))
       (s0 (mod0 s (expt 2 (fixnum-width))))
       (s1 (div0 s (expt 2 (fixnum-width))))))
  (values s0 s1))
```

(fx-/carry fx_1 fx_2 fx_3)   procedure

Returns the two fixnum results of the following computation:

```
      (let* ((d (- fx₁ fx₂ fx₃))
             (d0 (mod0 d (expt 2 (fixnum-width))))
             (d1 (div0 d (expt 2 (fixnum-width)))))
        (values d0 d1))
```

(fx*/carry fx_1 fx_2 fx_3)   procedure
Returns the two fixnum results of the following computation:

```
      (let* ((s (+ (* fx₁ fx₂) fx₃))
             (s0 (mod0 s (expt 2 (fixnum-width))))
             (s1 (div0 s (expt 2 (fixnum-width)))))
        (values s0 s1))
```

(fxnot fx)   procedure
Returns the unique fixnum that is congruent mod 2^w to the one's-complement of fx.

(fxand fx_1 ...)   procedure
(fxior fx_1 ...)   procedure
(fxxor fx_1 ...)   procedure
These procedures return the fixnum that is the bit-wise "and", "inclusive or", or "exclusive or" of the two's complement representations of their arguments. If they are passed only one argument, they return that argument. If they are passed no arguments, they return the fixnum (either −1 or 0) that acts as identity for the operation.

(fxif fx_1 fx_2 fx_3)   procedure
Returns the fixnum that is the bit-wise "if" of the two's complement representations of its arguments, i.e. for each bit, if it is 1 in fx_1, the corresponding bit in fx_2 becomes the value of the corresponding bit in the result, and if it is 0, the corresponding bit in fx_3 becomes the corresponding bit in the value of the result. This is the fixnum result of the following computation:

```
        (fxior (fxand fx₁ fx₂)
               (fxand (fxnot fx₁) fx₃))
```

(fxbit-count fx)   procedure
If fx is non-negative, this procedure returns the number of 1 bits in the two's complement representation of fx. Otherwise it returns the result of the following computation:

```
        (fxnot (fxbit-count (fxnot ei)))
```

(fxlength fx)   procedure
Returns the number of bits needed to represent fx if it is positive, and the number of bits needed to represent (fxnot fx) if it is negative, which is the fixnum result of the following computation:

```
(do ((result 0 (+ result 1))
     (bits (if (fxnegative? fx)
               (fxnot fx)
               fx)
           (fxarithmetic-shift-right bits 1)))
    ((fxzero? bits)
     result))
```

(fxfirst-bit-set *fx*)   procedure

Returns the index of the least significant 1 bit in the two's complement representation of *fx*. If *fx* is 0, then −1 is returned.

```
(fxfirst-bit-set 0)                    ⟹    -1
(fxfirst-bit-set 1)                    ⟹    0
(fxfirst-bit-set -4)                   ⟹    2
```

(fxbit-set? *fx*$_1$ *fx*$_2$)   procedure

Fx$_2$ must be non-negative. The fxbit-set? procedure returns #t if the *fx*$_2$th bit is
1 in the two's complement representation of *fx*$_1$, and #f otherwise. This is the result
of the following computation:

```
(if (fx>= fx₂ (fx- (fixnum-width) 1))
    (fxnegative? fx₁)
    (not
      (fxzero?
        (fxand fx₁
               (fxarithmetic-shift-left 1 fx₂)))))
```

(fxcopy-bit *fx*$_1$ *fx*$_2$ *fx*$_3$)   procedure

Fx$_2$ must be non-negative and less than $w - 1$. *Fx*$_3$ must be 0 or 1. The fxcopy-bit
procedure returns the result of replacing the *fx*$_2$th bit of *fx*$_1$ by *fx*$_3$, which is the
result of the following computation:

```
(let* ((mask (fxarithmetic-shift-left 1 fx₂)))
  (fxif mask
        (fxarithmetic-shift-left fx₃ fx₂)
        fx₁))
```

(fxbit-field *fx*$_1$ *fx*$_2$ *fx*$_3$)   procedure

Fx$_2$ and *fx*$_3$ must be non-negative and less than w. Moreover, *fx*$_2$ must be less than
or equal to *fx*$_3$. The fxbit-field procedure returns the number represented by the
bits at the positions from *fx*$_2$ (inclusive) to *fx*$_3$ (exclusive), which is the fixnum result
of the following computation:

```
(let* ((mask (fxnot
               (fxarithmetic-shift-left -1 fx3)))))
   (fxarithmetic-shift-right (fxand fx1 mask)
                             fx2))
```

(fxcopy-bit-field fx_1 fx_2 fx_3 fx_4)   procedure

Fx_2 and fx_3 must be non-negative and less than w. Moreover, fx_2 must be less than or equal to fx_3. The fxcopy-bit-field procedure returns the result of replacing in fx_1 the bits at positions from fx_2 (inclusive) to fx_3 (exclusive) by the bits in fx_4 from position 0 (inclusive) to position $fx_3 - fx_2$ (exclusive), which is the fixnum result of the following computation:

```
(let* ((to     fx1)
       (start fx2)
       (end   fx3)
       (from  fx4)
       (mask1 (fxarithmetic-shift-left -1 start))
       (mask2 (fxnot
                 (fxarithmetic-shift-left -1 end)))
       (mask (fxand mask1 mask2))
       (mask3 (fxnot (fxarithmetic-shift-left
                        -1 (- end start)))))
   (fxif mask
         (fxarithmetic-shift-left (fxand from mask3)
                                  start)
         to))
```

```
(fxcopy-bit-field #b0000001 2 5 #b11111000)
(fxcopy-bit-field #b0000001 2 5 #b00001201)
(fxcopy-bit-field #b0001111 2 5 #b00001311)
```

(fxarithmetic-shift fx_1 fx_2)   procedure

The absolute value of fx_2 must be less than w. If

```
(floor (* fx1 (expt 2 fx2)))
```

is a fixnum, then that fixnum is returned. Otherwise an exception with condition type &implementation-restriction is raised.

(fxarithmetic-shift-left fx_1 fx_2)   procedure
(fxarithmetic-shift-right fx_1 fx_2)   procedure

Fx_2 must be non-negative, and less than w. The fxarithmetic-shift-left procedure behaves the same as fxarithmetic-shift, and the expression

```
(fxarithmetic-shift-right fx1 fx2)
```

behaves the same as the expression (fxarithmetic-shift fx_1 (fx- fx_2)).

(fxrotate-bit-field fx_1 fx_2 fx_3 fx_4)   procedure
Fx_2, fx_3, and fx_4 must be non-negative and less than w. Fx_2 must be less than or
equal to fx_3. Fx_4 must be less than or equal to the difference between fx_3 and fx_2.
The fxrotate-bit-field procedure returns the result of cyclically permuting in
fx_1 the bits at positions from fx_2 (inclusive) to fx_3 (exclusive) by fx_4 bits towards
the more significant bits, which is the result of the following computation:

```
(let* ((n      fx1)
       (start fx2)
       (end   fx3)
       (count fx4)
       (width (fx- end start)))
  (fxcopy-bit-field n start end
    (fxior
      (fxarithmetic-shift-left
        (fxbit-field n start (fx- end count))
        count)
      (fxarithmetic-shift-right
        (fxbit-field n start end)
        (fx- width count)))))
```

(fxreverse-bit-field fx_1 fx_2 fx_3)   procedure
Fx_2 and fx_3 must be non-negative and less than w. Moreover, fx_2 must be less than
or equal to fx_3. The fxreverse-bit-field procedure returns the fixnum obtained
from fx_1 by reversing the order of the bits at positions from fx_2 (inclusive) to fx_3
(exclusive).

```
(fxreverse-bit-field #b1010010 1 4) ⟹ 88 ; #b1011000
```

11.3 Flonums

This section describes the (rnrs arithmetic flonums (6)) library.

This section uses fl, fl_1, fl_2, etc., as parameter names for arguments that must be
flonums, and ifl as a name for arguments that must be integer-valued flonums, i.e.,
flonums for which the integer-valued? predicate returns true.

(flonum? obj)   procedure
Returns #t if obj is a flonum, #f otherwise.

(real->flonum x)   procedure
Returns the best flonum representation of x.
The value returned is a flonum that is numerically closest to the argument.
Note: If flonums are represented in binary floating point, then implementations

should break ties by preferring the floating-point representation whose least significant bit is zero.

(fl=? fl_1 fl_2 fl_3 ...)	procedure
(fl<? fl_1 fl_2 fl_3 ...)	procedure
(fl<=? fl_1 fl_2 fl_3 ...)	procedure
(fl>? fl_1 fl_2 fl_3 ...)	procedure
(fl>=? fl_1 fl_2 fl_3 ...)	procedure

These procedures return #t if their arguments are (respectively): equal, monotonically increasing, monotonically decreasing, monotonically nondecreasing, or monotonically nonincreasing, #f otherwise. These predicates must be transitive.

(fl=? +inf.0 +inf.0)	$\Longrightarrow$	#t
(fl=? -inf.0 +inf.0)	$\Longrightarrow$	#f
(fl=? -inf.0 -inf.0)	$\Longrightarrow$	#t
(fl=? 0.0 -0.0)	$\Longrightarrow$	#t
(fl<? 0.0 -0.0)	$\Longrightarrow$	#f
(fl=? +nan.0 fl)	$\Longrightarrow$	#f
(fl<? +nan.0 fl)	$\Longrightarrow$	#f

(flinteger? fl)	procedure
(flzero? fl)	procedure
(flpositive? fl)	procedure
(flnegative? fl)	procedure
(flodd? $i\mathit{fl}$)	procedure
(fleven? $i\mathit{fl}$)	procedure
(flfinite? fl)	procedure
(flinfinite? fl)	procedure
(flnan? fl)	procedure

These numerical predicates test a flonum for a particular property, returning #t or #f. The flinteger? procedure tests whether the number object is an integer, flzero? tests whether it is fl=? to zero, flpositive? tests whether it is greater than zero, flnegative? tests whether it is less than zero, flodd? tests whether it is odd, fleven? tests whether it is even, flfinite? tests whether it is not an infinity and not a NaN, flinfinite? tests whether it is an infinity, and flnan? tests whether it is a NaN.

(flnegative? -0.0)	$\Longrightarrow$	#f
(flfinite? +inf.0)	$\Longrightarrow$	#f
(flfinite? 5.0)	$\Longrightarrow$	#t
(flinfinite? 5.0)	$\Longrightarrow$	#f
(flinfinite? +inf.0)	$\Longrightarrow$	#t

Note: (flnegative? -0.0) must return #f, else it would lose the correspondence with (fl< -0.0 0.0), which is #f according to IEEE 754 (IEEE754, 1985).

(flmax fl_1 fl_2 ...)   procedure
(flmin fl_1 fl_2 ...)   procedure

These procedures return the maximum or minimum of their arguments. They always return a NaN when one or more of the arguments is a NaN.

(fl+ fl_1 ...)   procedure
(fl* fl_1 ...)   procedure

These procedures return the flonum sum or product of their flonum arguments. In general, they should return the flonum that best approximates the mathematical sum or product. (For implementations that represent flonums using IEEE binary floating point, the meaning of "best" is defined by the IEEE standards.)

      (fl+ +inf.0 -inf.0) $\Longrightarrow$ +nan.0
      (fl+ +nan.0 fl) $\Longrightarrow$ +nan.0
      (fl* +nan.0 fl) $\Longrightarrow$ +nan.0

(fl- fl_1 fl_2 ...)   procedure
(fl- fl)   procedure
(fl/ fl_1 fl_2 ...)   procedure
(fl/ fl)   procedure

With two or more arguments, these procedures return the flonum difference or quotient of their flonum arguments, associating to the left. With one argument, however, they return the additive or multiplicative flonum inverse of their argument. In general, they should return the flonum that best approximates the mathematical difference or quotient. (For implementations that represent flonums using IEEE binary floating point, the meaning of "best" is reasonably well-defined by the IEEE standards.)

      (fl- +inf.0 +inf.0) $\Longrightarrow$ +nan.0

For undefined quotients, fl/ behaves as specified by the IEEE standards:

      (fl/ 1.0 0.0) $\Longrightarrow$ +inf.0
      (fl/ -1.0 0.0) $\Longrightarrow$ -inf.0
      (fl/ 0.0 0.0) $\Longrightarrow$ +nan.0

(flabs fl)   procedure

Returns the absolute value of fl.

(fldiv-and-mod fl_1 fl_2)   procedure
(fldiv fl_1 fl_2)   procedure
(flmod fl_1 fl_2)   procedure
(fldiv0-and-mod0 fl_1 fl_2)   procedure
(fldiv0 fl_1 fl_2)   procedure
(flmod0 fl_1 fl_2)   procedure

These procedures implement number-theoretic integer division and return the results of the corresponding mathematical operations specified in report section 11.7.4.

In the cases where the mathematical requirements in section 11.7.4 cannot be satisfied by any number object, either an exception is raised with condition type `&implementation-restriction`, or unspecified flonums (one for `fldiv flmod`, `fldiv0` and `flmod0`, two for `fldiv-and-mod` and `fldiv0-and-mod0`) are returned.

(fldiv fl_1 fl_2)	$\implies$ fl_1 div fl_2
(flmod fl_1 fl_2)	$\implies$ fl_1 mod fl_2
(fldiv-and-mod fl_1 fl_2)	$\implies$ fl_1 div fl_2, fl_1 mod fl_2
	; two return values
(fldiv0 fl_1 fl_2)	$\implies$ fl_1 div$_0$ fl_2
(flmod0 fl_1 fl_2)	$\implies$ fl_1 mod$_0$ fl_2
(fldiv0-and-mod0 fl_1 fl_2)	$\implies$ fl_1 div$_0$ fl_2, fl_1 mod$_0$ fl_2
	; two return values

(flnumerator fl)   procedure
(fldenominator fl)   procedure

These procedures return the numerator or denominator of fl as a flonum; the result is computed as if fl was represented as a fraction in lowest terms. The denominator is always positive. The denominator of 0.0 is defined to be 1.0.

(flnumerator +inf.0)	$\implies$	+inf.0
(flnumerator -inf.0)	$\implies$	-inf.0
(fldenominator +inf.0)	$\implies$	1.0
(fldenominator -inf.0)	$\implies$	1.0
(flnumerator 0.75)	$\implies$	3.0 ; probably
(fldenominator 0.75)	$\implies$	4.0 ; probably

Implementations should implement following behavior:

(flnumerator -0.0)	$\implies$	-0.0

(flfloor fl)   procedure
(flceiling fl)   procedure
(fltruncate fl)   procedure
(flround fl)   procedure

These procedures return integral flonums for flonum arguments that are not infinities or NaNs. For such arguments, `flfloor` returns the largest integral flonum not larger than fl. The `flceiling` procedure returns the smallest integral flonum not smaller than fl. The `fltruncate` procedure returns the integral flonum closest to fl whose absolute value is not larger than the absolute value of fl. The `flround` procedure returns the closest integral flonum to fl, rounding to even when fl represents a number halfway between two integers.

Although infinities and NaNs are not integer objects, these procedures return an infinity when given an infinity as an argument, and a NaN when given a NaN:

(flfloor +inf.0)	$\implies$	+inf.0
(flceiling -inf.0)	$\implies$	-inf.0
(fltruncate +nan.0)	$\implies$	+nan.0

(flexp *fl*)	procedure
(fllog *fl*)	procedure
(fllog *fl*$_1$ *fl*$_2$)	procedure
(flsin *fl*)	procedure
(flcos *fl*)	procedure
(fltan *fl*)	procedure
(flasin *fl*)	procedure
(flacos *fl*)	procedure
(flatan *fl*)	procedure
(flatan *fl*$_1$ *fl*$_2$)	procedure

These procedures compute the usual transcendental functions. The flexp procedure computes the base-*e* exponential of *fl*. The fllog procedure with a single argument computes the natural logarithm of *fl* (not the base ten logarithm); (fllog *fl*$_1$ *fl*$_2$) computes the base-*fl*$_2$ logarithm of *fl*$_1$. The flasin, flacos, and flatan procedures compute arcsine, arccosine, and arctangent, respectively. (flatan *fl*$_1$ *fl*$_2$) computes the arc tangent of *fl*$_1/$*fl*$_2$.

See report section 11.7.5 for the underlying mathematical operations. In the event that these operations do not yield a real result for the given arguments, the result may be a NaN, or may be some unspecified flonum.

Implementations that use IEEE binary floating-point arithmetic should follow the relevant standards for these procedures.

(flexp +inf.0)	$\Longrightarrow$ +inf.0
(flexp -inf.0)	$\Longrightarrow$ 0.0
(fllog +inf.0)	$\Longrightarrow$ +inf.0
(fllog 0.0)	$\Longrightarrow$ -inf.0
(fllog -0.0)	$\Longrightarrow$ *unspecified*
; if -0.0 is distinguished	
(fllog -inf.0)	$\Longrightarrow$ +nan.0
(flatan -inf.0)	$\Longrightarrow$ -1.5707963267948965
; approximately	
(flatan +inf.0)	$\Longrightarrow$ 1.5707963267948965
; approximately	

(flsqrt *fl*) procedure

Returns the principal square root of *fl*. For −0.0, flsqrt should return −0.0; for other negative arguments, the result may be a NaN or some unspecified flonum.

(flsqrt +inf.0)	$\Longrightarrow$ +inf.0
(flsqrt -0.0)	$\Longrightarrow$ -0.0

(flexpt *fl*$_1$ *fl*$_2$) procedure

Either *fl*$_1$ should be non-negative, or, if *fl*$_1$ is negative, *fl*$_2$ should be an integer object. The flexpt procedure returns *fl*$_1$ raised to the power *fl*$_2$. If *fl*$_1$ is negative and *fl*$_2$ is not an integer object, the result may be a NaN, or may be some unspecified flonum. If fl_1 and fl_2 are both zero, the result is 1.0. If fl_1 is zero and fl_2 is positive, the result is zero. If fl_1 is zero and fl_2 is negative, the result may be a NaN, or may be some unspecified flonum.

`&no-infinities`	condition type
`(make-no-infinities-violation)`	procedure
`(no-infinities-violation? obj)`	procedure
`&no-nans`	condition type
`(make-no-nans-violation)`	procedure
`(no-nans-violation? obj)`	procedure

These condition types could be defined by the following code:

```
(define-condition-type &no-infinities
    &implementation-restriction
  make-no-infinities-violation
  no-infinities-violation?)


(define-condition-type &no-nans
    &implementation-restriction
  make-no-nans-violation no-nans-violation?)
```

These types describe that a program has executed an arithmetic operations that is specified to return an infinity or a NaN, respectively, on a Scheme implementation that is not able to represent the infinity or NaN. (See report section 11.7.2.)

`(fixnum->flonum fx)`   procedure

Returns a flonum that is numerically closest to *fx*.

Note: The result of this procedure may not be numerically equal to *fx*, because the fixnum precision may be greater than the flonum precision.

11.4 Exact bitwise arithmetic

This section describes the `(rnrs arithmetic bitwise (6))` library. The exact bitwise arithmetic provides generic operations on exact integer objects. This section uses *ei*, ei_1, ei_2, etc., as parameter names that must be exact integer objects.

`(bitwise-not ei)`   procedure

Returns the exact integer object whose two's complement representation is the one's complement of the two's complement representation of *ei*.

`(bitwise-and ei_1 ...)`	procedure
`(bitwise-ior ei_1 ...)`	procedure
`(bitwise-xor ei_1 ...)`	procedure

These procedures return the exact integer object that is the bit-wise "and", "inclusive or", or "exclusive or" of the two's complement representations of their arguments. If they are passed only one argument, they return that argument. If they are passed no arguments, they return the integer object (either -1 or 0) that acts as identity for the operation.

(bitwise-if ei_1 ei_2 ei_3)   procedure
   Returns the exact integer object that is the bit-wise "if" of the two's complement representations of its arguments, i.e. for each bit, if it is 1 in ei_1, the corresponding bit in ei_2 becomes the value of the corresponding bit in the result, and if it is 0, the corresponding bit in ei_3 becomes the corresponding bit in the value of the result. This is the result of the following computation:

```
(bitwise-ior (bitwise-and ei₁ ei₂)
             (bitwise-and (bitwise-not ei₁) ei₃))
```

(bitwise-bit-count ei)   procedure
   If ei is non-negative, this procedure returns the number of 1 bits in the two's complement representation of ei. Otherwise it returns the result of the following computation:

```
(bitwise-not (bitwise-bit-count (bitwise-not ei)))
```

(bitwise-length ei)   procedure
   Returns the number of bits needed to represent ei if it is positive, and the number of bits needed to represent (bitwise-not ei) if it is negative, which is the exact integer object that is the result of the following computation:

```
(do ((result 0 (+ result 1))
     (bits (if (negative? ei)
               (bitwise-not ei)
               ei)
           (bitwise-arithmetic-shift bits -1)))
    ((zero? bits)
     result))
```

(bitwise-first-bit-set ei)   procedure
   Returns the index of the least significant 1 bit in the two's complement representation of ei. If ei is 0, then -1 is returned.

```
(bitwise-first-bit-set 0)        ⟹  -1
(bitwise-first-bit-set 1)        ⟹  0
(bitwise-first-bit-set -4)       ⟹  2
```

(bitwise-bit-set? ei_1 ei_2)   procedure
Ei_2 must be non-negative. The bitwise-bit-set? procedure returns #t if the ei_2th bit is 1 in the two's complement representation of ei_1, and #f otherwise. This is the result of the following computation:

```
(not (zero?
      (bitwise-and
        (bitwise-arithmetic-shift-left 1 ei₂)
        ei₁)))
```

(bitwise-copy-bit ei₁ ei₂ ei₃)   procedure
Ei_2 must be non-negative, and ei_3 must be either 0 or 1. The bitwise-copy-bit
procedure returns the result of replacing the ei_2th bit of ei_1 by ei_3, which is the result
of the following computation:

```
(let* ((mask (bitwise-arithmetic-shift-left 1 ei₂)))
  (bitwise-if mask
              (bitwise-arithmetic-shift-left ei₃ ei₂)
              ei₁))
```

(bitwise-bit-field ei₁ ei₂ ei₃)   procedure
Ei_2 and ei_3 must be non-negative, and ei_2 must be less than or equal to ei_3. The
bitwise-bit-field procedure returns the number represented by the bits at the
positions from ei_2 (inclusive) to ei_3 (exclusive), which is the result of the following
computation:

```
(let ((mask
        (bitwise-not
          (bitwise-arithmetic-shift-left -1 ei₃))))
  (bitwise-arithmetic-shift-right
    (bitwise-and ei₁ mask)
    ei₂))
```

(bitwise-copy-bit-field ei₁ ei₂ ei₃ ei₄)   procedure
Ei_2 and ei_3 must be non-negative, and ei_2 must be less than or equal to ei_3. The
bitwise-copy-bit-field procedure returns the result of replacing in ei_1 the bits
at positions from ei_2 (inclusive) to ei_3 (exclusive) by the bits in ei_4 from position
0 (inclusive) to position $ei_3 - ei_2$ (exclusive), which is the result of the following
computation:

```
(let* ((to      ei₁)
       (start   ei₂)
       (end     ei₃)
       (from    ei₄)
       (mask1
         (bitwise-arithmetic-shift-left -1 start))
       (mask2
         (bitwise-not
           (bitwise-arithmetic-shift-left -1 end)))
       (mask (bitwise-and mask1 mask2)))
```

```
(bitwise-if mask
        (bitwise-arithmetic-shift-left from
                                      start)
        to))
```

(bitwise-arithmetic-shift ei_1 ei_2)   procedure

Returns the result of the following computation:

(floor (* ei_1 (expt 2 ei_2)))

Examples:

```
(bitwise-arithmetic-shift -6 -1)  ⟹ -3
(bitwise-arithmetic-shift -5 -1)  ⟹ -3
(bitwise-arithmetic-shift -4 -1)  ⟹ -2
(bitwise-arithmetic-shift -3 -1)  ⟹ -2
(bitwise-arithmetic-shift -2 -1)  ⟹ -1
(bitwise-arithmetic-shift -1 -1)  ⟹ -1
```

(bitwise-arithmetic-shift-left ei_1 ei_2)   procedure
(bitwise-arithmetic-shift-right ei_1 ei_2)   procedure
Ei_2 must be non-negative. The bitwise-arithmetic-shift-left procedure returns
the same result as bitwise-arithmetic-shift, and

(bitwise-arithmetic-shift-right ei_1 ei_2)

returns the same result as

(bitwise-arithmetic-shift ei_1 (- ei_2)).

(bitwise-rotate-bit-field ei_1 ei_2 ei_3 ei_4)   procedure
Ei_2, ei_3, ei_4 must be non-negative, ei_2 must be less than or equal to ei_3, and ei_4 must
be non-negative. The bitwise-rotate-bit-field procedure returns the result of
cyclically permuting in ei_1 the bits at positions from ei_2 (inclusive) to ei_3 (exclusive)
by ei_4 bits towards the more significant bits, which is the result of the following
computation:

```
(let* ((n     $ei_1$)
       (start $ei_2$)
       (end   $ei_3$)
       (count $ei_4$)
       (width (- end start)))
  (if (positive? width)
      (let* ((count (mod count width))
             (field0
              (bitwise-bit-field n start end))
             (field1 (bitwise-arithmetic-shift-left
```

```
                 field0 count))
           (field2 (bitwise-arithmetic-shift-right
                    field0
                    (- width count)))
             (field (bitwise-ior field1 field2)))
        (bitwise-copy-bit-field n start end field))
      n))
```

(bitwise-reverse-bit-field ei_1 ei_2 ei_3)   procedure
Ei_2 and ei_3 must be non-negative, and ei_2 must be less than or equal to ei_3. The
bitwise-reverse-bit-field procedure returns the result obtained from ei_1 by
reversing the order of the bits at positions from ei_2 (inclusive) to ei_3 (exclusive).

(bitwise-reverse-bit-field #b1010010 1 4) $\implies$ 88 ; #b1011000

12 syntax-case

The (rnrs syntax-case (6)) library provides support for writing low-level macros
in a high-level style, with automatic syntax checking, input destructuring, output
restructuring, maintenance of lexical scoping and referential transparency (hygiene),
and support for controlled identifier capture.

12.1 Hygiene

Barendregt's *hygiene condition* (Barendregt, 1984) for the lambda calculus is an
informal notion that requires the free variables of an expression N that is to be
substituted into another expression M not to be captured by bindings in M when
such capture is not intended. Kohlbecker, et al (Kohlbecker *et al.*, 1986) propose
a corresponding *hygiene condition for macro expansion* that applies in all situations
where capturing is not explicit: "Generated identifiers that become binding instances
in the completely expanded program must only bind variables that are generated at
the same transcription step". In the terminology of this document, the "generated
identifiers" are those introduced by a transformer rather than those present in the
form passed to the transformer, and a "macro transcription step" corresponds to a
single call by the expander to a transformer. Also, the hygiene condition applies to
all introduced bindings rather than to introduced variable bindings alone.

This leaves open what happens to an introduced identifier that appears outside the
scope of a binding introduced by the same call. Such an identifier refers to the lexical
binding in effect where it appears (within a syntax ⟨template⟩; see section 12.4)
inside the transformer body or one of the helpers it calls. This is essentially the
referential transparency property described by Clinger and Rees (Clinger & Rees,
1991a). Thus, the hygiene condition can be restated as follows:

A binding for an identifier introduced into the output of a transformer call from the
expander must capture only references to the identifier introduced into the output of the same

transformer call. A reference to an identifier introduced into the output of a transformer refers to the closest enclosing binding for the introduced identifier or, if it appears outside of any enclosing binding for the introduced identifier, the closest enclosing lexical binding where the identifier appears (within a `syntax` ⟨template⟩) inside the transformer body or one of the helpers it calls.

Explicit captures are handled via `datum->syntax`; see section 12.6.

Operationally, the expander can maintain hygiene with the help of *marks* and *substitutions*. Marks are applied selectively by the expander to the output of each transformer it invokes, and substitutions are applied to the portions of each binding form that are supposed to be within the scope of the bound identifiers. Marks are used to distinguish like-named identifiers that are introduced at different times (either present in the source or introduced into the output of a particular transformer call), and substitutions are used to map identifiers to their expand-time values.

Each time the expander encounters a macro use, it applies an *antimark* to the input form, invokes the associated transformer, then applies a fresh mark to the output. Marks and antimarks cancel, so the portions of the input that appear in the output are effectively left unmarked, while the portions of the output that are introduced are marked with the fresh mark.

Each time the expander encounters a binding form it creates a set of substitutions, each mapping one of the (possibly marked) bound identifiers to information about the binding. (For a `lambda` expression, the expander might map each bound identifier to a representation of the formal parameter in the output of the expander. For a `let-syntax` form, the expander might map each bound identifier to the associated transformer.) These substitutions are applied to the portions of the input form in which the binding is supposed to be visible.

Marks and substitutions together form a *wrap* that is layered on the form being processed by the expander and pushed down toward the leaves as necessary. A wrapped form is referred to as a *wrapped syntax object*. Ultimately, the wrap may rest on a leaf that represents an identifier, in which case the wrapped syntax object is also referred to as an *identifier*. An identifier contains a name along with the wrap. (Names are typically represented by symbols.)

When a substitution is created to map an identifier to an expand-time value, the substitution records the name of the identifier and the set of marks that have been applied to that identifier, along with the associated expand-time value. The expander resolves identifier references by looking for the latest matching substitution to be applied to the identifier, i.e., the outermost substitution in the wrap whose name and marks match the name and marks recorded in the substitution. The name matches if it is the same name (if using symbols, then by `eq?`), and the marks match if the marks recorded with the substitution are the same as those that appear *below* the substitution in the wrap, i.e., those that were applied *before* the substitution. Marks applied after a substitution, i.e., appear over the substitution in the wrap, are not relevant and are ignored.

An algebra that defines how marks and substitutions work more precisely is given in section 2.4 of Oscar Waddell's PhD thesis (Waddell, 1999).

12.2 Syntax objects

A *syntax object* is a representation of a Scheme form that contains contextual
information about the form in addition to its structure. This contextual information
is used by the expander to maintain lexical scoping and may also be used by an
implementation to maintain source-object correlation (Dybvig *et al.*, 1992).

A syntax object may be wrapped, as described in section 12.1. It may also be
unwrapped, fully or partially, i.e., consist of list and vector structure with wrapped
syntax objects or nonsymbol values at the leaves. More formally, a syntax object is:

- a pair of syntax objects,
- a vector of syntax objects,
- a nonpair, nonvector, nonsymbol value, or
- a wrapped syntax object.

The distinction between the terms "syntax object" and "wrapped syntax object" is
important. For example, when invoked by the expander, a transformer (section 12.3)
must accept a wrapped syntax object but may return any syntax object, including
an unwrapped syntax object.

Syntax objects representing identifiers are always wrapped and are distinct from
other types of values. Wrapped syntax objects that are not identifiers may or may
not be distinct from other types of values.

12.3 Transformers

In define-syntax (report section 11.2.2), let-syntax, and letrec-syntax forms
(report section 11.18), a binding for a syntactic keyword is an expression that
evaluates to a *transformer*.

A transformer is a *transformation procedure* or a *variable transformer*. A transformation procedure is a procedure that must accept one argument, a wrapped syntax
object (section 12.2) representing the input, and return a syntax object (section 12.2)
representing the output. The transformer is called by the expander whenever a
reference to a keyword with which it has been associated is found. If the keyword
appears in the car of a list-structured input form, the transformer receives the entire
list-structured form, and its output replaces the entire form. Except with variable
transformers (see below), if the keyword is found in any other definition or expression context, the transformer receives a wrapped syntax object representing just the
keyword reference, and its output replaces just the reference. Except with variable
transformers, an exception with condition type &syntax is raised if the keyword
appears on the left-hand side of a set! expression.

(make-variable-transformer *proc*)   procedure
Proc should accept one argument, a wrapped syntax object, and return a syntax
object.

The make-variable-transformer procedure creates a *variable transformer*. A
variable transformer is like an ordinary transformer except that, if a keyword

associated with a variable transformer appears on the left-hand side of a `set!` expression, an exception is not raised. Instead, *proc* is called with a wrapped syntax object representing the entire `set!` expression as its argument, and its return value replaces the entire `set!` expression.

Implementation responsibilities: The implementation must check the restrictions on *proc* only to the extent performed by applying it as described. An implementation may check whether *proc* is an appropriate argument before applying it.

12.4 Parsing input and producing output

Transformers can destructure their input with `syntax-case` and rebuild their output with `syntax`.

```
(syntax-case ⟨expression⟩ (⟨literal⟩ ...)                                      syntax
    ⟨syntax-case clause⟩ ...)
-                                                                     auxiliary syntax
...                                                                   auxiliary syntax
```

Syntax: Each ⟨literal⟩ must be an identifier. Each ⟨syntax-case clause⟩ must take one of the following two forms.

> (⟨pattern⟩ ⟨output expression⟩)
> (⟨pattern⟩ ⟨fender⟩ ⟨output expression⟩)

⟨Fender⟩ and ⟨output expression⟩ must be ⟨expression⟩s.

A ⟨pattern⟩ is an identifier, constant, or one of the following.

```
(⟨pattern⟩ ...)
(⟨pattern⟩ ⟨pattern⟩ ... . ⟨pattern⟩)
(⟨pattern⟩ ... ⟨pattern⟩ ⟨ellipsis⟩ ⟨pattern⟩ ...)
(⟨pattern⟩ ... ⟨pattern⟩ ⟨ellipsis⟩ ⟨pattern⟩ ... . ⟨pattern⟩)
#(⟨pattern⟩ ...)
#(⟨pattern⟩ ... ⟨pattern⟩ ⟨ellipsis⟩ ⟨pattern⟩ ...)
```

An ⟨ellipsis⟩ is the identifier "..." (three periods).

An identifier appearing within a ⟨pattern⟩ may be an underscore (_), a literal identifier listed in the list of literals (⟨literal⟩ ...), or an ellipsis (...). All other identifiers appearing within a ⟨pattern⟩ are *pattern variables*. It is a syntax violation if an ellipsis or underscore appears in (⟨literal⟩ ...).

_ and ... are the same as in the (rnrs base (6)) library.

Pattern variables match arbitrary input subforms and are used to refer to elements of the input. It is a syntax violation if the same pattern variable appears more than once in a ⟨pattern⟩.

Underscores also match arbitrary input subforms but are not pattern variables and so cannot be used to refer to those elements. Multiple underscores may appear in a ⟨pattern⟩.

A literal identifier matches an input subform if and only if the input subform is an identifier and either both its occurrence in the input expression and its occurrence in the list of literals have the same lexical binding, or the two identifiers have the same name and both have no lexical binding.

A subpattern followed by an ellipsis can match zero or more elements of the input.

More formally, an input form F matches a pattern P if and only if one of the following holds:

- P is an underscore (_).
- P is a pattern variable.
- P is a literal identifier and F is an equivalent identifier in the sense of `free-identifier=?` (section 12.5).
- P is of the form $(P_1 \ldots P_n)$ and F is a list of n elements that match P_1 through P_n.
- P is of the form $(P_1 \ldots P_n . P_x)$ and F is a list or improper list of n or more elements whose first n elements match P_1 through P_n and whose nth cdr matches P_x.
- P is of the form $(P_1 \ldots P_k \ P_e \ \langle \text{ellipsis} \rangle \ P_{m+1} \ldots P_n)$, where $\langle \text{ellipsis} \rangle$ is the identifier $\ldots$ and F is a proper list of n elements whose first k elements match P_1 through P_k, whose next $m-k$ elements each match P_e, and whose remaining $n-m$ elements match P_{m+1} through P_n.
- P is of the form $(P_1 \ldots P_k \ P_e \ \langle \text{ellipsis} \rangle \ P_{m+1} \ldots P_n . P_x)$, where $\langle \text{ellipsis} \rangle$ is the identifier $\ldots$ and F is a list or improper list of n elements whose first k elements match P_1 through P_k, whose next $m-k$ elements each match P_e, whose next $n-m$ elements match P_{m+1} through P_n, and whose nth and final cdr matches P_x.
- P is of the form $\#(P_1 \ldots P_n)$ and F is a vector of n elements that match P_1 through P_n.
- P is of the form $\#(P_1 \ldots P_k \ P_e \ \langle \text{ellipsis} \rangle \ P_{m+1} \ldots P_n)$, where $\langle \text{ellipsis} \rangle$ is the identifier $\ldots$ and F is a vector of n or more elements whose first k elements match P_1 through P_k, whose next $m-k$ elements each match P_e, and whose remaining $n-m$ elements match P_{m+1} through P_n.
- P is a pattern datum (any nonlist, nonvector, nonsymbol datum) and F is equal to P in the sense of the `equal?` procedure.

Semantics: A `syntax-case` expression first evaluates $\langle \text{expression} \rangle$. It then attempts to match the $\langle \text{pattern} \rangle$ from the first $\langle \text{syntax-case clause} \rangle$ against the resulting value, which is unwrapped as necessary to perform the match. If the pattern matches the value and no $\langle \text{fender} \rangle$ is present, $\langle \text{output expression} \rangle$ is evaluated and its value returned as the value of the `syntax-case` expression. If the pattern does not match the value, `syntax-case` tries the second $\langle \text{syntax-case clause} \rangle$, then the third, and so on. It is a syntax violation if the value does not match any of the patterns.

If the optional $\langle \text{fender} \rangle$ is present, it serves as an additional constraint on acceptance of a clause. If the $\langle \text{pattern} \rangle$ of a given $\langle \text{syntax-case clause} \rangle$ matches the input value, the corresponding $\langle \text{fender} \rangle$ is evaluated. If $\langle \text{fender} \rangle$ evaluates to a true value, the clause is accepted; otherwise, the clause is rejected as if the pattern had failed to match the value. Fenders are logically a part of the matching process, i.e., they specify additional matching constraints beyond the basic structure of the input.

Pattern variables contained within a clause's ⟨pattern⟩ are bound to the corresponding pieces of the input value within the clause's ⟨fender⟩ (if present) and ⟨output expression⟩. Pattern variables can be referenced only within `syntax` expressions (see below). Pattern variables occupy the same name space as program variables and keywords.

If the `syntax-case` form is in tail context, the ⟨output expression⟩s are also in tail position.

(syntax ⟨template⟩) syntax
Note: #'⟨template⟩ is equivalent to (syntax ⟨template⟩).

A `syntax` expression is similar to a `quote` expression except that (1) the values of pattern variables appearing within ⟨template⟩ are inserted into ⟨template⟩, (2) contextual information associated both with the input and with the template is retained in the output to support lexical scoping, and (3) the value of a `syntax` expression is a syntax object.

A ⟨template⟩ is a pattern variable, an identifier that is not a pattern variable, a pattern datum, or one of the following.

> (⟨subtemplate⟩ ...)
> (⟨subtemplate⟩ ... . ⟨template⟩)
> #(⟨subtemplate⟩ ...)

A ⟨subtemplate⟩ is a ⟨template⟩ followed by zero or more ellipses.

The value of a `syntax` form is a copy of ⟨template⟩ in which the pattern variables appearing within the template are replaced with the input subforms to which they are bound. Pattern data and identifiers that are not pattern variables or ellipses are copied directly into the output. A subtemplate followed by an ellipsis expands into zero or more occurrences of the subtemplate. Pattern variables that occur in subpatterns followed by one or more ellipses may occur only in subtemplates that are followed by (at least) as many ellipses. These pattern variables are replaced in the output by the input subforms to which they are bound, distributed as specified. If a pattern variable is followed by more ellipses in the subtemplate than in the associated subpattern, the input form is replicated as necessary. The subtemplate must contain at least one pattern variable from a subpattern followed by an ellipsis, and for at least one such pattern variable, the subtemplate must be followed by exactly as many ellipses as the subpattern in which the pattern variable appears. (Otherwise, the expander would not be able to determine how many times the subform should be repeated in the output.) It is a syntax violation if the constraints of this paragraph are not met.

A template of the form (⟨ellipsis⟩ ⟨template⟩) is identical to ⟨template⟩, except that ellipses within the template have no special meaning. That is, any ellipses contained within ⟨template⟩ are treated as ordinary identifiers. In particular, the template (... ...) produces a single ellipsis. This allows macro uses to expand into forms containing ellipses.

The output produced by syntax is wrapped or unwrapped according to the following rules.

- the copy of $(\langle t_1 \rangle \; . \; \langle t_2 \rangle)$ is a pair if $\langle t_1 \rangle$ or $\langle t_2 \rangle$ contain any pattern variables,
- the copy of $(\langle t \rangle \; \langle \text{ellipsis} \rangle)$ is a list if $\langle t \rangle$ contains any pattern variables,
- the copy of #($\langle t_1 \rangle \; \ldots \; \langle t_n \rangle$) is a vector if any of $\langle t_1 \rangle, \ldots, \langle t_n \rangle$ contain any pattern variables, and
- the copy of any portion of $\langle t \rangle$ not containing any pattern variables is a wrapped syntax object.

The input subforms inserted in place of the pattern variables are wrapped if and only if the corresponding input subforms are wrapped.

The following definitions of or illustrate syntax-case and syntax. The second is equivalent to the first but uses the #' prefix instead of the full syntax form.

```
(define-syntax or
  (lambda (x)
    (syntax-case x ()
      [(_) (syntax #f)]
      [(_ e) (syntax e)]
      [(_ e1 e2 e3 ...)
       (syntax (let ([t e1])
                 (if t t (or e2 e3 ...))))])))
```

```
(define-syntax or
  (lambda (x)
    (syntax-case x ()
      [(_) #'#f]
      [(_ e) #'e]
      [(_ e1 e2 e3 ...)
       #'(let ([t e1])
           (if t t (or e2 e3 ...)))])))
```

The examples below define *identifier macros*, macro uses supporting keyword references that do not necessarily appear in the first position of a list-structured form. The second example uses make-variable-transformer to handle the case where the keyword appears on the left-hand side of a set! expression.

```
(define p (cons 4 5))
(define-syntax p.car
  (lambda (x)
    (syntax-case x ()
      [(_ . rest) #'((car p) . rest)]
      [_ #'(car p)])))
p.car                                    ⟹ 4
(set! p.car 15)                          ⟹ &syntax exception
```

```
(define p (cons 4 5))
(define-syntax p.car
  (make-variable-transformer
    (lambda (x)
      (syntax-case x (set!)
        [(set! _ e) #'(set-car! p e)]
        [(_ . rest) #'((car p) . rest)]
        [_ #'(car p)]))))
(set! p.car 15)
p.car                                    ⟹ 15
p                                        ⟹ (15 . 5)
```

12.5 Identifier predicates

(identifier? *obj*)   procedure

Returns #t if *obj* is an identifier, i.e., a syntax object representing an identifier, and #f otherwise.

The identifier? procedure is often used within a fender to verify that certain subforms of an input form are identifiers, as in the definition of rec, which creates self-contained recursive objects, below.

```
(define-syntax rec
  (lambda (x)
    (syntax-case x ()
      [(_ x e)
       (identifier? #'x)
       #'(letrec ([x e]) x)])))

(map (rec fact
       (lambda (n)
         (if (= n 0)
             1
             (* n (fact (- n 1))))))
     '(1 2 3 4 5))                       ⟹ (1 2 6 24 120)

(rec 5 (lambda (x) x))                   ⟹ &syntax exception
```

The procedures bound-identifier=? and free-identifier=? each take two identifier arguments and return #t if their arguments are equivalent and #f otherwise. These predicates are used to compare identifiers according to their *intended use* as free references or bound identifiers in a given context.

(bound-identifier=? *id₁* *id₂*)   procedure

Id₁ and *id₂* must be identifiers. The procedure bound-identifier=? returns #t if a binding for one would capture a reference to the other in the output of the transformer, assuming that the reference appears within the scope of the binding, and #f otherwise. In general, two identifiers are bound-identifier=? only if both are present in the original program or both are introduced by the same transformer application (perhaps implicitly—see datum->syntax). Operationally, two identifiers are considered equivalent by bound-identifier=? if and only if they have the same name and same marks (section 12.1).

The bound-identifier=? procedure can be used for detecting duplicate identifiers in a binding construct or for other preprocessing of a binding construct that requires detecting instances of the bound identifiers.

(free-identifier=? id_1 id_2)   procedure

Id_1 and id_2 must be identifiers. The free-identifier=? procedure returns #t if and only if the two identifiers would resolve to the same binding if both were to appear in the output of a transformer outside of any bindings inserted by the transformer. (If neither of two like-named identifiers resolves to a binding, i.e., both are unbound, they are considered to resolve to the same binding.) Operationally, two identifiers are considered equivalent by free-identifier=? if and only the topmost matching substitution for each maps to the same binding (section 12.1) or the identifiers have the same name and no matching substitution.

The syntax-case and syntax-rules forms internally use free-identifier=? to compare identifiers listed in the literals list against input identifiers.

```
(let ([fred 17])
  (define-syntax a
    (lambda (x)
      (syntax-case x ()
        [(_ id) #'(b id fred)])))
  (define-syntax b
    (lambda (x)
      (syntax-case x ()
        [(_ id1 id2)
         #`(list
             #,(free-identifier=? #'id1 #'id2)
             #,(bound-identifier=? #'id1 #'id2))])))
  (a fred))                              ⟹ (#t #f)
```

The following definition of unnamed let uses bound-identifier=? to detect duplicate identifiers.

```
(define-syntax let
  (lambda (x)
    (define unique-ids?
      (lambda (ls)
        (or (null? ls)
            (and (let notmem?
                   ([x (car ls)] [ls (cdr ls)])
```

```
          (or (null? ls)
              (and (not (bound-identifier=?
                          x (car ls)))
                   (notmem? x (cdr ls)))))
              (unique-ids? (cdr ls))))))
      (syntax-case x ()
        [(_ ((i v) ...) e1 e2 ...)
         (unique-ids? #'(i ...))
         #'((lambda (i ...) e1 e2 ...) v ...)])))
```

The argument #'(i ...) to unique-ids? is guaranteed to be a list by the rules given in the description of syntax above.

With this definition of let:

```
    (let ([a 3] [a 4]) (+ a a))          ⟹ &syntax exception
```

However,

```
    (let-syntax
      ([dolet (lambda (x)
                (syntax-case x ()
                  [(_ b)
                   #'(let ([a 3] [b 4]) (+ a b))]))])
      (dolet a))                          ⟹ 7
```

since the identifier a introduced by dolet and the identifier a extracted from the input form are not bound-identifier=?.

The following definition of case is equivalent to the one in section 12.4. Rather than including else in the literals list as before, this version explicitly tests for else using free-identifier=?.

```
(define-syntax case
  (lambda (x)
    (syntax-case x ()
      [(_ e0 [(k ...) e1 e2 ...] ...
          [else-key else-e1 else-e2 ...])
       (and (identifier? #'else-key)
            (free-identifier=? #'else-key #'else))
       #'(let ([t e0])
           (cond
             [(memv t '(k ...)) e1 e2 ...]
             ...
             [else else-e1 else-e2 ...]))]
      [(_ e0 [(ka ...) e1a e2a ...]
          [(kb ...) e1b e2b ...] ...)
       #'(let ([t e0])
           (cond
             [(memv t '(ka ...)) e1a e2a ...]
```

```
     [(memv t '(kb ...)) e1b e2b ...]
     ...))])))
```

With either definition of case, else is not recognized as an auxiliary keyword if an enclosing lexical binding for else exists. For example,

```
(let ([else #f])
  (case 0 [else (write "oops")])) ⟹ &syntax exception
```

since else is bound lexically and is therefore not the same else that appears in the definition of case.

12.6 Syntax-object and datum conversions

(syntax->datum *syntax-object*)   procedure

Strips all syntactic information from a syntax object and returns the corresponding Scheme datum.

Identifiers stripped in this manner are converted to their symbolic names, which can then be compared with eq?. Thus, a predicate symbolic-identifier=? might be defined as follows.

```
(define symbolic-identifier=?
  (lambda (x y)
    (eq? (syntax->datum x)
         (syntax->datum y))))
```

(datum->syntax *template-id datum*)   procedure

Template-id must be a template identifier and *datum* should be a datum value. The datum->syntax procedure returns a syntax-object representation of *datum* that contains the same contextual information as *template-id*, with the effect that the syntax object behaves as if it were introduced into the code when *template-id* was introduced.

The datum->syntax procedure allows a transformer to "bend" lexical scoping rules by creating *implicit identifiers* that behave as if they were present in the input form, thus permitting the definition of macros that introduce visible bindings for or references to identifiers that do not appear explicitly in the input form. For example, the following defines a loop expression that uses this controlled form of identifier capture to bind the variable break to an escape procedure within the loop body. (The derived with-syntax form is like let but binds pattern variables—see section 12.8.)

```
(define-syntax loop
  (lambda (x)
    (syntax-case x ()
      [(k e ...)
       (with-syntax
```

```
    ([break (datum->syntax #'k 'break)])
  #'(call-with-current-continuation
     (lambda (break)
       (let f () e ... (f)))))])))

(let ((n 3) (ls '()))
  (loop
    (if (= n 0) (break ls))
    (set! ls (cons 'a ls))
    (set! n (- n 1))))          ⟹ (a a a)
```

Were loop to be defined as

```
(define-syntax loop
  (lambda (x)
    (syntax-case x ()
      [(_ e ...)
       #'(call-with-current-continuation
          (lambda (break)
            (let f () e ... (f))))])))
```

the variable break would not be visible in e ....

The datum argument *datum* may also represent an arbitrary Scheme form, as demonstrated by the following definition of include.

```
(define-syntax include
  (lambda (x)
    (define read-file
      (lambda (fn k)
        (let ([p (open-file-input-port fn)])
          (let f ([x (get-datum p)])
            (if (eof-object? x)
                (begin (close-port p) '())
                (cons (datum->syntax k x)
                      (f (get-datum p))))))))
    (syntax-case x ()
      [(k filename)
       (let ([fn (syntax->datum #'filename)])
         (with-syntax ([(exp ...)
                        (read-file fn #'k)])
           #'(begin exp ...)))])))
```

(include "filename") expands into a begin expression containing the forms found in the file named by "filename". For example, if the file flib.ss contains (define f (lambda (x) (g (* x x)))), and the file glib.ss contains (define g (lambda (x) (+ x x))), the expression

```
(let ()
```

```
(include "flib.ss")
(include "glib.ss")
(f 5))
```

evaluates to 50.

The definition of include uses datum->syntax to convert the objects read from the file into syntax objects in the proper lexical context, so that identifier references and definitions within those expressions are scoped where the include form appears.

Using datum->syntax, it is even possible to break hygiene entirely and write macros in the style of old Lisp macros. The lisp-transformer procedure defined below creates a transformer that converts its input into a datum, calls the programmer's procedure on this datum, and converts the result back into a syntax object scoped where the original macro use appeared.

```
(define lisp-transformer
  (lambda (p)
    (lambda (x)
      (syntax-case x ()
        [(kwd . rest)
         (datum->syntax #'kwd
           (p (syntax->datum x)))]))))
```

12.7 Generating lists of temporaries

Transformers can introduce a fixed number of identifiers into their output simply by naming each identifier. In some cases, however, the number of identifiers to be introduced depends upon some characteristic of the input expression. A straightforward definition of letrec, for example, requires as many temporary identifiers as there are binding pairs in the input expression. The procedure generate-temporaries is used to construct lists of temporary identifiers.

(generate-temporaries *l*)   procedure

L must be be a list or syntax object representing a list-structured form; its contents are not important. The number of temporaries generated is the number of elements in *l*. Each temporary is guaranteed to be unique, i.e., different from all other identifiers.

A definition of letrec equivalent to the one using syntax-rules given in report appendix B is shown below.

```
(define-syntax letrec
  (lambda (x)
    (syntax-case x ()
      ((_ ((i e) ...) b1 b2 ...)
       (with-syntax
           (((t ...) (generate-temporaries #'(i ...))))
         #'(let ((i <undefined>) ...)
```

```
         (let ((t e) ...)
           (set! i t) ...
           (let () b1 b2 ...)))))))))
```

This version uses `generate-temporaries` instead of recursively defined helper to
generate the necessary temporaries.

12.8 Derived forms and procedures

The forms and procedures described in this section can be defined in terms of the
forms and procedures described in earlier sections of this chapter.

(with-syntax ((⟨pattern⟩ ⟨expression⟩)) ...) ⟨body⟩)   syntax

   The `with-syntax` form is used to bind pattern variables, just as `let` is used to
bind variables. This allows a transformer to construct its output in separate pieces,
then put the pieces together.

   Each ⟨pattern⟩ is identical in form to a syntax-case pattern. The value of each
⟨expression⟩ is computed and destructured according to the corresponding ⟨pattern⟩,
and pattern variables within the ⟨pattern⟩ are bound as with syntax-case to the
corresponding portions of the value within ⟨body⟩.

   The `with-syntax` form may be defined in terms of `syntax-case` as follows.

```
(define-syntax with-syntax
  (lambda (x)
    (syntax-case x ()
      ((_ ((p e0) ...) e1 e2 ...)
       (syntax (syntax-case (list e0 ...) ()
                 ((p ...) (let () e1 e2 ...))))))))
```

The following definition of cond demonstrates the use of `with-syntax` to support
transformers that employ recursion internally to construct their output. It handles
all cond clause variations and takes care to produce one-armed `if` expressions where
appropriate.

```
(define-syntax cond
  (lambda (x)
    (syntax-case x ()
      [(_ c1 c2 ...)
       (let f ([c1 #'c1] [c2* #'(c2 ...)])
         (syntax-case c2* ()
           [()
            (syntax-case c1 (else =>)
              [(else e1 e2 ...) #'(begin e1 e2 ...)]
              [(e0) #'e0]
              [(e0 => e1)
               #'(let ([t e0]) (if t (e1 t)))]
              [(e0 e1 e2 ...)
```

```
                    #'(if e0 (begin e1 e2 ...))])]
            [(c2 c3 ...)
             (with-syntax ([rest (f #'c2 #'(c3 ...))])
               (syntax-case c1 (=>)
                 [(e0) #'(let ([t e0]) (if t t rest))]
                 [(e0 => e1)
                  #'(let ([t e0]) (if t (e1 t) rest))]
                 [(e0 e1 e2 ...)
                  #'(if e0
                        (begin e1 e2 ...)
                        rest)])))])))])))
```

(quasisyntax ⟨template⟩)	syntax
unsyntax	auxiliary syntax
unsyntax-splicing	auxiliary syntax

The quasisyntax form is similar to syntax, but it allows parts of the quoted text to be evaluated, in a manner similar to the operation of quasiquote (report section 11.17).

Within a quasisyntax *template*, subforms of unsyntax and unsyntax-splicing forms are evaluated, and everything else is treated as ordinary template material, as with syntax. The value of each unsyntax subform is inserted into the output in place of the unsyntax form, while the value of each unsyntax-splicing subform is spliced into the surrounding list or vector structure. Uses of unsyntax and unsyntax-splicing are valid only within quasisyntax expressions.

A quasisyntax expression may be nested, with each quasisyntax introducing a new level of syntax quotation and each unsyntax or unsyntax-splicing taking away a level of quotation. An expression nested within n quasisyntax expressions must be within n unsyntax or unsyntax-splicing expressions to be evaluated.

As noted in report section 4.3.5, #`⟨template⟩ is equivalent to (quasisyntax ⟨template⟩), #,⟨template⟩ is equivalent to (unsyntax ⟨template⟩), and #,@⟨template⟩ is equivalent to (unsyntax-splicing ⟨template⟩).

The quasisyntax keyword can be used in place of with-syntax in many cases. For example, the definition of case shown under the description of with-syntax above can be rewritten using quasisyntax as follows.

```
(define-syntax case
  (lambda (x)
    (syntax-case x ()
      [(_ e c1 c2 ...)
       #`(let ([t e])
           #,(let f ([c1 #'c1] [cmore #'(c2 ...)])
               (if (null? cmore)
                   (syntax-case c1 (else)
                     [(else e1 e2 ...)
                      #'(begin e1 e2 ...)]
```

```
           [((k ...) e1 e2 ...)
            #'(if (memv t '(k ...))
                  (begin e1 e2 ...))])
         (syntax-case c1 ()
           [((k ...) e1 e2 ...)
            #`(if (memv t '(k ...))
                  (begin e1 e2 ...)
                  #,(f (car cmore)
                       (cdr cmore)))])))))])))
```

Uses of unsyntax and unsyntax-splicing with zero or more than one subform are valid only in splicing (list or vector) contexts. (unsyntax *template* ...) is equivalent to (unsyntax *template*) ..., and (unsyntax-splicing *template* ...) is equivalent to (unsyntax-splicing *template*) .... These forms are primarily useful as intermediate forms in the output of the quasisyntax expander.

Note: Uses of unsyntax and unsyntax-splicing with zero or more than one subform enable certain idioms (Bawden, 1999), such as #,@#,@, which has the effect of a doubly indirect splicing when used within a doubly nested and doubly evaluated quasisyntax expression, as with the nested quasiquote examples shown in section 11.17.

Note: Any syntax-rules form can be expressed with syntax-case by making the lambda expression and syntax expressions explicit, and syntax-rules may be defined in terms of syntax-case as follows.

```
     (define-syntax syntax-rules
       (lambda (x)
         (syntax-case x ()
           [(_ (lit ...) [(k . p) t] ...)
            (for-all identifier? #'(lit ... k ...))
            #'(lambda (x)
                (syntax-case x (lit ...)
                  [(_ . p) #'t] ...))])))
```

Note: The identifier-syntax form of the base library (see report section 11.19) may be defined in terms of syntax-case, syntax, and make-variable-transformer as follows.

```
(define-syntax identifier-syntax
  (syntax-rules (set!)
    [(_ e)
     (lambda (x)
       (syntax-case x ()
         [id (identifier? #'id) #'e]
         [(_ x (... ...)) #'(e x (... ...))]))]
    [(_ (id exp1) ((set! var val) exp2))
     (and (identifier? #'id) (identifier? #'var))
     (make-variable-transformer
```

```
(lambda (x)
  (syntax-case x (set!)
    [(set! var val) #'exp2]
    [(id x (... ...)) #'(exp1 x (... ...))]
    [id (identifier? #'id) #'exp1])))]))
```

12.9 Syntax violations

(syntax-violation *who message form*)   procedure
(syntax-violation *who message form subform*)   procedure
Who must be #f or a string or a symbol. *Message* must be a string. *Form* must
be a syntax object or a datum value. *Subform* must be a syntax object or a datum
value. The syntax-violation procedure raises an exception, reporting a syntax
violation. *Who* should describe the macro transformer that detected the exception.
The *message* argument should describe the violation. *Form* should be the erroneous
source syntax object or a datum value representing a form. The optional *subform*
argument should be a syntax object or datum value representing a form that more
precisely locates the violation.

If *who* is #f, syntax-violation attempts to infer an appropriate value for the
condition object (see below) as follows: When *form* is either an identifier or a list-
structured syntax object containing an identifier as its first element, then the inferred
value is the identifier's symbol. Otherwise, no value for *who* is provided as part of
the condition object.

The condition object provided with the exception (see chapter 7) has the following
condition types:

- If *who* is not #f or can be inferred, the condition has condition type &who, with
  who as the value of its field. Otherwise, the condition does not have condition
  type &who.
- The condition has condition type &message, with *message* as the value of its
  field.
- The condition has condition type &syntax with *form* and *subform* as the value
  of its fields. If *subform* is not provided, the value of the subform field is #f.

13 Hashtables

The (rnrs hashtables (6)) library provides a set of operations on hashtables. A
hashtable is a data structure that associates keys with values. Any object can be used
as a key, provided a *hash function* and a suitable *equivalence function* is available.
A hash function is a procedure that maps keys to exact integer objects. It is the
programmer's responsibility to ensure that the hash function is compatible with the
equivalence function, which is a procedure that accepts two keys and returns true
if they are equivalent and #f otherwise. Standard hashtables for arbitrary objects

based on the eq? and eqv? predicates (see report section 11.5) are provided. Also, hash functions for arbitrary objects, strings, and symbols are provided.

This section uses the *hashtable* parameter name for arguments that must be hashtables, and the *key* parameter name for arguments that must be hashtable keys.

13.1 Constructors

(make-eq-hashtable)   procedure
(make-eq-hashtable *k*)   procedure

Returns a newly allocated mutable hashtable that accepts arbitrary objects as keys, and compares those keys with eq?. If an argument is given, the initial capacity of the hashtable is set to approximately *k* elements.

(make-eqv-hashtable)   procedure
(make-eqv-hashtable *k*)   procedure

Returns a newly allocated mutable hashtable that accepts arbitrary objects as keys, and compares those keys with eqv?. If an argument is given, the initial capacity of the hashtable is set to approximately *k* elements.

(make-hashtable *hash-function equiv*)   procedure
(make-hashtable *hash-function equiv k*)   procedure

Hash-function and *equiv* must be procedures. *Hash-function* should accept a key as an argument and should return a non-negative exact integer object. *Equiv* should accept two keys as arguments and return a single value. Neither procedure should mutate the hashtable returned by make-hashtable. The make-hashtable procedure returns a newly allocated mutable hashtable using *hash-function* as the hash function and *equiv* as the equivalence function used to compare keys. If a third argument is given, the initial capacity of the hashtable is set to approximately *k* elements.

Both *hash-function* and *equiv* should behave like pure functions on the domain of keys. For example, the string-hash and string=? procedures are permissible only if all keys are strings and the contents of those strings are never changed so long as any of them continues to serve as a key in the hashtable. Furthermore, any pair of keys for which *equiv* returns true should be hashed to the same exact integer objects by *hash-function*.

Implementation responsibilities: The implementation must check the restrictions on *hash-function* and *equiv* to the extent performed by applying them as described. *Note:* Hashtables are allowed to cache the results of calling the hash function and equivalence function, so programs cannot rely on the hash function being called for every lookup or update. Furthermore any hashtable operation may call the hash function more than once.

13.2 *Procedures*

(hashtable? *obj*)   procedure
    Returns #t if *obj* is a hashtable, #f otherwise.

(hashtable-size *hashtable*)   procedure
    Returns the number of keys contained in *hashtable* as an exact integer object.

(hashtable-ref *hashtable key default*)   procedure
    Returns the value in *hashtable* associated with *key*. If *hashtable* does not contain
an association for *key*, *default* is returned.

(hashtable-set! *hashtable key obj*)   procedure
    Changes *hashtable* to associate *key* with *obj*, adding a new association or replacing
any existing association for *key*, and returns unspecified values.

(hashtable-delete! *hashtable key*)   procedure
    Removes any association for *key* within *hashtable* and returns unspecified values.

(hashtable-contains? *hashtable key*)   procedure
    Returns #t if *hashtable* contains an association for *key*, #f otherwise.

(hashtable-update! *hashtable key proc default*)   procedure
Proc should accept one argument, should return a single value, and should not
mutate *hashtable*. The hashtable-update! procedure applies *proc* to the value
in *hashtable* associated with *key*, or to *default* if *hashtable* does not contain an
association for *key*. The *hashtable* is then changed to associate *key* with the value
returned by *proc*.

    The behavior of hashtable-update! is equivalent to the following code, but
may be implemented more efficiently in cases where the implementation can avoid
multiple lookups of the same key:

```
(hashtable-set!
 hashtable key
 (proc (hashtable-ref
        hashtable key default)))
```

(hashtable-copy *hashtable*)   procedure
(hashtable-copy *hashtable mutable*)   procedure
    Returns a copy of *hashtable*. If the *mutable* argument is provided and is true, the
returned hashtable is mutable; otherwise it is immutable.

(hashtable-clear! *hashtable*)   procedure
(hashtable-clear! *hashtable k*)   procedure
    Removes all associations from *hashtable* and returns unspecified values.

If a second argument is given, the current capacity of the hashtable is reset to approximately *k* elements.

(hashtable-keys *hashtable*)   procedure

Returns a vector of all keys in *hashtable*. The order of the vector is unspecified.

(hashtable-entries *hashtable*)   procedure

Returns two values, a vector of the keys in *hashtable*, and a vector of the corresponding values.

```
(let ((h (make-eqv-hashtable)))
  (hashtable-set! h 1 'one)
  (hashtable-set! h 2 'two)
  (hashtable-set! h 3 'three)
  (hashtable-entries h))        ⟹ #(1 2 3) #(one two three)
        ; two return values
        ; entries may be in different order
```

13.3 Inspection

(hashtable-equivalence-function *hashtable*)   procedure

Returns the equivalence function used by *hashtable* to compare keys. For hashtables created with make-eq-hashtable and make-eqv-hashtable, returns eq? and eqv? respectively.

(hashtable-hash-function *hashtable*)   procedure

Returns the hash function used by *hashtable*. For hashtables created by make-eq-hashtable or make-eqv-hashtable, #f is returned.

(hashtable-mutable? *hashtable*)   procedure

Returns #t if *hashtable* is mutable, otherwise #f.

13.4 Hash functions

The equal-hash, string-hash, and string-ci-hash procedures of this section are acceptable as the hash functions of a hashtable only if the keys on which they are called are not mutated while they remain in use as keys in the hashtable.

(equal-hash *obj*)   procedure

Returns an integer hash value for *obj*, based on its structure and current contents. This hash function is suitable for use with equal? as an equivalence function.
Note: Like equal?, the equal-hash procedure must always terminate, even if its arguments contain cycles.

`(string-hash` *string*`)`   procedure
    Returns an integer hash value for *string*, based on its current contents. This hash function is suitable for use with `string=?` as an equivalence function.

`(string-ci-hash` *string*`)`   procedure
    Returns an integer hash value for *string* based on its current contents, ignoring case. This hash function is suitable for use with `string-ci=?` as an equivalence function.

`(symbol-hash` *symbol*`)`   procedure
    Returns an integer hash value for *symbol*.

14 Enumerations

This chapter describes the `(rnrs enums (6))` library for dealing with enumerated values and sets of enumerated values. Enumerated values are represented by ordinary symbols, while finite sets of enumerated values form a separate type, known as the *enumeration sets*. The enumeration sets are further partitioned into sets that share the same *universe* and *enumeration type*. These universes and enumeration types are created by the `make-enumeration` procedure. Each call to that procedure creates a new enumeration type.

    This library interprets each enumeration set with respect to its specific universe of symbols and enumeration type. This facilitates efficient implementation of enumeration sets and enables the complement operation.

    In the descriptions of the following procedures, *enum-set* ranges over the enumeration sets, which are defined as the subsets of the universes that can be defined using `make-enumeration`.

`(make-enumeration` *symbol-list*`)`   procedure
Symbol-list must be a list of symbols. The `make-enumeration` procedure creates a new enumeration type whose universe consists of those symbols (in canonical order of their first appearance in the list) and returns that universe as an enumeration set whose universe is itself and whose enumeration type is the newly created enumeration type.

`(enum-set-universe` *enum-set*`)`   procedure
    Returns the set of all symbols that comprise the universe of its argument, as an enumeration set.

`(enum-set-indexer` *enum-set*`)`   procedure
    Returns a unary procedure that, given a symbol that is in the universe of *enum-set*, returns its 0-origin index within the canonical ordering of the symbols in the universe; given a symbol not in the universe, the unary procedure returns #f.

```
(let* ((e (make-enumeration '(red green blue)))
       (i (enum-set-indexer e)))
  (list (i 'red) (i 'green) (i 'blue) (i 'yellow)))
          ⟹ (0 1 2 #f)
```

The enum-set-indexer procedure could be defined as follows using the memq procedure from the (rnrs lists (6)) library:

```
(define (enum-set-indexer set)
  (let* ((symbols (enum-set->list
                    (enum-set-universe set)))
         (cardinality (length symbols)))
    (lambda (x)
      (cond
        ((memq x symbols)
         => (lambda (probe)
              (- cardinality (length probe))))
        (else #f)))))
```

(enum-set-constructor *enum-set*)   procedure

Returns a unary procedure that, given a list of symbols that belong to the universe of *enum-set*, returns a subset of that universe that contains exactly the symbols in the list. The values in the list must all belong to the universe.

(enum-set->list *enum-set*)   procedure

Returns a list of the symbols that belong to its argument, in the canonical order of the universe of *enum-set*.

```
(let* ((e (make-enumeration '(red green blue)))
       (c (enum-set-constructor e)))
  (enum-set->list (c '(blue red))))   ⟹ (red blue)
```

(enum-set-member? *symbol enum-set*)   procedure
(enum-set-subset? *enum-set₁ enum-set₂*)   procedure
(enum-set=? *enum-set₁ enum-set₂*)   procedure

The enum-set-member? procedure returns #t if its first argument is an element of its second argument, #f otherwise.

The enum-set-subset? procedure returns #t if the universe of *enum-set₁* is a subset of the universe of *enum-set₂* (considered as sets of symbols) and every element of *enum-set₁* is a member of *enum-set₂*. It returns #f otherwise.

The enum-set=? procedure returns #t if *enum-set₁* is a subset of *enum-set₂* and vice versa, as determined by the enum-set-subset? procedure. This implies that the universes of the two sets are equal as sets of symbols, but does not imply that they are equal as enumeration types. Otherwise, #f is returned.

```
(let* ((e (make-enumeration '(red green blue)))
       (c (enum-set-constructor e)))
  (list
    (enum-set-member? 'blue (c '(red blue)))
    (enum-set-member? 'green (c '(red blue)))
    (enum-set-subset? (c '(red blue)) e)
    (enum-set-subset? (c '(red blue)) (c '(blue red)))
    (enum-set-subset? (c '(red blue)) (c '(red)))
    (enum-set=? (c '(red blue)) (c '(blue red)))))
              ⟹ (#t #f #t #t #f #t)
```

(enum-set-union *enum-set₁* *enum-set₂*)   procedure
(enum-set-intersection *enum-set₁* *enum-set₂*)   procedure
(enum-set-difference *enum-set₁* *enum-set₂*)   procedure

Enum-set₁ and *enum-set₂* must be enumeration sets that have the same enumeration type.

The enum-set-union procedure returns the union of *enum-set₁* and *enum-set₂*. The enum-set-intersection procedure returns the intersection of *enum-set₁* and *enum-set₂*. The enum-set-difference procedure returns the difference of *enum-set₁* and *enum-set₂*.

```
(let* ((e (make-enumeration '(red green blue)))
       (c (enum-set-constructor e)))
  (list (enum-set->list
          (enum-set-union (c '(blue)) (c '(red))))
        (enum-set->list
          (enum-set-intersection (c '(red green))
                                 (c '(red blue))))
        (enum-set->list
          (enum-set-difference (c '(red green))
                               (c '(red blue))))))
                        ⟹ ((red blue) (red) (green))
```

(enum-set-complement *enum-set*)   procedure

Returns *enum-set*'s complement with respect to its universe.

```
(let* ((e (make-enumeration '(red green blue)))
       (c (enum-set-constructor e)))
  (enum-set->list
    (enum-set-complement (c '(red)))))
                        ⟹ (green blue)
```

`(enum-set-projection` *enum-set*$_1$ *enum-set*$_2$`)`   procedure

Projects *enum-set*$_1$ into the universe of *enum-set*$_2$, dropping any elements of *enum-set*$_1$ that do not belong to the universe of *enum-set*$_2$. (If *enum-set*$_1$ is a subset of the universe of its second, no elements are dropped, and the injection is returned.) The result has the enumeration type of *enum-set*$_2$.

```
(let ((e1 (make-enumeration
            '(red green blue black)))
      (e2 (make-enumeration
            '(red black white))))
  (enum-set->list
    (enum-set-projection e1 e2))))
                              ⟹ (red black)
```

`(define-enumeration` ⟨type-name⟩   syntax
    `(`⟨symbol⟩ `...)`
    ⟨constructor-syntax⟩`)`

The `define-enumeration` form defines an enumeration type and provides two macros for constructing its members and sets of its members.

A `define-enumeration` form is a definition and can appear anywhere any other ⟨definition⟩ can appear.

⟨Type-name⟩ is an identifier that is bound as a syntactic keyword; ⟨symbol⟩ ... are the symbols that comprise the universe of the enumeration (in order).

(⟨type-name⟩ ⟨symbol⟩) checks at macro-expansion time whether the name of ⟨symbol⟩ is in the universe associated with ⟨type-name⟩. If it is, (⟨type-name⟩ ⟨symbol⟩) is equivalent to ⟨symbol⟩. It is a syntax violation if it is not.

⟨Constructor-syntax⟩ is an identifier that is bound to a macro that, given any finite sequence of the symbols in the universe, possibly with duplicates, expands into an expression that evaluates to the enumeration set of those symbols.

(⟨constructor-syntax⟩ ⟨symbol⟩ ...) checks at macro-expansion time whether every ⟨symbol⟩ ... is in the universe associated with ⟨type-name⟩. It is a syntax violation if one or more is not. Otherwise

    (⟨constructor-syntax⟩ ⟨symbol⟩ ...)

is equivalent to

```
((enum-set-constructor (⟨constructor-syntax⟩))
   '(⟨symbol⟩ ...)).
```

Example:

```
(define-enumeration color
  (black white purple maroon)
```

```
    color-set)
```

`(color black)`	⟹ black
`(color purpel)`	⟹ &syntax *exception*
`(enum-set->list (color-set))`	⟹ ()
`(enum-set->list`	
`  (color-set maroon white))`	⟹ (white maroon)

Note: In (⟨type-name⟩ ⟨symbol⟩) and (⟨constructor-syntax⟩ ⟨symbol⟩ ...) forms, only the names of the ⟨symbol⟩s are significant.

15 Composite library

The (rnrs (6)) library is a composite of most of the libraries described in this report. The only exceptions are:

- (rnrs eval (6)) (chapter 16)
- (rnrs mutable-pairs (6)) (chapter 17)
- (rnrs mutable-strings (6)) (chapter 18)
- (rnrs r5rs (6)) (chapter 19)

The library exports all procedures and syntactic forms provided by the component libraries.

All of the bindings exported by (rnrs (6)) are exported for both run and expand; see report section 7.2.

16 eval

The (rnrs eval (6)) library allows a program to create Scheme expressions as data at run time and evaluate them.

(eval *expression environment*)   procedure

Evaluates *expression* in the specified environment and returns its value. *Expression* must be a syntactically valid Scheme expression represented as a datum value, and *environment* must be an *environment*, which can be created using the environment procedure described below.

If the first argument to eval is determined not to be a syntactically correct expression, then eval must raise an exception with condition type &syntax. Specifically, if the first argument to eval is a definition or a splicing begin form containing a definition, it must raise an exception with condition type &syntax.

(environment *import-spec* ...)   procedure

Import-spec must be a datum representing an ⟨import spec⟩ (see report section 7.1). The environment procedure returns an environment corresponding to *import-spec*.

The bindings of the environment represented by the specifier are immutable: If eval is applied to an expression that is determined to contain an assignment to one of the variables of the environment, then eval must raise an exception with a condition type &syntax.

```
(library (foo)
  (export)
  (import (rnrs)
          (rnrs eval))
  (write
    (eval '(let ((x 3)) x)
          (environment '(rnrs)))))
      writes 3


(library (foo)
  (export)
  (import (rnrs)
          (rnrs eval))
  (write
    (eval
      '(eval:car (eval:cons 2 4))
      (environment
        '(prefix (only (rnrs) car cdr cons null?)
                 eval:)))))
      writes 2
```

17 Mutable pairs

The procedures provided by the (rnrs mutable-pairs (6)) library allow new values to be assigned to the car and cdr fields of previously allocated pairs.

(set-car! *pair obj*)   procedure

Stores *obj* in the car field of *pair*. The set-car! procedure returns unspecified values.

```
(define (f) (list 'not-a-constant-list))
(define (g) '(constant-list))
(set-car! (f) 3)              ⟹   unspecified
(set-car! (g) 3)              ⟹   unspecified
    ; should raise &assertion exception
```

If an immutable pair is passed to set-car!, an exception with condition type &assertion should be raised.

(set-cdr! *pair obj*)   procedure

Stores *obj* in the cdr field of *pair*. The set-cdr! procedure returns unspecified values.

If an immutable pair is passed to set-cdr!, an exception with condition type &assertion should be raised.

```
(let ((x (list 'a 'b 'c 'a))
      (y (list 'a 'b 'c 'a 'b 'c 'a)))
  (set-cdr! (list-tail x 2) x)
  (set-cdr! (list-tail y 5) y)
  (list
   (equal? x x)
   (equal? x y)
   (equal? (list x y 'a) (list y x 'b))))) ⟹ (#t #t #f)
```

18 Mutable strings

The string-set! procedure provided by the (rnrs mutable-strings (6)) library allows mutating the characters of a string in-place.

(string-set! *string k char*)   procedure

K must be a valid index of *string*. The string-set! procedure stores *char* in element *k* of *string* and returns unspecified values.

Passing an immutable string to string-set! should cause an exception with condition type &assertion to be raised.

```
(define (f) (make-string 3 #\*))
(define (g) "***")
(string-set! (f) 0 #\?)          ⟹   unspecified
(string-set! (g) 0 #\?)          ⟹   unspecified
           ; should raise &assertion exception
(string-set! (symbol->string 'immutable)
             0
             #\?)                ⟹   unspecified
           ; should raise &assertion exception
```

Note: Implementors should make string-set! run in constant time.

(string-fill! *string char*)   procedure

Stores *char* in every element of the given *string* and returns unspecified values.

19 R⁵RS compatibility

The features described in this chapter are exported from the (rnrs r5rs (6)) library and provide some functionality of the preceding revision of this report (Kelsey *et al.*, 1998) that was omitted from the main part of the current report.

```
(exact->inexact z)                                          procedure
(inexact->exact z)                                          procedure
```
These are the same as the inexact and exact procedures; see report section 11.7.8.

```
(quotient n₁ n₂)                                            procedure
(remainder n₁ n₂)                                           procedure
(modulo n₁ n₂)                                              procedure
```
These procedures implement number-theoretic (integer) division. N_2 must be non-zero. All three procedures return integer objects. If n_1/n_2 is an integer object:

$$
\begin{array}{ll}
\texttt{(quotient } n_1 \ n_2) & \Longrightarrow n_1/n_2 \\
\texttt{(remainder } n_1 \ n_2) & \Longrightarrow 0 \\
\texttt{(modulo } n_1 \ n_2) & \Longrightarrow 0
\end{array}
$$

If n_1/n_2 is not an integer object:

$$
\begin{array}{ll}
\texttt{(quotient } n_1 \ n_2) & \Longrightarrow n_q \\
\texttt{(remainder } n_1 \ n_2) & \Longrightarrow n_r \\
\texttt{(modulo } n_1 \ n_2) & \Longrightarrow n_m
\end{array}
$$

where n_q is n_1/n_2 rounded towards zero, $0 < |n_r| < |n_2|$, $0 < |n_m| < |n_2|$, n_r and n_m differ from n_1 by a multiple of n_2, n_r has the same sign as n_1, and n_m has the same sign as n_2.

Consequently, for integer objects n_1 and n_2 with n_2 not equal to 0,

```
(= n₁ (+ (* n₂ (quotient n₁ n₂))
         (remainder n₁ n₂)))
```
$$\Longrightarrow \ \texttt{\#t}$$

provided all number object involved in that computation are exact.

```
(modulo 13 4)                        ⟹  1
(remainder 13 4)                     ⟹  1

(modulo -13 4)                       ⟹  3
(remainder -13 4)                    ⟹  -1

(modulo 13 -4)                       ⟹  -3
(remainder 13 -4)                    ⟹  1

(modulo -13 -4)                      ⟹  -1
(remainder -13 -4)                   ⟹  -1

(remainder -13 -4.0)                 ⟹  -1.0
```

Note: These procedures could be defined in terms of div and mod (see report section 11.7.9) as follows (without checking of the argument types):

```
(define (sign n)
  (cond
    ((negative? n) -1)
    ((positive? n) 1)
    (else 0)))

(define (quotient n1 n2)
  (* (sign n1) (sign n2) (div (abs n1) (abs n2))))

(define (remainder n1 n2)
  (* (sign n1) (mod (abs n1) (abs n2))))

(define (modulo n1 n2)
  (* (sign n2) (mod (* (sign n2) n1) (abs n2))))
```

(delay ⟨expression⟩)   syntax
The delay construct is used together with the procedure force to implement
lazy evaluation or *call by need*. (delay ⟨expression⟩) returns an object called a
promise which at some point in the future may be asked (by the force procedure)
to evaluate ⟨expression⟩, and deliver the resulting value. The effect of ⟨expression⟩
returning multiple values is unspecified.

(force *promise*)   procedure
Promise must be a promise. The force procedure forces the value of *promise*. If no
value has been computed for the promise, then a value is computed and returned.
The value of the promise is cached (or "memoized") so that if it is forced a second
time, the previously computed value is returned.

```
(force (delay (+ 1 2)))                          ⟹   3
(let ((p (delay (+ 1 2))))
  (list (force p) (force p)))
                                                 ⟹   (3 3)


(define a-stream
  (letrec ((next
             (lambda (n)
               (cons n (delay (next (+ n 1))))))))
    (next 0)))
(define head car)
(define tail
  (lambda (stream) (force (cdr stream))))


(head (tail (tail a-stream)))
                                                 ⟹   2
```

Promises are mainly intended for programs written in functional style. The following examples should not be considered to illustrate good programming style, but they illustrate the property that only one value is computed for a promise, no matter how many times it is forced.

```
(define count 0)
(define p
  (delay (begin (set! count (+ count 1))
                (if (> count x)
                    count
                    (force p)))))
(define x 5)
p                                  ⟹  a promise
(force p)                          ⟹  6
p                                  ⟹  a promise, still
(begin (set! x 10)
       (force p))                  ⟹  6
```

Here is a possible implementation of `delay` and `force`. Promises are implemented here as procedures of no arguments, and `force` simply calls its argument:

```
(define force
  (lambda (object)
    (object)))
```

The expression

```
(delay ⟨expression⟩)
```

has the same meaning as the procedure call

```
(make-promise (lambda () ⟨expression⟩))
```

as follows

```
(define-syntax delay
  (syntax-rules ()
    ((delay expression)
     (make-promise (lambda () expression))))),
```

where `make-promise` is defined as follows:

```
(define make-promise
  (lambda (proc)
    (let ((result-ready? #f)
          (result #f))
      (lambda ()
        (if result-ready?
            result
            (let ((x (proc)))
```

```
(if result-ready?
    result
    (begin (set! result-ready? #t)
           (set! result x)
           result))))))))
```

(null-environment *n*)   procedure
N must be the exact integer object 5. The null-environment procedure returns
an environment specifier suitable for use with eval (see chapter 16) representing
an environment that is empty except for the (syntactic) bindings for all keywords
described in the previous revision of this report (Kelsey *et al.*, 1998), including
bindings for =>, ..., else, and _ that are the same as those in the (rnrs base
(6)) library.

(scheme-report-environment *n*)   procedure
N must be the exact integer object 5. The scheme-report-environment procedure
returns an environment specifier for an environment that is empty except for the bindings for the identifiers described in the previous revision of this report (Kelsey *et al.*,
1998), omitting load, interaction-environment, transcript-on, transcript-off,
and char-ready?. The variable bindings have as values the procedures of the same
names described in this report, and the keyword bindings, including =>, ..., else,
and _ are the same as those described in this report.

PART THREE
Non-Normative Appendices

Abstract

This document contains non-normative appendices to the *Revised*[6] *Report on the Algorithmic Language Scheme*. These appendices contain advice for users and suggestions for implementors on issues not fit for standardization, in particular on platform-specific issues.

This document frequently refers back to the *Revised*[6] *Report on the Algorithmic Language Scheme* and the *Revised*[6] *Report on the Algorithmic Language Scheme — Libraries —*; references to the report are identified by designations such as "report section" or "report chapter", and references to the library report are identified by designations such as "library section" or "library chapter".

A Standard-conformant mode

Scheme implementations compliant with the report may operate in a variety of modes. In particular, in addition to one or more modes conformant with the requirements of the report, an implementation may offer non-conformant modes. These modes are by nature implementation-specific, and may differ in the language and available libraries. In particular, non-conformant language extensions may be available, including unsafe libraries or otherwise unsafe features, and the semantics of the language may differ from the semantics described in the report. Moreover, the default mode offered by a Scheme implementation may be non-conformant, and such a Scheme implementation may require special settings or declarations to enter the report-conformant mode. Implementors should clearly document the nature of the default mode and how to enter a report-conformant mode.

B Optional case insensitivity

In contrast with earlier revisions of the report (Kelsey *et al.*, 1998), the syntax of data distinguishes upper and lower case in identifiers and in characters specified via their names. For example, the identifiers X and x are different, and the character #\space cannot be written #\SPACE.

Implementors may wish to support case-insensitive syntax for backward compatibility or other reasons. If they do so, they should adopt the following directives to control case folding.

```
#!fold-case
#!no-fold-case
```

These directives may appear anywhere comments may appear and are treated as comments, except that they affect the reading of subsequent lexemes. The #!fold-case causes the reader to case-fold (see library section 1.2) each ⟨identifier⟩ and ⟨character name⟩. The #!no-fold-case directive causes the reader to return to the default, non-folding behavior.

C Use of square brackets

Even though matched square brackets are synonymous with parentheses in the syntax, many programmers use square brackets only in a few select places. In particular, programmers should restrict use of square brackets to places in syntactic forms where two consecutive open parentheses would otherwise be common. These are the applicable forms specified in the report and the library report:

- For cond forms (see report section 11.4.5), a ⟨cond clause⟩ may take one of the follow forms:

    [⟨test⟩ ⟨expression₁⟩ ...]
    [⟨test⟩ => ⟨expression⟩]
    [else ⟨expression₁⟩ ⟨expression₂⟩ ...]

- For case forms (see report section 11.4.5), a ⟨case clause⟩ may take one of the follow forms:

    [(⟨datum₁⟩ ...) ⟨expression₁⟩ ⟨expression₂⟩ ...]
    [else ⟨expression₁⟩ ⟨expression₂⟩ ...]

- For let, let*, letrec, letrec* forms (see report section 11.4.6), ⟨bindings⟩ may take the following form:

    ([⟨variable₁⟩ ⟨init₁⟩] ...)

- For let-values and let-values* forms (see report section 11.4.6), ⟨mv-bindings⟩ may take the following form:

    ([⟨formals₁⟩ ⟨init₁⟩] ...)

- For syntax-rules forms (see report section 11.19), a ⟨syntax rule⟩ may take the following form:

    [⟨srpattern⟩ ⟨template⟩]

- For identifier-syntax forms (see report section 11.19), the two clauses may take the following form:

    [⟨id₁⟩ ⟨template₁⟩]
    [(set! ⟨id₂⟩ ⟨pattern⟩) ⟨template₂⟩]

- For do forms (see library section 5), the variable bindings may take the following form:

    ([⟨variable₁⟩ ⟨init₁⟩ ⟨step₁⟩] ...)

- For case-lambda forms (see library section 5), a ⟨case-lambda clause⟩ may take the following form:

    [⟨formals⟩ ⟨body⟩]

- For guard forms (see library section 7.1), a ⟨cond clause⟩ may take one of the follow forms:

```
[⟨test⟩ ⟨expression₁⟩ ...]
[⟨test⟩ => ⟨expression⟩]
[else ⟨expression₁⟩ ⟨expression₂⟩ ...]
```

- For `syntax-case` forms (see library chapter 12.4), a ⟨syntax-case rule⟩ may take one of the following forms:

```
[⟨pattern⟩ ⟨output expression⟩]
[⟨pattern⟩ ⟨fender⟩ ⟨output expression⟩]
```

D Scripts

A *Scheme script* is a top-level program (see report chapter 8) which is packaged such that it is directly executable by conforming implementations of Scheme, on one or more plaforms.

D.1 Script interpreter

Where applicable, implementations should provide a *script interpreter* in the form of an executable program named `scheme-script` that is capable of initiating the execution of Scheme scripts, as described below.

Rationale: Distributing a Scheme program that is portable with respect to both Scheme implementations and operating systems is challenging, even if that program has been written in standard Scheme. Languages with a single or primary implementation can at least rely on a standard name for their script interpreters. Standardizing the name of the executable used to start a Scheme script removes one barrier to the distribution of Scheme scripts.

D.2 Syntax

A Scheme *script* is a delimited piece of text, typically a file, which consists of an optional script header, followed by a top-level program. A script header has the following syntax:

⟨script header⟩ ⟶ ⟨shebang⟩ /usr/bin/env ⟨space⟩
    `scheme-script` ⟨linefeed⟩
⟨shebang⟩ ⟶ #! | #! ⟨space⟩

D.2.1 Script header

The *script header*, if present on the first line of a script, is used by Unix-like operating systems to identify the interpreter to execute that script.

The script header syntax given above is the recommended portable form that programmers should use. However, if the first line of a script begins with #!/ or

`#!`⟨space⟩, implementations should ignore it on all platforms, even if it does not conform to the recommended syntax.

Rationale: Requiring script interpreters to recognize and ignore the script header helps ensure that Scheme scripts written for Unix-like systems can also run on other kinds of systems. Furthermore, recognizing all `#!/` or `#!`⟨space⟩ combinations allows local customizations to be performed by altering a script header from its default form.

D.2.2 Example

```
#!/usr/bin/env scheme-script
#!r6rs
(import (rnrs base)
        (rnrs io ports)
        (rnrs programs))
(put-bytes (standard-output-port)
           (call-with-port
               (open-file-input-port
                 (cadr (command-line)))
             get-bytes-all))
```

D.3 Platform considerations

Many platforms require that scripts be marked as executable in some way. The platform-specific details of this are beyond the scope of this report. Scripts that are not suitably marked as executable will fail to execute on many platforms. Other platform-specific notes for some popular operating systems follow.

D.3.1 Apple Mac OS X

The Mac OS X operating system supports the Unix-like script header for shell scripts that run in the Terminal. Depending on the intended usage, it may be advisable to choose a file name ending in `.command` for a script, as this makes the script double-clickable.

D.3.2 Unix

Scheme scripts on Unix-like operating systems are supported by the presence of the script header. Scripts that omit the script header are unlikely to be directly executable on Unix-like systems.

To support installation of the Scheme script interpreter in non-standard paths, scripts should use the `/usr/bin/env` program as specified in the recommended script header syntax. (Note that on many Unix-like systems, this also allows the script interpreter itself to be implemented as a shell script.)

D.3.3 Microsoft Windows

The Windows operating system allows a file extension to be associated with a script interpreter such as `scheme-script`. This association may be configured appropriately by Scheme implementations, installation programs, or by the user.

D.3.4 Selecting an implementation

If multiple implementations of Scheme are installed on a machine, the user may wish to specify which implementation should be used to execute Scheme scripts by default. Most platforms support some mechanism for choosing between alternative implementations of a program. For example, Debian GNU/Linux uses the `/etc/alternatives` mechanism to do this; Microsoft Windows uses file extension associations. Implementations are expected to configure this appropriately, e.g., as part of their installation procedure. Failing that, users must perform any necessary configuration to choose their preferred Scheme script interpreter.

E Source code representation

The report does not specify how source code is represented and stored. The only requirement the report imposes is that the source code of a top-level program (see report section 8.1) or a script (see section D.2) be delimited. The source code of a library is self-delimiting in the sense that, if the beginning of a library form can be identified, so can the end.

Implementations may take radically different approaches to storing source code for libraries, among them: files in the file system where each file contains an arbitrary number of library forms, files in the file system where each file contains exactly one library form, records in a database, and data structures in memory.

Similarly, programs and scripts may be stored in a variety of formats. Platform constraints may restrict the choices available to an implementation, which is why the report neither mandates nor recommends a specific method for storage.

Implementations may provide a means for importing libraries coming from the outside via an interface that accepts a UTF-8 text file in Unicode Normalization Form C where line endings are encoded as linefeed characters. Such text files may contain an arbitrary number of library forms. (Authors of such files should include an `#!r6rs` comment if the file is written purely with the lexical and datum syntax described in the report. See report section 4.2.3.) After importing such a file, the libraries defined in it should be available to other libraries and files. An implementation may store the file as is, or convert it to some storage format to achieve this.

Similarly, implementations may provide a means for executing a program represented as a UTF-8 text file containing its source code. Again, authors of such files should include an `#!r6rs` comment if the file is written purely with the lexical and datum syntax described in the report. This report does not describe a file format that allows both libraries and programs to appear in the same file.

F Use of library versions

Names for libraries may include a version. An ⟨import spec⟩ may designate a set of acceptable versions that may be imported. Conversely, only one version of each library should be part of a program. This allows using the "name part" of a ⟨library name⟩ for different purposes than the ⟨version⟩.

In particular, if several different variants of a library exists where it is feasible that they coexist in the same program, it is recommended that different names be used for the variants. In contrast, for compatible versions of a library where coexistence of several versions is unnecessary and undesirable, it is recommended that the same name and different versions be used. In particular, it is recommended that new versions of libraries that are conservative extensions of old ones differ only in the version, not in the name.

Correspondingly, it is recommended that ⟨import spec⟩s do not constrain an import to a single version, but instead specify a wide range of acceptable versions of a library.

Implementations that allow two libraries of the same name with different versions to coexist in the same program should report when processing a program that actually makes use of this extension.

G Unique library names

Programmers should choose names for distributed libraries that do not collide with other libraries' names. This appendix suggests a convention for generating unique library names, similar to the convention for Java (Gosling et al., 2005).

A unique library name can be formed by associating the library with an Internet domain name, such as mit.edu. The lower-case components of the domain are reversed to form a prefix for the library name. Adding further name components to establish a hierarchy may be advisable, depending on the size of the organization associated with the domain name, the number of libraries to be distributed from it, and other organizational properties or conventions associated with the library.

Programmers should use library names that are suitable for use as part of file names. Special characters in domain names that do not fit conventions of commonly used file systems should be replaced by hyphens or suitable "escape sequences" that, as much as possible, are suitable for avoiding collisions. Here are some examples for possible library names according to this convention:

```
(edu mit swiss cheese)
(de deinprogramm educational graphics turtle)
(com pan-am booking passenger)
```

The name of a library does not necessarily indicate an Internet address where the package is distributed.

References

Abelson, Harold, Sussman, Gerald Jay, & Sussman, Julie. (1996). *Structure and interpretation of computer programs.* second edn. Cambridge, Mass.: MIT Press.

Backus, J. W., Bauer, F.L., J.Green, Katz, C., Naur, J. McCarthy P., Perlis, A. J., Rutishauser, H., Samuelson, K., Wegstein, B. Vauquois J. H., van Wijngaarden, A., & Woodger, M. (1963). Revised report on the algorithmic language Algol 60. *Communications of the ACM,* **6**(1), 1–17.

Barendregt, Henk P. (1984). Introduction to the lambda calculus. *Nieuw archief voor wisenkunde,* **4**(2), 337–372.

Bawden, Alan. 1999 (Jan.). Quasiquotation in Lisp. *Pages 4–12 of:* Danvy, Olivier (ed), *Proceedings acm sigplan workshop on partial evaluation and semantics-based program manipulation pepm '99.* BRICS Notes Series NS-99-1.

Bawden, Alan, & Rees, Jonathan. (1988). Syntactic closures. *Pages 86–95 of: ACM conference on Lisp and functional programming.* Snowbird, Utah: ACM Press.

Bradner, Scott. 1997 (Mar.). *Key words for use in RFCs to indicate requirement levels.* `http://www.ietf.org/rfc/rfc2119.txt`. RFC 2119.

Burger, Robert G., & Dybvig, R. Kent. (1996). Printing floating-point numbers quickly and accurately. *Pages 108–116 of: Proceedings of the ACM SIGPLAN '96 conference on programming language design and implementation.* Philadelphia, PA, USA: ACM Press.

Clinger, Will, Dybvig, R. Kent, Sperber, Michael, & van Straaten, Anton. (2005). *SRFI 76: R6RS records.* `http://srfi.schemers.org/srfi-76/`.

Clinger, William. 1985 (1985). *The revised revised report on Scheme, or an uncommon Lisp.* Tech. rept. MIT Artificial Intelligence Memo 848. MIT. Also published as Computer Science Department Technical Report 174, Indiana University, June 1985.

Clinger, William. (1998). Proper tail recursion and space efficiency. *Pages 174–185 of:* Cooper, Keith (ed), *Proceedings of the 1998 on programming language design and implementation.* Montreal, Canada: ACM Press. Volume 33(5) of SIGPLAN Notices.

Clinger, William, & Rees, Jonathan. (1986). Revised[3] report on the algorithmic language Scheme. *SIGPLAN notices,* **21**(12), 37–79.

Clinger, William, & Rees, Jonathan. (1991a). Macros that work. *Pages 155–162 of: Proceedings 1991 ACM sigplan symposium on principles of programming languages.* Orlando, Florida: ACM Press.

Clinger, William, & Rees, Jonathan. (1991b). Revised[4] report on the algorithmic language Scheme. *Lisp pointers,* **IV**(3), 1–55.

Clinger, William D. (1990). How to read floating point numbers accurately. *Pages 92–101 of: Proceedings on programming language design and implementation '90.* White Plains, New York, USA: ACM.

Clinger, William D, & Sperber, Michael. (2005). *SRFI 77: Preliminary proposal for R6RS arithmetic.* `http://srfi.schemers.org/srfi-77/`.

Cohen, Danny. 1980 (Apr.). *On holy wars and a plea for peace.* `http://www.ietf.org/rfc/ien/ien137.txt`. Internet Engineering Note 137.

Davis, Mark. (2006). *Unicode Standard Annex #29: Text boundaries.* `http://www.unicode.org/reports/tr29/`.

Dybvig, R. Kent. (2003). *The Scheme programming language.* third edn. Cambridge: MIT Press. `http://www.scheme.com/tspl3/`.

Dybvig, R. Kent. (2005). *Chez Scheme version 7 user's guide.* Cadence Research Systems. `http://www.scheme.com/csug7/`.

Dybvig, R. Kent. (2006). *SRFI 93: R6RS* `syntax-case` *macros.* `http://srfi.schemers.org/srfi-93/`.

Dybvig, R. Kent, Hieb, Robert, & Bruggeman, Carl. (1992). Syntactic abstraction in Scheme. *Lisp and symbolic computation*, **5**(4), 295–326.

Felleisen, Matthias, & Flatt, Matthew. (2003). *Programming languages and lambda calculi.* http://www.cs.utah.edu/plt/publications/pllc.pdf.

Fessenden, Carol, Clinger, William, Friedman, Daniel P., & Haynes, Christopher. (1983). *Scheme 311 version 4 reference manual.* Indiana University. Indiana University Computer Science Technical Report 137, Superseded by (Friedman *et al.*, 1985).

Flatt, Matthew. 2006 (July). *PLT MzScheme: Language manual.* Rice University, University of Utah. http://download.plt-scheme.org/doc/352/html/mzscheme/.

Flatt, Matthew, & Dybvig, Kent. (2005). *SRFI 83: R6RS library syntax.* http://srfi .schemers.org/srfi-83/.

Flatt, Matthew, & Feeley, Marc. (2005). *SRFI 75: R6RS unicode data.* http://srfi.schemers .org/srfi-75/.

Friedman, Daniel P., Haynes, Christopher, Kohlbecker, Eugene, & Wand, Mitchell. 1985 (Jan.). *Scheme 84 interim reference manual.* Indiana University. Indiana University Computer Science Technical Report 153.

Gosling, James, Joy, Bill, Steele, Guy, & Bracha, Gilad. (2005). *The Java^{TM} language specification.* Third edn. Addison-Wesley.

IEEE754. (1985). *IEEE standard 754-1985. IEEE standard for binary floating-point arithmetic.* Reprinted in SIGPLAN Notices, 22(2):9-25, 1987.

Kelsey, Richard, Clinger, William, & Rees, Jonathan. (1998). Revised[5] report on the algorithmic language Scheme. *Higher-order and symbolic computation*, **11**(1), 7–105.

Kohlbecker, Eugene E., Friedman, Daniel P., Felleisen, Matthias, & Duba, Bruce. (1986). Hygienic macro expansion. *Pages 151–161 of: Proceedings of the 1986 ACM conference on Lisp and functional programming.*

Kohlbecker Jr., Eugene E. 1986 (Aug.). *Syntactic extensions in the programming language lisp.* Ph.D. thesis, Indiana University.

Leach, P., Mealling, M., & Salz, R. 2005 (July). *A Universally Unique IDentifier (UUID) URN namespace.* http://www.ietf.org/rfc/rfc4122.txt. RFC 4122.

Matthews, Jacob, & Findler, Robert Bruce. 2005 (Sept.). An operational semantics for R5RS Scheme. *Pages 41–54 of:* Ashley, J. Michael, & Sperber, Michael (eds), *Proceedings of the sixth workshop on scheme and functional programming.* Indiana University Technical Report TR619.

Matthews, Jacob, & Findler, Robert Bruce. (2007). An operational semantics for Scheme. *Journal of functional programming.* From http://www.cambridge.org/journals/JFP/.

Matthews, Jacob, Findler, Robert Bruce, Flatt, Matthew, & Felleisen, Matthias. (2004). A visual environment for developing context-sensitive term rewriting systems. *Proceedings 15th conference on rewriting techniques and applications.* Aachen: Springer-Verlag.

MIT Department of Electrical Engineering and Computer Science. 1984 (Sept.). *Scheme manual, seventh edition.*

Rees, Jonathan A., & IV, Norman I. Adams. (1982). T: a dialect of lisp or lambda: The ultimate software tool. *Pages 114–122 of: ACM conference on Lisp and functional programming.* Pittsburgh, Pennsylvania: ACM Press.

Rees, Jonathan A., IV, Norman I. Adams, & Meehan, James R. 1984 (Jan.). *The T manual.* fourth edn. Yale University Computer Science Department.

Scheme Charter. 2006 (Mar.). *Scheme standardization charter.* http://www.schemers.org/ Documents/Standards/Charter/mar-2006.txt.

Sperber, Michael, Dybvig, R. Kent, Flatt, Matthew, van Straaten, Anton, Kelsey, Richard,

Clinger, William, & Rees, Jonathan. (2007a). *Revised*[6] *report on the algorithmic language Scheme (Libraries)*. `http://www.r6rs.org/`.

Sperber, Michael, Dybvig, R. Kent, Flatt, Matthew, & van Straaten, Anton. (2007b). *Revised*[6] *report on the algorithmic language Scheme (Rationale)*. `http://www.r6rs.org/`.

Steele Jr., Guy Lewis. 1978 (May). *Rabbit: a compiler for Scheme*. Tech. rept. MIT Artificial Intelligence Laboratory Technical Report 474. MIT.

Steele Jr., Guy Lewis. (1990). *Common Lisp: The language*. second edn. Burlington, MA: Digital Press.

Steele Jr., Guy Lewis, & Sussman, Gerald Jay. 1978 (Jan.). *The revised report on Scheme, a dialect of Lisp*. Tech. rept. MIT Artificial Intelligence Memo 452. MIT.

Sussman, Gerald Jay, & Jr., Guy Lewis Steele. 1975 (Dec.). *Scheme: an interpreter for extended lambda calculus*. Tech. rept. MIT Artificial Intelligence Memo 349. MIT.

Texas Instruments. 1985 (Nov.). *TI Scheme language reference manual*. Texas Instruments, Inc. Preliminary version 1.0.

Unicode Consortium, The. (2007). *The Unicode standard, version 5.0.0.* defined by: *The Unicode Standard, Version 5.0* (Boston, MA, Addison-Wesley, 2007. ISBN 0-321-48091-0).

Waddell, Oscar. 1999 (Aug.). *Extending the scope of syntactic abstraction*. Ph.D. thesis, Indiana University. `http://www.cs.indiana.edu/~owaddell/papers/thesis.ps.gz`.

Waite, William M., & Goos, Gerhard. (1984). *Compiler construction*. Springer-Verlag.

Wright, Andrew, & Felleisen, Matthias. (1994). A syntactic approach to type soundness. *Information and computation*, **115**(1), 38–94. First appeared as Technical Report TR160, Rice University, 1991.

Alphabetic index of definitions of concepts, keywords, and procedures

Printed in the United States
by Baker & Taylor Publisher Services